GATHERING INFORMATION FROM OTHER SOURCES

Conducting interviews
Administering a questionnaire or a survey
• *Using e-mail and the Internet to administer questionnaires*
Examining government records
Other kinds of primary research

D0153551

DEVELOPING A THESIS AND A WORKING OUTLINE

WRITING YOUR FIRST DRAFT

REVISING YOUR PAPER

PREPARING YOUR FINAL COPY

The Bedford Guide
to the Research Process

THIRD EDITION

The Bedford Guide to the Research Process

Jean Johnson

*University of Maryland
at College Park*

Bedford Books ≈ **Boston**

For Bedford Books

President and Publisher: Charles H. Christensen
General Manager and Associate Publisher: Joan E. Feinberg
Managing Editor: Elizabeth M. Schaaf
Developmental Editor: Beth Castrodale
Editorial Assistant: Joanne Diaz
Production Editor: Heidi L. Hood
Production Assistant: Ellen C. Thibault
Copyeditor: Rosemary Winfield
Text Design: George McLean
Cover Design: Richard Emery Design, Inc.
Cover Illustration: Maureen Kehoe, copyright 1996.

Library of Congress Catalog Card Number: 96–84936

For information, write: Bedford Books, 75 Arlington Street, Boston, MA 02116
(617-426-7440)

ISBN: 0–312–11967–4

Acknowledgments

Stephen Barrett M.D., from "Commercial Hair Analysis: Science or Scam?" in *JAMA: The Journal of the American Medical Association* 1985: 254: 1042, 1044. Copyright © 1985, American Medical Association. Reprinted by permission of *JAMA: The Journal of the American Medical Association.*

Bibliographic Index, "Falklands War" entry. *Bibliographic Index,* 1989. Copyright © 1989 by The H. W. Wilson Company. Material reproduced with permission of the publisher.

Elizabeth Bishop, lines from "Arrival at Santos," "Brazil, January 1, 1502," "Exchanging Hats," "In the Waiting Room," "The Man-Moth," "The Moose," "The Riverman," and "Roosters." From *The Complete Poems 1927–1979* by Elizabeth Bishop. Copyright © 1979, 1983 by Alice Helen Methfessel. Reprinted with permission of Farrar, Straus & Giroux, Inc.

Book Review Digest, "Drinka, George Frederick" entry. *Book Review Digest,* 1985. Copyright © 1985 by The H. W. Wilson Company. Material reproduced with permission of the publisher.

Truman Capote, from *Writers at Work,* George Plimpton, editor. New York: Penguin, 1981. Reprinted with permission.

Acknowledgments and copyrights are continued at the back of the book on pages 442–43, which constitute an extension of the copyright page. It is a violation of the law to reproduce these selections by any means whatsoever without the written permission of the copyright holder.

Preface

The love of the search seems to be common to all people. Much of human history consists of accounts of exploration: the people living around the Mediterranean Sea set out in ships to explore their world, eventually sailing across the Atlantic. Hsüan-tsang of China traveled to India and perhaps farther west in the seventh century. Our fascination with exploration is reflected in great search stories, such as Sir Galahad's quest for the Holy Grail and Ahab's pursuit of Moby Dick. That fascination continues in modern times impelling researchers, such as primatologist Jane Goodall, to make new discoveries in nature, science, and medicine. And we are so eager to satisfy our curiosity about outer space that we are willing to spend billions of dollars to find out who or what is out there.

Like its previous editions, *The Bedford Guide to the Research Process,* Third Edition, helps students harness that basic enthusiasm as a motivating force. It helps them see that research is not an esoteric activity conducted only by scholars in libraries and prescribed only in schools but a necessary and constant function of everyday life. What students already know about this process can aid them in their current research project; what they learn here can be applied to the acquisition of knowledge not only in the college classroom but anywhere and at any time in their lives.

Organization

This edition, like the first two, serves students in two ways: as a step-by-step guide to the research process for a course in which a research paper is assigned and as a reference for writing papers both in college and after graduation. Chapter 1 provides help with choosing a topic — for some students the hardest part of writing a research paper in college. Chapter 2 helps students plan the paper and design a search strategy. Chapters 3, 4, and 5 present detailed guidelines for collecting information from library sources and the Internet as well as through questionnaires, e-mail, interviews, oral history, court documents, and government archives. Students are also shown how to keep accurate notes and records using a computer as well as how to paraphrase, summarize, quote, and document sources in their papers while avoiding plagiarism.

The principles and practice of re-searching and outlining are discussed in Chapter 6. Then, to emphasize that more than one draft is needed in writing a research paper and that each draft serves a special rhetorical purpose, students are guided through three writing stages: a first exploratory draft (Chapter 7), the revising process (Chapter 8), and preparation of the final copy (Chapter 9). At each stage of the process, examples from student writing in a wide range of subjects, from engineering, biology, psychology, and geology to computer science, history, music, and literature, provide scholars with a sense of how others have worked in areas related to their own. Besides illustrating each stage of the process, these examples serve as a background chorus of fellow researchers — human voices in what can at times seem like a wilderness of books, periodicals, computer files, notes, and drafts.

Chapters 10, 11, and 12 offer guidelines for citing and documenting sources in the updated versions of three major styles: MLA or author-page style, used primarily in the humanities; APA or author-date style, favored by writers in the social sciences; and citation-sequence style, used by writers in the sciences. (The style manual of the Council of Biology Editors, on which the discussion of citation-sequence method is based, also offers advice on the name-year and alphabet-number methods of documentation; these systems are also discussed in Chapter 12.) For those who prefer to use footnotes or endnotes, Appendix 2 contains guidelines for using the *Chicago Manual of Style* format. MLA, APA, CBE, and *Chicago* have all published new style guidelines since the second edition of *The Bedford Guide to the Research Process,* and this revision collects all of the updated guidance in one convenient place.

Included in Chapters 10, 11, and 12 are four annotated student papers from different academic disciplines that illustrate MLA-, APA-, and CBE-style documentation and the range of sources that might be cited in these disciplines. Three of these papers (for MLA, APA, and CBE style) are new, and an additional MLA paper, on the repatriation of Native American remains and artifacts, has been extensively revised and updated and includes new references to current government documents — an important resource for students.

Features Retained and Strengthened

The features that instructors and students appreciated in earlier editions, such as the step-by-step procedures, the optional search log, the end-of-chapter exercises containing suggestions for peer collaboration, and the examples of student writing from many disciplines are retained and improved. The following features were also strengthened:

Updated Advice on Using Computers throughout the Research Process.
Because computers have dramatically changed the way papers are re-
searched and written, the third edition of *The Bedford Guide to the Research Process* features up-to-date advice on using computers in every
stage of the research process. It provides the latest guidance on using
electronic catalogs and other library databases, composing and designing papers and graphics on a computer, and citing information obtained from electronic sources.

Extensive Coverage of Summarizing and Paraphrasing.   In response
to requests from users, the advice on summarizing and paraphrasing
includes more examples to help students understand these critical
tasks.

Expanded Appendixes with More Resources.   The annotated list of
references in Appendix 1, a cross-curricular feature that many instructors found to be one of the most helpful parts of the first edition, has
been revised and updated and now includes Internet sources. Appendix 3, an index of style manuals in various disciplines, has also been updated and expanded.

New Features

In response to suggestions from those who used the second edition
and to developments in the fields of research and composition, several
new features have been introduced.

Advice on Using the Internet and Other Electronic Resources.   Although computers have been used for researching and composing for
some time, this edition reflects the striking revolution in the way information is now commonly conveyed — that is, electronically. The third
edition includes new coverage of the World Wide Web, Gopher, WAIS,
and Archie; advice on using the Internet critically; suggestions for
using e-mail and newsgroups; additional documentation models for
electronic sources; and a list of Internet references in Appendix 1.

New Exercises for Computerized Classrooms.   In addition to exercises
for researching, writing, and peer review, the third edition offers new
exercises to help students working in computer labs or on networks.
Many of these encourage further collaboration among students.

Stronger Treatment of Critical Thinking and Rhetorical Argument.
Because critical thinking is necessary at each stage of the research
process, new student examples are included to demonstrate thinking
skills and logical argumentation. In addition to discussing the popular Toulmin model for analyzing arguments, the book now discusses

common logical fallacies and how the sample papers in Chapters 10 and 11 employ the techniques of rhetorical argument to explore two controversial subjects: the repatriation of Native American remains and artifacts and the increase in pathological gambling.

Acknowledgments

This new edition would not have been possible without the help of many people. For taking the time to answer a questionnaire on how the second edition worked in their classrooms, I am very grateful to Pompa Banerjee, University of Colorado; Francine Canfield, University of Nebraska at Kearney; Patrice Dodd, Portland Community College; Marta O. Dmytrenko-Ahrabian, Wayne State University; Lorraine J. Duggin, Iowa Western Community College; Marilyn Francis, Washington State University; Tamara Fritze, Washington State University; Bill Hardwis, University of Illinois at Chicago; Deborah Healey, Oregon State University; Karl Kilborn, University of California at Irvine; Shelley Kirkpatrick, St. Francis College; Michael Pringle, Washington State University; Norma L. Rudinsky, Oregon State University; Bedford M. Vestal, University of Oklahoma; and Margaret J. K. Watson, Quinsigamond Community College. I am also grateful to those who reviewed the book in depth: Barbara Fister, Gustavus Adolphus College; David Hartman, St. Petersburg Junior College; and Candy Schwartz, Simmons College Graduate School of Library and Information Science. Barbara Fister deserves my special thanks for helping to update Appendix 1.

I would like to thank all of my colleagues in the Professional Writing Program at the University of Maryland who have served as exemplars of good writing teachers and who have shared their techniques with me in many ways, including our brown-bag symposia and casual discussions. I owe special thanks to colleagues Kathleen Staudt, George Oliver, and Shirley Logan and to staff members Dominique Raymond and Rosalie Lynn.

A book like this could not be written without the help of librarians. My special thanks to Courtenay Shaw, Robert Merikangas, and other librarians at the University of Maryland's McKeldin Library, who were always helpful in answering my many questions and particularly in explaining the use of electronic sources. Barbara Fister and Candy Schwartz, mentioned above, also provided invaluable advice on electronic information. Finally, I would like to thank John Dorsey of the Boston Public Library for his help in providing reference materials.

My gratitude goes to all of those at Bedford Books who attended so competently to the many details connected with publication. Once again my special thanks to Charles Christensen, whose idea this was from the beginning, and to Joan Feinberg, whose advice and support were always helpful. Beth Castrodale was a great source of suggestions and encouragement for the third edition, and Heidi Hood and Eliza-beth Schaaf ably shepherded the book through production, providing much helpful advice along the way. Joanne Diaz, Ellen Thibault, and Verity Winship offered invaluable editorial and production assistance. I would also like to thank copy editor Rosemary Winfield for her sharp eye and many helpful suggestions.

My best teachers have been the students in my classes. I am particu-larly grateful to Jamie Dietz, Walker Han, Keith Hannon, Jonathan Leung, and Ted Shih for giving me permission to use parts of their work in this third edition.

Contents

12   Writing a Paper in Science or Technology: The Citation-Sequence and Name-Year Systems   *347*

APPENDIXES   *379*

1   Annotated List of References   *379*

2   Using Footnotes or Endnotes to Document Your Paper   *432*

The Bedford Guide
to the Research Process

PART I

Searching

Research: Searching, Re-Searching, and Writing

Why We Do Research

Searching, exploring, discovering — we associate these words with excitement and pleasure, and for good reasons. We like the idea of uncovering what has been hidden, of turning the unknown into the known, whether we are exploring our inner space, like Plato or Freud, or the space beyond us, like Christopher Columbus or Sally Ride. Then, after we have made our discoveries, we like to tell others about them. Our choice of medium can be anything from film or newspapers to novels or poems. One of the most common media — and the one you will be mastering — is the research paper.

Why do we search? Searching seems to be a result of our natural curiosity, our desire to find answers to problems, our urge to question what others have told us, or perhaps just our need to know more about the unknown. We want to know how to cure AIDS or how to get a job; we want to know how things work — how plants grow or how the human mind functions. But we may not have a specific goal. We may just want to collect information — to find out what is inside the earth, what is on the moon, or how children behave at the age of two. Collecting such information and analyzing it may lead to questions about it and to further searches.

Sometimes we search to find answers to controversial social questions. As members of a community, we may find our beliefs in conflict with those of others. Should abortion be legal? Should convicted murderers be executed? How much should we be taxed? Answering such questions requires that we check the validity of our assumptions, inform ourselves adequately about the subject, and analyze the information thoughtfully. It requires that we think creatively and critically — and not become just passive receptors of someone else's obvious or popular conclusion.

Whatever our motivation is, when we search for information, we must think creatively and critically during the whole process. We must first choose a subject that will yield information likely to be valuable to ourselves or to others. Then we must find and evaluate the most reliable sources, using or rejecting the information we find. Next we must analyze that information to find its meaning, and finally we must weigh its value and implications.

With the research paper, as with all exploration, the search is as important as the telling, but when a search is compelling and absorbing for the searcher, there is an almost equally compelling urge to tell or write about it. And not simply to tell about it, but to tell it so well that the reader or listener can participate in the experience and learn what the writer found during the search. The more interested you are in your project, the better chance you have of producing an interesting paper. There are other benefits besides this tangible result. Because you direct your own search, you will gain knowledge that is important to you and that can even change your life — as, in varying degrees, all learning does.

In doing his research paper, one student, Iori Miller, discovered an area of knowledge that he wanted to continue to explore professionally. When the research paper was assigned, Miller considered plants as a possible subject. At first he thought he would concentrate on ferns. He had always admired the different kinds of ferns in the woods near his home and thought he would like to find out more about them. While looking for information about them, he came across a book on cacti and became fascinated by them. He began reading books about cacti and enrolled in a botany course. The following year he became a student assistant in the botany lab and eventually went on to do graduate work in botany.

As Miller's experience shows, a search like this has no predictable pattern and no predictable results; if they were predictable, there would be no point in undertaking the search. Henry David Thoreau (1817–1862), whom we remember as the author of *Walden*, chose a large subject for his search — he wanted to discover the meaning of life. He decided to live alone in a cabin in the woods to collect his information. Later, in *Walden*, he explained his purpose:

> I went to the woods because I wished to live deliberately. . . . I wanted to drive life into a corner, and reduce it to its lowest terms, and, if it proved to be mean, why then to get the whole and genuine meanness of it, and publish its meanness to the world; or if it were sublime, to know it by experience, and be able to give a true account of it.

Notice that Thoreau's purpose was not only to gather information for himself. He also wanted to "publish" it "to the world"; he wanted to "give a true account of it." During his two years at Walden Pond, Thoreau kept a journal in which he recorded his observations of the animals, the people, the lake, the trees, and the sky and the thoughts that these observations inspired. In dated entries in his journal he recorded his observations and thoughts as he experienced them. These were his data, his raw material. Natural events, in other words, were the books in which Thoreau did his research on life.

> I start a sparrow from her three eggs in the grass, where she had settled for the night. The earliest corn is beginning to show its tassels now, and I scent it as I walk — its peculiar dry scent. . . . I smell the huckleberry bushes. I hear a human voice — some laborer singing after his day's toil. . . . The air is remarkably still and unobjectionable on the hilltop, and the whole world below is covered as with a gossamer of moonlight. It is just about as yellow as a blanket.

Seven years after he left Walden Pond, he published *Walden*, in which he selected parts of his journal and reordered them topically under such headings as "Reading," "Sounds," "Visitors," and "The Pond in Winter." This type of organization allowed him to focus on the aspects of his experience that had the most meaning for him and to explain what that meaning was. The observations in his journal, when reviewed, gave new meaning to his subject: the sparrow instructed Thoreau in his subject, life.

> The first sparrow of spring! The year beginning with younger hope than ever! . . . the symbol of perpetual youth, the grass-blade, like a long green ribbon, streams from the sod into the summer. . . . So our human life but dies down to its root, and still puts forth its green blade to eternity.

Charles Darwin (1809–1882), an amateur naturalist from England, set out in 1831 on a five-year voyage around the world on the HMS *Beagle*. Like Thoreau, he kept a journal recording his observations of natural life in minute detail. His *Journal of Researches into the Geology and Natural History of the Various Countries Visited by HMS Beagle, 1832–36* was published after he returned. From the notes in his journal he developed a theory on the formation of coral reefs and a theory of evolution by natural selection. The latter revolutionary theory he explained in *On the Origin of Species*, published in 1859.

Each of these kinds of writing — the journal and the book created from it — has its own organizational form; each has its own value.

Like Thoreau's observations in *Walden* and Darwin's in his *Origin of Species*, what you discover while researching and writing this paper may be important not only to you but also to someone else. Peter DeGress, a student, did a study to find out whether solar energy would be a practical source of heat for his uncle's house. After finding out the costs of installation and computing the savings, he concluded that only solar hot-water heating would save his uncle money. He then drew plans for such a system and presented his results to his uncle as well as to the class.

The aunt of Rhonda Martin, another student, wondered whether a soldier with a name similar to hers who was mentioned in books on the Civil War was a relative. Martin decided to find out. She did much of her research in the genealogical section of the Library of Congress in Washington, D.C. (she happened to live nearby), and she also made a trip to a town in Maryland to look at court documents from the Civil War. She discovered that the soldier was indeed a relative, and she was able to find out a good deal more about where he had lived and worked than the family had known before. Martin's aunt paid her a small amount for her report.

Courtenay Coogan heard her microbiology instructor refer to a little-known organism, Pseudomonas pseudomallei, that was causing a hard-to-detect and usually fatal disease in Vietnam veterans. She wanted to find out what research had been conducted on this organism and to determine whether anything could be done to diagnose the disease more accurately. She was able to report to her classmates on the growing danger of this disease and the steps that can be taken to prevent it.

Joan Keller, also a student, examined different types of computers to determine which would be best for her office to buy. Because computers are expensive, she had to do her research carefully and thoroughly. She visited computer stores and talked to sales people to learn the prices and features of computers. She interviewed managers of companies who had purchased computer systems to find out actual time and money benefits as well as their ease of operation and repair records. Through her research she was able to help her company make a decision that would increase staff efficiency and save money.

How We Do Research

Searching: Finding Answers to Your Questions

The first stage in writing a paper — searching or exploring — is an activity you began very early in life, probably shortly after you were born. By the age of two you were in high gear, trying to find out everything you could about your world. "The love of the chase is an inherent delight in man — a relic of an instinctive passion," wrote Darwin as he looked back at his journey on the *Beagle.* A two-year-old is probably the preeminent human explorer, akin in many ways to the likes of Darwin or Thoreau. Watch a two-year-old on his or her own for fifteen minutes, and you'll get some idea of the single-mindedness, determination, and zest that distinguish the successful researcher. Because of these characteristics, the two-year-old will learn at an astonishingly rapid rate. Later, other search-and-find activities begin to interest us — games of hide-and-seek and treasure hunts. In school we continue our search for information with the help of others. As we get older, we may search for special kinds of seashells, antiques, or buried treasure. As professionals we continue to search: as archaeologists we seek evidence of past civilizations; as ornithologists we look for rare birds; as immunologists we try to find the cure for a disease; as business managers we search for ways to improve a product or service; as lawyers we examine records for pertinent cases. In fact, we often define ourselves or our interests according to the area in which we choose to search.

The search is as important to the searcher as is the written account. Without the interest in the search itself, the product will be of little value or interest either to the researcher or to others. For the true searcher, the product, like the extent of the search, is unpredictable, at least at the beginning. Thoreau's goal was not to write *Walden*; Darwin was not planning to write *On the Origin of Species.* They searched and observed and kept journals. Students, on the other hand, may know they will be writing a report, but what they don't know is the exact *content* of their report.

Choosing Your Topic.   As you begin to choose the subject you will explore, you should ask yourself not only "What *subject* do I want to explore?" but also "What subject do I want to be an explorer of?" You ask these questions because your result will be not only a paper but also an addition to your personal store of knowledge: each helps to define you as a person.

Chances are you already have your subject in mind — that is, in your mind. You just haven't uncovered it yet or selected one of the many subjects you have in mind. Take some time to listen to the questions you ask yourself daily about the subjects you are studying or about what is going on around you. Thoreau asked himself, "What is life?" Darwin asked, "What animals and plants exist in other parts of the world?" Peter DeGress asked, "Can my uncle heat his home with solar energy?"

Finding Sources.   Two of the benefits of writing this paper will be discovering new information and, more important, discovering new ways of finding information. As you begin, you may think first of the process often used by beginning researchers in finding information: going to the library, looking in the *Readers' Guide* and the library catalog, checking out a few books, photocopying a few articles, and then beginning to write. In doing this paper you will learn how to expand this process. No matter what size your community is, you have many sources available to you. Libraries provide books, articles, pamphlets, computer databases, microfilms, videotapes, records, and often other resources. You can probably find experts on your subject on your campus or in your town. For some types of historical research, interviews with people who have had relevant experience may be the best source. The local courthouse or statehouse has documents available to the public; museums store documents and artifacts. You may even find that you are able to access records and databases through your home computer. The dedicated researcher, in other words, looks under the stones that others merely walk around.

Collecting Information. When you select for your search one of the many subjects you are interested in, you have your first direction — the first clue in your search. The thoroughness of your search determines the amount of information you have to work with and thus, to a large extent, the quality of your paper. Peter DeGress had to find out the cost of solar space-heating systems and solar water-heating systems. He had to analyze the structure of his uncle's house and family's needs to see how these matched up with available systems. To determine whether a solar heating system would save his uncle money, he had to learn about costs of other fuels and returns on other possible investments of the money that would be spent on the heating system. Then he had to compute the effects of these expenditures and savings on his uncle's tax liabilities. Some of this information he could collect directly: as an engineering major, he could study the structure of his uncle's house and take the necessary measurements. For some information he had to rely on other people: he had to read books, pamphlets, and periodicals and make judgments about the reliability of his materials, such as how accurate a pamphlet published by a manufacturer was or whether an article by a consumer affairs group would be more reliable. And for a technical subject like this, the information had to be up to date; a book published in 1981 was not likely to be of much value. As he collected his information, he recorded it on cards or drew diagrams.

The research paper often requires you to be more an observer of events than a participant in them. You will probably be getting most of your information from the work and experiences of others — experts who may have spent years studying, observing, and examining the same things you want to know about. You'll find this information in books, articles, or databases or by conducting interviews. However, you may find that making your own observations or conducting your own experiments is more rewarding or appropriate. Whatever your method of research, your collecting of information will be *purposeful* and *directed* — you'll want to find out more about a specific subject or answer a specific question.

Keeping Records. In previous papers you've written, you assimilated the information you gathered through your senses or perhaps by listening to others and then re-searched it (found what was significant in it) and wrote it down. Even if you were only recording your experience, you were ordering and selecting and therefore giving significance to some part of your experience rather than another. With your research paper you will be gathering your information from other people's experience and knowledge, and you will have to document those sources.

Recording Two Kinds of Information: Keeping a Search Log and Taking Notes. Since you will probably be using more than your own experience as a source of information, you must learn new techniques for gathering and storing information. You won't be able to rely on your memory to store everything you learn; you'll have to write it down as you go along. And because you will be learning a process as you gather data, you will be collecting two kinds of information: *wht you do* and *what you find.* To keep track of both, you'll need to keep two kinds of records.

First, you'll be keeping a record of what you do — where you go, what kinds of sources you discover, whom you interview, and so on — in a *search log* (much as the captain of a ship keeps a log) so that you will know where you have been and what you still have to do. You can buy a small notebook for this or use a part of your loose-leaf binder. If you use a computer, jot down in a notebook what you do and then record it later in a file in your computer. Besides summarizing what you have done each day, you can put down your thoughts and feelings about your project as well as your questions or problems. It's so much easier and faster to write on a computer that you're likely to write more if you use one. Talking to yourself on a computer about your project can help you understand more clearly what you are doing and where you are going. If you have a portable computer, your job will be even easier.

This record can also be helpful when you do research in the future. Although logs or journals are commonly used to record various kinds of data, including personal experience, and are meant for a limited audience, they are sometimes interesting enough to be published (as were Darwin's and parts of Thoreau's) because often the story of the search is as exciting as what is found. When scientists Francis Crick and James Watson discovered the structure of DNA, they explained *what* they found in a scientific article, "Molecular Structure of Nucleic Acids" (1953), in the journal *Nature.* In 1968 Watson published *The Double Helix,* an account of *how* he and Crick conducted their search that was written for the general public and became a best seller. Marie Curie described the scientific work for which she won the Nobel Prize in her book *The Discovery of Radium.* So what you do can be as interesting as what you find. If you enjoy the search, you will more likely enjoy writing about what you find and thus write an interesting paper. You will probably be "publishing" only the results of your search, though you may share parts of your search log with your classmates as you go along.

Second, what you find — the information you discover — will go on note cards or separate pieces of paper so you can organize that information for easy use when you begin to write your research paper. It may be even more efficient, however, to put this information into the computer immediately. For more information on how to take notes on cards and on the computer, see Chapter 4.

Re-Searching: The Search for Meaning

The mere collecting and recording of information is only the first stage. *Re-searching* is looking back over that information and making sense of it, seeing how it fits together and how it links up with what you already know. The two-year-old is searching (exploring); she gathers and stores information but doesn't find the meaning in it as an adult would. In other words, *search* plus *re-search* equals *research*.

Of course, you have gone through this process many times. You research when you look for the scores of your favorite baseball team (the searching stage) and then analyze why they played so poorly or so well (the re-searching stage). You use the process when you plan a trip: in the searching stage you decide what route to follow, what supplies to bring, how much time to allot; and in the re-searching stage you decide whether you have the time or the money to go. Or you might decide to buy a new CD player. As part of your searching stage you would read the ads in the newspaper, ask a friend whether he likes his new CD player, and perhaps read an article in *Consumer Reports*. Then you would re-search the subject: you would put all this information together with what you already have observed about CD players and make your decision.

Writing the Research Paper

Exchanging Information. Writing down the results of your findings is naturally the next step in this process. As you research and as you write, you're finding out what significance your information has for you and what conclusions you've reached, and you're putting them in a form that will make them available to others. There's a generosity about bothering to write down the results of your search, just as there is a generosity about orally sharing your information and thoughts. Personal relations are enhanced by giving and receiving information. (Peter DeGress gave his results to his uncle, Rhonda Martin gave hers to her aunt, and Joan Keller shared hers with her office staff; all of them shared their information with other members of their class.) Communities of interest (scientific, academic, agricultural, political, religious, and sports, for example) are built and maintained through this sharing of information.

Collaborative Writing.   Besides exchanging with your classmates the information you've gathered, you might want to assist one another in all parts of the process — in effect becoming collaborators on your projects. If you do, the writing classroom, where you have the opportunity to exchange information and ideas, can also serve as a writing workshop. You have an opportunity presented to you that may not occur again: it's not easy to assemble outside the classroom a group of people with similar goals who will meet regularly for several weeks to concentrate on writing.

To be a helpful member of this group you don't have to be an expert on writing (your instructor is), but you can act as a surrogate or intermediary audience for your classmates. Each of you can provide reactions and feedback to one another at all points of the research and writing process. You might also be able to provide information and sources to each other. When everyone in the class is aware of the topics being researched by other class members, the class becomes a network of searchers that can report back relevant information found in their daily reading of newspapers, magazines, and books.

There are many other ways you can collaborate. As you go through the process outlined in this book, you will find exercises suggested for working in groups that will help you to give and receive help in writing. If you have e-mail or are linked to classmates by a computer network, you might find the "For the Computerized Classroom" exercises helpful.

The Writing Process.   Of course, you already know from doing other assignments that writing a paper is not just a simple matter of sitting down one night, recording what you know or think about a topic, and handing it in to your teacher the next day. First you need a written plan — an outline — to organize the information you have collected so that it is logical and understandable. When you sit down to write, an outline will save you time because you won't have to decide what to write next. In your first draft you need only fill in the structure of your outline with details that further shape and make meaning out of your materials. Most people need (1) a second draft to refine the organization, to add further details or support where necessary, and to check the effectiveness of paragraphs, sentences, and words; and (2) a final draft to check the documentation of sources and to solve problems of punctuation, grammar, spelling, and the like. Some parts may have to be rewritten more than twice. Starting early and following a carefully planned schedule will make it possible for you to write a good paper and meet your deadline.

The Importance of Abundance.   Start thinking now of providing more than you need at each stage of your research process. Abundance — even overabundance — is part of nature's backup system, and you can benefit from it too. Start with a list of more subjects to choose from than you need for your paper. Collect more information than you think you can use. Write more drafts than you plan to. And, if you can possibly manage it, plan to spend more time than you think it may take you to complete the project.

Even when it comes to using paper, be generous. If you're not using a computer, using both sides of sheets and cards without leaving margins may save you some money, but it will cost you a lot of time. Instead, leave plenty of space so that you can add material if you want to, and write on only one side of the paper or card. Smaller amounts of information on more cards or pieces of paper will also make sorting and organizing much easier.

Building overabundance into your process means that you must be willing to discard what you don't need. (Place your discarded paper in one of the receptacles for recycling now available on most campuses.) Producing more than you need will save you time in the long run and make your product better because it will give you choices. In case something does not work — a subject, source, piece of information, sentence, paragraph — you will have a backup. Space missions operate on this theory. When people are launched into space, they carry extra equipment with them. So as you begin your exploration, plan for leftovers. You'll end up with a better paper and save time as well.

C H A P T E R 1

Choosing Your Topic

Choosing a topic is often regarded as something that is done only at term paper or essay writing time. But we are choosing topics to explore every day. We may explore something as mundane as the taste of a new kind of cheese or as exciting as a mountain. And we're not only choosing topics; we're also rejecting many that we would like to investigate because we don't have time or they aren't important enough.

Choosing a topic is not a one-time act, like picking a carton of milk off the shelf. Choosing a topic is more of an evolutionary process that coincides with the beginning of your search. There's a bit of a Catch-22 feeling at first: you can't begin your search until you have a topic, but you can't decide on a topic until you've done some research. You need to find out

1. what the scope of the subject is,
2. what information is available,
3. whether you can find the information in the required time, and
4. whether the time required to explore the subject adequately and write your results corresponds to the time you have.

In the early stages of your search, your topic and your information direct each other: your topic tells you where to find your information (for example, in books, from people, or by observation), and your information helps shape your topic or perhaps leads you to abandon one topic and choose another. Because it's important to have a clearly defined topic as soon as possible, it is a good idea to begin your search as early as you can.

Before you can decide on a specific *topic* for your paper, you will probably want to explore one or more *subjects,* or general areas of study.

These subjects interest you because of what you have read or heard or because of what has happened to you or to someone you know. Of course, the intensity of your interest will vary from one subject to another. Now is the time to look at some of those overlooked subjects. Although your choice of subject for a research paper will depend on other things besides your interest in it, interest is certainly the main criterion and the one to consider first. The intensity of your desire to know more about your subject will keep you searching even when obstacles arise — when information seems hard to find, when you are busy with other things, and when the necessary time doesn't seem to be there. The first step in writing a good research paper, then, is to recall some of the subjects that attract you and to choose the most suitable for this occasion.

When You're Assigned a Subject.   "But what if I'm assigned a subject to write on?" you may be asking. "Then I can't write about what *I'm* interested in." Yes, usually you can. You need to find the part of that subject that relates to something you are interested in. Let's say that your American history instructor asks you to write a paper on Custer's last stand — the Battle of the Little Bighorn. Before you say that this subject doesn't appeal to you, ask yourself questions about the event that relate to other interests of yours until you find an aspect of it that you think you might like to explore. If you are taking a course in which this subject is relevant, you probably already have some information about it. Questions like the following might occur to you: Was it Custer's fault that the battle was lost? Was he a good military strategist? What was Custer's ability to command men? What was the role of the Battle of the Little Bighorn in settling the West? What is known about Custer's personal life? What fictional treatments have there been of Custer? What films have been made about this battle or about Custer? How does this battle figure into the way Native Americans have been treated by the government? After asking yourself questions like these you might come up with the following possible topics:

> Custer's military strategy
> The role of the Battle of the Little Bighorn in settling the West
> Treatment of Native Americans in settling the West
> The effect of the battle on relations with Native Americans
> The treatment of Custer in films
> The treatment of Custer in fiction

Because any subject can be treated from many angles, the steps outlined in the following pages for helping you find a subject that intrigues you can be adapted to your own use, even if you are starting with someone else's initial selection.

As you follow the steps given in this chapter, you'll notice that you begin not with choosing a single topic for your paper but with choosing a number of *general subjects* from which you can derive a more specific and manageable topic. Having more possibilities than you need will help you find a better topic. The steps outlined in the following pages are designed to help you find a subject that you will enjoy exploring and writing about and that will result in a paper you and others will enjoy reading. Record the results in your search log, where you will be able to refer to them as a guide as you go through the process of deciding on a topic.

Making a List of Subjects

Set aside an hour or more, sit down at your computer or go to a quiet place with your notebook, and let your mind range over the subjects that interest you. To aid your exploration and direct your thinking, use categories such as experiences, course work, and hobbies. Give your entry a title and a date, say "Subjects for research paper — September 28." Write down the categories you've chosen, and under each category record your thoughts about it and possible related subjects.

Writing on the Computer. If you use a computer, you may write more, and writing more than you need can be helpful at this stage. The ideas that come to you first are not always the best; besides, the more you write, the more choices you'll have. As you're writing your *thoughts,* try darkening the monitor so you won't focus on what is on the screen; you don't want to be thinking about spelling or grammar right now. Then, as you write down the *subjects,* try using boldface, so that you can easily distinguish them from other ideas later. Print out the results when you've finished.

Don't hurry this step. You are not trying to come up with a final topic; you are trying to find out what interests you and get your ideas down. If some subjects are too broad, you may reduce them to specific topics later. You'll be given suggestions for this. Just let your mind wander freely as you contemplate each one of these areas. Here are some examples:

- **Experiences:** What experiences of yours (or someone close to you) have raised questions in your mind that you couldn't answer?

    Thoughts: "I had a friend who was an alcoholic. I wonder why. I wonder if he could have been helped."

    Possible subjects: The causes and control of alcoholism. How friends can help an alcoholic.

- **School subjects:** What subjects have you studied that you wish you had time to learn more about?

    Thoughts: "My psych teacher mentioned gestalt psychology. It sounds interesting, but what is it?"

    Possible subjects: The origins of gestalt psychology. The role of gestalt psychology in mental therapy.

- **Hobbies:** What do you like to do in your spare time? Which of these would you like to find out more about?

  Thoughts: "I planted a few tomatoes last year, but I'd like to have more plants next year — a small garden maybe. Do I have enough space? Do I have enough sunlight? What would I plant? What plants grow well together? Should I use chemical fertilizers?"

  Possible subjects: Planting a small garden. Chemical fertilizers versus organic gardening.

- **Reading and television:** What television programs have you seen that made you want to learn more? What books, newspapers, or magazine articles have you read that made you want to learn more about a subject?

  Thoughts: "I saw a television program on Alzheimer's disease. My grandmother has Alzheimer's. I wonder what this means and whether there is a cure. . . . I've been watching a series of programs on China — about Buddhism and Confucianism, about the Chinese use of acupuncture, about the practice of tai chi and other martial arts to keep fit. I've always wanted to know more about China."

  Possible subjects: Alzheimer's disease. How to keep the brain from aging. The use of acupuncture in modern China. The practice of tai chi and how it keeps your body healthy.

- **Current controversial issues:** What social or ethical problems have you discussed recently with your friends? What are some current issues that you haven't been able to make up your mind about?

  Thoughts: "The use of drugs is certainly a problem that seems to be getting out of hand. Should the use of drugs be made legal? What would be the consequence of legalization? Should employees be tested for drugs? Should certain groups be tested? It's confusing."

  Possible subjects: Legalization of drugs. Mandatory drug testing in the workplace. Mandatory drug testing of college students.

Now that you've started your list, add to it as possible subjects occur to you. With the added awareness your search has already given you, you'll find that your list will increase.

Choosing Possible Topics

Reread your list carefully, putting a check mark beside the subjects that seem most interesting to you. Then reread those you have checked. Pick two that appeal to you most, and make each into a sentence beginning "I want to know more about. . . ." Then complete the following exploratory sentences for each.

1. I already know that _____.
2. I want to find out who _____.
3. I want to find out what _____.
4. I want to find out where _____.
5. I want to find out when _____.
6. I want to find out why _____.
7. I want to find out how _____.

Write these sentences in your search log. Here is an example.

Subject sentence: I want to know more about UFOs.
Exploratory sentences:

I already know
 that a lot of people say they have seen them.
 that the air force says they don't exist.
 that there are a lot of theories about what they are.

I want to find out
 why the air force thinks they don't exist.
 why there haven't been any reported recently.
 where they have been seen.
 how they are propelled.
 who has reported seeing them.
 how reliable these witnesses are.

After writing down your sentences, you should revise your subject sentence so that it more accurately reflects what you want to find out. Begin this time with "I want to know. . . ."

 Revised subject sentence: I want to know whether UFOs exist.

At this point, try rephrasing the sentence as a question to focus your topic further. "I want to know whether UFOs exist" may become "Do UFOs exist?" And "I want to find out why the air force thinks they don't exist" may become "Why does the air force think there are no UFOs?" These sentences make it clear that you are looking for answers to questions and that your paper will give the answers.

 Your question "Do UFOs exist?" now leads you to the topic "The UFO: Fantasy or Fact?" The subheadings relating to their existence (such as "why the air force thinks they don't exist") will now become more important, and a subheading such as "how they are propelled" will become less important, though it may still be included in your search.

The Controlling Idea or Thesis Statement

After you have done some of your research, you might be able to compose a sentence about the existence of UFOs or visitors from outer space, such as "UFOs do not exist." "Many people have reported visits from extraterrestrials," or "The existence of UFOs cannot be proved or disproved." Such a statement will help you further focus your search. Although you probably are not yet able to arrive at the controlling idea that directs your writing stage, you should be alert at each step to the possibility of making your topic more specific. As with other stages, you will find yourself engaged in a back-and-forth process: as you look further into your subject, you will be able to define it better; as you define it better, you will be able to direct your search more economically. With a controversial topic like visitors from outer space, you may not feel you can compose a thesis statement (a sentence that states the main point of your paper) until you have collected most of your information. Of course, even as you are writing, you are continuing to focus your topic; focusing is something to be aware of through each stage. (For more information on composing a thesis, see Chapter 6.)

Critical Thinking

Now is a good time to use your critical abilities to analyze your subject. What aspects of your subject have you failed to consider? What assumptions have you made in choosing your subject that may need to be checked for their validity?

Student Alice Denton chose as her subject the deterioration of the family in the United States. She wanted to know why family structure has declined and what the effects of this decline have been. In her "I already know" statements she wrote that the extended family was the norm in the nineteenth and early twentieth centuries; grandparents, aunts, and uncles were available for support. Then in the mid-twentieth century came the nuclear family with only father, mother, and children. Now, she wrote, the divorce rate is up, and there are more single-parent families and families with stepparents. Drug use and crime rates are up.

First Denton had to identify the assumptions she had made. What she claimed to "know" were really beliefs that she held without knowing whether they were true. After rereading her statements and discussing them with her classmates, she realized that she had made the following assumptions without careful examination:

1. *Families have gotten smaller and their composition has changed.* She did not have any data to show that families are smaller or different. In fact, one of her classmates pointed out that his great-grandparents had immigrated to this country around 1900. They were a nuclear family that in later generations became an extended family; their family became larger, not smaller. It seemed likely that many families had had a similar experience.

2. *Family structure has declined because family size and composition have changed.* First she has assumed that the quality of family life has declined and then that the size and composition of the family are related to the quality of family life. But she had no evidence that either of these was so. She also needed to define what she meant by *decline.*

3. *The decline of the family is responsible for social ills such as drug use and crime.* She realized that she had no proof that social ills are related to family composition. They might be, but there could be other reasons for social problems as well.

Denton decided to do more preliminary research on the family before making these or any other assumptions. She needed to find answers to the following questions:

1. What are the composition and size of the average family, and what changes have occurred in family structure over the last century?
2. What are the criteria for determining the quality of family life?
3. What is the judgment of sociologists about the quality of family life: do they believe that that quality has changed over the years? Why?

In fact, examining her assumptions now became the central part of Denton's research.

Dealing with Special Problems

Perhaps you know so little about your subject that you have trouble completing your exploratory sentences. Or perhaps your mind goes blank instead of overflowing with ideas. Here are three ways of solving these problems. If one doesn't work, try the others, or try all three using the same subject.

1. *Look up your subject in a general reference source.* You can use the *Encyclopaedia Britannica,* the *Encyclopedia Americana,* or an encyclopedia that specializes in one area of knowledge. (General and special encyclopedias and other reference works are discussed in Chapter 3.) One student heard gestalt therapy referred to in psychology class and decided she would like to look into the possibility of using this therapy as a research subject. The reference librarian directed her to the *Encyclopedia of Psychology* (5 vols., 1994). Under "Gestalt Therapy" she found a three-page article explaining its origins, with Fritz Perl discussing the theory, the philosophy behind it, and the techniques used by its practitioners. As she read the article, she realized that she was most interested in the techniques used in therapy. They were explained in the following paragraphs:

TECHNIQUES OF GESTALT THERAPY

Gestalt therapists have described a variety of techniques — some of them powerful and dramatic — that they use to sharpen direct experience, heighten conflicts and polarities, foster freer expression, or to bring into awareness blocks and avoidance mechanisms. Perls cautioned therapists, however, not to become technicians depending on a bag of tricks or "gimmicks." Claudio Naranjo writes, "Practically every technique in Gestalt therapy might be seen as a particularized embodiment of the broad prescription: 'be aware.' This prescription, in turn, is an expression of the therapist's belief and experience that only with awareness can there be true living" (Naranjo, 1973, p. 4).

Continuum of awareness is a technique which encourages the patient to focus on the now, the ever-shifting midpoint of experience. The Gestalt therapist will ask questions that begin with "what" (What is your present awareness?) and "how" (How do you experience this?), avoiding "why" questions which encourage theorizing, rationalizing, and justifying. If the patient attempts to diminish feelings (sadness, anger, fear) through deflection, intellectualizing, or other avoidance mechanisms, the therapist may encourage the patient instead to "stay with" whatever is in the foreground and bring full awareness to the experience. The resolution of an unpleasant situation lies in experiencing it fully, not trying to avoid it. In *Awareness* John Stevens offers an extensive compendium of Gestalt awareness exercises for individuals, pairs, and groups.

In addition to awareness, *experimentation* is encouraged so as to make sufficient contact with the environment to determine the suitability of a contemplated action. For example, when a patient avoids being critical of others for fear of rejection, the Gestalt therapist may suggest he experiment by making critical statements and noticing the results. The patient can then discover how this feels to him and what responses he actually gets from others.

In Gestalt therapy as practiced by Fritz Perls, *taking the "hot seat"* indicated a person's willingness to engage with the therapist. In this case the hot seat was a chair facing the therapist. An additional "empty chair" next to the patient might be used to imagine the presence of a significant other or disowned part of self for the purpose of initiating a dialogue. The technique of *dialogues* is helpful in identifying projected and denied parts of the personality. If, for example, a patient is conflicted between a part of herself with high expectations for achievement and another part which procrastinates, making promises and excuses — a particular personality split which Perls labeled "top dog/underdog" — the therapist might suggest a dialogue between these two parts. By using two chairs and moving back and forth between them, the patient carries out a "conversation" by speaking alternately from each position. As the interplay between these polar opposites is heightened and more fully experienced, integration through greater self-acceptance becomes possible.

The Gestalt therapist attends to the full range of a patient's expression, not just words. *Nonverbal cues* such as body posture, gestures, or tone of voice often reflect an aspect of functioning outside the patient's awareness. The therapist may ask a patient to exaggerate or repeat a gesture, for example, and through this intensification allow the patient to discover its function or significance.

The Gestalt method of *dream-work* grew out of Perls' belief that dreams are among our most spontaneous productions. Each dream is thought to contain an existential message — an expression of aspects of the dreamer's present state of being. By becoming every object and character in the dream (both animate and inanimate), the dreamer can identify with and thereby reown projections, conflicts, and unfinished situations reflected in the dream.

After rereading these paragraphs, the student made a list of the techniques that might be used in a therapy session: *continuum of awareness, experimentation, taking the "hot seat," dialogues, nonverbal cues, and dream work.* She thought she might not have time to investigate all of these, so she chose the last one. Her topic became "How dreams are used in gestalt therapy." As a result of reading the article, she had not only a topic but also a framework in which to place that topic: she knew a little about the history and the philosophy of the movement, and she had a general idea about the techniques used. In addition, the references mentioned in the text and the bibliography at the end of the article (Figure 1.1) gave her some sources with which to start her search.

With the flexibility this knowledge from her preliminary research gave her, she was able to expand or redirect her topic in response to the information that she had found. Although she decided to concentrate on dream techniques, she might have chosen any of the other techniques that looked interesting. She also might have included a brief summary of the history and philosophy of the theory at the beginning of her paper. With this map of her subject, she began her search with confidence. She had a clear sense of direction with flexibility enough to adapt to whatever other information she might find. In her search log she recorded a map of her mental journey so far (see Figure 1.2).

2. *Use special categories to help you analyze your subject.* We are all familiar with the physical habits we've developed — waking up at the same time, eating the same foods, and so on. We are not always this aware of our mental habits because our minds are caught in the same daily grooves. A characteristic of the good researcher is the ability to see

FIGURE 1.1 Sample Bibliography

FURTHER REFERENCES

Fagan, M. J., & Shepherd, I. L. *Gestalt therapy now: Theory, techniques, applications.*

Perls, F. S. *In and out the garbage pail.*

Perls, F. S. *The gestalt approach and eyewitness to therapy.*

Perls, F. S., Hefferline, R. E., & Goodman, P. *Gestalt therapy: Excitement and growth in the human personality.*

Shepard, M. *Fritz: An intimate portrait of Fritz Perls and gestalt therapy.*

FIGURE 1.2 Search Log Entry

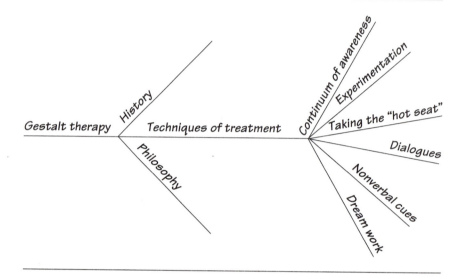

things in several ways. The following exercise helps stimulate your thinking processes by looking at a subject from various points of view. You don't have to be a scientist to find it useful to think about a subject from a scientific point of view. Just thinking about a subject this way may suggest something completely different to you because it will help you break down your traditional thinking habits and improve your mental agility. Try applying these exploratory categories — personal or psychological, sociological, political, historical, scientific, and any others you wish to include — to any of your subjects. The following examples illustrate how to use such categories to stimulate new ways of thinking.

Subject: Dropping the bomb on Hiroshima

Personal: Who were the people in the airplane that dropped the bomb? What was their reaction to the explosion and its aftermath? How do they feel about it now? How do the Japanese who survived the attack feel toward the United States?

Sociological: What were the effects of the bomb on the people of Japan? Did it affect the Japanese social structure?

Political: Was the attack justified? What were its short- and long-term political repercussions in the United States? How did it affect relations between the United States and Japan after the war?

Historical: What was the historical significance of this event? How did it affect Japanese history? What are the current attitudes in Japan toward this attack?

Scientific: How was the bomb developed? Was there any scientific value in this act? What medical treatment were victims of the attack given?

Trying to answer such questions on this subject might lead to the following topics.

The effect on the people who flew in the plane of dropping the bomb
Why the bomb should not have been dropped
Why President Truman made the right decision
The development of nuclear arms in the future
The current relationship between the United States and Japan

3. *Try talking to your computer.* Some computer programs (often called *prewriting* or *preinvention programs*) prompt your thinking with questions about the purpose of your topic or your reasons for selecting it. Your computer may even answer you on the screen. If you don't have a special program, try talking to yourself and writing the conversation on the computer.

"Why can't I come up with a topic I like?"
"Because I've got two or three good topics and I can't make up my mind which one to settle on."
"Well, why not?"
"Maybe if I had more time. That's not really it. I like one but I don't know if the teacher would like it. But it would be popular with my classmates."
"But why don't you pick the one *you* want to find out about? And what is it about this topic that makes you want to choose it?"

Keep going. Press yourself to say what's on your mind. Talk about the pros and cons of the topics you're considering.

If you are linked to other students in your class through a computer network, try sending them some of your ideas. You might find that others have knowledge or insights that can help you. An online conversation on health foods might go something like this:

KERRY P.   As long as I can remember, health food has been a pretty big deal. The whole health food movement interests me, but I'm not sure what to focus on. Any ideas?

MARTA C.   Did you know that the inventor of Kellogg's Cornflakes was an early health food enthusiast? I learned that last year in a class where we read *The Road to Wellville.* Some pretty interesting characters have been part of the health food movement.

KERRY P.   That's cool. Maybe I could focus on the history of the movement or on some of the key players throughout history.

CARLOS T.   Hey, I read that graham crackers were invented as a health food too. You might want to check that out.

KERRY P.   Thanks!

Some people — even those who have never used a computer before — feel that a computer allows them more freedom to play with an idea than a pen or pencil does.

Choosing a Topic

Choose one of your two topics as the subject in which you will do your research, using your own interest or the approval of your instructor as your guide. Keep your second subject in reserve. When you start a search, you are embarking on the unknown or at least on what is largely unknown to you: that is the nature of the activity. You must do some planning on the basis of what you know and what others have told you, but until you get there, you don't know whether your plans will work. Therefore, you need both a first-choice topic to begin your search with as well as a backup topic.

Turn to your backup topic if the answer to any of the following questions about your first-choice topic is yes.

1. *Is your topic so new that little has been written on it?* Topics aimed at exploring recent technical developments, newly discovered diseases, or new solutions to old medical problems often prove frustrating because information on them is scarce.

2. *Can the answer to your main question be found only in a single source?* If you rely on only one source, instead of writing a research paper you will end up paraphrasing or summarizing a book or an article. Such a problem often arises with a process topic that may be covered in a manual ("How to Set Up a Salt Water Aquarium") or with a general historical topic that may be adequately summarized in a good encyclopedia ("Events Leading up to the Revolutionary War"). Historical subjects that are more limited or that have produced different points of view may work better (for example, "How Pennsylvania Came to Enter the Revolution" or "The Importance of French Assistance in the Revolutionary War").

3. *Are you unable to find the information you need in your library?*

4. *Is the information you need contained in highly technical journals written in language you don't understand?* Translating technical articles (for example, articles from the *IEEE Transactions of Quantum Electronics*), takes too much time.

5. *Will you need more time than you have to find information about your topic?* You might, for example, have to write to a government agency that cannot promise you a reply in time. Or you might have to get your materials through interlibrary loan. You can avoid the latter problem by checking your library for sources as soon as possible and, if interlibrary borrowing is necessary, finding out how long it will take to receive the publication you want.

Sometimes you can anticipate these problems before you choose a topic. Your instructor, who has had more experience than you, can also be helpful. But sometimes it is impossible to know what your problems are until you start your search. Kathy Matthews, in a narrative she wrote explaining her research process, tells what happened to her.

> The hardest part of the research paper for me was getting the right topic. I had several criteria to meet: (1) the topic had to be approved by my history teacher; (2) it had to be large enough so that I could write a ten- to fifteen-page paper on it; and (3) it had to be interesting enough to help get me through several otherwise tedious weeks of research. After making lists of subjects I was interested in, I finally settled on "The Effects of Agent Orange on Vietnam Veterans." I figured that periodicals and government documents would be my chief sources of information.
>
> What I didn't know until I started my search was that the campus library has very few government documents. I discovered that all of the military documents on defoliation are still classified and unavailable to civilians. A few newspaper articles had been written, but they seemed to have the same problems I did — little solid information. Fortunately I had a second choice — "Is Melatonin Really a Wonder Drug?" This topic, though I had to get my information primarily from newspapers and periodicals, worked out successfully.

After you begin your search and complete your preliminary bibliography (see suggestions given in Chapter 3), you should be firmly committed to your topic. To turn back at this point will make it difficult for you to finish your paper on time.

EXERCISES

1. **FOR YOUR SEARCH LOG**

   a. Record the subject you have chosen to search.
   b. Identify and list the assumptions you made as you selected your subject. Leave several spaces between each.
   c. After each assumption, write down the information on which you have based your assumption.

   You may want to ask your classmates to help you locate and examine these assumptions.

2. **FOR THE COMPUTERIZED CLASSROOM**   You can do this exercise in collaborative writing in a computer lab in groups of three or four, depending on the capacity of your networking software. If your class is equipped for online conferencing, you can broadcast to the whole class. Place one of your subject sentences and several of your exploratory sentences

on the screen. Ask your classmates to answer the following questions onscreen:

a. Are there other parts of this subject that would be interesting to explore?
b. What do you know about this subject that might help me?
c. Where can I find more information?

Print out the answers if you wish and if your system permits, or note the most helpful suggestions in your search log.

3. **FOR PEER RESPONSE** Read part of a recent daily newspaper or newsmagazine, and list any interesting research subjects that the articles suggest to you. Choose five subjects, read them to your classmates, and discuss their possibilities as subjects for research. If members of your class agree to read the same selections, you may prefer to do this exercise in small groups.

CHAPTER 2

Planning Your Search

Creating a Search Strategy

Now that you have chosen a topic, you will want to plan your search, much as you would plan a trip. You'll need an itinerary or search strategy showing where you will go, what you will do, and in what order you will undertake the search. Such a strategy will ensure that you can conduct your search in the most effective and efficient way possible. Of course, your plans are always subject to change as you learn more about your subject and about the sources available. Explorers sometimes have to change directions, and you too may find new areas to explore. You also may find that some places you had planned to go to no longer interest you. Although you need a firm plan to follow, you need to be ready to alter that plan when new information requires it. So before you begin your search, complete the following tasks:

1. Make a timetable.
2. Compose a preliminary outline.
3. Adjust the scope of your project.
4. List possible sources of information.
5. Develop a search strategy.
6. Assemble your materials.

Record the timetable, outline, and list of information sources in your search log. The rest of this chapter provides suggestions to help you.

Making a Timetable

A timetable will help you allocate enough time to each part of your project so that you meet your deadlines and end up with a good paper. As you make your estimates, consider your writing habits, the amount of time you will be able to spend on the paper, and the recommendations given here (which are based on an average of about two working hours a day). Although it is difficult to make such a plan — it is especially hard to judge how much time to set aside for gathering your information — setting up the framework and then revising it as circumstances require will help you finish your paper on time.

Divide your work into the following stages: (1) searching, (2) re-searching, (3) writing, (4) revising, and (5) preparing the final copy (each of these stages is discussed in a separate chapter). Estimate how long it will take you to do each part, starting with the due date and working your way back to the present. You will thus allot time first to those tasks whose required time is easiest to estimate and leave the remaining time for searching, the most difficult stage to predict. Such a timetable will be most effective if you work a few hours each day or each week instead of concentrating on your project for a week or two and then neglecting it for a few weeks. If you don't maintain continuity, you will have to rethink your project each time you start to work on it.

Remember that these stages enable you to plan; the actual process will probably be recursive. For example, as you re-search or as you write, you may discover that you lack necessary information and need to return to the library. As you move steadily forward, maintain your flexibility.

1. The searching stage (see Chapters 3, 4, and 5) is the most difficult to estimate at the beginning because you don't know yet what you need to find, what you will find, and where you need to go to find it. Will you be conducting interviews? You will need to arrange them. Will you be administering a questionnaire? You will have to design and administer it. Because the time required for this stage is so unpredictable, it's a good idea to start your search as soon as possible. The first step will be to compile a preliminary list of sources; then you need to find out whether the sources are available. You should make these determinations as soon as possible — within a few days of beginning your search. If all goes well, you can proceed with your search. On the other hand, if you decide that your topic will not work, you will have time to change it. The recommended minimum time for searching (assuming you can spend six hours a week) is one month — more if you have it.

2. At the next stage, re-searching (see Chapter 6), you have completed your searching and will now be organizing your material, writing a detailed and accurate outline, and developing or revising your controlling idea or argument. The recommended minimum time for re-searching is six to eight hours, divided between two days.

3. The third stage is writing the first draft (see Chapter 7). Most people like to write the first draft of a ten- to fifteen-page paper at one or two sittings. If your paper is shorter or longer, adjust your time accordingly. Try to reserve two consecutive days for this work — four or five hours a day. The recommended minimum time for this process is ten hours divided between two days.

4. In the revising stage (see Chapters 8 and 9) you have to make a judgment about your writing habits. Some people revise as they write the first draft; most people write two or three drafts before the final draft. Leave time between your drafts for "incubation" and for doing other classwork. Two weeks is the recommended minimum time for revising.

5. Preparing the final copy (see Chapters 10, 11, and 12) is the final stage. Your answers to these questions will help you estimate the time required for this step: If you are using your college's computer system, can you arrange for computer and printer time when you want it? Will other papers be due at the same time? When are final exams scheduled? Allow time, too, for proofreading and photocopying. The recommended minimum time for final preparation is three days for a ten- to fifteen-page paper. Adjust your schedule to fit the length of your paper.

Adapt these suggestions to fit your own needs, and count back from the time your paper is due to determine specific dates. Mark these dates on your calendar. Here is a typical schedule for an assignment received early in the semester.

Searching: February 15 to March 22
   By February 22, complete preliminary list of sources and make final decision on choice of topic.
   February 23 to March 22, conduct search.
Re-searching: March 23 to April 1
Writing: April 2 to April 15
   Incubation: April 16 to April 19
Revising: April 25
Keyboarding final copy: April 26 to May 1
   Proofreading, correcting, and photocopying: April 30 to May 2
   Paper due: May 3

If your paper must be completed in a shorter time, you should scale down this timetable to suit your needs. Here's a suggested shortened timetable of about a month. To finish a paper in this length of time, you may have to spend more time each day and on weekends.

Searching: April 1 to April 14
Re-searching: April 15 to April 18
Writing: April 19 to April 25
    Incubation: April 16
Revising: April 27 to April 30
Keyboarding final copy: May 1 to May 2
    Proofreading, correcting, and photocopying: May 2
    Paper due: May 3

If you are working within a quarterly system, use the following timetable as a guide.

Searching: March 27 to May 19
Re-searching: May 20 to May 25
Writing: May 26 to June 8
    Incubation: June 9
Revising: June 10 to June 17
Keyboarding, proofreading, correcting, and photocopying: June 18
    to June 21
    Paper due: June 22

Composing a Preliminary Outline

Reread the exploratory sentences you wrote in your notebook or your computer file when you were choosing possible topics. By grouping and rearranging them, you can create a brief outline to help you organize your search. If your subject is "rheumatoid arthritis," you might have the following exploratory sentences.

I already know
    that RA occurs because the body reacts against its own immune
        system.
    that the specific cause of the problem has not been identified.
    that those affected usually have swelling of the joints.
I want to find out
    how the immune system works.
    the physical characteristics of those who have RA.
    current theories about the cause of RA.
    how RA differs from other types of arthritis.
    the groups of people most affected by RA.
    the treatments or cures.

The first step in organizing these headings is to group them. They seem to fall into three main groups: the causes of RA, the symptoms of RA, and treatment of those with RA. By arranging your subheadings according to these groups, you produce the following outline. Numbers and letters for a traditional outline are included in brackets to indicate that you can choose either a formal or informal structure at this point.

[I.] Rheumatoid arthritis: Background
    [A.] Physical symptoms
    [B.] Populations affected
[II.] Causes of RA
    [A.] Normal immune response
    [B.] Immune response in those with RA
    [C.] Possible causes of RA
[III.] Treatments for RA

Adjusting the Scope of Your Subject

Once you have divided your subject this way, you can usually limit it by dropping one or more of the headings or subheadings according to what you find as you begin your search. You might discover, for example, that certain data are limited or nonexistent or that it takes so long to gather the information on one of your important points that you begin to run out of time. If your topic is UFOs, for instance, you might need to write to the air force for information about its investigations or you might want to conduct interviews. Because these efforts are time-consuming, perhaps you would decide to concentrate your time and energy on these sources instead of newspaper investigations. You should also add to your outline as you discover topics you weren't aware of. For example, you might discover that the sighting of UFOs is not a contemporary phenomenon and that similar stories have been told throughout history.

Listing Possible Sources of Information

Make a list in your search log of all the places where you think you might find information on your subject. From what you know about your subject, you should have some general ideas about where you will find most of your information. Joe Collins, who decided to evaluate gas-saving devices for cars, knew that he was going to acquire most of his information from examining and testing the devices himself. In addition, he had seen at least one article on such devices and thought there might be more. Margaret Little, in researching the effects of caffeine, realized that she would not be able to do her own experiments on the subject and would have to rely on reports from original researchers. She guessed she would find her information primarily in periodicals and perhaps books.

Here are some sources that have been successfully used by student researchers. You will find items on this list that don't apply to your subject, or you may know of places not on this list where you can get the information you need. You cannot, of course, be completely sure what sources will be helpful until you try them. See Chapter 3 for details on how to use the library.

Library sources:
General reference works (encyclopedias, biographical sources, indexes, dictionaries, handbooks)
Specific books on the subject
Periodicals (journals, magazines, newspapers, newsletters)
Government documents
Pamphlets and brochures
Computer databases: online or CD-ROM
Films
Recordings
Videotapes
Reference librarians

See Chapter 5 for details on the following sources:

Other sources:
Lectures (public or academic)
Museums
Television and radio programs
Interviews
Letters
Questionnaires
Personal observations, tests, or experiments

The list for a paper on UFOs might look like this:

Library sources:
Encyclopedias
Indexes
Periodicals, newspapers
Specific books on the subject
Government documents (for Air Force studies)
Reference librarians

Other sources:
Television and radio programs

The Computer as a Search Tool.   Most topics can be researched in print or microform sources, but computer searching has advantages that have resulted in increasing use of this research tool. Perhaps its greatest benefit is saving time. In a few minutes, you can search through the equivalent of many volumes of print sources merely by typing key words. In addition, more and more libraries are subscribing to computer services instead of, or in addition to, print sources.

Some narrowly defined topics require a computer search. For example, because electronic databases can be searched with many more terms than print sources, you might use such a search to find sources on adult education programs for immigrants. Such a narrowly defined topic would be difficult to search in printed indexes with their limited terminology and cross-references.

Another advantage of computer searching is that because electronic databases are constantly updated, they are more likely than print sources to have recent information in them. A computer search provides current information on such subjects as recent political events, new scientific discoveries, or contemporary literary criticism. The printed version of the *Readers' Guide to Periodical Literature,* for example, is updated semimonthly for six months of the year and monthly for the other six months, but the database version of the *Readers' Guide to Periodical Literature* is updated daily.

At many college libraries users now have the option of making computer searches on CD-ROM (a compact disc with read-only memory) as well as online (via a connection to a large computer containing many databases). In most libraries the CD-ROMs are installed in the computers; you'll be directed to the one with the database you want.

If you have a home computer and a modem, you may be able to access your library's online database system, including the library catalog as well as other databases that the library subscribes to. Your college or university system may also provide access to the Internet, which you can use to search hundreds of databases and communicate with other users. (For more information on the Internet, see p. 73.) If you do your research at the library, you may have the option of printing out the information you receive or downloading it onto your own disk.

Developing a Search Strategy

After you complete your list of possible sources of information, decide what order you will use in exploring these sources. Devise a strategy that will consider the needs of your topic, the materials available, and the requirements of the assignment. Estimate how long each step in your search will take — whether you will have to make advance appointments or request material by mail, for example, and how important to your project such information would be. Of course, you will have only a rough idea at the beginning of your search of what your sources might be. As your search progresses, you will revise your strategy to fit your experience. The reordered list for a paper on UFOs might look like this:

1. Encyclopedias
2. Government documents (These are an important source that might take some time to obtain.)
3. Television and radio programs (These may be of questionable importance and would take time to find and review.)
4. Indexes (electronic or printed)
5. Specific books on the subject

6. Reference librarians (This source might be consulted earlier if you encounter difficulty.)

A researcher relying primarily on personal observation might have quite a different set of priorities. Marian Glass, writing on the image of the elderly as portrayed on television, expected to gather her information for her paper from watching television programs. Written sources would be secondary. Her ordered list looked like this:

1. Television programs (These are an ongoing source.)
2. Lectures (She would reread her notes from a psychology lecture on the way different age groups are portrayed on TV.)
3. Interviews (She would call immediately to see whether she could schedule an interview with the local newspaper's reviewer of TV programs. For a discussion of interviewing, see Chapter 5.)
4. Periodicals (She would check electronic databases.)
5. Pamphlets (These might contain recent studies of television programs.)
6. Books (These were the least likely to be useful because the information in them was probably outdated.)

Assembling Your Materials

As you do your research, you acquire two kinds of learning: knowledge about a subject you're interested in and knowledge about a process — how to search for, find, record, and organize information from your observation and from outside sources. Because you won't be able to contain all of this information in your head, you'll need to keep the following records: (1) the data from your sources, written on cards or on your computer, and (2) an account of the process you use, recorded in your search log.

Taking some time now to decide what materials to use and buying them if necessary will make your work easier and save you time later. Here are some items to consider.

Writing Implements. Writing on a computer is much faster than handwriting, and the copy is easier to read. You may be able to use a library computer or even take a portable computer to the library. If not, take your books out of the library, and photocopy or request copies of articles from other libraries. Then take your notes. (Do not, however, use photocopying as a substitute for note taking: it's only an intermediate step.) If you must handwrite your notes, use pen and not pencil because pencil smudges easily and is generally more difficult to read.

Writing Materials. If you use a computer, you may need to buy only one type of paper for everything — for note taking as well as for printing out your paper. Most writers, however, will probably take some notes by hand. Cards are easy to carry and easy to sort later; use 4-by-6 inch or 5-by-8 inch cards for notes (3-by-5-inch cards are useful for recording your sources). You might choose to take notes in small notebooks the size of note cards. Finally, you might use ordinary 8½-by-11-inch notebook paper divided evenly into two or three horizontal sections. When you're ready to write your paper, cut the pieces apart and rearrange them. (How to record information on these cards is discussed and illustrated in Chapters 3, 4, and 5.)

Planning for Efficiency. When doing research, use the most efficient materials available, unless you have an unlimited amount of time to spend on your project. With the proper software, notes made on a computer can be inserted directly into your paper. Some programs make it possible to divide the screen so that you can read a note and type it or parts of it into your draft at the same time. With note cards, you can write one piece of information on each card and then order them according to your outline before you begin writing your paper. Cards are easier to arrange and more durable than paper.

The following hints will make your work more efficient and will save you time and money in the long run.

- *Do not take notes on random scraps of paper.* This practice may result in lost material or too many items on a page.
- *Do not write your notes continuously in a notebook.* If you write your notes under headings, you will have less difficulty organizing them later.
- *Do not write on both sides of your paper.* If you use only one side, you will be able to look at all of your notes at once.
- *Do not use photocopying as a substitute for taking notes.* Note taking is an important part of thinking critically about your material. Photocopy only when you don't have time to read and take notes on the material in the library or when you are storing your information in a home computer.

EXERCISES

1. **WRITING** Use the entries in your search log to write a two-page paper for your instructor based on the following information:

   a. The topic of your research paper (make it as specific as you can at this time),
   b. Your reasons for choosing this subject,
   c. Knowledge you already have of this subject,
   d. Information you want to obtain about this subject, and
   e. Possible sources to consult.

2. **FOR PEER RESPONSE** Before the whole class or in small groups, read your paper to your classmates, and ask them whether there are other

aspects of your subject that interest them and that also might interest you. They may have suggestions about additional sources of information, as well.

3. **FOR THE COMPUTERIZED CLASSROOM** In groups of three or four, take turns displaying papers on group members' computer screens. Group members should comment onscreen on the following aspects of each paper:

a. Is enough information likely to be available on this subject?

b. Is all of the information needed likely to be available in one book or one article? If so, you do not have a topic for a research paper.

c. Will you be able to find the information you need in the time you have?

C H A P T E R   3

Compiling Your Working Bibliography

Where to Start Looking

There is no single best place to start a search for information. You can start by interviewing someone who knows about your subject, by gathering information through observation, by distributing a questionnaire, by checking the Internet, or by going to the library to extract information from books and electronic sources. Two considerations are important in deciding where to start: you want to find some general information about your subject so that you have a framework within which to operate, and you want to give priority to those types of information that take more time to obtain. Each of the following students started searching in a different place.

Bob Larkin, who wanted to study the culture of the Mayan Indians, began his search in an encyclopedia to see what was generally known about the Mayas and to get some bibliographic leads. Siti Salim, who planned to investigate learning disabilities in children, went first to the psychology teacher who had mentioned the subject in class and talked further with him about specific areas she might study. Besides giving her some good advice on how to structure her project, he gave her a list of helpful books on the subject. She also obtained some helpful suggestions from participants in an Internet newsgroup on learning disabilities. Moira Jones wanted to examine the disposal of hazardous wastes, so she visited a company engaged in that business. John Exley, whose subject was the use of steroids by college athletes and who wanted to send a questionnaire to college coaches, concluded that he needed to design and send his questionnaire as quickly as possible to receive the returns in time to include them in his paper.

What You Can Find in the Library

For many students, the library is the best place to start a search, and compiling a *working bibliography* — making a list of possible information sources — is their first step. In addition to printed information (including books, journals, newspapers, and pamphlets), your library may have films, CDs, records, and videotapes. Some libraries have paintings, photographs, and collections of private papers. Printed matter is sometimes accessible on microforms — either microfiche (a film sheet that usually reduces the size of the material contained on it) or microfilm (35-mm film rolls). Bibliographic information, abstracts, and even complete texts are available on computers at many libraries. To aid you in finding your way, many libraries offer tours, both guided and unguided, and most have a directory or map. Taking advantage of these services will save you time in the long run.

The information given here about libraries applies primarily to academic or other research libraries. Most public libraries will not have all of the specialized indexes, dictionaries, and professional journals that are collected in college libraries. However, they sometimes have books of general interest that college libraries would not have, so you may want to look in both places.

Making a List of Sources

Before you begin to read and take notes in the library, you should compile a list of possible sources — your working bibliography. It will change as you begin to read: you may drop some sources that are not relevant and add others that are suggested by your reading.

The information given in this chapter will provide a guide for most of the information sources in the library, as well as in the Internet, which lets you search beyond the library. The detailed discussions of each group of sources will help you decide which of them apply to your project and which you can omit.

As you locate your sources, keep three kinds of records: (1) a record of the sources you have found, (2) an account of where you went and what you did, and (3) notes on your reading for use in your paper.

Recording Bibliographic Information

Identifying information about books, periodicals, pamphlets, and other sources that are potentially useful should be recorded in a computer file or on 3-by-5-inch cards. You can record such information in a notebook if you write on one side of the page so you can easily cut notes apart and rearrange them. Putting them in a computer file allows you to type them according to the documentation style you will use in your paper. This list will be your working bibliography. (See Figure 3.1 for examples from a working bibliography in APA style.) Because the list will contain only those sources in which substantive information for your paper is found, it won't include titles of indexes (the *Readers' Guide to Periodical Literature,* for example). However, it may include indexes containing abstracts (such as *Psychological Abstracts*) if you plan to use the information contained in the abstracts. The list will also include those encyclopedias or dictionaries that provide you with enough information to use in your paper. Encyclopedias and dictionaries used only for background reading or for bibliographic leads are usually not listed in a bibliography. Record useful information from an encyclopedia or from indexes on 4-by-6-inch or 5-by-8-inch note cards or in your computer. (See Chapter 4 for more suggestions on taking notes.)

Be sure you record all the bibliographic information about your sources that you will need later for full, scholarly documentation of your paper. Decide now which of the three main documentation systems you

FIGURE 3.1 Selections from a Working Bibliography (Author-Date Style)

Bandini, L. G., & Dietz, W. H. (1992). Myths about childhood obesity. <u>Pediatric Annals, 21,</u> 648.

Dietz, W. H. (1994). Critical periods in childhood for the development of obesity. <u>American Journal of Clinical Nutrition, 59,</u> 955-959.

Marcus, Erin. (1990, September 5). Study finds children risk high blood pressure if fat. <u>The Washington Post,</u> p. A3.

Pfanner, P., & Marcheschi, M. (1992). Psychological aspects of childhood obesity. In P. L. Giorgi, R. M. Suskind, & C. Catassi (Eds.), <u>The obese child</u> (pp. 149-154). Basel, Switzerland: Karger.

Rosenthal, Elisabeth. (1990, January 4). New insights on why some children are fat offer clues on weight loss. <u>The New York Times,</u> pp. B7, B8.

Schwartz, M. W. (Ed.). (1989). <u>Pediatric primary care: A problem-oriented approach.</u> Chicago: Random House.

will be using (see Chapters 10, 11, and 12 and Appendix 2) so that you can record the data in the appropriate order. However, although each system orders the bibliographic data in a slightly different way and uses different styles of punctuation, all systems require the following information.

Books.   Record the call number, author(s), title and subtitle, editor, translator, edition, volume number of book or total volumes in the book, name of the series, place of publication, publisher, and date. You will find this information on the title and copyright pages. Copy the facts down exactly as you find them. If only the author and title are given in a database, record these on a card, and fill in the other details when you look up the book in the library catalog. (See "Finding Information in the Library Catalog," p. 44.

Articles.   For articles in periodicals, record the author(s), title of article, name of periodical, volume number (omit for popular magazines), date or issue, and page numbers. Add a note indicating where you found this reference. If you found it in an index or database, give its name; you might want to return to the same source for further references.

It may be tempting to list books and articles on one sheet of paper at this early stage, but it's best to put every work on a separate card or in your computer file, even if you don't know yet whether you will use it. When you actually find the work, you can add extra information that might help you, such as details from the table of contents, titles of relevant chapters, a summary of the abstract, or the fact that it has a bibliography. That way if you decide not to use a work, you'll know why. Eventually, of course, you will arrange your sources in the order in which you record them in your list of references at the end of your paper.

Other Sources.   For sources other than books and articles, record any other information — in addition to author, title, date, edition, and so on — that identifies the source. For example, if you are considering using a source retrieved through a computer network such as the Internet, be sure to record the electronic address of the source. If you plan to use government documents, remember to record the issuing agencies and any document numbers provided.

Recording the Bibliography on a Computer.   If you locate your sources in a print index, you can put them on cards and transfer them to your computer file later. If you are using a computer database — either online or on CD-ROM (see p. 49) — the computer may have an attached printer on which you can print a copy of sources you want to save; or you may be able to download the information to your own disk. As you add to your list, your computer may be able to arrange the entries in alphabetical or numerical order. Check your computer software for a Sort command. If it has this capability, you will be able later, if you wish, to move the list as a single document into its final position at the end of your paper. Of course, you may have to change the style of the entries to fit the bibliographic style you are using. Figure 3.1 shows excerpts from a working bibliography kept in a computer file. The main types of bibliography cards are shown in Figure 3.2, and a computer file containing those same sources is shown in Figure 3.3. While typing in the sources in your computer file, try to use the documentation style that you will use in your paper, and enter sources in alphabetical order by sources' last names. That way, you can transfer the bibliography directly to your paper later on. (Notes like those in brackets at the end of the entries in Figure 3.3 should be deleted when you prepare your final list of works cited.)

After making a list of your sources, record in your search log the

FIGURE 3.2   Bibliography Recorded on Cards (Author-Page Style)

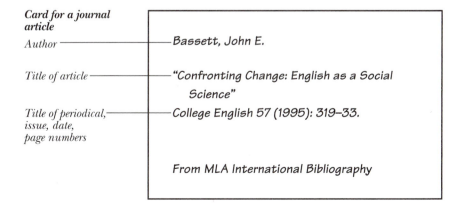

Card for a book

Library of Congress —————— PE1068.U5E47   1990
call number

Author ——————————— Elbow, Peter.
Title ——————————————— What Is English?

Place of publication, —————— New York: MLA, 1990.
publisher, date

From MLA International Bibliography, online

Card for a journal
article

Author ——————————— Bassett, John E.

Title of article ———————— "Confronting Change: English as a Social
                              Science"

Title of periodical, —————— College English 57 (1995): 319–33.
issue, date,
page numbers

From MLA International Bibliography

FIGURE 3.3   Bibliography Recorded on Computer (Author-Page Style)

Bassett, John E. "Confronting Change: English as a Social Science." *College English* 57

(1995): 319–33. [From MLA International Bibliography, CD-ROM.]

Elbow, Peter. *What Is English?* New York: MLA, 1990. [From MLA International

Bibliography, online library catalog.]

institution(s) you used, the bibliographic sources you examined, the date you examined them, and any other comments you might want to include about your search. (See Figure 3.4.)

Finally, record any information you think you may use and photocopy articles for later reading. Although you will probably take most of your notes later as you read books, articles, and other sources, you may

FIGURE 3.4   Search Log Entry

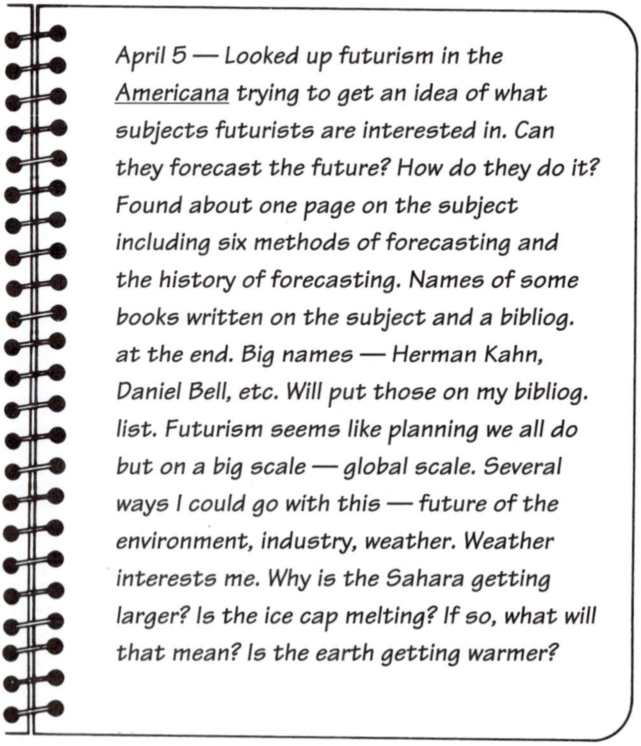

April 5 — Looked up futurism in the *Americana* trying to get an idea of what subjects futurists are interested in. Can they forecast the future? How do they do it? Found about one page on the subject including six methods of forecasting and the history of forecasting. Names of some books written on the subject and a bibliog. at the end. Big names — Herman Kahn, Daniel Bell, etc. Will put those on my bibliog. list. Futurism seems like planning we all do but on a big scale — global scale. Several ways I could go with this — future of the environment, industry, weather. Weather interests me. Why is the Sahara getting larger? Is the ice cap melting? If so, what will that mean? Is the earth getting warmer?

FIGURE 3.5   Brief Exploratory Entry from an Encyclopedia

Subheading from outline

Author, title of article

Name of encyclopedia, volume number, page number

This note combines direct quotes and paraphrase. (See Chapter 4.)

> Robert Fitch, "Futurism"   Types of
> Americana, Vol. 12, p. 209   forecasts
>
> "Exploratory forecasting" — working from the present; furturists try to predict what will happen.
> "Normative forecasting" — using this type, futurists imagine a desirable result and try to figure out how to achieve that.

find some information worth recording through your exploratory reading in encyclopedias (see Figure 3.5). (For suggestions on taking notes and for further models of note cards, see Chapter 4.)

Beginning Your Library Search

You will save time if you familiarize yourself with the arrangement of library resources before actually starting your search. Then you will be able to go directly to those rooms or sections that have the information you need. Most college libraries offer tours, either guided by a librarian or self-guided. A typical college library contains the following areas:

- A room that provides access to the *library catalog,* either by computer terminals (the *online catalog*) or by cards (the *card catalog*). Terminals for periodical databases in specific subject areas such as business, education, law, and medicine will probably be located here also. (Of course, if you have a modem and personal computer, you can search the online catalog as well as other databases that may be accessible through it, from home.)
- A *reference* section, which contains encyclopedias, print indexes, handbooks, and other reference books that can't be checked out of the library.
- A *periodicals* area or room, which contains current and bound periodicals (bound periodicals are shelved by call number) and possibly microfilm machines for viewing periodicals on tape. (Many libraries offer computerized periodical indexes.)
- A section called the *stacks* where books that can be checked out are shelved.

- An *audiovisual* section, which contains CDs, records, audiotapes, videotapes, and films.
- Rooms for *special collections* where items such as government documents, maps, music, and rare books are stored.

Large institutions may have separate libraries that store information relevant to specific disciplines such as computer science, engineering, chemistry, music, drama, or art.

You can begin your search in any of these areas. If your subject is very general, you may want to focus it by looking it up in a general encyclopedia such as the *Encyclopaedia Britannica* or in a specialized encyclopedia such as the *Encyclopedia of Anthropology*. For most researchers, though, the online catalog (or PAC, public-access catalog) may be the best place to start. (See "The Library Catalog," p. 47.)

As you gain more experience in the library, you will find that researching is an exploratory, recursive process. The references you find in your early searching will lead you back to more sources; periodical articles will yield lists of other relevant articles; encyclopedia articles will provide further sources. You may find that even after you start to write, you need to return to the library to gather more information, so be sure to build some time into your schedule for return trips. Even though the research process is not a simple trip from one point to another, constructing a simple road map at the beginning may help you keep your bearings as you progress.

A Typical Library Search

Of course, each person's search strategy will be different, but a typical library search might proceed in this order:

1. To the *library catalog and other databases* to find the titles and locations of encyclopedias, books, and periodicals;
2. To the *reference section* to find articles in encyclopedias or to consult other reference books;
3. To the *periodical room* to read current articles or articles in bound volumes, on microfilm, or databases;
4. To the *stacks* to locate books; and
5. To *special collections* to consult government documents or nonprint sources.

Finding Information in the Library Catalog

Each book in the library is given a unique call number so that it can be easily distinguished from all other books. This call number appears on the book and on the pertinent cards in the card catalog or in entries in the online catalog. Two classification systems, Dewey decimal and Library of Congress, are in common use.

Dewey Decimal System

This system classifies books by using numbers and decimal points. All information is divided into the following ten groups:

000–099	General Works	600–699	Technology
100–199	Philosophy		(Applied Sciences)
200–299	Religion	700–799	The Arts
300–399	Social Sciences	800–899	Literature
400–499	Language	900–999	History
500–599	Pure Science		

Each of these classes is further divided into groups of ten, each of these groups into more subdivisions, and so on. Decimal points are added to increase the number of subdivisions. Here are the ten main subdivisions of Technology:

600	Technology	650	Management
	(Applied Sciences)	660	Chemical Technology
610	Medical Sciences	670	Manufactures
620	Engineering	680	Miscellaneous Manufactures
630	Agriculture	690	Buildings
640	Home Economics		

Printed below a specific number and its divisions (for example, 610.73, which includes books about nursing) is a combination of letters and numbers that represents the individual book's author and title. For example, Ronald Philip Preston's *The Dilemmas of Care* has been classified this way:

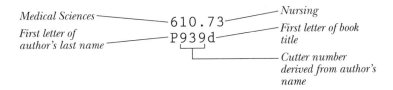

Medical Sciences ——— 610.73 ——— *Nursing*
First letter of author's last name ——— P939d ——— *First letter of book title*
——— *Cutter number derived from author's name*

Library of Congress System

This system was developed to make even more categories possible than are allowed under the Dewey decimal system. Instead of the ten basic divisions of knowledge of the Dewey system, the Library of Congress system maintains twenty basic divisions corresponding to the letters of the alphabet (I, O, W, X, and Y are omitted, and E and F are both reserved for North and South American History):

A	General Works	K	Law
B	Philosophy, Psychology, Religion	L	Education
		M	Music
C	History and Auxiliary Sciences	N	Fine Arts
		P	Language and Literature
D	History and Topography (except North and South America)	Q	Science
		R	Medicine
		S	Agriculture
E–F	History: North and South America	T	Technology
		U	Military Science
G	Geography and Anthropology	V	Naval Science
		Z	Bibliography and Library Science
H	Social Sciences		
J	Political Science		

An additional letter subdivides these divisions. Medicine, for example, is divided into the following categories:

R	Medicine (General)	RL	Dermatology
RA	Public Aspects of Medicine	RM	Therapeutics
RB	Pathology	RS	Pharmacy and Materia Medica
RC	Internal Medicine		
RD	Surgery	RT	Nursing
RE	Ophthalmology	RV	Botanic, Thomsonian, and Eclectic Medicine
RF	Otorhinolaryngology		
RG	Gynecology and Obstetrics	RX	Homeopathy
RJ	Pediatrics	RZ	Other Systems of Medicine
RK	Dentistry		

Other letters and numbers that follow the decimal point provide further subdivisions. Here is the call number for *Rehabilitation Medicine* by Howard A. Rusk:

Medicine ————————	**RM** ———————	*Therapeutics*
Cutter number derived from author's —————	**700** ———————	*Physical medicine, physical therapy*
name	**.R8**	

Library of Congress Subject Headings

Most college and university libraries use the Library of Congress classification system for cataloging their books and for arranging the contents of both the online and the card catalogs. They may also use the index system of the Library of Congress to organize their library catalogs. Therefore, you may save yourself some time if you consult the *Library of Congress Subject Headings (LCSH),* usually located near the library catalog, before you begin your search to find out whether the words you have used to identify your subject are the same terms that the library has used to identify it. For example, if your subject is "solar heat," you will not find books under that subject in the library catalog. If you have looked first in the *LCSH,* you will know that instead of "solar heat," the Library of Congress uses the heading "Solar heating:"

> Solar heat
> USE Solar heating
> Sun—Temperature

Under "Solar heat" in the *LCSH,* you will find other subject headings that might be helpful (See Figure 3.6). The front pages of the *LCSH* contain a complete list of symbols and abbreviations.

The Library Catalog

The *library catalog* (also known as the *PAC* or *public-access catalog*) is usually *online* and located on the first floor. Most colleges have moved their old *card catalogs* to a remote location where they can still be used by those who are looking for older sources. Although libraries that have switched to online catalogs usually don't keep card catalogs up-to-date, the terms used in the card catalog for cross-referencing are helpful when you search online as well.

The online catalog stores information about all the library's holdings in a large database, which you can access at a terminal consisting of a keyboard and a screen monitor. The database contains the call numbers of all the books in the library's reference room and stacks; special collections may be recorded in a separate catalog. The database

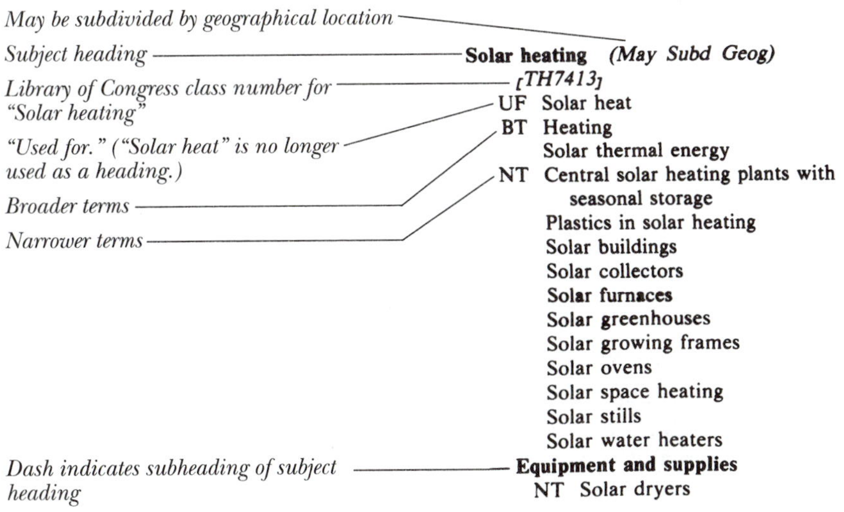

FIGURE 3.6 Entry from the Library of Congress Subject Heading

also may provide connections to other online databases. (If you have your own computer with a modem, you won't have to go to the library to access the catalog.)

To begin your catalog search, type in either the author's name, the book's title, the subject, or a key word. The *Library of Congress Subject Headings (LCSH)* can save you time by giving you the term closest to your subject (see p. 46). If you want to narrow a key-word search, you may enter another term. When Yusef Price started a catalog search under the subject "animation," he found far more titles than he could use. Because he was mainly concerned with the history of animation, he added the term "history." This narrowed his search and provided him with titles that were more suited to his topic. When he called up the first title on the screen, the heading for classifying that book and books like it appeared, which gave him further help with finding the best search term.

If you add a term to narrow your search but the screen still shows a large number of titles available, you can select the Display command, and the computer will show sources in reverse chronological order. Usually you will want the most recent information, anyway. You may get ideas for new terms from the titles displayed.

Besides providing the call number, complete title, name of author(s), and publication data for each source, the screen usually will show whether a book has been checked out and, if it has, when it is due. Also, you may be able to place a hold on a book to give you time to pick it up — a great convenience, especially when you are not searching at a terminal in the library. If your online catalog includes the catalogs of nearby libraries, it may be possible to have a book sent to your library for you as an interlibrary loan. Figure 3.7 shows a catalog entry displayed in a search under the subject "human gene mapping."

Finding Indexes.   You can use the online catalog to locate periodical indexes in your subject. Here are some suggestions:

- Find the title of an index in your subject area. (A list of indexes by subject area appears in Appendix 1 in this book.) Then perform a title search in the catalog to find the call number and location of the index.
- Search the catalog using your subject heading. The indexes will appear after the subject with the subheadings "periodicals — indexes." For example: "Biology — periodicals — indexes."

Getting Help.   Most college libraries offer classes in the operation of the online catalog; if these are available, you will save time by attending. When you do encounter problems during your library search, ask for help from a librarian. You don't want to spend a lot of time looking for information when a librarian can give immediate assistance.

FIGURE 3.7   Screen from a Subject Search of the Online Catalog

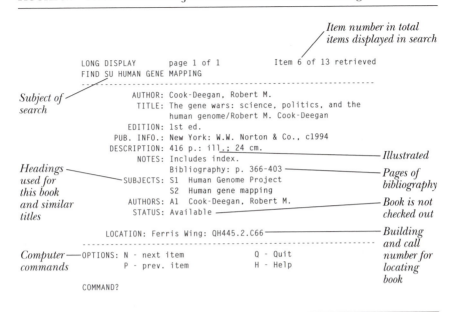

Other Library Databases

Other databases, either online or on a laser disc called a CD-ROM (compact disc with read-only memory), may be available at stand-alone terminals near the catalog stations. Printers may be attached to some terminals so that you can print out relevant sources or, in some cases, abstracts or complete articles from periodicals. At some terminals you may be able to download information onto your own disk. If you locate a magazine or journal article that you would like to read but that can't be downloaded, you may be able to order a copy onscreen and have it mailed or faxed to you or to your library. There probably will be a charge for this service. (For descriptions of databases by discipline, see Appendix 1.)

Searching Online.   At an online computer terminal, you can search for periodical titles, book titles, or even full texts of multivolume works (encyclopedias, for example). Among the databases available online are BIOSIS (biology), *Business Periodicals Index,* ERIC (education), *General Science Index, Humanities Index,* LEXIS (law), LEGI-SLATE (government documents), MEDLINE (medicine), *MLA International Bibliography* (arts and humanities), the *National Newspaper Index,* and PsycLIT (psychology).

Searching on CD-ROM Discs.   Many of the databases available online are also stored on CD-ROM and preinstalled on a computer.
When a computer has several discs covering different years, the years
covered will be listed onscreen. The library subscribes to CD-ROM
databases just as it subscribes to print indexes. Because the vendor provides updated discs at intervals of only one to three months, CD-ROM
information is usually less current than online information, but for
most research projects it is adequate.

In most cases onscreen directions will help you find the information
you want in these databases. If you need more help, check the shelves
near the computer terminals for explanatory booklets. If an onscreen
tutorial is provided, it may be worth your time to use it.

The computer printout in Figure 3.8 shows an excerpt from the
PsycLIT database, which is available on CD-ROM. With this database
searchers can use their own terms as well as the descriptors suggested

FIGURE 3.8   Printout from a CD-ROM Search

Vendor or distributor — SilverPlatter 3.11

Database — PsycLIT Journal Articles

Dates of journals included — (1/90-9/95)

Indicates second record out of 17 — 2 of 17

Title of article — TI: Agoraphobia: The interface between anxiety and personality disorder.

Author — AU: Pam,-Alivin; Inghilterra,-Karen; Munson,-Catherine; Jacqueline

Institution — IN: Bronx Psychiatric Ctr, NY, US

Journal — JN: Bulletin-of-the-Menninger-Clinic; 1994 Spr Vol 58(2) 242-261

IS: 00259284 — *ISSN: International Standard Serial Number*

Year of publication

Inclusive pages

Language of publication — LA: English

Date of issue

Publication year — PY: 1994

Volume and issue

Abstract: a short summary of the article — AB: Suggests that the etiology of agoraphobia can be attributed to a predisposing antecedent character structure. The initial panic attacks are triggered by a stressor, but patients can then use these symptoms to further intensify and justify avoidant and dependent behavior. An autobiographical account of a 52-yr-old agoraphobic woman is presented and discussed. The "fear of fear" characteristic of agoraphobia is readily traced in the S's history to a family background in which she was conditioned to feel that she could not manage without the direct support of her father. (PsycLIT Database Copyright 1994 American Psychological Assn, all rights reserved)

Key phrase — KP: predisposing character structure & fear of fear; 52 yr old female with agoraphobia

Descriptors — DE: AGORAPHOBIA-; ETIOLOGY-

Population described in this entry — CC: 3215; 32 — *Classification code*

PO: Human

Age of subject — AG: Adult

UD: 9410 — *Volume of* Psychological Abstracts *and abstract number*

AN: 81-37605

JC: 1142 — *Journal code*

Update code

in the *Thesaurus of Psychological Index Terms.* The searcher here entered two terms — "agoraphobia" and "etiology"— so both terms had to be found in the title or the abstract in order for the article to be cited. The more terms you use, the narrower your search will be.

Finding Information in the Reference Area

The reference area, often near the online terminals, is a good place to continue your search. As you enter the room, look for a display rack containing handouts. College libraries often prepare lists of commonly used sources in specific disciplines as well as lists of electronic reference sources identified by subject area. Such lists can be timesavers because the library has completed the first steps of your research for you.

The following list shows the printed materials usually available in a library's reference room. Consulting the sources in the order presented here — from general to more specific — works best for most search projects, but you can adapt this list to your own needs.

Encyclopedias: general encyclopedias, such as the *Encyclopaedia Britannica,* or a specific encyclopedia, such as the *Encyclopedia of Philosophy,* or both

General sources of bibliographic information, such as *Books in Print*

Biographical indexes, such as the *Dictionary of American Biography*

Periodical indexes, such as the *Humanities Index* and the *General Science Index*

Dictionaries

Indexes to government documents

Handbooks and directories

If, for example, your topic is "The Role of the Ku Klux Klan during the Civil Rights Movement," you might compile this list of sources to consult, in order, in the reference area:

Encyclopedia Americana
Essay and General Literature Index
New York Times Index
Social Sciences Index
Sociological Abstracts
Readers' Guide to Periodical Literature
A Dictionary of Politics
Congressional Record

All of these will probably be available in print in the reference room. Most of them will also be available on computer databases.

Computer-Aided Searching
in the Reference Area

Although print indexes still have their uses, most of your bibliographic information will probably be obtained from a computerized database. The bibliographic databases — those containing indexes and abstracts — are the ones you should use as you begin. You may also be able to search reference works such as encyclopedias and dictionaries at a computer terminal in your library. Some of these probably are connected to a printer. In some cases you may be able to download information onto your own disk.

Choosing the Best Format.   Because many indexes in the library are available in more than one format — online, CD-ROM, or print — you should consider the advantages and disadvantages of each form.

ONLINE
Advantages: Because online databases are updated frequently, in some cases daily, they provide more up-to-date information than other formats. In addition, you can search several years at once, combine two or more topics in one search, and print the results. As the number of online databases increases, even more information is likely to become available. Some databases can be accessed through the college online catalog. Full texts of articles may be available.

Disadvantages: Some libraries require an appointment or waiting period for a terminal, and others may charge for each minute of use. Online searching may not be available in smaller libraries.

Best use: Online databases are good for extensive research projects, for projects requiring very current information, and for in-depth searching of narrow or complicated subjects.

CD-ROM
Advantages: Access to CD-ROMs is easy, although you may have to sign up for them in advance. Instructions are provided onscreen. Use is free. The information that you select can be printed out.

Disadvantages: Information is usually not as current as what is available online, although it is more current than print sources. Small libraries may have a limited selection of CD databases.

Best use: CD-ROM indexes are good for most undergraduate research projects in libraries with a variety of databases.

PRINT
Advantages: More indexes, especially less commonly available ones such as the *Biography Index* and the *Essay and General Literature Index,* are available in this form than any other. All libraries have

some print indexes; they allow random browsing and are easy for the inexperienced searcher to use. Also, they require no waiting time and no fee. Print indexes are the only available source for articles published before 1980.

Disadvantages: It takes much more time to search through several volumes of different print indexes than to use either of the electronic index formats. Print indexes are less current than electronic databases. Sources found in print indexes have to be copied by hand or photocopied.

Best use: Print indexes are the only choice in libraries without computerized facilities. They are useful for a broad search or for searching that requires only a few sources. They are the best choice for a quick search for a single item.

For more information on computerized research, see "Finding Information through the Internet" (p. 73).

Some of the most frequently consulted print sources are discussed next. (For a full listing of computerized and print resources by discipline, see Appendix 1.)

Encyclopedias

General Encyclopedias. Unless your subject is an event or discovery that occurred very recently, the best place for you to start your search for information may be a general encyclopedia. There you might discover facets of your subject that you hadn't thought of, and such discoveries may lead you to expand or narrow your search or to change direction. An encyclopedia article also shows how your specific topic fits within the framework of the subject as a whole. General encyclopedias attempt to give summaries of knowledge about everything — an impossible task, of course — and in order to make this knowledge easily accessible, most of them are organized alphabetically. Finally, most encyclopedia articles conclude with helpful bibliographies. Be sure to check the publication date of the encyclopedia; even the most recent edition may not be current enough for your needs.

The *New Encyclopaedia Britannica* (32 vols., new printing yearly; also available online and on CD-ROM) consists of the *Micropaedia: Ready Reference* (vols. 1–12), the *Macropaedia: Knowledge in Depth* (vols. 13–29), the *Propaedia: Outline of Knowledge* (1 vol.), and the Index (2 vols). The *Britannica* has attempted to counteract the fragmentation that occurs with alphabetical organization of subjects. In the *Propaedia,* a volume-length outline of subjects discussed in the *Micropaedia* and *Macropaedia,* the editors try to show the interrelatedness of all knowledge. They divide knowledge into ten areas (such as "Matter and Energy," "The Earth," and "Human Society") and explain in an introductory essay, "A Circle of Learning," their belief that knowledge is circular, not linear.

A table of contents at the beginning of the volume directs you to the part of the outline in the *Propaedia* in which you can find the subject you are interested in. After each section of the outline, you are referred to relevant articles in the *Micropaedia* and *Macropaedia*.

There are no articles in the *Propaedia* except for introductory essays to each of the ten sections. Browsing in this volume might help you to determine the part of a subject you would like to research and also give you valuable perspective — a framework for your research. For example, if you're interested in the theater but aren't sure what aspect of theater to study, you could look under "Part Six, Art." Under "Section 622. Theatre," you would find a detailed outline followed by a list of articles given in the *Micropaedia* and *Macropaedia*. See Figure 3.9 for an excerpt from this outline and Figure 3.10 for a list of subject headings on this subject to be found in the *Macropaedia* and *Micropaedia*. In addition, the *Propaedia* contains a directory of the full names and professional affiliations of the authors of articles in the *Micropaedia* and *Macropaedia* (in the latter volumes authors are identified only by their initials).

The *Micropaedia* contains short articles that summarize a subject and refer you to related articles in the *Macropaedia*. The *Macropaedia* contains longer signed articles on broader subjects with bibliographies at the end. You will find more on a specific subject in the *Micropaedia*, but in the *Macropaedia* that subject is discussed in a larger context — perhaps in several different articles. For example, if your subject were the Italian novelist and playwright Luigi Pirandello, you could look up his

FIGURE 3.9   Part of the Outline for "Theatre" in the *Propaedia*

Section 622.	**Theatre**

A. The art of theatre

    1. The nature and origins of theatre as an art

    2. Functions of theatre and theatrical production; *e.g.,* theatre as social, moral, or religious expression; theatre as entertainment

    3. Problems of theatre and theatrical production

    4. Interrelation of theatrical performance and audience

    5. The arts of design in the theatre: staging and the design of stages, sets, lights, costumes, and makeup

Reference to section C within this outline —— [see C.2., below]

    6. Directing

    7. Acting

    8. The roles of other arts in the theatre: literature, music, dance, painting, and architecture [see C., below]

B. Kinds and methods of theatrical production

Reference to section elsewhere in the Propaedia ——

    1. Diverse kinds of theatrical production

      a. Kinds defined by the nature of the production itself

        i. The traditional dramatic forms or genres; *e.g.,* tragedy, comedy [for these forms as literature, see 621.C.3.]

FIGURE 3.10 Subject Headings in the *Macropaedia* and the *Micropaedia*

MACROPAEDIA: Major articles dealing with the theatre

African Arts	Folk Arts	Theatre, The Art	Theatrical
American Peoples, Arts of Native	Oceanic Arts	of the	Production
	Puppetry	Theatre, The	
Central Asian Arts	South Asian Arts	History of	
Circus	Southeast Asian	Western	
East Asian Arts	Arts		

MICROPAEDIA: Selected entries of reference information

General subjects

dramatic conventions and techniques:	chorus	Stanislavsky method	biomechanics
agon	courtyard theatre	stock company	Cruelty, Theatre of
lazzo	directing	summer theatre	environmental theatre
soliloquy	hanamichi	theatre	Fact, Theatre of
elements of theatrical production:	open stage	theatre-in-the-round	little theatre
acting	proscenium	*movements and tendencies:*	Living Newspaper
actor-manager	régisseur	Absurd, Theatre	theatricalism
system	repertory theatre	of the	
	skene		

name in the Index, where you would see references to articles in the *Micropaedia* and *Macropaedia* (see Figure 3.11).

If you looked up the reference following his name, you would find in the *Micropaedia* (vol. 9) a summary of his life and professional accomplishments along with a bibliography. Under the first subheading you would find an article in the *Micropaedia* about his association with a contemporary novelist, Capuana. The second subheading, "contribution to," introduces articles in both the *Micropaedia* and *Macropaedia* on Pirandello's contribution to Italian literature in general and on his specific contributions to Italian theater, novel, and tragicomedy. The last line refers the reader to the list of recent Nobel Prize winners in volume 8 of the *Micropaedia*. There the reader learns that Pirandello received the Nobel Prize for Literature in 1934, two years before he died.

FIGURE 3.11 *Encyclopaedia Britannica* Index Entry

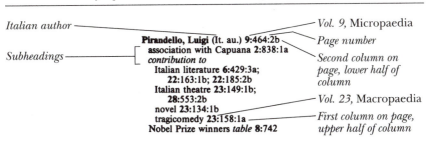

The *Encyclopedia Americana* (30 vols., new printing yearly) contains an index volume, which is helpful if you haven't used the same terminology as the *Americana* has for your subject. This encyclopedia is known for its attention to North American affairs and to scientific and technical subjects; in recent editions it has expanded its coverage of international subjects as well. The editors consult with school curriculum designers and attempt to keep up with the current needs of American students, a goal that may account for the relatively large amount of space given to biographies. However, in general it is not kept as up-to-date as the *Britannica*. The final paragraph and the bibliography of the *Americana*'s discussion on Pirandello are illustrated in Figure 3.12.

Examples of a bibliography note and a textual note derived from an encyclopedia article are shown in Figures 3.13 and 3.14. In Figure 3.14, notice that the volume and page numbers aren't given; these are unnecessary for notes from encyclopedias that are organized alphabetically. Significant words in Figure 3.14 are enclosed in quotation marks.

The *Columbia Encyclopedia* is an excellent one-volume work providing concise articles in most academic areas. It is a good choice if you want a short summary of a subject along with a brief bibliography. The entry on Pirandello gives a brief account of his life, names his main novels and plays, and lists four authors who have written about him.

You may want to consult more than one of these encyclopedias, depending on your purpose: the *New Encyclopaedia Britannica* for establishing the interrelationships of your subject with other areas of knowledge; the *Americana* for science and technology, American studies, and biographies; and the *Columbia Encyclopedia* for a brief introduction to your subject.

FIGURE 3.12   Last Paragraph and Bibliography from the Pirandello Entry in the *Encyclopedia Americana*

A few of Pirandello's contemporaries failed to understand the subtlety of his thought and technique and tended to dismiss his theater as a clever hoax. Most serious critics, however, expressed great admiration for it and valued highly his contribution, despite a recurrent weakness in his dramatic structure. Commentators in Italy engaged in controversies concerning the validity of Pirandello's ideas, but even those who accused him of excessive "cerebral" qualities granted him a high place as a theatrical innovator, ". . . an artist at the center of our time."

THOMAS W. BISHOP
Author of "Pirandello and the French Theater"

Bibliography

Bentley, Eric, *The Pirandello Commentaries* (Northwestern Univ. Press 1986).
Bishop, Thomas W., *Pirandello and the French Theater* (1960; N.Y. Univ. Press 1970).
Paolucci, Anne, *Pirandello's Theater: The Recovery of the Modern Stage for Dramatic Art* (Southern Ill. Univ. Press 1974).
Sogliuzzo, A. Richard, *Luigi Pirandello, Director: The Playwright in the Theatre* (Scarecrow 1982).
Vittorini, Domenico, *The Drama of Luigi Pirandello*, 2d ed. (1959; reprint, Russell & Russell 1969).

FIGURE 3.13 Bibliography Note for an Encyclopedia Article

Author ——————————— Bishop, Thomas W.
"Pirandello," <u>Americana</u>

Editions are ——————— 1995 ed.
published yearly

Note on content ——————— Bibliography of five items

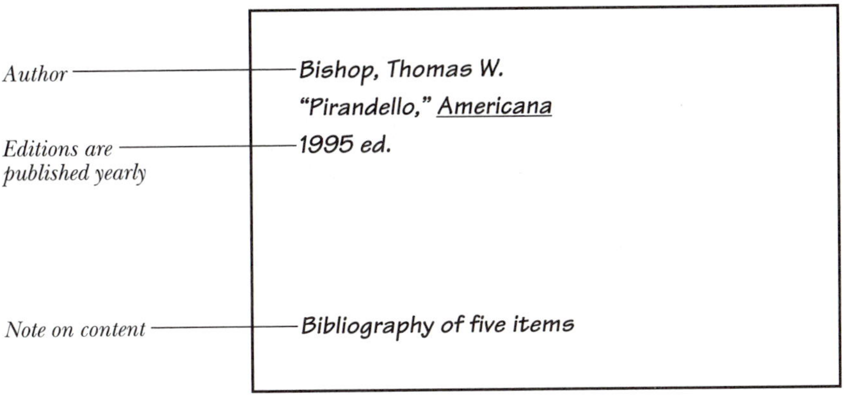

Specialized Encyclopedias. An encyclopedia dealing only with your subject, such as the *Encyclopedia of Educational Research* or the *Encyclopedia of Anthropology*, may give you specific information unavailable in other, more general encyclopedias. For instance, if you want to know about the religion of the Hittites, who lived about 1000 B.C., consult the *Encyclopedia of Religion and Ethics*, which contains an extensive discussion along with a bibliography.

The *Encyclopedia Judaica* is a good source for articles on Jewish culture and history. The *Dictionary of the Middle Ages* (20 vols.) provides articles on topics ranging from farming and medicine to philosophers and rulers. The *McGraw-Hill Encyclopedia of Science and Technology* and the *New Grove Dictionary of Music and Musicians* (20 vols.) cover their subjects in more depth than do general encyclopedias. The *Encyclopedia of*

FIGURE 3.14 Note from an Encyclopedia Article (Record on a card or in your computer.)

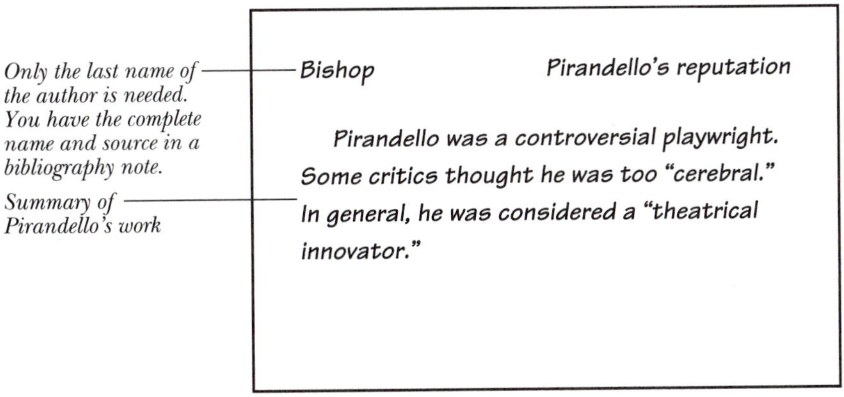

Only the last name of ——— Bishop   Pirandello's reputation
the author is needed.
You have the complete
name and source in a   Pirandello was a controversial playwright.
bibliography note.
                               Some critics thought he was too "cerebral."
Summary of ———————
Pirandello's work   In general, he was considered a "theatrical

                               innovator."

Associations provides the names of organizations that issue newsletters and other publications, maintain libraries, and conduct research. George Forte received helpful information in writing his paper (see Chapter 10) from Native American associations, such as the Native American Rights Fund (NARF), listed in this encyclopedia and shown in Figure 3.15. You can find other specialized encyclopedias and reference books in Appendix 1.

You might also enjoy exploring the new multimedia encyclopedias, like *Microsoft Encarta* and *Grolier's.* Multimedia encyclopedias typically allow for more search options than print encyclopedias and are enlivened by video clips, sound files, and animations. They may include atlases or timelines. In a multimedia encyclopedia it is easy to jump from one topic to a related one and to print or download information. However, many of the most popular are designed for a broad audience and may not provide the depth you require. *Microsoft Encarta,* for example, is designed for ages nine through adult, so its articles tend to be written at a level a nine-year-old child can understand.

General Sources of Bibliographic Information

You may be looking for a bibliography on your subject to give you a start in your research. If you are, look in an index of bibliographies — a bibliography of bibliographies. Here are some of the most commonly used general bibliographic guides. (For print and electronic indexes and bibliographies on specific subjects refer to Appendix 1 of this book.)

Bibliographic Index: A Cumulative Bibliography of Bibliographies is published quarterly with a yearly cumulative index. It cites not only periodical articles that contain bibliographies but also books with substantial bibliographic information and separately published bibliographies. By

FIGURE 3.15 Entry from the *Encyclopedia of Associations*

Reference number

Title of association, with abbreviation

★15813★ NATIVE AMERICAN RIGHTS FUND (NARF)

Address and phone

1506 Broadway
Boulder, CO 80302
John E. Echohawk, Dir.
PH: (303)447-8760 FX: (303)443-7776

Fax number

Description, including staff and budget information

Founded: 1970. **Staff:** 44. **Budget:** $4,900,000. Represents Indian individuals and tribes in legal matters of national significance. Provides legal counsel in the protection of Indian lands and resources. Areas of concern are: tribal existence; protection of tribal resources; human rights, including educational matters and religious freedom; accountability of federal, state, and tribal governments; Indian law development. Serves as National Indian Law Support Center to legal service programs. **Libraries:** Type: reference. Holdings: 5,000. Subjects: Indian law cases, studies, hearings.

Publications and subscription information

Publications: *Indian Law Support Center Reporter*, monthly. Newsletter. Provides local legal services attorneys with information on developments in the area of Indian law. Includes summaries of recent court decisions. Price: $36.00/year. Advertising: not accepted • *Legal Review*, semiannual. Newsletter. Covers NARF's involvement in Indian legal issues. Price: free. Advertising: not accepted • *National Indian Law Library Catalogue*, quarterly • Also publishes index to *Indian Claims Commission Decisions*.

Information about meetings

Conventions/Meetings: semiannual board meeting - always May and November, Boulder, CO.

FIGURE 3.16 Entry from the *Bibliographic Index*

Main heading —— Falkland Islands War, 1982
 Miller, E. Willard (Eugene Willard), and Miller, Ruby M. —— Subtitle of book
Authors of book —— The Third World - Argentina and Uruguay; a bibliography.
 (Public administration series, bibliography P-2913) Vance
Title of book —— Bibls. 1990 31p
 Diplomatic history —— Subdivision by topic
 Kinney, Douglas. National interest/national honor; the
Date of publication diplomacy of the Falklands crisis; published in cooperation
 with the Institute for the Study of Diplomacy, Georgetown —— Pages containing
Publisher —— University. Praeger Pubs. 1989 p357-64 bibliography

looking up either a subject or an author, you will find sources that contain bibliographies. Figure 3.16 shows a sample entry under the major heading "Falkland Islands War" and tells you where you can obtain a list of sources on that subject.

Published in London, *Walford's Guide to Reference Material* (3 vols.) is a source for international bibliographies, indexes, dictionaries, encyclopedias, and directories. The word *Material* in the title indicates that, besides books, *Walford's* lists periodical articles and databases and that the format may be print, microform, online, or CD-ROM. A separate index of online and database services is provided. For information on your subject, use the table of contents to find the appropriate section and browse through it, or look up your subject in the index. Bibliographies for science and technology are listed in Volume 1 (1994); those for social and historical sciences, philosophy, and religion, in Volume 2 (1994); and those for generalia, language and literature, and the arts, in Volume 3 (1987). Figure 3.17 shows an entry from Volume 2 for databases in psychology.

FIGURE 3.17 Entry from *Walford's Guide to Reference Material*, Volume 2, Social and Historical Sciences, Philosophy and Religion

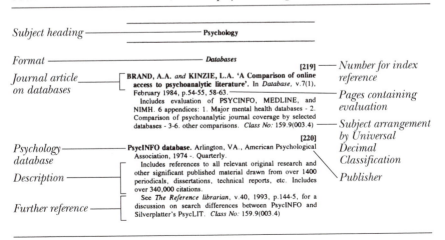

Trade Bibliographies and Bibliographies of Books

Books in Print (with new editions yearly) is a multivolume index of the books currently available for sale by book agents in the United States. (It is also available online and on CD-ROM.) If an important source book on your topic is not on the library shelf or has been ordered but not yet cataloged, *Books in Print* will supply you with complete bibliographic information, including publisher's name and address. Books are classified by subject, title, and author. The subject listing for Martin Luther King, shown in Figure 3.18, lists the first six of the many books about him.

If you're looking for books outside of the United States, try the *Cumulative Book Index,* published monthly, with a bound cumulative volume each year. It includes primarily books published in English; entries are listed by author, subject, and title. Both *Books in Print* and the *Cumulative Book Index* are available online, on CD-ROM, and in print.

Ulrich's International Periodicals Directory (5 vols. in print; also available online and on CD-ROM), published annually, can answer many questions you may have about periodicals related to your topic. The main section, "Classified List of Serials," contains periodicals arranged by subject; the "Title Index" lists periodicals by title with a cross-reference to the main section. Use *Ulrich's* if you do not know the titles of periodicals in your subject area or if you know the titles but don't know where they are indexed. For each periodical listed, *Ulrich's* provides such information as the first year of publication, the publisher or sponsor, where it is indexed, and whether it is available online or on CD-ROM. It even gives telex and fax numbers if they are available. *Ulrich's* provides the notation "Refereed Serial" for periodicals (usually profes-

FIGURE 3.18   Entry from Subject Index to *Books in Print*

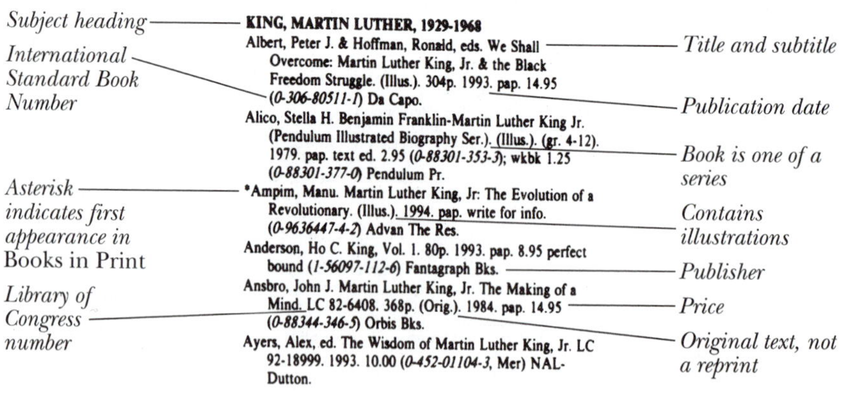

sional journals) whose articles are evaluated by peer reviewers before acceptance. The example in Figure 3.19 shows an entry from *Ulrich's* for a scholarly journal.

Ulrich's also includes a User's Guide to daily and weekly newspapers of general interest published in the United States (vol. 5). Newspapers are listed alphabetically by state, city, and name. Volume 5 is a good place to look for sources of information on local affairs in any town or city in the United States. Subject-oriented newspapers published in other countries are classified by subject along with other periodicals in Volumes 1 through 4.

Paperbound Books in Print, organized by author, title, and subject, lists books available in paperback editions or in both paperbound and hardcover copies. The *Essay and General Literature Index* (from 1900, issued three times a year with a yearly cumulative volume) contains citations to essays and parts of books in the humanities that are generally not listed in other indexes. Material is indexed by author, subject, and sometimes title. Figure 3.20 gives an example.

Biographical Indexes

The *Biography Index* is a good source if you want to find out what books and articles have been written about a famous person. It includes famous people, living or dead — from basketball players ("Abdul-Jabbar, Kareem") to authors ("Zola, Émile"). For biographies

FIGURE 3.19 Entry from *Ulrich's International Periodicals Directory*

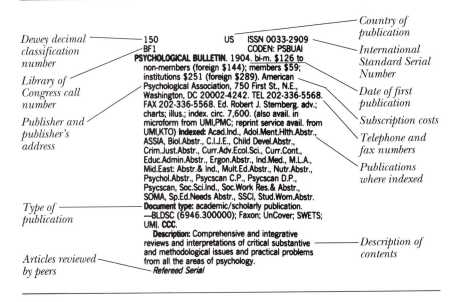

FIGURE 3.20   Entry from the *Essay and General Literature Index*

Author/subject heading ——— **Atwood, Margaret, 1939-** ——————————— Author's birth year
Biographobia: some personal reflections
on the act of biography. (*In* Nineteenth-
Heading for essays about ——— century lives; ed. by L. S. Lockridge, J.
Maynard, and D. D. Stone p1-8)
Atwood **— About**
Author ——— Grace, S. E. Quest for the peaceable king- ⎤ — Title of chapter in book
dom: urban/rural codes in Roy, Laurence, │
and Atwood. (*In* Women writers and the ⎦
Editor ——— city; ed. by S. M. Squier p193-209) ——— Title of book
About individual works
Work by Atwood ———————**Bodily harm**
——— Irvine, L. The here and now of Bodily — Title of chapter in book
Author of chapter about ——— harm. (*In* Margaret Atwood: vision and —
Bodily Harm forms; ed. by K. VanSpanckeren and J. — Title of book
G. Castro p85-100)

of popular and prominent Americans only, check the latest issue of
Current Biography, issued monthly and cumulated annually. Another
biographical index, *Who's Who in America,* first issued in 1889, might fit
your needs if you're interested only in living and famous Americans.
For a guide to all biographical sources, consult the *Biographic and
Genealogical Master Index,* an index to biographical information in reference books. For other sources of biographical information, see the annotated list in Appendix 1.

Periodical Indexes

Periodicals are publications that appear at regular intervals; magazines, journals, newspapers, and newsletters are all periodicals. A *magazine* is a periodical containing articles on popular subjects not
necessarily written by experts *(Vogue, Time). Journal* is the term usually
used to refer to a periodical that contains articles written by and for
professionals in the field *(Journal of American Folklore, American Mathematical Monthly).* The term *serials* is often used by libraries to refer to
publications that appear in successive parts, often at irregular intervals,
and that may be issued by organizations and research institutions. *Serials* is also used generically to refer to all of these publications.

Articles in periodicals are indexed in print, in microform, online, or
on CD-ROM, with the subjects, titles, and authors organized alphabetically. To decide whether you want to look in a magazine or a journal
for your information, consider the differences between the two. Magazine articles are designed to help sell a particular magazine; their quality and reliability vary, from those in the respected *New Yorker* and
Harper's to those in primarily entertainment magazines like *Vogue* and
Life. However, they are much easier to understand than journal articles
because they're not written for the expert. In addition, they may contain more up-to-date information than articles in journals, which, be-

cause of their high professional quality and the time limitations of non-commercial publishing, are often slower to produce. Journals are usually published by nonprofit professional organizations or academic institutions; before being accepted, an article is usually approved by a panel of expert referees. The professional status or brief biography of the author that is usually given in a journal article is a further clue to its authoritativeness, and the articles are fully and professionally documented.

Before consulting a periodical index, check the explanatory material in the front of the book or at the beginning of the database to find the abbreviations you need for citing information, such as volume and page numbers, date, and the periodicals that the index includes.

If you find that the periodical article you want is listed in the online catalog as available at another library, you may be able to order a copy online. To receive it, you will have to provide a fax number and pay for it with a credit card. To order paper copies of a periodical article or to borrow books, see the librarian in your library, who will usually arrange for the items to be sent to the library for you to pick up.

Magazine Indexes. The *Readers' Guide to Periodical Literature,* in print, online, and on CD-ROM, indexes about 200 magazines from 1900 to the present, including *Newsweek,* the *New Yorker, Rolling Stone,* and *Scientific American.* Print supplements are issued semimonthly. Bound cumulative volumes are issued for each year, and some libraries may have back issues available on microfilm or as bound volumes. Articles are indexed by subject and author. There is a book review section at the end of each volume; movie reviews are indexed under "Motion picture reviews — Single Works." The *Readers' Guide* uses subheadings to group related articles under the main subject. In Figure 3.21, for example, the subject "Skin" is divided by topic and by subtopic. In addition, places in the United States are listed by state. Figure 3.22 shows an author entry.

FIGURE 3.21   Subject Entry from the *Readers' Guide to Periodical Literature*

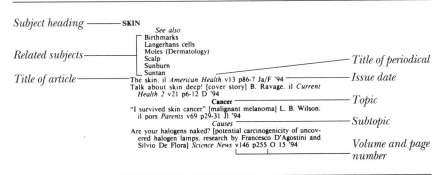

FIGURE 3.22 Author Entry from the *Readers' Guide to Periodical Literature*

Author heading ——————— **BISHOP, ELIZABETH, 1911-1979** ——————— *Author's birth and*
                    The art of losing [excerpt from One art; with introd. by Alice   *death dates*
Title of article ———   Quinn]; ed. by Robert Giroux. il *The New Yorker* v70
                    p82-9 Mr 28 '94
                    The map [poem] *Orion* v13 p17 Spr '94   *Title of periodical*
Subheading for ————————————————— **Bibliography**
bibliography   Exile's return. A. Bernard. il *The New York Review of Books*   *Contains illustrations*
            v41 p15-19 Ja 13 '94
Volume, page, ——————————————————————————— *Author of article*
and date of article

Magazine Index, available in many libraries online or in microform, covers a greater number of popular magazines — more than 400 — than the *Readers' Guide,* including, for example, more computer magazines, such as *PC Magazine* and *PC Week. Magazine Index* indexes by title, subject, and also product and brand name.

Journal Indexes. In professional journals you can often find articles on your subject written by experts for other experts. Such articles are likely to be more detailed and more authoritative than those found in a popular magazine. The disadvantage is that technical terms unfamiliar to the layperson are often used. If, for example, you want to find out the latest developments in heart transplants, you may have to learn the meanings of unfamiliar medical terms. If you need to look up only a few words, you'll probably find the article useful. But if the article requires an extensive background that you don't have, you'll probably be more successful with magazines aimed at a less specialized audience. Many professional journals, however, present few problems to the college student. Here are four of the most commonly used print indexes to professional journals.

The *Humanities Index* (April 1974–) is published yearly with quarterly updates; it is also available online and on CD-ROM. It indexes by author and subject 400 periodicals on art, drama, literature, history, philosophy, music, film, and folklore. For information before 1974, see the *International Index* (1907–1965) and the *Social Sciences and Humanities Index* (1965–1974), both of which were superseded by the *Humanities Index.* As Figure 3.23 shows, the format of the entries in the *Humanities Index* is similar to that in the *Readers' Guide.*

The *MLA International Bibliography of Books and Articles on the Modern Languages and Literatures* (1921–), also online and on CD-ROM, is published annually in two volumes: *Classified Listings with Author Index* — containing citations under four categories (national literatures, linguistics, general literature, and folklore) — and *Subject Index.* To find entries in the *Classified Listings,* look either in the *Subject Index* (organized alphabetically) or in the *Classified Listings,* finding first the appropriate section or national literature, then the time period of your subject (for

FIGURE 3.23   Entry from the *Humanities Index*

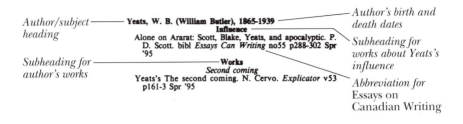

example, the nineteenth century), and finally the author (if your subject is a writer) listed alphabetically. Figure 3.24 shows the references you will find if you look up "Feminist novel" in the *Subject Index*. Figure 3.25 presents the entry you would find if you looked up the reference to Toni Morrison in the *Classified Listings*.

The *Public Affairs Information Service Bulletin (PAIS)* (1915–), in print, online, and on CD-ROM, indexes 1,400 worldwide publications in six languages in such subjects as economics, political science, business, law, finance, education, and social work using the *Readers' Guide* index entry format. *PAIS* in print is published semimonthly, with cumulative volumes issued four times a year and bound volumes annually.

The *Social Sciences Index* (April 1974–) consists of yearly volumes updated quarterly and contains guides to about 415 English-language periodicals on sociology, psychology, environmental affairs, economics, political science, geography, and anthropology. Like *PAIS*, it uses the *Readers' Guide* citation format. (From 1907 to 1965, this index was called the *International Index*, and from 1964 to 1974, the *Social Sciences and Humanities Index*.)

Citation Indexes.   Three citation indexes have a special type of organization in print that enables you to quickly build a network of authoritative sources on your subject.

FIGURE 3.24   Entry from the *MLA International Bibliography, Subject Index*

Main subject heading

FEMINIST NOVEL

Primary subheading

American literature. Novel. 1900-1999.
— Morrison, Toni. *Song of Solomon.* As FEMINIST NOVEL. 1-10445.

Secondary subheading

English literature. Novel: FEMINIST NOVEL (1890-1899). 1800-1899: Victorian period.
Treatment of feminism as activism. Historical approach. Dissertation abstract.

Volume in Classified Listings, *with citation number*

1-2868.

FIGURE 3.25 Entry from the *MLA International Bibliography, Classified Listings with Author Index*

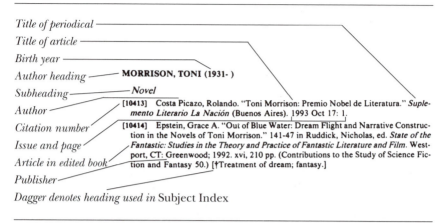

The *Social Sciences Citation Index* (1972–), also available online and on CD-ROM, is useful for subjects in the social, behavioral, and related sciences such as urban planning and development. The print version is divided into four parts: Citation, Source, Permuterm Subject, and Corporate. Any of these may be used to begin a search, but the usual place to begin is the Citation Index. Perhaps you have the name of an authority in your field from an encyclopedia article or one of your textbooks. For example, if you look up the name of W. S. Churchill, former prime minister of Great Britain, in the Citation Index, you will find the names of other writers who have cited this figure and who are probably writing about the same subject (See Figure 3.26). This list can help you build a bibliography of experts in your subject area.

FIGURE 3.26 Entry from the *Social Sciences Citation Index*, Citation Index

Cited author ——— **CHURCHILL WS** ———
```
                    23 WORLD CRISIS      6   695
                    JORAVSKY D    AM HIST REV    99  837  94 R
                    38 WORLD CRISIS 1911 19   1  185
                    BREEMER JS   J STRATEGIC   17   33  94
                    48 GATHERING STORM  p147                        ——— Book by Churchill
                    LEGRO JW     INT SECUR     18  108  94              cited by Legro
                    48 THOUGHTS ADVENTURES  p28
                    GARNETT MA   GOVT OPPOS    29   97  94         Volume, page, and
                    48 2ND WORLD WAR    1  180                     year of source citing
                    GREENWOO.S   J STRATEGIC   17   17  94         author
Churchill's 1948 —— ⌈ 48 2ND WORLD WAR    1  186
collection The      ⌊ GRAY CS     J STRATEGIC   17    7  94
Second World War    49 THEIR FINEST HOUR 2N   1  571
cited by Gray in    GORDON A     J STRATEGIC   17   63  94
Journal of Strategic 50 2ND WORLD WAR    v3
Studies             KLABBERS J   COM MKT L R   31  997  94
                    50 2ND WORLD WAR    4  121
                    LAMBAKIS S   COMP STRAT    13  211  94
                    51 2ND WORLD.WAR  p296
                    BUSH JA      COLUMB LAW    93 2022  93 B
                    61 GATHERING STORM  p186
                    SCHWELLE.RL  INT SECUR     19   72  94 R
```

Let's say that after looking up Churchill in the Citation Index, you decide to look up Gray, who cites Churchill's 1948 collection, *The Second World War,* in the *Journal of Strategic Studies.* In the Source Index, you find that Gray referred to Churchill in a review of a book (*The Search for Strategy: Politics and Strategic Vision* by G. L. Guertner), referred to him in an article ("Villains, Victims, and Sheriffs: Strategic Studies and Security for an Interwar Period") (see Figure 3.27). You also find the names of other authors referred to by Gray. You can look up any of these authors as well as other authors who cite Churchill. Following these steps, you will quickly build a bibliography of experts in your subject area.

The Permuterm Subject Index enables you to search a subject by pairing significant related words from titles of articles. If you are interested in drug use by adolescents, this index will provide authors who have written on the subject (Figure 3.28). For publication details, look up these authors in the Citation Index.

The Corporate Index can be especially valuable for college students. It arranges items in the Source Index geographically. Thus you can find out what articles have been published by authors affiliated with organizations in your city or state, or you can find out what is being published by authors in other countries. Locations in the United States are alphabetized by state. If you would like to find out recent articles

FIGURE 3.27 Entry from the *Social Sciences Citation Index,* Source Index

Source author — **GRAY CS**
THE SEARCH FOR STRATEGY - POLITICS AND STRATEGIC — *Gray reviewed a*
Title of source — VISION - GUERTNER,GL ♦ BOOK REVIEW *book by Guertner*
COMP STRAT 13(3):347-348   94   PD675
UNIV HULL,DEPT POLIT,CTR SECUR STUDIES, KINGSTON HULL HU6 *Source journal year*
7RX, N HUMBERSIDE, ENGLAND
Items citing Churchill — VILLAINS, VICTIMS, AND SHERIFFS - STRATEGIC STUDIES
book   AND SECURITY FOR AN INTERWAR PERIOD *Number of*
COMP STRAT   13(4):353-369   94   50R   PV253 *references*
UNIV HULL,CTR SECUR STUDIES, KINGSTON HULL HU6 7RX, N
HUMBERSIDE, ENGLAND
Abbreviation for the   [ANON)   94 ECONOMIST   0108   25 *Number for*
journal Comparative   ♦FAS   84 37 PUBL INT REP   3 *ordering articles*
Strategy   ANDERSON P   CITED INDIRECTLY *from the Institute*
ANGELL N   09 GREAT ILLUSION STUDY *for Scientific*
ASPIN L   93 BOTTOM UP REV *Information*
BAILEY KC   91 DOOMSDAY WEAPONS HAN   7
BERLIN I   57 HEDGEHOG FOX ESSAY T   5
BETTS RK   92 INT SECURITY   17   18
BOOTH K   91 NEW THINKING STRATEG   467
BRODIE B   49 WORLD POLIT   1   12
BULL H   91 SECURITY ANARCHY UTO   11
FOX R   92 NATIONAL INTERES WIN
FRIEDMAN G   91 WAR JAPAN
GIBBON   DECLINE FALL ROMAN E   84
GIBBON E   09 HIST DECLINE FALL RO   1 85
GLUBB JB   64 GREAT ARAB CONQUESTS
GLYNN P   92 CLOSING PANDORAS BOX
GOULD SJ   87 TIMES ARROW TIMES CY
GRAY CS   82 STRATEGIC STUDIES CR   61
"   92 HOUSE CARDS ARMS CON
"   93 WEAPONS DONT MAKE WA   95
"   94 POLITICAL STUDIES   42   25
HAMMOND GT   93 PLOWSHARES SWORDS AR
HITCH C   66 EC DEFENSE NUCLEAR A
HOLLIS M   91 EXPLAINING UNDERSTAN
JERVIS R   89 MEANING NUCLEAR REVO   177
"   91 INT SECURITY   16   39
KAEGI WE   92 BYZANTIUM EARLY ISLA
KAHN H   60 THERMONUCLEAR WAR
KAISER D   90 POLITICS WAR EUROPEA
KELLERT SH   93 WAKE CHAOS UNPREDICT
KENNEDY P   87 RISE FALL GREAT POWE
KNOCK TJ   92 END WARS W WILSON QU
KOESTLER A   70 GHOST MACHINE   177
KRAEMER SF   90 STRATEGIC REV   18   1
LEFFLAND E   91 KNIGHT DEATH DEVIL   208
LEVY JS   89 BEHAVIOUR SOC NUCLEA   1 295
LEWIS R   84 HITLERS MISTAKES
MANN SR   92 PARAMETERS   22   54

Gray's bibliographic — *references*

Year, journal, volume, and page — reference

FIGURE 3.28   Entry from the *Social Sciences Citation Index*, Permuterm
Subject Index

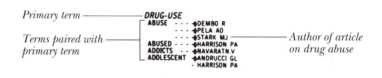

published by writers in Gettysburg, for example, you would look under
the state, Pennsylvania, and then under the city. Figure 3.29 shows references to journals containing articles by authors affiliated with Gettysburg College in Gettysburg. For further information on these authors,
you would look them up in the Source Index.

If you do not know the location of an organization, you can find it in
the index of this volume. All organizations and institutions in the
index are listed alphabetically along with their locations.

The *Science Citation Index* (1961–), also available online and on CD-
ROM, and the *Arts and Humanities Citation Index* (1977–), available online, can be used in the same way as the *Social Sciences Citation Index* to
build a network of sources. If an article that you believe to be important to your study is referred to in one of these citation indexes but
your library does not carry it, then you can order it from the publisher,
the Institute for Scientific Information. You will have to pay for this service, but delivery is prompt.

You can save time by searching these citation indexes online or on
CD-ROM because you do not have to handle several different volumes
to follow up a citation. Your library may offer this service.

FIGURE 3.29   Entry from the *Social Sciences Citation Index*, Corporate
Index

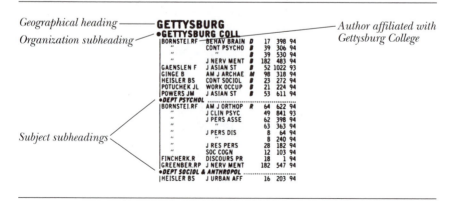

Indexes for Specific Disciplines. Indexes for journals in specific disciplines are listed and annotated in Appendix 1. Look in one of these specialized indexes — such as the *Music Index* or the *Index Medicus* — if your topic is highly technical or if you have trouble finding references in the general indexes.

Newspaper Indexes. Newspapers provide current accounts of subjects as well as contemporary views of historical events. The following newspapers publish their own indexes (items are indexed by subject only): the *Christian Science Monitor, Los Angeles Times, New York Times, Wall Street Journal, Washington Post,* and London *Times.* The *National Newspaper Index* (available online, on CD-ROM, and on microfilm) is a guide to articles in the *Christian Science Monitor, Los Angeles Times, New York Times, Wall Street Journal,* and *Washington Post.* Each index covers two and a half years, and the *Index* is updated frequently; old films are on microfiche. The *National Newspaper Index* is also available online as part of the database *NewSearch* and on CD-ROM through the *General Periodicals Index.* (For more information on periodical indexes, see Appendix 1.)

Dictionaries

Webster's Unabridged Dictionary of the English Language is often in a prominent place in the reference area for easy access. It can be useful for a quick search for a word's usage, pronunciation, or spelling.

If the way a word has been used over the years is important in your search, see the *Oxford English Dictionary* (20 vols., also online and on CD-ROM). Known as the *OED,* this dictionary illustrates the history of each word it defines by giving quotations in historical order beginning with the first known usage. Supplements keep the *OED* up to date. Figure 3.30 shows the changing meanings of the word *educate.* One of its uses in the early seventeenth century — to rear children and animals by supplying their physical needs — is now obsolete. But it's interesting to notice that Shakespeare's use of the word as early as 1588 was much the same as our use of it is today. After listing a word, the *OED* gives the pronunciation, part of speech, derivation, and grammatical use. Each numbered section provides a meaning of the word followed by the date, author, title of work, and quotation illustrating the word.

The word you want may be in a special dictionary, such as the *McGraw-Hill Dictionary of Scientific and Technical Terms.* Some dictionaries, such as the *Dictionary of Symbols* by J. E. Cirlot, are much like encyclopedias, with extended entries on a single subject. If you're interested in computers, the *New Hacker's Dictionary,* published by MIT Press, will help you update your terminology. Other dictionaries explain the terminology of politics, anthropology, engineering, law, medicine, or other professions. To find the dictionary that best fits your

FIGURE 3.30 Entry from the *Oxford English Dictionary,* Second Edition

---

educate ('ɛdjʊkeɪt), *v.* [f. L. *ēducāt-* ppl. stem of *ēducāre* to rear, bring up (children, young animals), related to *ēdūcĕre* to lead forth (see EDUCE), which is sometimes used nearly in the same sense.] *trans.* or *absol.*

† **1.** To rear, bring up (children, animals) by supply of food and attention to physical wants. *Obs.*

1607 TOPSELL *Four-f. Beasts* 229 The Epirotan & Siculian horses are not to be despised, if they were well bred & educated. **1651** WITTIE tr. *Primrose's Pop. Err.* 292 A boy of a good habit of body, with large veines, well and freely educated. **1690** [see EDUCATED]. **1818** [see 2].

2. To bring up (young persons) from childhood, so as to form (their) habits, manners, intellectual and physical aptitudes.

1618 BOLTON *Florus* I. i. 3 Himselfe delighting in the Rivers and Mountaines, among which he had beene educated. **1818** CRUISE *Digest* VI. 336 A devise .. to the intent that with the profits he should educate his daughter. **1839** tr. *Lamartine's Trav. East* 168/1 The principal amongst them [Greeks] have their children educated in Hungary. **1875** JOWETT *Plato* (ed. 2) V. 40 The youth of a people should be educated in forms and strains of virtue.

b. To instruct, provide schooling for (young persons).

1588 SHAKS. *L.L.L.* v. i. 84 Do you not educate youth at the Charg-house on the top of the Mountaine? **1863** MARY HOWITT tr. *F. Bremer's Greece* I. i. 13 It has educated, and

it educates to this day, a great portion of the Athenian female youth of all classes. **1863** A. TYLOR *Educ. & Manuf.* 40 It costs 8*d.* per week to educate a child.

3. To train (any person) so as to develop the intellectual and moral powers generally.

1849 KINGSLEY *Lett.* (1878) I. 198 In my eyes the question is not what to teach, but how to Educate. **1875** JOWETT *Plato* (ed. 2) V. 120 Elder men, if they want to educate others, should begin by educating themselves. **1886** *Pall Mall G.* 10 July 4/2 Our artists are not educated at all, they are only trained.

4. To train, discipline (a person, a class of persons, a particular mental or physical faculty or organ), so as to develop some special aptitude, taste, or disposition. Const. *to,* also *inf.*

1841-4 EMERSON *Ess. Hist.* Wks. (Bohn) I. 11 And the habit of supplying his own needs educates the body to wonderful performances. **1847** —— *Repr. Men.* v. *Shaks.* ibid. I. 359 Our ears are educated to music by his rhythm. **1867** DISRAELI in *Scotsman* 30 Oct., I had to prepare the mind of the country, and to educate,—if not too arrogant to use such a phrase,—our party. *Mod.* He is educating himself to eat tomatoes.

b. To train (animals).

1850 LANG *Wand. India* 2 No horses, except those educated in India, would crawl into these holes cut out of the earth and rock. **1856** KANE *Arct. Expl.* I. xxix. 389 The dogs of Smith's Sound are educated more thoroughly than any of their more southern brethren.

---

needs, consult *Dictionaries, Encyclopedias, and Other Word-Related Books* (2 vols.), edited by Annie M. Brewer, or browse in the online catalog using your subject area and the word *dictionaries.*

Handbooks and Manuals

Handbooks and manuals (the terms are virtually synonymous) present information about a specialized subject usually in a concise format. (The *Handbook of North American Indians,* a fifteen-volume work, is an exception.) Besides background information, handbooks may give instructions and references to other sources. They are useful when you want a review of established information and not necessarily the latest developments in a field. There are handbooks for just about any subject, including advertising, aging, alcohol and drug abuse, eating disorders, electronics, human sexuality, Irish folklore, Latin American literature, lobbying, marriage, music, nursing, radio, real estate, statistics, and women's history. To find a handbook on your subject, search in the online catalog using "handbook" or "manual" and your subject area.

Indexes to Government Documents

If you need information on American history, government, or law, federal government documents can provide interesting firsthand reports of committee findings, congressional debates over bills, and much other information about what goes on in Congress and elsewhere in government. Government documents also can provide information in a wide range of subjects, including health (*Health Effects of Global Warming,* 1992), science (*The Genome Project: The Ethical Issues of Gene Patenting,* 1993), and business *(Export Assistance Efforts for Small Business,* 1995).

Many college libraries are repositories for government documents (a library must have at least 15,000 titles in its catalog to qualify as a repository). One repository in each state (a regional repository) receives all government documents; other repositories (selective repositories) choose the documents they wish to receive. Selective repositories may obtain any document they do not have from the nearest regional repository. Although some government documents can be checked out of the library, most do not circulate, and they may be stored in either print or microform. Small collections of government documents might be kept in the reference area, but large collections will probably be located in their own room or department.

Libraries with large collections of government documents usually do not list them in the library catalog and therefore do not use the classification systems used for other material. (Libraries with limited numbers of government documents may, however, integrate them into their regular cataloging system.) Instead, government documents in repository libraries are assigned a SuDoc (Superintendent of Documents) number that looks like this: Y 10.2:W29/2. Consult your librarian for indexes to the documents and their location. Here are the chief indexes.

The *Monthly Catalog of U.S. Government Publications,* issued by the U.S. Government Printing Office in print, online, and on CD-ROM (as *GPO and Government Documents Catalog*), describes all the publications sent to repository libraries. The contents are indexed in the back of the catalog by author, title, subject, series, stock number, and title key word. These cumulative indexes are issued semiannually and annually. Documents published before 1971 are indexed somewhat differently and may best be located in two commercial publications: the *Cumulative Subject Index to the Monthly Catalog, 1900–1971* (15 vols.), by William W. Buchanan and Edna M. Kanely, and the *Decennial Cumulative Personal Author Index* (3 vols.), edited by Edward Przebienda and covering the years 1941 to 1970. As the title of the Buchanan–Kanely index indicates, you can locate information by looking up a subject. You can also find some authors by looking up "Addresses, Lectures," where speakers' names are listed in alphabetical order. Przebienda indexes material only by author.

The *CIS/Index to Publications of the United States Congress,* online and on CD-ROM as *Congressional and Masterfile I* and *Congressional Masterfile II,* is issued monthly in two parts — Abstracts and Indexes — with quarterly and annual cumulative volumes. Items are indexed by subject, name, title, document number, and committee chairman. To find information in this volume, look up your subject in the Indexes volume and find the number of the document you want; then find the abstract in the Abstracts volume of the *CIS/Index*. Figure 3.31 presents a sample abstract entry from the *CIS/Index*.

The *American Statistics Index (ASI)* is a guide to government publications containing statistical information. It follows the same format as the *CIS/Index*.

The Statistical Abstract of the United States, published yearly and usually shelved in the library's reference collection, is a one-volume source of statistics covering a variety of topics. Other sources of statistics include the *Census of Population and Housing*, published every ten years after the census is collected. (Census statistics are also available online through Gopher and the World Wide Web. See Appendix 1.) *The National Trade Data Bank* is a popular information source that includes foreign trade statistics and a review of the year in trade, and *The National Economic, Social, and Environmental Data Bank*, on CD-ROM, focuses on regional and state economic data.

If your research requires information on United States law, you might want to consult *U.S. Reports*, which contains the text of all of the decisions of the U.S. Supreme Court.

The *Congressional Record*, a daily record of proceedings in the U.S. House of Representatives and the U.S. Senate, is usually shelved in the reference room or in the government documents section. Published daily, the *Congressional Record* is indexed biweekly, with a yearly bound

FIGURE 3.31   Abstract Entry from the *CIS/Index to Publications of the United States Congress*

| *CIS accession number* | **S181–9** | **NATIONAL AERONAUTICS AND SPACE ADMINISTRATION SPACE STATION PROPOSAL, FY88, Special Hearing.** | *Title of document* |

CIS accession number — **S181–9**
Date
Number of pages
Price from U.S. Government Printing Office
GPO stock number
Bullet indicates that publication is sent to a depository library. Number is for paper copy.
Abstract

NATIONAL AERONAUTICS AND SPACE ADMINISTRATION SPACE STATION PROPOSAL, FY88, Special Hearing.
May 1, 20, 1987.   100-1.
iii+273+v p. il. Index.
GPO $8.50
S/N 552-070-03126-0.
CIS/MF/5
•Item 1033; 1033-A.
S. Hrg. 100-328.
°Y4.Ap6/2:S.hrg.100-328.
LC 88-601109.

Hearings to examine NASA planning for design and applications of a manned space station.
    Includes submitted statements and correspondence (p. 4-8, 165-166).
    Also includes a subject index (p. iii-v).

Title of document
Congress and session
Includes illustrations
Contents are available on 5 microfiche
Superintendent of Documents number for microfiche
Senate hearing number
Superintendent of Documents classification number
Library of Congress card number

CIS accession number for testimony — **S181–9.1:** May 1, 1987. p. 11-63.
Witnesses: **SAGAN, Carl,** astronomy and space sciences prof; dir, Planetary Studies Lab, Cornell Univ.
VAN ALLEN, James A., physics prof emeritus, Univ of Iowa.

Date and page numbers of testimony

cumulative issue. Material is indexed by author and subject. It is available on microfilm from 1873.

(For information on searching state and county records and federal archives, see Chapter 5.)

Interlibrary Loans

If you find that some promising articles or books are not available in your library, your reference librarian may be able to get them through interlibrary loan. A computer network, such as OCLC (Online Computer Library Center), which links the catalogs of subscribing libraries, may be able to assist you in finding a library that has the source you want. If you want a book, arrangements may be made to borrow it for you. You may also arrange for photocopies of periodical articles to be sent to you, for which you will probably pay a small fee. Before you ask for such a service, however, determine the relevance of your article by reading an abstract of it in an index of abstracts if one is available for your subject. You will find indexes of abstracts along with other indexes in Appendix 1. Although OCLC is the largest of these networks, other online networks are available to libraries that want to participate, including RLIN (Research Libraries Information Network), a network of large academic research libraries such as Cornell, Harvard, Stanford, and the University of California; WLN (Washington Library Network), a network of Pacific Northwest libraries; and UTLAS (University of Toronto Library Automation System), a Canadian libraries system.

Before you leave the reference room, take a few minutes to review your records. You should have a list of possible sources on cards or note paper and, in your search log, a record of where you went and what you did, including names of indexes you searched.

Finding Information
through the Internet

The Internet, a loosely organized global network of computers connected by telephone lines, can be a useful source of information on almost any subject. A student working on a music history paper posted a question to an Internet Shakespeare discussion group, asking how sixteenth-century music was being used in modern performances. Within a few days, she received a dozen or so responses from Shakespeare scholars, theater directors, and performers. Another student researching Brazilian national parks found a database in Brazil that included texts relating to the government's policies on natural resources.

Because of its scope and complexity, the Internet can be a confusing place for the novice. If your library or campus computing center offers training sessions, you should take advantage of them. The following overview, however, will introduce you to the possibilities of four major Internet search systems: the World Wide Web (often called "the Web"), Gopher, Archie, and the Wide Area Information Service (WAIS). Each system has features that will make it more or less useful to you, depending on your research needs.

Your computer may be equipped with programs that provide direct access to these systems. If not, you may use Telnet, an application that allows you to log on to other computers by remote. Your campus computing center or Internet service provider should be able to give you instructions for using Telnet and other Internet services. Or you can consult one of the books listed on page 79. (See Appendix 1 for addresses of Internet resources in your subject area.)

World Wide Web

The World Wide Web is the most advanced — and probably the most enjoyable and user-friendly — Internet search tool. The Web links Internet information providers across the world and is accessed with "browsers" (such as Mosaic or Netscape Navigator), which provide interfaces between you and the many available sites (estimated at 7 million in a 1996 article in *PC World* magazine and still growing.)

A key feature of the Web is hypertext, which links related documents, whether these documents are texts, pictures, or some other type of data. From the home page of a Web site, you can select a link (or "hot word") that interests you and follow it to another page of information, which may offer links to further pages. Simple Web pages consist of plain text with links in color or otherwise highlighted using bold, italics, underlining, or more elaborate formatting or graphics. Browsers such as Mosaic or Netscape Navigator are good at handling hypertext links and are especially good at combining text with images, sounds, and even video clips.

While doing a research paper on college students' attitudes toward affirmative action programs, Patrice Tyler found several college newspapers that were available on the Web. Figure 3.32 shows a home page for one of the newspapers she found.

By clicking on the opinion button, Patrice was able to search through back issues for editorials on affirmative action, a few of which she used for quotations and statistics.

Gopher

Gopher, which links more than a thousand information servers around the world, allows you to browse a series of menus to find sources relevant to your topic. (The service originated at the University of Minnesota, home of the football team the "Golden Gophers," and it can "go-fer" the information you want.) Because Gopher is easy to use and provides broad access to a variety of texts, documents, and pictures, you'll find it one of the most useful of the automated search sys-

FIGURE 3.32   A World Wide Web Home Page for a College Newspaper

tems. With Gopher, for example, you can look for resources related to your topic in online library catalogs across the country; you can even retrieve files from those libraries.

Because each Gopher server uses its own terminology for filing information, Gopherspace lacks the consistency of libraries, which are organized according to the Dewey decimal system or the Library of Congress system. However, most Gopher menus are fairly easy to understand and use. Figure 3.33 shows an example of a Gopher server's root directory.

FIGURE 3.33   Root Directory from an Internet Gopher Server

```
            Internet Gopher Information Client v1.13x


                         Root Directory


    ---> 1. Frequently Asked Questions.

         2. Discussion Groups/

         3. News/

         4. Software and Data Sources/

         5. Information about Other Information Servers/

         6. Search Gopher Titles at This Server <?>

         7. Campus Information/


Press ? for Help, q to Quit, u to go up a menu              Page: 1/1
```

On this menu, the slashes after entries 2, 3, 4, 5, and 7 indicate that these entries contain another, more specific menu of information. You select menus (or directories) by entering their line numbers. (Graphical systems — like those available through Macintosh or Windows — offer menu items that are labeled with icons. You can select items by pointing at and clicking on icons with a mouse.) Eventually, the menus you select will lead you to specific resources that you can choose to read or retrieve.

Veronica, so-named because it works much in the way that Archie does (see below), is a system that allows you to search menus of Gopher servers worldwide by typing in a wordstring related to your topic. Often, individual Gopher servers will allow you to select a Veronica search from their menus.

Archie

Archie, a system that locates files available to the public through the Internet, is most useful when you know that a certain file exists but don't know how to access it. For example, if you think that a new piece of software or a document from a public archive may be available through the Internet, you could contact an Archie server and type a wordstring that's likely to be in the file name. The server will then return to you the names of any matching files and their locations.

If you don't have a specific file name in mind, you can use a Whatis command to search a descriptive index that links file names to key words. Just enter a descriptive wordstring after the Whatis command; Archie will return the names and locations of any matching files.

At the start of a research project, you'll probably find it easier to use a tool like the Web, which lets you browse numerous databases to uncover a variety of sources that are relevant to your topic.

Wide Area Information Service (WAIS)

The Wide Area Information Service or WAIS (pronounced "ways") is a convenient way to search indexed databases on the Internet. Unlike Archie, which searches for file names, WAIS searches for key words and phrases that are embedded within indexed files and returns to you a list of any texts containing those words. It also scores texts according to how many times they mention your key words; the more frequently the words are mentioned, the higher the score. Further, if WAIS uncovers a document that is perfect for your needs, you can ask it to look for others like it.

Although WAIS is a powerful tool that helps you search full texts in hundreds of databases, you might find it easier to use Gopher or the World Wide Web. WAIS is most handy for tracking down sources that haven't yet been indexed through Gopher or the World Wide Web.

Other Uses for the Internet

In addition to allowing searches of millions of databases, the Internet lets you communicate with Internet users across your campus and around the world. You can send and receive electronic mail, or e-mail, and you can add your name to a mailing list that allows people with a shared interest to exchange messages. You can subscribe by contacting the list's administrator, often a program known as listserv. Some writing centers will respond to students' writing questions — and even to full texts of papers — via e-mail. Ask your instructor or writing center about the availability of such a service.

Through the Internet you can also access Usenet, a worldwide network of electronic bulletin boards — known as newsgroups or discussion groups — where users read and post information on specific topics. If you are beginning a research project on how computers are used as tools in scientific research, you could post a message to sci.comp-aided, a newsgroup concerned with this topic, and ask members about new developments or research leads. (Some Internet handbooks contain lists of key newsgroups; your campus computing center may keep print copies of such lists.)

Wading through the Internet

With the overwhelming amount of information available on the Internet, it can be difficult to know where to begin your research and how to conduct it in the most efficient manner. Fortunately, a growing number of Internet service providers are developing World Wide Web sites that can make your job easier. These sites provide electronic directories for searches on general topics and search engines for more focused investigations. Following is a brief overview.

General Searches. If you are just beginning your research and want to browse through Internet sites dealing with a big topic like Alzheimer's disease or the Vietnam War, general Internet directories might be your best bet. The most popular of these is probably Yahoo **(http://www.yahoo.com/),** which covers thousands of Web sites, Gopher sites, and newsgroups. Yahoo breaks down Internet sites into general topics that you can click on with your mouse to select subtopics. To find more general directories that might help you with your search, consider consulting the Clearinghouse for Subject-Oriented Internet Resource Guides at the University of Michigan **(http://www.lib.umich.edu/chhomee.html).**

Focused Searches. As your research progresses and you find yourself needing more specific information (for example, if you are trying to find current statistics on the number of Alzheimer's diagnoses in your state), you might want to use search engines — specialized Web pages that allow you to search for Internet sites relevant to your topic by entering key words or phrases — much as you do when you search the online catalog at the library (see p. 47). After you enter key words or phrases (a query string), the engine returns a list of sites to you, ranked according to their relevance to your search string. (Often, relevance is calculated according to the number of times the key words or phrases appear in files.) Many search engines are available on the Web, and you might want to ask your campus computing center about the ones that would be best for your research project. Here are a few popular engines to investigate:

ENGINE	ADDRESS
Excite NetSearch	http://www.excite.com/
InfoSeek	http://www.infoseek.com/
Lycos	http://lycos.cs.cmu.edu/

When entering search strings, keep the following tips in mind:

- Consider using the limiting word NOT, which tells the engine to ignore terms that you do not want to include in your search (for example, "artificial sweeteners NOT saccharin").
- Use terms that are as technical and specific as possible (for example, "lepidopteran" instead of "butterfly").
- Use more than one engine to broaden your options. You may find that some engines are more successful for you than others.
- If your search terms don't seem to be working, try synonyms or look for other key words in articles, indexes, or other sources that you've found on your subject.

Using the Internet Critically

The scope, diversity, and open access of the Internet constitute its greatest strength — and its greatest weakness. Because anyone can contribute to the Internet and because no central board of editors decides what can be published, you must evaluate carefully and critically both the sources and the information you obtain through the Internet. (For more advice on evaluating all types of sources, see Chapter 4.)

- *Evaluate databases.* When you are interested in a particular database, find out what you can about the organization or individual who compiled it, perhaps by consulting an established reference (such as one of the Internet books listed on p. 79). Databases often offer descriptions of themselves that can help you determine whether the source really suits your research needs.
- *Evaluate the information you get from databases, e-mail, and newsgroups.* As you should with any other source you consult for a research proj-

ect, find out what you can about the credentials and authority of an electronic text's author. How reliable are the author's sources? How well, and with what kind of facts and statistics, does the author support assertions? You may be able to check facts against other sources.

- *Evaluate the information you get from Web pages.* Many Web pages are sponsored by companies or groups that wish to advertise their products or get publicity. Before using information from the Web, find out who sponsored and wrote the Web page (or pages) and evaluate the credentials of the source. Is the information biased to suit the sponsor's needs? Have sources been provided for facts and statistics?

For most research projects, it's best to think of mailing lists and newsgroups as informal means of finding preliminary leads and learning about possible sources, not as sources themselves.

Books about the Internet

Most libraries have guides to the Internet in their reference sections. The following can help you get started:

The Internet for Dummies. 3rd ed. Foster City, CA: IDG Books, 1995.
The Internet for Dummies: Quick Reference. 2nd ed. Foster City, CA: IDG Books, 1995.
The Internet Guide for New Users. 2nd ed. New York: McGraw-Hill, 1995.
The Internet Yellow Pages. 3rd ed. New York: Osborne McGraw-Hill, 1995.
The Official Internet World Internet Yellow Pages. Medford, NJ: Information Today, 1996.
Riding the Internet Highway. Indianapolis: New Riders, 1994.
The Whole Internet User's Guide. 2nd ed. Sebastopol, CA: O'Reilly, 1994.
Zen and the Art of the Internet: A Beginner's Guide. 3rd ed. Englewood Cliffs, NJ: Prentice Hall, 1994.

Taking Stock

You are now ready to locate the books, periodicals, and other sources you have identified by searching print references, databases, and other materials. If you used the Internet to help you compile your working bibliography, you might already have retrieved full text files of articles and documents that interest you. Help in evaluating your sources and taking notes will be given in Chapter 4, but before you begin that process, it would be wise for you to answer these questions: Where am I? Where have I been? Where am I going?

As you followed the steps in compiling your bibliography, you were constantly finding references to related subjects. Beginning with the encyclopedia, you found that you could take a number of directions. When you looked through the indexes, you found more possibilities. Then as you searched the library catalog, you had to choose from various subject headings. Some of your decisions about choices of direction you made consciously; others, unconsciously. Now, before you begin to locate your sources, it's time to review your progress and note where you are headed.

Widening or Narrowing?

First review your original outline or list of subtopics and add possibilities you may have found in encyclopedias, indexes, periodical listings, and the catalog or other databases. Then choose from this expanded list the subtopics you want to cover. In deciding which ones to include, consider their relevance to your main topic, your interests, and the time and sources available to you. The list you make now will guide you as you look up and examine your sources. (It may also help you realize that you need to investigate still more sources.) Use the subtopics from your outline as headings for your note cards, or use them to organize notes you've taken on your computer.

Focusing a Topic

A subject — any subject — is a little like a Fourth of July sparkler: it gives off sparks of light in all directions. Sometimes when you're starting to investigate a subject, these sparks seem to be multiplying at an uncontrollable rate. Marvin Kohl started to write a paper on pornography. He wanted to know answers to these questions: What is pornography? Is it harmful? Should anything be done about it? He went first to the *Encyclopaedia Britannica's Micropaedia* where he found, besides a brief definition, two reasons for laws against pornography: it corrupts morals and it causes crime. In the *Macropaedia* he found a discussion of the following subjects: censorship, laws against pornography and obscenity, a history of such laws, laws in other countries, and book banning. He then looked up his subject in the *Encyclopedia Americana* and found that this source concentrated on American obscenity laws and referred to congressional hearings. To organize all these ideas and others that were occurring to him, he drew a diagram (Figure 3.34) to show how one subject suggested another. From this diagram he selected the topics he was most interested in: laws passed in the United States and elsewhere and the effects of pornography.

His next step was to search the *Encyclopedia of Psychology*, where he found an article that referred to reports of the Commission on Obscenity and Pornography. In the *Readers' Guide* he spotted a reference to an article that attacked pornography on the grounds that it violates women's rights. Next the reference librarian recommended the *Ency-*

FIGURE 3.34 Focusing a Topic

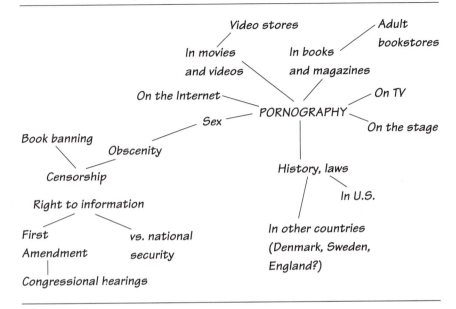

clopaedia of Crime and Justice, which, as it turned out, was an excellent suggestion because the article on pornography discussed the two aspects of the subject he was mainly interested in — behavioral and legal. It was a lengthy article with a long bibliography. On the basis of this article, he decided to concentrate on photographic pornography. Kohl was now ready to compose a working title, preliminary outline, and a hypothesis or tentative thesis.

The Social Effects of Photographic Pornography

Possible bad effects (to be verified or disproven)
    Involves the exploitation of children
    Leads to the exploitation of women
    Causes increase in crime
    Results in moral corruption

Possible good effects (to be verified or refuted)
    Can be used in sex education and treatment programs
    Helps in preventing some crimes

Laws relating to pornography
    Legalization of pornography in Denmark
    Laws against pornography in the United States
    First Amendment protection of freedom of speech

He next read over his outline to ensure that the topics and subtopics were listed in the order of most to least important. On review, Kohl thought he might have trouble covering all these topics in the time available; but he decided that if necessary, he could drop "Laws relating to pornography" and still produce a paper with a valid argument.

What he had read so far about pornography's exploitation of women and children was causing him to lean toward advocating the outlawing of pornography. But the issue was turning out to be less clear-cut than he had thought it would be. A major question was whether pornography could or should be protected under the First Amendment, which grants freedom of speech. He decided he needed to do more reading before he could clearly formulate his thesis statement, but for now he developed this working thesis, or hypothesis: pornography that exploits women or children should be illegal.

As you assess your position, refer to the following summary of steps for help in deciding which direction to take.

1. List all the possible subtopics you might cover.
2. Choose the ones you want to include in your search.
3. Reexamine your purpose and restate your topic.
4. Rewrite your list of subtopics according to your revised topic to make a working outline; that is, put the subtopics in logical order and group them under headings to demonstrate their relationships.
5. If possible, formulate a working thesis, but don't rush to judgment.

This kind of decision making is, as you have found, a continual part of your search. Searching, or exploring, always means going into unknown territory. It means setting out on a Lewis and Clark expedition with some general guidelines and an idea of the ground to be covered but also with the need to constantly reassess your strategy and direction.

Keeping a Search Log: A Student Example

Be sure to record in your search log what you did in trying to focus your topic. Such a record will make it possible for you to resume your search quickly even if you have to stop for other assignments for a few days. The following student's account of her search was written on the basis of records kept in her search log.

Norma Stefano's search for a working bibliography on her topic, "The Hazards of Smoking," was difficult to begin. Here is her account.

> When I went to the library to begin my search, I wasn't sure where to start. The reference area offered so many possibilities — rows of computer stations labeled with the electronic database or system that could be searched there. I saw signs for NEXIS/LEXIS, PsycLIT, BIOSIS, Art Index, ERIC, and about fifteen others.
>
> Then I saw another row of computers that offered access to the online college catalog. I decided to start there. It seemed like a good idea to first find a general medical encyclopedia that would give me some background

using terms I could understand. I typed the words *medicine* and *encyclopedia,* and the screen told me that there were eighty-eight items using these words. But I knew they were arranged in reverse chronological order — the most recent first — so I pressed the button for display. The screen showed *The New Complete Medical and Health Encyclopedia* (1993) along with the call number, which showed that it was in the reference room. I looked up smoking and found an article on "Smoking and Disease." It had some interesting information on how cells in the body react to nicotine and what substances in tobacco smoke cause cancer. But the articles were short and pretty general; I needed articles with more depth.

I noticed a rack near the reference desk with handouts explaining the information available in the library. One contained a list of electronic databases available. I chose MEDLINE, which was listed under medical sciences. I typed my terms *smoking* and *hazards* into the computer using the Browse command, but I got titles of articles on smoke pollution.

So I decided to ask the librarian for help, and she showed me a book on a shelf in the reference room called *Permuted Medical Subject Headings* (1996). The entries that came closest to what I wanted were "Smoking" and "Smoking Cessation." Using those, I found several articles, and one, called "The Global Tobacco Epidemic" by Bartecchi in *Scientific American* (May 1995), looked especially interesting and helpful. I ordered a copy to be delivered to me by e-mail. A couple of other articles also drew my attention: "AMA Calls for Curbs on the Tobacco Industry: Companies 'Duped' U.S. Public, Doctors Say," an editorial in *JAMA,* the journal of the American Medical Association, and "Tobacco Should Be Regulated," from the *New York Times* (July 13, 1995). The possibility that legal steps might be taken against tobacco companies interested me, especially since I'm thinking of going to law school after graduation. So I began to shift the focus of my topic. I typed *smoking tobacco industry* and found a number of interesting articles, including one titled "Lawyers' Control of Internal Scientific Research to Protect Against Products Liability Lawsuits" in *JAMA* (July 19, 1995).

Now I was cooking. Continuing my search, I found a reference to an article in the British medical journal *Lancet* discussing lawsuits against tobacco companies and an onscreen summary of the article. Following up on a reference to the bodily harm that smoking could cause, I found an article titled "Tobacco as a Cause of Angina Pectoris" by Carl Bartecchi in the medical journal *Primary Cardiology* (July 1995). References were made to articles on smoking as a cause of cancer that I would check out later.

I decided to head for the LEXIS database to pursue the legal angle. There I learned that the state of Florida was filing a class action suit and that individuals were filing suit against tobacco companies. I wrote down the names of the articles.

Now I could see my paper as having two parts. In the first part I would provide evidence from medical journals that smoking was harmful; in the second part, I would explore how this issue was being addressed in the courts. My search had now become more than just an assignment; I was really getting excited about it. I found titles of all the articles I could on both the medical and the legal sides. Some had abstracts onscreen. I printed out the reference information and some of the abstracts on printers next to the library's computers. Then, thinking I would need some current information from newspapers, I headed toward the NEXIS database station. There were plenty of articles — more than I needed. I chose the most recent ones.

Finally, I went to the reference area to look up the articles. I photocopied the relevant ones or parts of them that had useful information. Then at home, I opened the bibliography file I already had created on my computer and added the references I found useful; I made sure to put down all the information I needed — author, title of article, title of journal, volume, date, and page number. My computer alphabetized them for me. Later I would add the most useful information from my references to my computer files, which were organized according to my revised outline. I felt great. I knew I was on the right track now.

EXERCISES

1. Make a list of other sources that Norma Stefano might have used in her bibliographic search on the hazards of smoking.

2. Write a two- or three-page memorandum to your instructor explaining the topic you have chosen and your reasons for choosing it. Discuss the most difficult parts of your search so far, outline problems you have encountered, and explain the next steps you will take in your research. Finally, attach your working bibliography. Use this memo format:

   To: [your instructor's name]
   From: [your name]
   Subject: [topic for your research paper]
   Date: [today's date]

3. **FOR YOUR SEARCH LOG**   Write a narrative account of your search up to this point. Use the informal style of Norma Stefano. Or make a list in your search log of all the metaphors for searching that occur to you, such as exploring a cave, climbing a mountain, going to the moon, snorkeling. Then write an account of your library search using the terms of one of those metaphors.

4. **FOR THE COMPUTERIZED CLASSROOM**   Post a memo, similar to the one outlined in Exercise 2, to your classmates using a listserv mailing list and ask them to suggest sources of information on your subject. Ask also if they know any people who might have helpful information and who might be willing to talk to you.

Recording Information from Print and Electronic Sources

The Library [is] a wilderness of books. . . . It is necessary to find out exactly what books to read on a given subject. Though there may be a thousand books written upon it, it is only important to read three or four; they will contain all that is essential, and a few pages will show which they are.   — H. D. Thoreau, *A Writer's Journal*

If you have followed the suggestion in the Introduction to build abundance into your search process, you have perhaps not the thousand books that Thoreau mentions but many more books, articles, and other sources on your list than you will need or can use. Here are the next steps:

1. Locate your sources in the library or download them from the Internet.
2. Evaluate your sources and select the most useful and reliable.
3. Take notes on your reading.

Locating Sources

Books, unless they are reference books such as encyclopedias, dictionaries, and the like, are shelved in the library stacks according to their call numbers. These stacks are open in most college libraries; that is, you may locate books yourself and take them to the checkout desk. (In some large public libraries, you must hand in your book requests and wait for your books to be delivered to you.) An advantage of open stacks is that you may see other books on the subject that interest you while you are looking for the ones on your list. To simplify your search for books, arrange your working bibliography according to the classification system used by your library. If your library uses the Library of Congress classification system, put all of your PF cards together, your QPs together, and so forth, and then arrange them in alphabetical order, according to library practice.

Bound volumes of periodicals may be located in a separate room or in the book stacks by call number (see Chapter 3). You may want to photocopy short articles from them to read later (be sure to record complete publication data on these copies so that you can identify them). Microforms may also be stored separately, along with the machines for using them; some of these machines may print copies of the microforms.

Of course, you might have found potential sources by browsing the Internet, a kind of virtual library (see Chapter 3). You may print full-text files from online sources or download them onto your own computer for later reading.

Once you have located your sources, you are ready to evaluate, read, and take notes. Skillful reading and note taking are crucial to the writing of a good research paper.

Evaluating Your Sources

As you evaluate your working bibliography, you will find out which sources will be the most useful and reliable for your paper. You have probably already begun this process by noticing the copyright date (if currentness is important to you), by paying special attention to authors who have been recommended, and by reading abstracts of books and articles. The evaluation process, which, like other parts of searching, is continuous, is especially useful at this stage, when you have assembled your bibliography and are about to begin reading. The following suggestions will help to eliminate sources that are not worth your time to read.

Some sources may be of limited value to you, others so unreliable as to be misleading and deceptive, and still others hard to evaluate until you begin to read them. *But you should keep in mind that the integrity of your paper depends to a great extent on the reliability or authenticity of your sources.* If your subject is controversial, you will want to make sure that you use unbiased sources or, at least, that you are aware of their biases. Although all standards of reliability are relative and subject to error, the *copyright date, author, source* in which an article appears, *recommendations and reviews,* and *content* provide you with the information necessary to make a reasonable judgment. Although you may not be able to judge the content adequately until you start reading, you can learn about it to some extent beforehand. If you evaluate your sources according to the following guidelines, you will be able to begin your reading and note taking with reliable and useful sources.

Copyright Date

The publication, or copyright, date of a source is important for any research project. In the sciences, for instance, researchers build on the information of their predecessors because knowledge in these subjects is increasing at a rate that produces obsolescence almost overnight. For a paper on the uses of artificial satellites, for example, most sources more than five years old are of limited value; new uses for satellites in communications and new reports from satellites used as observatories are reported almost daily. In the social sciences, too, the date may be crucial: a study on the methods of achieving school integration should look at contemporary data; currently, instead of busing, many school districts are integrating through the use of magnet schools. Although sources in the humanities tend to age more slowly than those in the sciences, new information or new documents sometimes emerge that shed new light on a subject. For example, a study focusing on the Brontë sisters would be limited without attention to the many articles and books that have been published about them over the last five years.

You will usually find the publication date on the copyright page (the page following the title page) or sometimes on the title page itself. The number of dates may be confusing, but the significant date, the one you would use in your bibliography, is the latest copyright date, which is the date of the last revision. Additional printings do not necessarily indicate changes in the text — only new *editions* acquire new copyright dates. Figure 4.1 shows examples of copyright dates from two different publications. (Electronic texts may also include copyright dates. See the CD-ROM printout in Figure 3.8 on page 50.)

FIGURE 4.1 Sample Copyright Dates

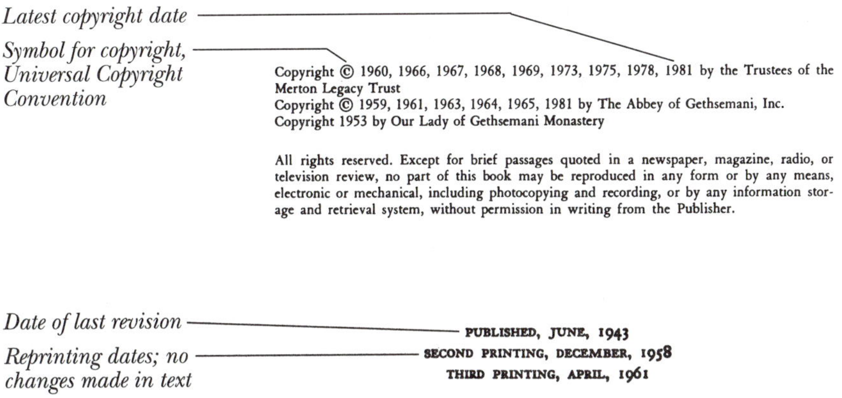

Latest copyright date

Symbol for copyright,
Universal Copyright
Convention

Copyright © 1960, 1966, 1967, 1968, 1969, 1973, 1975, 1978, 1981 by the Trustees of the Merton Legacy Trust
Copyright © 1959, 1961, 1963, 1964, 1965, 1981 by The Abbey of Gethsemani, Inc.
Copyright 1953 by Our Lady of Gethsemani Monastery

All rights reserved. Except for brief passages quoted in a newspaper, magazine, radio, or television review, no part of this book may be reproduced in any form or by any means, electronic or mechanical, including photocopying and recording, or by any information storage and retrieval system, without permission in writing from the Publisher.

Date of last revision — PUBLISHED, JUNE, 1943

Reprinting dates; no — SECOND PRINTING, DECEMBER, 1958
changes made in text — THIRD PRINTING, APRIL, 1961

Once in a while you may come across a book that does not give a publication date. In that case, check the library catalog; a copyright date may be given on the computer screen or card. (The abbreviation *c* before a date in a catalog entry means "copyright.")

Author

The status, experience, and professional position of an author are clues to the reliability of the writing. You may learn about an author's background in such sources as *Who's Who in America* (there are similar books for other countries). Those in academic disciplines and professions may be found in the appropriate subject volume of the *Who's Who* series, which includes American history, arts and literature, commerce and industry, economics, electronics, engineering, finance and industry, government, law, music, nursing, opera, politics, religion, technology, and theater. For biographies of writers, consult *Contemporary Authors* (updated volumes appear regularly) and the *Directory of American Scholars*. Credentials of scientists can be checked in *Modern Scientists and Engineers* and *American Men and Women of Science*. All these sources are usually shelved in the reference area.

You can also tell something about the professional status of writers by how often they are mentioned by other experts. For example, if your subject is in the social sciences, see the *Social Sciences Citation Index* for names of other writers who have cited the author of a book or article on your list (Chapter 3 describes this index in detail). Although these citations are not recommendations in themselves, their appearance in professional sources is some indication of the author's importance. As you proceed with your reading, watch for references to other writers; then look up these names in the index that applies to their discipline (the *MLA Bibliography*, for example, if they are writing on literary subjects) and study their publishing record.

Professional Journals

Articles in professional journals are usually more trustworthy than those in widely circulating magazines. Published by professional associations or by academic institutions, they are approved for publication by specialists in a field and are written for an audience knowledgeable in that field. As a result, such articles are usually well documented and carefully reasoned. However, articles in some commercially published magazines and newspapers, although they are not as formally documented as those in scholarly journals, can also supply bibliographic information and can be equally reliable.

Every periodical possesses its own point of view to attract its audience. If you use an article that discusses only one side of an issue, you should at least be aware of that bias and try to find other points of view.

Moreover, whatever the bias of an article, you should always judge the writing by the presentation of facts and the conclusions based on them. *Magazines for Libraries* evaluates both journals and magazines and explains the kinds of articles most often published by them as well as any detectable biases. It also gives the circulation size, which may indicate a limited audience. See Figure 4.2 for reviews of two magazines with different political views.

Also be on guard against bias by reading the masthead of a magazine or periodical (usually found on the same page as the table of contents) to see who publishes it. Many lobbying organizations, such as the Sierra Club or the National Rifle Association, issue their own publications in which the point of view of their organization is promoted.

Recommendations and Reviews

You may also determine the reliability of a book or article by the source that recommended the material to you. College faculty, librarians, and others knowledgeable about your subject are dependable sources. Bibliographies in printed sources, such as encyclopedias or books by known professionals, are usually reliable. The presence of a book or periodical in a college library may also recommend it because such material is often chosen by instructors in the field or by librarians who have studied reviews. However, some books of doubtful validity do make their way into college libraries, so double-checking may be necessary.

Book Review Digest provides excerpts from book reviews by professionals writing in about 200 periodicals such as *Commentary,* the *New York Review of Books,* and *Science,* as well as in scholarly journals such as the *American Journal of Sociology* and *Modern Language Journal.* The reviews cited have appeared in at least two periodicals and within eighteen

FIGURE 4.2 Reviews from *Magazines for Libraries*

5412. The Nation. [ISSN: 0027-8378] 1865. w. $48. Victor Navasky. Nation Co., 72 Fifth Ave., New York, NY 10011. Index, adv. Sample. Circ: 95,000. Vol. ends: June & Dec. Microform: PMC, UMI. Reprint: Pub., UMI. *Indexed:* API, MI, PAIS, RG. *Bk. rev:* 4, 1,000 words, signed. *Aud:* Ga, Ac.

The Nation and *The New Republic* represent two of the foremost liberal/left-wing journals currently available. Although the two publications represent the same side of the political spectrum, they each seem to take pride in being different from the other and in claiming higher readership, therefore supremacy. As with *Time* and *Newsweek,* chosing between them can be a matter of personal preference. *The Nation,* which is the oldest continually published weekly in the United States, is an unabashedly liberal/left-wing publication and yet doesn't take itself so seriously that it won't include the occasional tongue-in-cheek piece. The writing is crisp and concise, a joy to read. The "Reading Around" column in particular is great fun. The column discusses other publications and what they are printing, a good way to keep an eye on titles not received or being considered for purchase. *The Nation* is a valuable resource for any library.

5413. National Review: a journal of fact and opinion. [ISSN: 0028-0038] 1955. bi-w. $57. John O'Sullivan. National Review, 150 E. 35th St., New York, NY 10016. Illus., index, adv. Sample. Circ: 163,800. Vol. ends: No. 25. CD-ROM: Pub. Microform: MIM, UMI. Reprint: UMI. Online: DIALOG, ISI. *Indexed:* MI, RG. *Bk. rev:* 4, 1,000 words, signed. *Aud:* Ga, Ac.

National Review is the standard to which all other conservative periodicals should be held. It maintains the verve and sting that have been its hallmark and is currently feasting on the foibles of President Clinton's administration. In addition to its pointedly right-wing editorials, each issue features a number of short articles on items of current interest, a longer feature article, and reviews of the arts. Another feature of note is the political cartoons scattered throughout each issue. This title should be considered a necessity in academic and public libraries.

months of a book's publication. Although you may not find it necessary to look up a review of every book you find on your subject, you might want to research further a book that deals with a controversial subject or that is central to your paper. Figure 4.3 presents excerpts from reviews of a book on the history of neurosis from *Book Review Digest.*

If you do not find the work you are looking for in *Book Review Digest,* you might try *Book Review Index,* which indexes almost 450 publications, from the *Atlantic* and the *New York Times* to scholarly journals such as the *Journal of Asian Studies* and the *American Historical Review.* Because the *Index* functions only as a referral, you must look up the original review in the source cited. Two other helpful works that index reviews are the *Index to Book Reviews in the Humanities* and the *Index to Book Reviews in the Social Sciences.*

Choice, an American Library Association monthly publication used by many librarians and faculty to evaluate books for academic libraries, is another good source for checking the reliability of your sources. Unlike *Book Review Digest* or *Book Review Index, Choice* contains complete, short reviews by experts as well as bibliographic essays that discuss books written on a subject of current interest; these essays are indexed in *Library Literature.* Figure 4.4 provides an example.

Content

The most important indication of the reliability of an article or book is, of course, its content. Primary sources are more reliable than secondary sources. They may be either firsthand accounts (autobiographies

FIGURE 4.3 Reviews from *Book Review Digest*

DRINKA, GEORGE FREDERICK. The birth of neurosis; myth, malady, and the Victorians. 431p il $21.95 1984 Simon & Schuster
616.85 1. Psychiatry 2. Neuroses 3. Medicine—Europe
ISBN 0-671-44999-0 LC 84-10563

This is a "history of the study and treatment of nervous disorders in the nineteenth century." (Atlantic) Bibliography. Index.

"Rousseau's noble savage was one of the myths and railway spine was one of the maladies confronting the physicians Dr. Drinka describes. Some of those early neurologists were as eccentric as their patients, but while some of their theories seem quite daft, others have been proved correct by modern researchers using instruments unavailable to the pioneers. It is a fascinating and often amusing story that Dr. Drinka has to tell, and he presents it well."
—*Atlantic* 254:128 S '84. Phoebe-Lou Adams (120w)

"This study of pre-Freudian Victorian notions about neurosis and psychopathology ranges widely, exploring the works of Charcot, Krafft-Ebing, Janet, and other major neurologists and psychiatrists. . . . This is a fascinating area that lends itself to further work; the material will therefore be of interest to a broad range of scholars. It is therefore unfortunate that the book tends to be rambling and unfocused, without a clearly developed thesis, jumping back and forth between difficult clinicians in a confusing way. Henri F. Ellenberger's The Discovery of the Unconscious [BRD 1971] is a more coherent overview of the development of modern psychiatry."
Libr J 109:1854 O 1 '84. Paul Hymowitz (120w)

Ms 18:14 O '84. Margaret McDonald (700w)

FIGURE 4.4 Review from *Choice*

Author ——————— NEITZKE, Frederic William. A software law primer. Van Nostrand
Reinhold, 1984. 157p index 83-23508. 24.95 ISBN 0-442-26866-1.
CIP

Title
Publisher

Date of publication —————
Number of pages ———
Contains an index ———

Written for the computer software author, this book provides a basic
introduction to the legal issues that can arise in any of several areas. Initially
Neitzke deals with the question of legal protection for software and discusses the advantages and disadvantages of patent, copyright, and trade
secret protection. He then moves on to trademark, employer relationship,
business, contract, and tort law considerations. No area is covered in detail,
but the major areas for concern are pointed out and a range of examples is
presented showing how the courts have resolved these difficulties. Underly-
ing Neitzke's treatment are his feelings about the judicial system's incompe-
tence in handling the issues that are connected to computer software. The
final chapter in the book dealing with the Betamax home videotaping case
was written before the US Supreme Court's recent decision and adds
nothing to this monograph. There is a glossary of legal terms, a table of
cases cited, and a detailed index. Recommended for corporate, public, and
undergraduate academic libraries.—*M. Silverman, University of Pittsburgh Law Library*

Price

*Library of Congress
call number*

Reviewer

and eyewitness reports); original research based on questionnaires, interviews, observations, personal experiences, or experiments; or poems,
novels, plays, and other original creations of an author. However, secondary sources — articles, books, speeches, and so on — derived from
primary sources are also important. In fact, an expert's commentary on
primary sources is sometimes more valuable to a nonexpert than information gained through primary research. For a college writer, a combination of these two kinds of sources is desirable. Use the following
questions to help you evaluate the content of a source.

1. *If information is gathered through original research, are the problem and
the search strategy or method clearly stated?* A scientific article detailing an
experiment usually follows a four-part format: an introduction states the
problem and reviews previous work on the subject; an explanation of
methods and materials includes how the research was conducted and
provides the details that make evaluation possible; a description outlines the results; and a discussion or conclusion analyzes those results.
Figure 4.5, from an article in the *Journal of the American Medical Association,* shows how such details are explained. The problem being investi-
gated is whether commercial hair analysis is a scientific process. From
the methods section, readers can judge whether the writers selected
their samples carefully and evaluated their statistics fairly.

In *Consumer Reports,* aimed at a more general audience than the *Journal of the American Medical Association,* the experiments are less formal
in presentation, but they contain similar information. Notice that in
the excerpt (Figure 4.6) the methodology, purpose of the study, results, and discussion of the results are all given.

2. *If the information you find in a book or article is based on someone else's
original research or experience, are the sources and method of research explained
well enough to validate the findings? Or are the secondary sources authoritative
enough to be convincing without further explanation?* In the magazine

FIGURE 4.5   Methods Section of a Scientific Article

METHODS
Laboratory Communications

Each of the laboratories in this study was contacted by a "doctor" interested in doing hair analysis on his patients. All responded with instructions for submitting specimens, and most included literature on the supposed value of the test. Additional viewpoints were gathered from articles and advertisements in chiropractic journals and health food industry trade publications.

Preparation of Hair Samples

The specimens consisted of shoulder-length hair from two apparently healthy 17-year-old girls. The hairs varied in length up to about 15 cm. One sample weighed 60 g, while the other weighed 36 g. Each was rinsed 20 times in tap water, allowed to dry, cut into 1- to 2-cm lengths, and mixed thoroughly so that hair from different locations would be selected for inclusion into each laboratory specimen. Twenty-six specimens of 0.5 to 2.0 g each were then prepared from each hair sample according to instructions from each laboratory; some were measured into envelopes, some were measured using a teaspoon, and others were prepared with a balance card supplied by the laboratory.

One sample per subject was sent to each laboratory, under an assumed name, and this process was repeated using different names about three weeks later, so that 52 reports were obtained. Each report presented mineral levels in parts per million or milligrams per 100 g, and indicated in some way whether these values were "low," "normal," or "high" compared with the laboratory's standards. Tables 2 and 3 summarize the values for each mineral. The Figure illustrates portions of the reports from five laboratories.

Statistical Analysis

The degree of concordance between matched pairs for each mineral in the four samples sent to each laboratory was assessed using Cohen's κ, a standard coefficient of agreement.[7] A κ value of 1.00 would signify perfect agreement. A value of .75 or more is usually regarded as a high level of agreement; .41 to .74, moderate agreement; and .40 or less, low agreement. The 13 laboratories scored as follows: laboratory A, .70; laboratory B, .42; laboratory C, .24; laboratory D, .40; laboratory E, .73; laboratory F, .83; laboratory G, .28; laboratory H, .83; laboratory I, −.06; laboratory J, .66; laboratory K, .78; laboratory L, .62; laboratory M, .90.

American Health (June 1995) Trina Chang wrote a brief article about carotenoids, "a class of pigments that occur naturally in many fruits and vegetables." Chang describes these pigments — including the best known, beta-carotene — and refers to their "supposed health benefits." Then she writes, "But a 1994 study of smokers found a *higher* rate of lung cancer among those taking beta-carotene supplements" and concludes that the "best strategy, researchers currently believe, is to eat a variety of carotenoids." The readers of this article do not know who did the study or where the information was first published. The editors apparently believe that readers are willing to rely on the reputation of the magazine and that they are more interested in the findings than in the source or the methodology used.

Some popular magazines and newspapers, however, when giving research results, give the title of the journal that first published the infor-

FIGURE 4.6   Extract from *Consumer Reports*

Methodology —

Purpose —

Staffers in a lather

To see how soaps stacked up against one another, we rounded up 42 of the best-selling brands: beauty soaps, deodorant soaps, and products that dare to call themselves simply "soap." We bought both liquids, in plastic pump-bottles, and bath-sized bars, usually white. Some of the soaps come in colors other than the ones we tested, and *Dove* comes in scented and unscented versions. Because the variants' formulas are identical to those of the soaps we chose, their effectiveness should be the same, too.

We recruited a score of staffers to visit our chemistry lab twice a day to get their hands dirty, then wash them. In their morning visits, the panelists wore a surgical glove on their right hand and soiled their left with a gooey smear of finely powdered clay mixed with light mineral oil. In the afternoon, they reversed hands.

Panelists used as much soap and took as much time washing as they needed. We carefully removed or covered the name of each product so as not to prejudice our hand-washers.

Panelists judged how well the soaps cleaned and how their hands felt after soaping. They also assessed how well the soaps lathered up. We weighed soaps before and after use to gauge how long they last and how much they actually cost to use. And we paraded the products under the sensitive proboscis of one of our chemists for a scent profile.

Coming clean

None of the soaps were judged less than good in cleaning or in the way they left the hands feeling. But some clearly performed better than others. *Dove Unscented White*, a penny-a-wash bar containing moisturizing cream, won the panel's highest marks for both cleaning and feel—and for its lathering and ease of rinsing. We've check-rated it. *Liquid Dial Antibacterial* emerged as the best liquid. But liquids generally didn't feel as good on the skin as bar soap, probably because they're more likely to contain detergent, which tends to feel harsher than soap. (The Ratings Comments tell which brands have detergent, soap, or both.)

The biggest differences among soaps were in price and longevity. The Ratings give the price we paid for a bar or pump-bottle, the unit price (price per ounce), and the number of hand-washes we reckon you'd get from an ounce. The key figure is the cost per wash—the price per ounce divided by the number of washes per ounce.

The cost ranged all the way from half a cent per wash with *Lux* to 31 cents per wash with *Eau de Gucci*. We wish we could tell you why *Eau de Gucci* might be worth 60 times more than *Lux*. But it landed dead last in our blind tests, so we're stumped.

— Results

— Discussion

mation and perhaps the date. Such information validates the content of the article and also makes it possible for readers to find the original to get more details or to determine the accuracy of the second-hand source. It's best for you, as a researcher, to look up the original article, which is clearly more authentic and reliable.

3. *Is consideration given to both sides of a controversial subject? If not, can you find another source that supplies the opposing point of view?* It is impossible to find completely unbiased sources. We all have our own ways of looking at events because of our past experiences and knowledge. Even the objectivity of science has come under criticism; for example, see Jackson Albrecht's article "Social Context of Policy Research" in *Sociological Methods & Research* (Feb. 13, 1985) in which he speaks of "the myth of value-free science." Universities, he points out, often have their research funded by government agencies or business firms. Politics often determines what research will be funded within the government. "Researchers," he declares, "carry their values into any study they begin." What is the solution? He urges scientists to "openly [declare] their assumptions and biases, stating the research objectives of the funding agency, investigators, and audience, and describing the location, time, and context of the study." As a student, rather than a professional researcher, you may have difficulty discerning subtle influences of values, but you should be aware of the obvious ones. It is wise, for example, to carefully examine studies by tobacco companies that describe the effects of tobacco on health. Also remember that you as a researcher and an individual have your own biases and you should recognize them.

4. *Are statistics used accurately and are they interpreted fairly?* The use of statistics is like the use of other evidence in research: their collection and interpretation is subject to bias. In his book *A Primer of Statistics for Non-Statisticians,* Abraham N. Franzblau warns:

> First and foremost, the consumer [reader of statistics] should beware of statistics with a built-in bias — statistics, in other words, which aim to serve a vested interest. He should look routinely to the source of every statistic offered and carefully scrutinize the purpose for which it was compiled. He should be wary of sales inducements, clouded contexts, partial truths, and slanted findings. . . .
>
> The consumer of statistics should also beware of large conclusions drawn from small facts. How was the sample selected? Was it large enough? . . . Are the generalizations which are made justifiable?

It's often difficult for the nonexpert to determine whether statistics are being used fairly. Many times, though, plain common sense will come to your aid. Suppose you find in your research the following "evidence": in random interviews a reporter asked five people on the street whether they think the government is handling a current crisis well. The implication in the story is that their views are representative of those of many other people — how many is never stated. But common sense tells you that this is not a fair sample of the beliefs of a whole country or even a small part of it. Experienced poll takers take samples according to tested poll-taking techniques. But even they recognize that they are unlikely to be completely accurate in making claims for large groups on the basis of evidence from small groups. Consequently, they allow for margins of error. The figures of a professional, experienced poll taker should be regarded as good evidence, but no sampling is as reliable as a survey of the whole group. Because you will not be able to examine the way statistics were gathered and compiled, you frequently will have to rely on the credibility or reputation of your source.

5. *Are generalizations based on sufficient evidence?* You may have heard a claim like this: "Cigarette smoking isn't harmful. My grandfather smoked every day and he lived to be eighty." One person's experience may be considered, but it cannot be used alone as representative of a group. Individual experiences and examples are valuable for making generalizations understandable but not for proving them. In other words, each piece of evidence should be given appropriate weight.

Source Evaluation: Student Examples

The examples that follow demonstrate how two students evaluated their research sources.

George Forte's Source Evaluation. Because he was writing on a subject that is controversial — Native Americans' rights to their ancestral remains — George Forte had to get the views of reliable experts on both sides of the issue (Native Americans and museum officials) as well as the views of those who were not directly involved. He was fortunate that the issue had been argued in hearings before Congress, where committees had selected experts from both sides to testify. The testimony in such hearings is easy to locate in government documents. He also found books on relevant historical and archaeological research published by university presses, and he located articles in magazines (*National Geographic* and *Harper's*) whose information is usually reliable. An editorial in the *New York Times* provided arguments from a reputable neutral source on the side of Native Americans. Finally, he himself evaluated all of the arguments and evidence according to the Toulmin guidelines (see p. 148).

Melanie Reynolds's Source Evaluation. Melanie Reynolds's paper on the effects of environmental tobacco smoke (Chapter 12) required a somewhat different type of validation. It presents statistics on the kinds and percentages of harmful elements in second-hand smoke. Then it presents data showing the resulting harmful effects on the health of those who inhaled it. To be convincing to readers, the sources of the data had to be recognized as authoritative. Reynolds relied primarily on three groups of sources: books published by university presses, such as the Oxford University Press and Johns Hopkins University Press; professional journals in medicine and biology, such as *JAMA* and the *New England Journal of Medicine;* and government documents, including reports from two surgeons general and from the Environmental Protection Agency. The magazine *Science News,* another cited source, receives a favorable review in *Magazines for Libraries* (C. Katz and L. S. Katz) as an authoritative source of science information for young people.

Reading

Finding information is a little like searching for gold. First you have to search to find out where the likely places are — you can't dig everywhere — and then you have to dig carefully and thoroughly. When you have finally located sources of information, you need to read efficiently. You can save time by scanning the whole article or book to see whether it is worth reading at all and, if it is, by deciding which parts you want to scan and which you want to read closely. Then you must read carefully the material that you have decided is important and record the relevant material in your notes.

Scanning a Book

To scan a book, look first at the title and subtitle. You have already written down the title, but you may not have noticed the subtitle, which is often more descriptive of the contents. *Wishes, Lies, and Dreams* by Kenneth Koch is a rhythmic and evocative title, but it does not indicate what the book is about as clearly as the subtitle does — *Teaching Children to Write Poetry*. Record both on your bibliography card or type them into your computer. Next read the table of contents to discover the scope of the book and to see whether any chapters or parts of chapters deal with your subject or your preliminary list of sources. If you are doing a report on the capacity of the human brain, you might consult Carl Sagan's *The Dragons of Eden: Speculations on the Evolution of Human Intelligence*. A look at the table of contents shows three chapter titles referring to the brain:

Consulting the index to a book is another quick, useful way of determining contents. The index to Sagan's book includes this entry:

The table of contents gives you a general idea of what is in a book; the index gives specific citations or references. Be sure to include in your notes the chapter or page numbers that contain useful information. You may want to come back and read them later.

If the book seems to discuss relevant material, read the preface or introduction (some books have both). The preface usually explains the author's reason for writing the book and perhaps its organization or focus. Carl Sagan's preface gives the hypothesis on which his book is based: his belief "that man is descended from some lowly-organized form." The introduction may not be labeled as such; it may be just a part of the first chapter. The introduction prepares readers for the substance of the book by telling them what they need to know in order to understand the book's contents. In Sagan's introduction, preceding the first chapter, he defines his audience ("the interested layman"), states his fundamental premise (that the workings of the brain "are a consequence of its anatomy and physiology, and nothing more"), and explains that he will outline the evolution of human intelligence. After reading such an introduction, you would be able to decide whether you wanted to continue.

In some cases, you might also want to glance at the conclusion, especially if you plan to read a substantial part of the book. Like the introduction, the conclusion may not be labeled; it may be just the last part of the book. In *The Dragons of Eden,* the last chapter, "Knowledge Is Our Destiny," sums up the author's beliefs, forecasts the discovery of extraterrestrial intelligence, and suggests how the brains of extraterrestrial beings might be constructed.

Finally, if the book has a bibliography, note this fact in your bibliographic notes. Then check the bibliography to see if any of the sources listed seem relevant to your research. If you find any, record them on separate bibliography cards or put them in a separate list in your computer so that you can look at them later.

Scanning an Article

To scan an article, note first the biographical facts about the author, often given at the beginning or sometimes at the end; these facts will help you further evaluate the article. Then read the first two or three paragraphs, which usually state the scope and argument or thesis of the article. (Journal articles in the sciences and other disciplines may be preceded by an abstract that summarizes the author's major points. If available, an abstract is one of the quickest ways to determine how useful an article will be for your research.) Finally, you may want to glance at the last paragraph, which usually states the results or conclusions reached. Scanning these elements will give you a kind of map to follow, making it easier to understand the article if you decide to read it closely.

Suppose you are writing a paper on early women poets and you locate an article by Elizabeth A. Nist in *College English*. The first page of the article is reproduced in Figure 4.7.

First, note the author's credentials at the bottom; her professional position and publications are given. The first paragraph of the article is a quotation that can be skimmed quickly by reading the first line and glancing over the rest, just for a general understanding. The main point comes in the fourth paragraph — particularly in the first sentence. Here the author tells about the good poetry women wrote in the sixteenth century. Finally, a footnote supplies a short bibliography of anthologies of early women writers. If these interest you, enter them in your working bibliography.

Turning to the end of the article, you notice four concluding paragraphs (Figure 4.8). The first sentence of this group of paragraphs is almost the same as the thesis statement at the beginning: "Women wrote and wrote well during the Elizabethan period." The second paragraph is

FIGURE 4.7   Scanning an Article: The First Page

"Men might consider that women were not created to be their slaves or vassals, for as they had not their origin out of his head, (thereby to command him), so it was not out of his foot to be trod upon, but in a (medium) out of his side to be his fellow-feeler, his equal and companion."

When and by whom was this written? It sounds like some turn of the century suffragist, or, with a little more contemporary diction and syntax, it could be a Bible-belt feminist during the ERA campaign of the 1970s. Probably it goes as far back as some pioneer woman in Nebraska or Utah in the 1870s, but, at the very least, surely it was written after 1700, because even Virginia Woolf admits that "nothing is known about women before the eighteenth century and certainly no woman wrote a word of that extraordinary Elizabethan literature when every other man, it seemed, was capable of song or sonnet." The contents of all our anthologies of British literature suport Virginia Woolf's surmises.

But our opening quote did not come from the "modern" women's movement. It was published in 1640 in London in *The Women's Sharpe Revenge . . . Performed by Mary Tattle-well and Ione Hit-him-home, Spinsters*. A little digging shows these pseudonymous co-authors were not alone in their opinions or their talent for forcefully expressing them.

Women wrote and wrote well during the Elizabethan period. A surprising number of manuscripts have been preserved, but they are not readily available to readers and scholars. Most are held in the British Library, private collections, or university rare book collections and can generally be read only on microfilm. Even though a few good anthologies of women's literature have been published in the past ten years,[1] most professors and teachers of literature remain unaware of these works.

1. Three recent anthologies of early women writers are particularly outstanding: Ann Stanford, ed., *The Women Poets in English* (New York: McGraw-Hill, 1972); Mary R. Mahl and Helene Koon, eds., *The Female Spectator: English Women Writers Before 1800* (Bloomington: Indiana University Press and Old Westbury, N.Y.: The Feminist Press, 1977); and Fidelis Morgan, ed., *The Female Wits: Women Playwrights of the Restoration* (London: Virago Press, 1981).

Elizabeth A. Nist teaches at Utah Technical College. She has published essays, stories, and poems in many journals, and a book of her poems, *Now Is My Springtime*, was published in 1974.

College English, Volume 46, Number 7, November 1984

FIGURE 4.8 Scanning an Article: Concluding Paragraphs

It is obvious that Elizabethan women did write, and they wrote well. This essay presents only eleven of the more than fifty women whose work is known. Yet even from these few examples we get a glimpse of the variety and importance of their writings.

They have given us some wonderful lyric poetry that celebrates not only their joys but, even more significantly, expresses their sorrows and their pain. In their prose we not only have firsthand accounts of life at that time, but realistic and practical accounts. We also have the first attempts to create real-life characters and dialogue in English, along with realistic subplots. In drama we have the first play by a women in English, attracting the attention and respect of the other writers of her time.

These writers speak for themselves. Surely a true picture of our cultural heritage cannot be constructed without their contributions, but, despite the fact that all of these works were published in the sixteenth and seventeenth centuries (many in repeated and popular editions), they are virtually unknown by modern scholars.

That no women wrote before 1800 is a myth, and until women like Margaret More Roper, Mary Sidney Herbert, Elizabeth Cary, and Mary Sidney Wroth stand alongside their husbands, brothers, and uncles, the myth will continue. As Mary Tattle-well said, ''Men might consider that women were not created to be their slaves or vassals . . . but out of [their] sides to be [their] fellow-feelers, their equals and companions.''

a summary of the article, the third paragraph comments on the importance of these women, and the last paragraph makes an appeal for equality of women. After reading the introduction and conclusion of this article, you have a good idea of what it is about and what the author's point of view is. If you wish, you can read the rest of the article later.

In scanning, you save time by not reading everything. Instead, you read fast to find out where to read slowly and carefully. Try not to be distracted by interesting but irrelevant material unless you are in the early stages of your search and have time to change direction. In addition, do not waste time by reading sources that merely repeat factual information you already have. You may want to read several accounts of an important or controversial event, such as the assassination of John F. Kennedy, for a variety of viewpoints, but if you are looking for general information on, for example, the Battle of Bunker Hill, an encyclopedia article will give you the necessary facts that other sources would merely duplicate.

Close Reading

Close reading means reading each word and sentence to learn the author's exact meaning. The following suggestions will help you to read efficiently as well as thoroughly.

Reading with a Purpose. When you locate a chapter, a book, or an article that you want to read completely, read with a clear sense of what you want to find out. To sharpen this sense of purpose, read with certain questions in mind derived from rephrasing parts of your outline: What is agoraphobia? What causes it? Can agoraphobics be helped? You might look for the answer to one question in one article or book and the answer to another question somewhere else. As you read, be ready to encounter and absorb information that you did not anticipate with your questions. Reading for a paper on nutrition, Jeffrey Smerko began to encounter warnings about advertisers' misrepresentations on health food products, so he decided to add a section in his paper on this subject.

Entering the Mind of the Writer. Withhold judgment until you have enough evidence. When you are reading an article on one side of a question, try to follow the thoughts of the writer to understand how conclusions were reached. If you make up your mind too soon on a controversial subject, you may overlook important information.

Reading for Main Ideas. Keep the main idea or purpose of the author in mind, and try to associate each paragraph and sentence with this main idea. If an idea does not seem to fit, stop and figure out whether the fault is yours or the writer's.

Defining Technical Terms. Do not look up a word that you can figure out by the context unless you have plenty of time. Your goal is to keep your concentration intact.

Paraphrasing. Put key passages or arguments into your own words. This test determines whether you have understood the writer by making the writer's thoughts part of your own thinking and expanding your own knowledge factually and conceptually. Failure to achieve this understanding usually results in one of the following problems. First, much of what is called plagiarism (copying another's words and ideas) results not so much from design as from failure to comprehend the original. What you don't understand, you can't put into your own words; the alternative then is to use the words of the original writer simply because there are no other words available. When you do not acknowledge the source, you engage in plagiarism. Second, if you use quotations too frequently, your paper becomes a patchwork of other people's words, and the writer's voice — your voice — is not heard.

Taking Notes

Good notes are the bridge between reading and writing; they make it possible for you to retain all of the material you read. But they have a further advantage: with good notes, not only will you have easy access to what you've read, but you will also have begun the writing process. Photocopying is not a substitute for the mental activity that occurs when you take notes. Although it is a convenient device for taking restricted material out of the library so that you can read it later, photocopying really adds an extra step to the process because you will eventually need to take notes from the photocopies. If you attempt the shortcut of writing your paper directly from books or photocopied articles, it will be harder for you to write a good paper. The temptation to use the words of the original may eliminate the step of making the ideas part of your own thinking.

Good notes also tell you where you found your information so that documenting your sources later will be easier. Because taking notes is time-consuming and sometimes laborious, it is tempting to think that you will be able to recall the necessary bibliographic information when you need to assemble and record your sources. Try to resist this temptation. You will collect so much information that you will have trouble remembering it all, and it is unlikely that you will always remember the sources.

Before you start to take notes, decide whether you will put them on cards or on your computer (you can, of course, use a combination of the two). In any case, each note should include, besides the information itself, (1) where you got the information and (2) where it fits in your working outline. You need to know *where it came from and where it's going* so that you can put it in your paper in a logical order and give its source.

Taking Notes on Cards

If you're taking notes on cards, follow these guidelines.

1. *Place an abbreviated form of the source at the top of each card on the left.* Key this name to your working bibliography.

2. *Place a heading from your working outline on the top of each card on the right.* This will help you arrange your notes when you write your paper.

3. *Paraphrase or summarize most of your information.* Be sure to enclose in quotation marks any direct quotations you do write down. Add your own reactions to your reading and enclose them in brackets.

4. *Place the page number of the source following the information from that page.* If you are summarizing or paraphrasing, you may be taking information from more than one page, so be sure to give all the relevant pages. If you are quoting, you must be careful to match the quotation with the exact pages. If a quotation extends over more than one page, mark on your card where the page break is. When you are writing your paper, you may want to use only a part of the quotation.

5. *Use only one side of each card.* Because you will write from your cards, you might find it helpful to spread them out and study their contents or write from them without turning them over. If a single note covers more than one side of a card, use another card and number the cards consecutively in the heading.

6. *Put only information that belongs in the same part of your outline on the same card.* Do this even if you write only one or two lines on a card. If your subject, for instance, is the use of solar power for home heating and your source includes information on both design and cost, put the data on different cards so that you can later sort them by subject.

7. *Write with pen.* Pencil is hard to read and smudges when the cards rub together.

Figure 4.9 illustrates headings for note cards.

Taking Notes on a Computer

One of the main differences between taking notes on a computer and writing notes by hand is that most word processing programs can order each note as you enter it, if you type the necessary commands. If you follow your outline when you number your notes, your computer will arrange them in numerical order.

Before you begin, decide on a filing system for your information. You might have a different file for each major heading, with headings within this file corresponding to your subheadings. When you want to enter information under your major heading, open the file named for that heading and then find the subheading where your information belongs. Some computer systems allow you to group your files by folder; then the folders could be your major headings. Grouping files by folder makes it easy to open parts of your document.

FIGURE 4.9   Note Card Headings

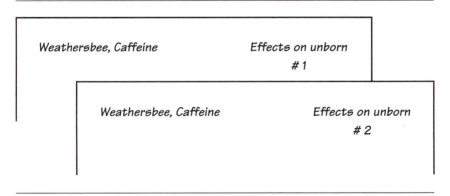

For each note, use guidelines similar to those for taking notes on cards.

1. At the beginning of each note, provide the source and the heading, keyed to your outline.
2. Include in each note only the information that relates to that heading.
3. Give page numbers at the end of each note. For direct quotations, identify page breaks (see guideline 4 on p. 101 in "Taking Notes on Cards").

Because the computer will organize your notes by subject as you take them, you'll be able to transfer them easily to your paper. You can retrieve them by opening files corresponding to your headings and subheadings or, within the file, by author, by title, or by word.

When you begin writing, you can print out your notes and read them as you type your paper. If your software program allows you to open more than one file at a time on your screen, you can use the Cut, Copy, and Paste commands to move text from one file to another. Some word processing programs allow you to save information on a clipboard so that you can insert it into another document later.

Recording Your Information

Note taking and close reading are interrelated. You need to read carefully, of course, to take notes; at the same time, note taking is a significant aid to reading with comprehension and retention. It isn't easy to decide what is relevant enough to record on note cards, especially at the beginning of your search when you are still defining your topic. Remember the researcher's safety policy: when in doubt, choose abundance, and plan to write down much more than it seems you need.

There are three main forms of recording information: paraphrasing, summarizing, and quoting. At first you will probably find yourself quoting quite a bit simply because you are not as familiar with your subject as you will be later. However, you will still save time by summarizing and paraphrasing as much as you can because these represent conversions of someone else's ideas into your own — a step closer to writing your paper. In addition to recording information on your cards, add comments and questions of your own, either on the same card or separately. These comments will also help you integrate your information and make it part of your own thinking. Be sure, though, that you differentiate between what is taken from your sources and what is your own thinking. One way to do this is by putting brackets around your own words or thoughts.

Paraphrase

Paraphrase is a kind of translation. If you can paraphrase something, you know you understand it. When you paraphrase, put the message that appears in someone else's language into your own, but always be sure to credit the actual author in your notes and paper. Paraphrase when you need the details of the original but don't want to quote the author: you want your own words to convey the sound of your own writing style. Helen Weathersbee, in her paper on caffeine, found this sentence in one of her sources: "Although soft drink manufacturers claim that they use caffeine strictly as a flavoring agent, some people are convinced that they add caffeine to their products in a deliberate effort to get children hooked on them." She paraphrased this sentence on her note card, as illustrated in Figure 4.10, and in her paper this note became the following sentence:

> Many consumers believe that soft drink manufacturers add caffeine to their products to cause children to become addicted to the caffeine in them.[6]

You might also want to paraphrase when your source is technical or scientific and your audience is unfamiliar with the language it uses. Weathersbee's audience was her college writing class, and most of the students were not science majors. In an article in *Medicine and Science in Sports,* she found the following passage:

> Since muscle glycogen depletion is considered responsible, in part, for exhaustion during prolonged exercise, slowing the rate of glycogen utilization should improve endurance performance (5, 8, 12). It has previously been established that the elevation of plasma FFA [free fatty acids] results in an increased rate of lipid metabolism and a diminished dependence on

FIGURE 4.10   Paraphrasing: A Sample Note Card

> *Jacobson, The Caffeine Catch*   *Caffeine Consumption*
>
> *Some people argue that caffeine is added to soft drinks so that children will become addicted to them.*
>
> *p. 21*

muscle glycogen in exercising skeletal muscle (5, 9, 14). In the present study, as in previous investigations, the ingestion of caffeine resulted in a 50 to 100% increase in plasma FFA (1, 7, 14).

On her note card, Weathersbee wrote this paraphrase:

> During exercise tests, the ingestion of caffeine raised the levels of fatty acids in the blood. Since high levels of fatty acids have been shown to slow the rate of carbohydrate depletion, which in turn leads to exhaustion, caffeine seems to help athletes' endurance.

In her paper, this information was reduced to a phrase in the section on the benefits of caffeine:

> In addition, caffeine has been found to enhance the speed and accuracy of those performing physical tasks such as typing[3]; it also increases endurance during exercise by reducing carbohydrate oxidation and increasing fat metabolism.[20]

In the early stages of his research for a paper on early conflicts between socialists and libertarians, Roger Tran paraphrased a key point of the conflict from an article in the *Dictionary of the History of Ideas*. Here is part of a passage that Tran found especially helpful:

> The socialist view was advanced in direct opposition to the more widely accepted belief that the rights of the individual against society and the state were inviolable. The most popular writers on political economy in the first half of the nineteenth century generally claimed that since individual liberty was the source of all progress, its enhancement must be the paramount aim of public policy. To interfere with the freedom of exchange was to infringe upon the rights of man and to place dangerous obstacles in the way of industry and prosperity.

On a note card, Tran paraphrased the passage this way:

> Socialism contradicted the popular notion that individual rights, seen as the source of innovation, should be upheld over the interests of the state and society. Supporters of individual rights believed that any restrictions on such rights would interfere with progress and industry.

Although Tran didn't end up citing this particular article in his paper, the process of reading and paraphrasing it improved his understanding of his subject.

Summary

When you paraphrase, you restate or translate a passage using about the same number of words. When you summarize, you reduce a long passage (a paragraph, page, or several pages) to a sentence or a few sentences. Writing a summary requires the ability to generalize — to extract the main ideas from a passage along with any significant details. You can see the difficulty in generalizing when you ask a child to ex-

plain a movie she has just seen. She will recount one detail after another without generalizing to show how all the details are related.

To summarize a long piece, first look for the headings, which announce the topics discussed, and then try to find the main sentence or the main idea in each paragraph. (In newspapers and popular magazines, paragraphs are so short that often they are not built around a central idea or main sentence. You may have to read several paragraphs to detect the general thought that ties them together.) The rest of the paragraph usually consists of details or elaborations of the central idea. Pick out any of these details that you want to mention in your paper. Take a moment to reflect, to make these ideas and details part of your own thinking, and then write a summary in your own words of what you have read.

If your article or book is photocopied, you can aid your reading and note taking by underlining or highlighting the main points as you read. Figure 4.11 presents an excerpt from the article "How the Milky Way Formed" in *Scientific American,* cited by Carl Rodriguez in his paper on galaxy formation. The article's title prepared him to find theories about how a particular galaxy, the Milky Way, formed. Working with a photocopy, he underlined these theories and other details he thought he could use in his report.

Figure 4.12 illustrates how Rodriguez summarized the material on his note card. Information from this summary and other note cards is combined in the following passage from his paper.

> Recently, scientists have questioned the hypothesis that the Milky Way galaxy was formed by a collapse of a single gas cloud. Some experts now believe that the galaxy might have formed when a "protogalactic" Milky Way, a conglomeration of gas cloud fragments, collapsed (p. 72). They have gained evidence for this and other conclusions by studying the color and luminosity of stars, which reveal everything from stars' age to their chemical composition.

While researching a paper on how and why the work of women and minority artists has been suppressed throughout history, Dena Howell found an interesting article on women abstract painters in *The Yale Journal of Criticism.* The article was especially helpful in explaining how women and minority painters in the Abstract Expressionist movement were overlooked in the mid-twentieth century. Here is one passage that caught Howell's attention:

> Universalism was what critics wanted to find when they urged artists not to pin their art down to one locality or nation. As early as 1939, critic Edwin Alden Jewell encouraged American artists to produce an art that was "universal, approaching finally the expression of a common human experience." Jewell's argument is a paradigmatic one, since in his longing for an art that is at once American and universal it illustrates the paradox that has plagued universalism's potential for opposing unjust hierarchies. The idea

FIGURE 4.11 Underlining Sample

Attempts to reconstruct how the Milky Way formed and began to evolve resemble an archaeological investigation of an ancient civilization buried below the bustling center of an ever changing modern city. From excavations of foundations, some pottery shards and a few bones, we must infer how our ancestors were born, how they grew old and died and how they may have helped create the living culture above. Like archaeologists, astronomers, too, look at small, disparate clues to determine how our galaxy and others like it were born about a billion years after the big bang and took on their current shapes. The clues consist of the ages of stars and stellar clusters, their distribution and their chemistry—all deduced by looking at such features as color and luminosity. The shapes and physical properties of other galaxies can also provide insight concerning the formation of our own.

The evidence suggests that our galaxy, the Milky Way, came into being as a consequence of the collapse of a vast gas cloud. Yet that cannot be the whole story. Recent observations have forced workers who support the hypothesis of a simple, rapid collapse to modify their idea in important ways. This new information has led other researchers to postulate that several gas cloud fragments merged to create the protogalactic Milky Way, which then collapsed. Other variations on these themes are vigorously maintained. Investigators of virtually all persuasions recognize that the births of stars and supernovae have helped shape the Milky Way. Indeed, the formation and explosion of stars are at this moment further altering the galaxy's structure and influencing its ultimate fate.

Much of the stellar archaeological information that astronomers rely on to decipher the evolution of our galaxy resides in two regions of the Milky Way: the halo and the disk. The halo is a slowly rotating, spherical region that surrounds all the other parts of the galaxy. The stars and star clusters in it are old. The rapidly rotating, equatorial region constitutes the disk, which consists of young stars and stars of intermediate age, as well as interstellar gas and dust. Embedded in the disk are the sweepingly curved arms that are characteristic of spiral galaxies such as the Milky Way. Among the middle-aged stars is our sun, which is located about 25,000 light-years from the galactic center. (When you view the night sky, the galactic center lies in the direction of Sagittarius.) The sun completes an orbit around the center in approximately 200 million years.

Source: From "How the Milky Way Formed" by Sidney van den Bergh and James E. Hesser. Copyright © 1993 by Scientific American, Inc. All rights reserved.

of the universal arises from particulars of people's experience which are subsequently noted to be strikingly similar. And it arises from the desire and effort to communicate, which predicates a common ground. It cannot exist without roots in subjective experience, in "nature," or in what can be called "difference." Its value lies in its potential to make both common ground and the historical and material specificity of its sources — sameness and difference — perceptible to its audience. What has frequently happened, however — and what happened in the institutionalization of Abstract Expressionism — is that the universal's oscillation between the general and the particular has often been stilled. Rather than seeing each as the guarantee and the condition of the other, and necessary to the

FIGURE 4.12 Summarizing: A Sample Note Card

> van den Bergh and Hesser,   Galaxy formation
> <u>Scientific American</u>
>
>
> New evidence about the creation of galaxies has made
> scientists reconsider their theory that the Milky Way
> formed when one big gas cloud collapsed. Some now
> think that a "protogalactic" Milky Way, made up of parts
> of gas clouds, collapsed to form the galaxy.
>
> p. 72

other's preservation, claims to a more permanent universalism were bolstered by elements of racism, homophobia, and misogyny sanctioned by postwar society in the U.S. These were used to repress the differences from which Abstract Expressionism was drawn. Between 1945 and 1955, it SEEMED as if a "universal" style did emerge. But by the mid-fifties, despite an impressively diverse roster of initial practitioners, its heroes and values were reductively and stereotypically heterosexual, male, and white.

Because Howell's preliminary outline organized examples of artistic suppression by time periods (for example, eighteenth century, nineteenth century, early twentieth century, and so on), she kept a "mid-twentieth century" note file in her portable computer in which she summarized this and other articles dealing with art in the 1940s and 1950s. Howell kept her outline in mind when she summarized the above passage.

> Universalism, which encouraged artists to explore similarities among humans instead of differences, eventually led to the suppression of women and minority artists. In the repressive climate of post-World War II America, Abstract Expressionism, which had been founded on the expression of differences, came to reflect the values of white, heterosexual males.

The following passage from Howell's paper draws on this and other notes:

> Some critics believe that even movements that were intended to include all of humanity eventually led to the exclusion of women and minority artists. The Universalist movement, for example, encouraged artists to create works that explored the similarities among all humans instead of particular differences. However, in the repressive environment of post-World War II

America, even Abstract Expressionism, which had been founded on the expression of differences, became dominated by the values of white, heterosexual males (Gibson 108).

Quotation

When you quote, you are using the exact words of someone else. However, because one of your purposes in writing a paper is to tell something in your own words, it doesn't make sense to overuse the words of other people. (You don't want to have to title your paper "A Collection of Quotations on the Use of Solar Energy.") Therefore, use quotations only when the exact wording is significant or necessary (see Chapter 7 for further suggestions on using and punctuating quotations). A quotation is the best choice (1) when you need to say exactly what was said in the original, (2) when the language of the original is metaphorical or highly individualistic, or (3) when the person quoted is an authority on the subject. Sometimes all three conditions apply.

Verbal precision is often important in technical subjects, such as law or medicine. Helen Weathersbee, taking notes on an article by Dr. E. R. Lutz on the effects of caffeine on the human body, quoted some of his words to provide a precise medical description of the symptoms (see Figure 4.13).

Highly individualistic or metaphorical language cannot usually be paraphrased adequately, as in Yogi Berra's statement "It ain't over till it's over." Language that has great emotional appeal or is associated with grand historical moments is also often quoted: "Give me liberty or give me death" (Patrick Henry) or Martin Luther King, Jr.'s "I have a

FIGURE 4.13 Quoting: A Sample Note Card

Lutz, Restless Legs   Effects of caffeine

Five percent of coffee drinkers have "restless legs
syndrome," a type of muscle spasm. The symptoms are
"unpleasant, creeping sensations in the lower legs
between the knee and ankle" and restlessness in the
arms and shoulders. Symptoms result from sedentary
pastimes, but victims feel the most discomfort in the
evenings and at night.

p. 693

dream" speech. Poetry or highly metaphorical prose is difficult to paraphrase or summarize. In the following passage from *Moby Dick* by Herman Melville, the metaphors and poetic sounds of the words make it
impossible to separate the words from the meaning.

> It was a clear steel-blue day. The firmaments of air and sea were hardly sepa-
> rate in that all-pervading azure; only, the pensive air was transparently pure
> and soft, with a woman's look, and the robust and man-like sea heaved with
> long, strong, lingering swells, as Samson's chest in his sleep.

The interest of a quotation may lie in the fact that it was spoken by
an authority on the subject or by a well-known person, such as the president of the United States. "A man paints with his brain and not with
his hands" is an interesting observation, but it has more significance
when the reader knows that it was said by Michelangelo.

An authority may be someone with firsthand experience. While
working on a paper about agoraphobia, Jean Carroll wrote down the
exact words of a person who had had a phobic attack. Figure 4.14
shows part of what Carroll recorded in her notes.

Personal Comments

Personal Observation.   As you consult your sources, you are consciously or unconsciously making connections between what you have
read before and what you are reading now. You are analyzing, making
judgments, and asking questions. While these thoughts are fresh in
your mind and you still remember clearly the readings on which they
are based, write them down to use when you are composing your
paper. Of course, you might write down brief comments as you record

FIGURE 4.14   Quoting: A Sample Note Card

Mansfield, <u>Wash. Post</u>   Interview

Mansfield interviewed Marjorie Goff, 64 yrs. old, who described
her first attack one Saturday in 1946 in a beauty shop where she
regularly had her hair done. "I was sitting under the dryer, and all
of a sudden this feeling swept over me. I'm losing my mind, I
thought. I'm going crazy. My heart started beating fast. My legs
felt weak. My body trembled. It was the most incredible feeling of
fear. I wanted to scream, to run out of there. I got up with all the
pins in my hair, slapped a five-dollar bill on the counter, and ran all
the way home."

p. G1

information from your sources, but there may be times when you want to make more lengthy or general observations on your work. Putting these comments on note cards (or in separate computer files) will enable you to order them along with your other notes. As he was reading sources for his paper on gambling (see Chapter 11), Donald Mower recorded his thoughts, indicating by brackets that they were his own (see Figure 4.15).

Descriptive Abstracts. A descriptive abstract is a personal note that describes or evaluates a source. Instead of summarizing content, you describe what an article or book contains and then perhaps evaluate it. Suppose you find a book early in your search and you aren't sure whether you want to use it. Write a descriptive abstract of the book, and file it with your notes for later reference.

Figure 4.16 presents a descriptive abstract of a book titled *Biofeedback: How to Control Your Body, Improve Your Health, and Increase Your Effectiveness,* by Robert M. Stern and William J. Ray. The writer made the note after reading the preface and the table of contents and after scanning the first chapter, "What Is Biofeedback?", and the reference pages.

As you take notes, write quotations in complete sentences or weave the pertinent lines in with your own words. Make sure, though, to quote your source accurately, including all marks of punctuation (see Chapter 7 for details). If you omit any words, use the marks of ellipsis (. . .). If the ellipsis marks fall at the end of a sentence, you need the three dots of ellipsis plus a period. Any addition of your own within a quotation, such as a comment or mark of punctuation added for clarity, should be enclosed in brackets.

FIGURE 4.15 Personal Observation: A Sample Note Card

Gambling in high schools   *Mar. 15*

[I am really amazed at how much gambling is being done in high schools these days. Students are even turning to crime to pay their gambling debts. I would like to find out how widespread this high school gambling is.]

FIGURE 4.16 Descriptive Abstract: A Sample Note Card

Stern and Ray
EF 319.5
B5 S73

S. & R. define biofeedback, describe procedures used, and then explain how it can be used to treat problems and illnesses such as high blood pressure, asthma, epilepsy, and headaches. Authors are psychologists who seem to have done a lot of research. Info. is in easy-to-read language. Their reference notes gave several good sources; I've added these to my bibliog. I'll explore these first because they are primary sources and I think they'll go into more detail than S. and R. Good glossary; I may use it if I run into trouble with vocabulary in some of the more tech. sources. May come back to this for gen. overview.

Avoiding Plagiarism

If you take notes carefully and record your sources accurately, you will be able to document your sources when you write your paper. You must give others credit when you use their words or when you paraphrase or summarize their original ideas. Failure to do so is called *plagiarism,* which means "literary theft" and may lead to a legal suit if the plagiarized material is published uncredited. Plagiarism is also unacceptable in student writing. The best way to avoid plagiarism is by converting the ideas of your source into your own words — as summary or paraphrase — as you take notes or, if you quote directly, by making sure that you use quotation marks. Whenever you write down any information from a source, be sure to note where you found it so that you can cite that source in your paper. If someone else's words are in your notes without identification, you may end up with the same words in your paper, which is unarguably plagiarism. You also may slip into plagiarism by failing to take notes at all and instead trying to write your paper directly from photocopied material or from books. Without the intermediate stage of putting the information into your own words in notes, it is easy to use the words of the original source without realizing it.

But, you might ask, do I have to document every bit of information I put into my paper? Must I have a footnote for every sentence? Because much of what you write will be yours and some of it will be general knowledge, you will not need to document every sentence in your paper, but you must, as a careful researcher, record your sources in your notes so that you will be able to give credit to their authors. Suggestions for documenting your paper to acknowledge your sources will be given in Chapter 7.

The preceding sections on paraphrasing and summarizing show how to take notes that do not plagiarize. You will not get into trouble if you make the information part of your own thinking and then put it down in your own words. Trouble arises when you take notes mechanically, without actually understanding what you are writing.

Here are some examples of different types of of plagiarism. The notes are based on the following passage from *The Greek Experience,* by C. M. Bowra.

> **ORIGINAL PASSAGE:** The essence of the heroic outlook is the pursuit of honour through action. The great man is he who, being endowed with superior qualities of body and mind, uses them to the utmost and wins the applause of his fellows because he spares no effort and shirks no risk in his desire to make the most of the gifts and to surpass other men in his exercise of them.

1. *Word-for-word transcription of the entire passage.* Using an exact quotation from a source in your paper without quotation marks and a citation is plagiarism.

2. *A paraphrase using the basic sentence structure of the source with a few of the words or phrases of the note taker substituted for those of the source.* In the following paraphrase, the writer keeps the basic structure of the original and merely changes a few of the words. This is plagiarism.

> **UNACCEPTABLE PARAPHRASE:** The main idea in the heroic outlook is striving to achieve honor by being active. The great man, having the highest qualities of body and mind, uses them to the greatest extent and is applauded by his comrades because he will pay any price in his desire to make the best of his gifts and to do better than other men in his use of them.

3. *A paraphrase using the note taker's sentence structure and many of his or her words but with key words of the author used without quotation marks.* The following note uses the note taker's sentence structure but borrows key words and phrases without quotation marks. This also is plagiarism.

> **UNACCEPTABLE PARAPHRASE:** The Greeks believed that the hero had superior qualities of body and mind. In his desire to make the most of his gifts the great man would spare no effort in his desire to use his gifts in surpassing other men.

The following paraphrases can be integrated into a paper with no danger of plagiarism.

> **ACCEPTABLE PARAPHRASE:** Heroism to the Greeks meant the demonstration of superiority through great deeds. The Greeks believed that the hero was a man who was superior to other men and who was willing to use his

great qualities even if he risked his life doing so. He deserves the praise he gets from his fellowmen.

ACCEPTABLE PARAPHRASE AND QUOTATION: The Greeks' idea of heroism was "the pursuit of honour through action." The hero has "superior qualities of body and mind," and he will take any risk in order to demonstrate his heroism to his fellowmen.

Of course, in both cases the source must be cited; instead of using a footnote, the writer might give the author's name in the text as part of the introduction to the passage. Notice that single words do not have to be put between quotation marks unless they show an original or distinctive use by the source. The word *superior* as used in the first acceptable paraphrase does not indicate a special use of the word, and so no quotation marks are necessary. Notice also that quoted material must be given exactly as it is in the original; in the second example the writer uses the British spelling of *honour,* as in the original.

EXERCISES

1. Write an evaluation of at least three of your sources, including both a book and an article if possible. Explain in detail how you arrived at your evaluation and the sources that guided you.

2. Write an evaluation of one of the authors in your working bibliography. Use the suggestions in this chapter.

3. **FOR YOUR SEARCH LOG**   Record the following in your search log:

   a. The most interesting bit of information you have learned about your subject so far
   b. The most frustrating experience you have had so far in your research
   c. The most enjoyable part of your research process until now

   Exchange your observations with your classmates.

4. **FOR THE COMPUTERIZED CLASSROOM** In computer-aided discussion groups of three to five members, have each member distribute photocopies of a short article or part of a long article that's relevant to his or her research. Take notes on the article primarily in your own words, interspersing a few words from the original if you wish (being careful to use quotation marks). E-mail your summaries to each other, and discuss how effective they are, answering the following questions:

   a. Is the summary accurate?
   b. Does it avoid plagiarism?

5. Read the following passage from a recent issue of *Scientific American*. Then read the lettered passages attempting to paraphrase it. Two of the

paraphrases plagiarize; one is acceptable. Identify the acceptable paraphrase, and indicate where the plagiarism occurs in each of the other passages.

ORIGINAL PASSAGE: Even if tighter marketing restrictions and higher excise taxes prove successful in decreasing tobacco smoking in the U.S., the [tobacco] industry has a means to counteract loss of revenue: exportation. Indeed, although total cigarette consumption in the U.S. has been declining for over a decade, domestic production has been buoyed by steadily increasing shipments overseas. . . . The U.S. currently leads the world in tobacco exports and has capitalized on the markets in underdeveloped countries, which have few if any restrictions on advertising or product labeling.

PARAPHRASES:

a. Even considering that tighter marketing restrictions and higher excise taxes may decrease smoking in the United States, the tobacco industry has a method to counterbalance the decline in revenue: exportation. Although total consumption of cigarettes in the United States has been declining for over ten years, domestic production has been propped up by increasing exportation. The United States now leads the world in tobacco exports and is focusing on the markets in underdeveloped countries, which have few if any restrictions on product labeling or advertising.

b. Although regulations and taxes may curtail smoking in the United States, American tobacco companies can offset lost sales by marketing their products overseas. In fact, production of cigarettes in the United States has grown as exports have increased, and the United States is now the top tobacco exporter in the world. Underdeveloped countries, where there are fewer advertising and labeling regulations, have been a special target of the tobacco industry's marketing efforts.

c. Although marketing regulations and higher excise taxes may decrease smoking in the United States, domestic production has been buoyed by steadily increasing shipments overseas, making the United States the top tobacco exporter in the world. U.S. tobacco companies are now concentrating on underdeveloped countries, where there are few restrictions on advertising and product labeling.

C H A P T E R   5

Gathering Information from Other Sources

Although we often think of research as something that we do only in libraries, we do most of our research outside them. Whether it's going to the moon, exploring caves, finding out about our own city, or just studying our own family tree, we don't limit our search to books. We want to know. We may find diaries, letters, or personal papers that no one else has yet seen, or we may discover information too recent to be in print, or even in a computer database. We are limited only by our inability to see what is there for us to discover and to figure out how to find it.

You can collect information outside the library by

- Interviewing
- Surveying and polling using questionnaires
- Recording oral history
- Reading diaries, letters, and personal papers
- Examining court and other government records
- Visiting museums, special collections, and organizations
- Observing, exploring, and experimenting

Interviewing

The holdings of a library record the experiences and thoughts of people as they have been collected in the past. In interviews you discover people's current thoughts, ideas, and attitudes. You can interview authorities — those who, like college professors, have been purposeful collectors of information — or talk to people about their own beliefs and experiences.

Although there are several kinds of interviews — the employment interview, the doctor-patient interview, the counseling interview, the journalistic interview, and others — you will be conducting an informational or research interview.

Personal Interviews

Personal interviews are usually more productive than telephone interviews or personal letters. Everyone has special information of some kind, and most people enjoy sharing it with others. When you're thinking about people to interview, look first in your home or college community and then widen your net.

Finding People to Interview. First talk to people in your neighborhood or school. To locate instructors in your subject, consult the college directory, which will tell you the department they are affiliated with. If you want to know about running a business, talk to the small restaurant owner or store owner in your neighborhood, or talk to the executive of a large corporation. Are you writing a paper about the influence of foreign cars on the American market? Ask the local car dealer for his or her point of view. What does your grandfather remember about World War II?

Use the telephone to inquire in your community. The phone book contains names of organizations and people who can help you. Most communities have a chamber of commerce, an association of businesspeople and merchants that promotes the business interests of a community; chambers of commerce usually publish a membership directory, another useful information source. In the yellow pages, look up "Social Service Organizations" to find phone numbers for groups like the Mental Health Association and the American Heart Association; organizations of ethnic groups, such as the Spanish Community Association, the Polish American Congress, or the Chinese Culture Services Center; political lobbying and information groups, such as the Consumer Product Safety Commission, Common Cause, or National Organization for Women; nonpartisan political information groups, like the League of Women Voters; and educational groups, such as the American Association of University Professors or American Association of University Women.

For a partisan point of view, call the local office of your congressional representative or senator and, of course, your local Democratic or Republican party organizations (you can call or write the national headquarters too). For national organizations that might be located in your area, consult the *Encyclopedia of Associations* in the reference room of the library; this source organizes associations alphabetically and geographically and includes social service, educational, hobby, government, scientific, cultural, and many other kinds of groups, both national and international. Whatever your interest, there is likely to be an organization of like-minded people.

Your phone book also has a special section that provides city and county government numbers. See the listings in areas such as environmental management, citizens' information, alcohol and drug programs, community affairs, status of women committees, consumer affairs, and recreation. You might find people at your local newspaper office or radio station, public school system, or police department who would be glad to talk to you. If you are interested in business or management, don't forget that your college or university is also a business, with managers, public relations officials, and others who may be willing to talk to you.

The thought of picking up the phone and calling someone you don't know may be intimidating, but an interview can result in a valuable experience. Stuart Levin, for instance, called a local radio station, explained that he wanted to learn about career possibilities in broadcasting, and was invited to talk to one of the managers. After a helpful discussion, he was given a tour of the station and invited to sit in on his favorite disk jockey's program.

Making the Appointment.   When you reach the person you want to talk to, state your name, the purpose of your call, and the specific information you are seeking: "My name is Steve Gorbush, and I'm a student at Valley State. I'm writing a paper on the New York Stock Exchange, and I wonder if you would have time to answer a few of my questions about it." In arranging a time, be sure to mention the times you will not be able to meet because of classes or other obligations, and then ask the person to set a time convenient for him or her. Indicate how long you need to talk (a half hour is generally sufficient for such an interview) so that your interviewee knows how much time to allow. Be sure to find out the exact location of the interview and any directions that you may need for getting there: you want to arrive on time.

Preparing for the Interview.   A good interview requires good preparation. First, clearly define your purpose. What do you want to find out, and how do you want to use this information? Review your working outline to see what you need to find out from the person you interview. And do some reading on your subject first. You will better understand the information given to you if you can put it in a context, and you won't waste time asking questions that can easily be answered by a book or article.

Then write out a list of questions whose answers will serve your purpose. Concentrate on the kinds of questions that can best be answered in an interview, such as questions on current topics like computer security or U.S. policy in the Middle East if that's the person's area of expertise, or questions that can be answered from the interviewee's experience, such as the amount of capital needed to start a small business. Instead of writing down questions, you may want to jot down subjects to cover. This list will remind you of your goals for the interview in case your interviewee begins to stray from the subject. At the same time, though, be prepared to let the interview branch out into areas that you didn't foresee but that might supply valuable information.

Find out as much as you can about the person you are going to interview. If you are interested in the way a lawyer handles *pro bono* or public-service cases, try to find out what cases the person you will be interviewing has handled. At the very least, you should know the person's complete name and job title, place of employment, and area of specialization.

Decide how you will record the information you obtain. You might take notes during the interview, tape-record the interview, or simply listen and record your notes later. All three methods have advantages and disadvantages. Writing can distract the speaker and also keep you from concentrating fully on what is being said. Tape-recording can inhibit the speaker even more but is more accurate and complete than taking notes. Tape recorders, though, can fail and leave you with no record at all. If you decide to tape your interview, practice with your machine beforehand so that you can operate it unobtrusively. Also, out of courtesy, ask your interviewee in advance for permission to tape-record.

Although some professional interviewers have trained themselves to listen carefully and memorize what is said in short interviews, most rely on a pen or pencil and a pad of paper. Be sure you take along extra pens. Some interviewers write on note cards, but most professionals find that it is more efficient to transcribe notes onto note cards or a computer after the interview to clarify sketchy notes and weed out irrelevant information. The best procedure is to take notes in your search log and then transfer relevant information to your notes later.

Conducting the Interview.   Arrive a few minutes early so that you are calm and relaxed and have a chance to look at your surroundings — they may give you some ideas for questions. A geologist, for example, may have photographs or rock samples decorating his or her office that would be of interest to you. Questions about these provide an informal, relaxed way to begin the interview. You might also begin with some questions about the background of your interviewee to give both of you time to get used to each other. Assume an attitude that tells your interviewee that you are interested in what he or she has to say. You do not want to act apologetic for taking the interviewee's time, but neither do you want to act as though you are a trial attorney interrogating a witness. Make the interview as conversational as possible, and let your interviewee set the direction as long as he or she does not stray too far from your subject. During pauses, always use your questions as a prompt. If you take notes, take them as unobtrusively as possible, using abbreviations and other means of shorthand when you can. Record the exact words of the speaker when something is said that you would like to quote in your paper. Unless you use a tape recorder, as a courtesy verify direct quotations with your interviewee before you leave. At the end of the time you have both agreed on, thank the person you've been talking with and leave.

Following Up.   As soon as you can, review your notes and add what you didn't have time to write down during the interview. This is also the time to decipher the scribblings that won't be legible the next day. Immediately after the interview it will seem so fresh that you may believe that you won't forget what took place, but within a few days you will forget many details. Transfer relevant information to your note cards or computer as soon as possible. Oral historians and sociologists who conduct interviews generally use tape recorders, but they also take notes on significant information as soon as possible after the interview. In addition, they keep a field log or journal in which they record information not included on tape, such as the surroundings, dress and demeanor of the person interviewed, the feelings of the interviewer, and the like. If your purpose is to collect data from the interviewee, such details are irrelevant, but do record them if you think they might be useful.

It's also a good idea to make a bibliography note for your interview because an interview is considered a source and should, in some systems of citation, be recorded in your list of works cited at the end of your paper. In others, you may acknowledge the help at the end of the paper or in a footnote. Besides the interviewee's name, include his or her position or area of expertise, and the place and date of the interview. You might also want to include a few biographical details.

Finally, within a day or two, write a brief thank-you note to the person who has taken the time to help you.

Ed Kovalcik's Interview with His Professor.   The following account of a personal interview was taken from a student's search log.

> I was sitting at my desk after my computer science class waiting for Professor G. to finish talking to the students crowded around his desk. I had made an appointment at the last class meeting to talk to him after class tonight. I wanted to ask him about the future of computers. What changes did he see coming? Where was the use of computers going? I felt the tension making my body a little stiff, making my heart beat a little faster. Why hadn't I interviewed a friend or relative? Too late to back out now. Then the last student's question was answered, and Professor G. came over and sat down near me.
>
>   There was a strong feeling of uneasiness in the air. It was my first interview — maybe it was his, too. I started out with some questions about his academic background. He said he had gotten his bachelor's and master's

degrees in mathematics from the Polytechnic Institute of Brooklyn and his Ph.D. from New York University. After a few more questions about his education, the anxiety in my voice and body began to ease and my confidence rose. This isn't too bad after all, I thought.

Knowing that he taught at the university only part-time, I asked him about his full-time job. He explained that he was in charge of research and development at COMSAT (Communications Satellites) Laboratories. "Right now we're working on a communications scheme that allows corporations to send up their information on a time-sharing basis." He continued to explain this process using words like "transducers" and "multiplexers." He was going so fast that I stopped taking notes and waited for him to slow down. He went to the chalkboard and drew a diagram depicting a theory for centralizing radio waves and pointing out the savings that could result for business.

When he came back to his desk, I began to question him about the future of computers — the subject I was most interested in. "Well, I believe that we'll see even more growth in 'smart' or 'intelligent' networks, which do a lot of the thinking that has usually been done by minicomputers, PCs, and Macs. Big companies like AT&T and IBM are already developing such networks." He was beginning to talk my language. I asked him how he thought computers would be used in college classrooms, and he said he believed more and more college classes would be conducted online — outside the classroom. Students could attend class from their own homes or rooms on campus. He called it "computer conferencing" and "asynchronous education." He foresaw that the exchange of information among students online would lead to a greater degree of collaborative learning. As he talked, he used terms like "networking," "course management tools," and "distributed learning environment." His prediction was that students would produce a kind of writing he called "interactive written discourse"— a hybrid of written and oral discourse. In the class of the future — the "cyberclass" — there would be more input by students and less lecturing by professors. Of course, the professor would provide materials and oversee all of the activity. It sounded pretty exciting.

I began to run out of questions, and we were running out of time. "Well, I guess that's it. Thank you," I said. "I appreciate your taking the time out of your busy schedule to talk to me." "I enjoyed it," he answered, shaking hands with me.

As I walked back to my dorm, I felt a sense of exhilaration. I had conquered a new experience. I had gotten to know a person through a new medium for me, an interview.

After this interview, Ed Kovalcik added another name to his bibliography and added the information to his computer file. (Figure 5.1).

Telephone, Mail, and Electronic Interviews

Telephone and mail interviews are usually more structured than personal interviews because you cannot observe the person's reactions to your questions and adjust your line of questioning accordingly. Of

FIGURE 5.1   Bibliography Card and Note Card for an Interview

Bibliography card

Grant, Edward M. Personal interview
18 February 1996
Professor, computer science at State University.
In charge of research and development at COMSAT.

Note card

Grant interview   Future impact of
                                                      computers

"Smart" networks will do much of the brainwork now
done by personal computers, and more college classes
will use computer conferencing.

course, on the phone you can tell something from the tone of voice. For a telephone interview, you may not need an appointment. You might, for example, call a professor during her office hours and say, "I wonder if you would have a few minutes to give me your reaction to the Supreme Court ruling in the *Missouri v. Jackson* case on school desegregation. You mentioned it in class the other day when you were talking about immigration problems." If you need more than a quick answer to a single question or two, call and make an appointment, just as you would for a personal interview.

Mail interviews make it possible for you to interview someone in another state or country. They also allow interviewees to answer questions at their own convenience. Depending on the medium you use, however, they may take more time. If you and your interviewees have access to e-mail, you can send your questions and receive responses quickly. If you or your interviewees do not have access to e-mail, you should allow more time for mailing your questions and receiving responses. Before you send out a set of questions by mail, you should call or e-mail the person and ask whether he or she will respond. Then carefully draft your questions. You may want to send the same questions to several different people. Be sure you explain on the questionnaire or in a cover letter when you need the answers returned. And if you are using regular mail, enclose a stamped envelope with your address on it. Be prepared to telephone or write with a reminder if your answers are not returned by the deadline.

Surveying and Polling Using Questionnaires

Surveys and Polls

When you interview members of a group (your fellow students, train engineers, the residents of Smalltown, North Dakota, or whatever group you want to find out about) for a survey or poll, you are not usually trying to acquire knowledge about a subject, such as the best treatment for leukemia. You would ask experts for that kind of information. Instead, you want to know some of the characteristics, behavior patterns, or attitudes of the group to develop statistical data. For example, you might want to know how many cars they own, how they spend their leisure time, or whether they believe physical punishment should be allowed in schools. Because you need to ask the same questions of everyone, you must design a set of questions or a questionnaire.

Using a Questionnaire. Questionnaires may be self-administered (and distributed by mail, via computer, or in person), or they can be administered by an interviewer in person or by phone. Because data from polls and surveys are extremely difficult to analyze, novice pollsters must be cautious about drawing firm conclusions about a group unless everyone in the group is questioned. Figures are sometimes used to prove what pollsters want them to prove. However, experts can do an "inferential statistical test" to confirm that results of surveys are typical of the group as a whole. (*A Journalist's Guide to Public Opinion Polls* by Sheldon R. Gawisha and G. Evans Witt [Westport, Conn.: Praeger, 1994] provides details on how to design and conduct reliable public opinion polls.)

If you are not an expert, the best thing to do is plan and describe your methodology carefully so that the reader of your paper has a basis for judging your reliability. For example, suppose that you want to know how many students in your school exercise daily. You do not have time to question everyone, so you decide to take a sample. How many students should you ask? The larger the sample, the more reliable your data will be. Still, even a large sample may be faulty if you poll only students going in and out of the gym or only those studying in the library. You want a random sample to ensure that every part of the student population is represented. Obtaining a random sample requires that you identify the different groups of the student population according to sex, age, number of courses taken, or other significant characteristics and then sample each of these groups at random. Likewise, you must take your samples at various locations and at different times of the day. Try to think of other ways to make your survey more representative.

Designing a Questionnaire.   When you ask for people's opinions on something, you may feel that you are getting the *truth* — that you are finding out what is really going on in people's minds. But designing an effective questionnaire is not easy. If you have never designed a questionnaire before, you might benefit from some reading on questionnaire development or talking to an expert. But if you keep your questionnaire relatively simple and short, you should be able to compose a serviceable one. Before you begin, ask yourself the following questions.

1. *What do I hope to find out from the results of this questionnaire?* Create a brief list — no more than five items, if possible — of your goals for the questionnaire. Use the list to focus your questions. Suppose you are doing a survey of health clubs in your area. You might make the following list of what you want to find out: (1) the kind of bodybuilding equipment the clubs have, (2) the exercise facilities they own (swimming pools, tennis courts, and so on), (3) the type of relaxing equipment they have (saunas, steam rooms, and so forth), (4) the kind of instruction that is available and the qualifications of the instructors, and (5) the fees and bonded status of the clubs.

2. *What people will most likely give me the information I need?* The answers to the questions about health clubs can easily be given by the managers of these clubs; furthermore, much of the information can be verified by a tour of the premises. However, if you ask different questions — say about the quality of the services offered — the patrons would be able to supply that information better.

3. *What kinds of questions will give me the information I want?* You can use open-ended questions, two-way questions (those that require choosing one of two alternatives), multiple-choice questions, or questions requiring a specific answer.

Open-ended questions are easy to ask, but they are more difficult to answer as well as to interpret. "What do you think of the registration procedure at the university?" is likely to produce vague answers. The advantage, of course, is that open-ended questions may provide you with interesting answers you did not anticipate.

Two-way questions are more focused ("Do you prefer objective tests or essay tests?") and provide quantifiable answers, but they do not leave room for replies that might fall somewhere between the two questions. A person who is asked, "Do you believe abortion should be legal?" might want to respond, "Well, yes and no."

If you think your subject cannot be reduced to only one of two answers, use *multiple-choice questions*. They are easily quantifiable and do not take much time to answer. One kind allows variations of degree ("Abortion should be outlawed. Circle the answer you prefer: strongly agree, agree somewhat, neither agree nor disagree, disagree somewhat, strongly disagree"). You can have as many alternatives as you wish, although a selection of five is the most common.

You can also use multiple-choice questions when you want to find out the extent of the respondents' knowledge (this is the type of multiple-choice question often used in school tests). For instance, you might want to learn how much the students in your school know about foreign affairs or perhaps about U.S. history or geography. Such questions must be carefully thought out so that the answer you want to obtain does not seem obvious. To avoid this problem, provide three or more answers that seem like genuine answers; for example, "In what state did the Wright brothers make the first airplane flight? Ohio, North Carolina, or Alaska." Most respondents would eliminate Alaska immediately, thus leaving only two possible choices. "Ohio" might be a better choice than Alaska because the Wrights lived and worked there. The correct answer, of course, is North Carolina.

Specific questions are the hardest ones to respond to because they require a specific answer: "Who said, 'The only thing we have to fear is fear itself'?" or "How many feet are there in a mile?" If the question deals with behavior rather than knowledge, it might not be as difficult: "How many hours of sleep do you get each night, on the average?"

Be cautious in using questions about behavior that respondents might find threatening. Such *unreliable questions* often result in unreliable answers because people don't like to admit doing things that others might disapprove of. One way to improve reliability is to use open-ended rather than two-way or multiple-choice questions. The question "How often do you drink beer?" might in some contexts carry the threat of criticism. If given a range, then, the respondent is likely to choose the lowest figure or none at all; in this case it would be better to leave the question open-ended (that is, allow the respondent to name a figure) rather than offer a range. Such a question is also "loaded": it assumes that the behavior exists. Thus it is less threatening than the question "Do you drink beer?" which may sound like an accusation and which may tempt the respondent to answer no. So the question "How often do you drink beer?" asked without a given range, or open-ended, is likely to produce more accurate answers. Another way to improve the accuracy of potentially threatening questions is to ask the respondent about the behavior of others: "Does your roommate smoke? How many cigarettes a day?" Such questions might be a better way to find out about the behavior of members of a group than asking the members directly about themselves.

Although the loading of the question about beer drinking is in the interest of validity, some loaded questions originate in the bias of the questioner and thus are designed to produce biased answers. "Do you believe in supporting the defense of our country by funding the _____ bill?" suggests that a no answer would come only from some-one unconcerned with national defense or from an unpatriotic citizen. People who don't want to think of themselves as unpatriotic would probably answer yes.

You can see that the wording of questions is crucial to the validity of a questionnaire. In summary, if you are writing a questionnaire for the first time, it is a good idea to keep it short, word your questions so that you get the information you want, and check your questions for bias. When writing your paper, explain your procedures to your readers; that is, tell them how many people you questioned, what groups these people belonged to, and the purpose of your questioning as well as the results you obtained. Include a copy of your questionnaire in the body of your paper or in the appendix.

Michelle Morrissey's Telephone Survey.   Michelle Morrissey, a stu-dent volunteer in a program to teach English as a second language (ESL), wanted to find out why so many tutors who took the training course either did not tutor or dropped out soon after training. She planned to prepare the results for the Literacy Council of Northern Virginia (LCNV), which trained the tutors, so that it could improve its program. Before she formulated her questions, she read books on preparing questionnaires and consulted with the LCNV staff and with another LCNV volunteer who was a statistician to discover what infor-mation they wanted her to gather. Here is part of the introduction to Morrissey's paper.

> After deciding to do a survey, I had to decide what type of survey would best suit my purposes. There are three major types of survey: the direct interview survey, the mail survey, and the telephone survey. The direct interview sur-vey was eliminated because the tutors were too widely dispersed geographi-cally, and the mail survey was unsuitable for such a small survey (300 tutors). The telephone survey, on the other hand, was ideally suited to LCNV needs because it is quick and inexpensive and allows for great flexi-bility in scheduling interviews. I drafted a short preliminary survey and called tutors to ask screening questions and make an appointment for a later call. I then divided this group into three subgroups — active tutors, tu-tors who have taught but are not teaching now, and trainees who never tutored — and designed a questionnaire for each of these groups. This pro-

cedure was time-consuming, but it permitted me to proceed with confidence with the longer interviews because the interviewees knew they were going to be interviewed and had given me a preferred time to call.

Morrissey included in her paper a copy of the short screening questionnaire that she used to identify those she would interview later at length (see Figure 5.2). Figure 5.3 illustrates the questionnaire Morrissey designed for trainees who had never tutored.

After analyzing the results of her questionnaire, Morrissey recommended the following measures: more stringent screening of prospective tutors, setting up information sessions before trainees commit themselves, and establishing a tutoring center instead of tutoring in homes.

Using E-Mail and the Internet to Administer Questionnaires. Now that more people can be reached through e-mail and the Internet, you might consider using these electronic resources to gather information. E-mail and the Internet allow you to cast a wide net and reach people who have an interest in the topic you are researching.

FIGURE 5.2 Screening Questionnaire for a Telephone Survey

PRELIMINARY SURVEY SAMPLE FORM
Michelle Morrissey

Identifying information (already known):

Date and hour of call _____

Name _____   Sex _____

Address _____   Phone _____

Date of training session _____

Questions to ask:

Hello, my name is Michelle Morrissey. I am calling on behalf of the Literacy Council of Northern Virginia. We are doing a survey of ESL tutors, and I have a few questions to ask you.

Are you tutoring now?   Yes _____   No _____

If no: Have you tutored at all since you took your training?

Yes _____   No _____

These are the only questions I am going to ask you now, but I may be calling you again in a few weeks for more questions. When is the best time to reach you?

Weekday evening _____   Saturday daytime _____

Sunday afternoon _____   Anytime _____

Thank you very much. Good-bye.

FIGURE 5.3 Questionnaire for a Telephone Survey

QUESTIONNAIRE FOR GROUP III

Date of training session _____

Name _____ Phone _____

Hello, my name is Michelle Morrissey. I am calling on behalf of the Literacy Council. You may remember that I called you earlier. I have a few questions to ask you. Is this a convenient time? If not, when? _____

Are you a member of LCNV now? Yes _____ No _____

Are you employed outside your home? Yes _____ No _____ If yes, PT _____ FT _____

If yes, are you a teacher or otherwise working in education? Yes _____ No _____

If not employed, are you retired? _____ staying at home? _____ seeking
   employment? _____

Do you have any preschool children at home? Yes _____ No _____
   of school age? Yes _____ No _____

In which age group do you belong? under 35? _____ between 35 and 49? _____
   between 50 and 60? _____ over sixty? _____

Did you take the LCNV training with the intent of tutoring? Yes _____ No _____

If no, why did you take the training? _____

If yes, why did you change your mind? _____

Would you be interested in tutoring eventually? Yes _____ No _____

If yes, would you want to attend a refresher course first? Yes _____ No _____

If yes, would you be interested in tutoring at a center where a group of tutors work with
   many students, either one-to-one or in small groups? Yes _____ No _____

If yes, would you use baby-sitting facilities if offered at the center? Yes _____ No _____

If yes, would you prefer to work there in the morning? _____ in the afternoon? _____
   in the evening? _____

Can you suggest any ways to improve the training? _____

Even though you have not tutored, do you feel the training was useful to you in other
   ways? Yes _____ No _____

If yes, specify: _____

That's all. Thank you very much for your assistance.

For a course in popular culture, Lilah Rossi decided to research the audience of a popular television sitcom, "Friends." She wanted to learn, among other things, whether fans believe that any serious political themes underlie "Friends" and how they respond to the show emotionally. Because Rossi wanted to obtain a variety of perspectives for her research, she posted some of her questions about "Friends" to an

Internet fan club for the show. Through her preliminary questioning, she was able to identify nearly forty serious fans of the show who were willing to respond to a longer questionnaire. The responses to the longer questionnaire provided Rossi with some detailed and intriguing audience information. However, she had to take into account the fact that the majority of her respondents were relatively young and, by a large percentage, male.

Recording Oral History

Not all interviews with groups are structured as those just discussed. Studs Terkel in his book *Working* interviewed people to find out their attitudes toward their jobs. He explains in his book why his interviews were relatively long and unstructured:

> I realized quite early in this adventure that interviews conventionally conducted were meaningless. Conditioned clichés were sure to come. The question-and-answer technique may be of some value in determining favored detergents, tooth-paste, and deodorants, but not in the discovery of men and women.

Because Terkel's interviews were open-ended — without a time limit — he could use a tape recorder effectively. His respondents eventually became used to it and talked freely in its presence. Terkel's books — including *Division Street, Hard Times,* and *Working,* in which he records the edited results of many taped interviews — have been called oral histories. *Oral historiography* or *folklore research* are terms used to refer to the study of the past through the recollections of living people recorded on tape or in questionnaires. Oral historical research has developed rapidly in the past few decades and has its own methodology and theoretical framework. You might want to interview grandparents, aunts, or uncles using this method to learn about your family history. Or observe the groups around you: they are living sources of historical information.

Students have recorded on tape the activities and customs of many groups, including city bus drivers, tattoo artists, coal miners, palm readers, neighborhood children, railroad workers, store owners, and musicians of all kinds. Projects can also be designed to ask a particular group to talk about a specific topic, such as weddings, folk songs, folk remedies, crafts, recipes, poetry, holiday customs, or rituals (baptisms, marriages, or funerals). Perhaps you can find someone on the college faculty who has done work in oral history and is willing to talk to you about a project. Further sources of information are *Principles for Oral*

Narrative Research by Olrik Axel (Bloomington: Indiana University Press, 1992) and *Oral Traditions and the Verbal Arts: A Guide to Research* by Ruth H. Finnegan (New York: Routledge, 1992).

Reading Diaries, Letters, and Other Personal Papers

Many families have writings of various kinds hidden away in boxes in the basement or attic that could provide information about family history. Sometimes personal papers providing local historical information are given to public libraries or local historical societies. Such papers can be used to supplement tape-recorded interviews or used independently like other written sources. One student wrote a biography of her great-grandmother, who married a West Point graduate in 1899 and kept diaries and letters that described in detail her military wedding and her life as an army wife. She wrote of a tour of duty in Idaho when the mines were put under military control after a strike and of her husband's death while riding horseback with the king of Italy. By researching parallel historical events, the student was able to show how the life of her great-grandmother was part of the history of the United States.

Examining Government Records

State and County Records

It can be fascinating to trace the history of the place where you live. Is there a historic event in your area that you would like to explore — perhaps a flood or a battle? Would you like to find out the history of a town or of a piece of land? Is there a trial or a court case you would like to learn more about? Marit Beecroft was interested in the history of a large park: some of the park had been farmland, and other parts of it were preserved as former Indian camping grounds. She found records of land sales and old maps in the county courthouse and traced the history of the area.

Perhaps you would like to learn more about one of your ancestors. State and county records contain large numbers of documents, including census figures, wills, deeds, tax rolls, military rolls, election results, and records of births, deaths, and marriages. Such records can help provide political, social, and economic information about the past as well as about specific persons. (Except for a few records that are sealed, such as adoption records, all court records are open for public examination.) County courthouses store records for their own jurisdictions; a state may maintain a separate archives building for its records.

If you want to examine these records, just go to the office of the clerk of court in the courthouse. Provide the name of the documents you want to see (for example, "land titles" if you are researching a piece of land), and they will be brought to you. If you do not know the name of a document or if you are not sure what areas you want to explore, you can look in the indexes — usually found in the clerk of court's office — to see what information the court has available and for what dates. (Some public documents offices now provide computer terminals that allow you to search for documents electronically. Usually, instructions on how to use these systems are posted onscreen or near the terminals. Clerks also should be able to help you.) If you want photocopies to take with you, most courts will provide them, although they tend to cost more than those at your local photocopier.

Federal Records

The National Archives. Do you like adventure? Do you like to explore the unexplored and discover the unexpected? If so, searching in the Archives may be for you. Billions of pages of "permanently valuable" national records are stored in National Archives Building I in Washington, D.C., in National Archives II in College Park, Md., in thirteen regional Archives branches, and in the ten presidential libraries. These buildings contain documents — some bound, some loose in boxes — that record life in the United States over the past two centuries, and if you are over sixteen, you can look at them. Besides documents, the Archives contain photographs, maps and charts, films, and recordings. If your subject has anything to do with diplomatic relations, land or Indian policies, law, foreign or domestic trade, navigation, military history or affairs, immigration, agriculture, transportation, communications, and many other areas, consider the National Archives. Consultants will help you find the information you are looking for, and although they will not do specific research for you, Archives staff members will answer concise requests for information by e-mail (at **inquire@nara.gov**). You will find specific information about Archives holdings in the following publications; these may be ordered from the Government Printing Office, but check at your library first.

> *Guide to the National Archives of the United States.* Available for purchase from the Superintendent of Documents, U.S. Government Printing Office, Washington, D.C. 20402
>
> *Select List of Publications of the National Archives and Records Service.* Available free from the National Archives Trust Fund, Publications Distribution, Room G3, Seventh and Pennsylvania Avenue, N.W., Washington, D.C. 20408

Some archival information is available through the World Wide Web (http://www.nara.gov) and gopher (gopher.nara.gov).

If you are not able to visit the National Archives Building in Washington, D.C., or College Park, Md., you may be near one of the regional branches in Waltham and Pittsfield, Mass.; New York; Philadelphia; Chicago; East Point, Ga.; Kansas City; Fort Worth; Denver; Laguna Niguel and San Bruno, Calif.; Seattle; or Anchorage, Alaska.

Although holdings do vary, in general the regional branches contain many documents, including records from the district courts, U.S. courts of appeals, the Bureau of Indian Affairs, and the Bureau of Customs, and they provide researchers with reading rooms, microfilm reading equipment, and photocopying machines.

Of special value to college students is the collection of documents on microfilm stored in regional branches and available through interlibrary loan. These include some of the most significant government records in subjects such as history, economics, public administration, political science, law, and genealogy. To learn whether information you need has been recorded on microfilm, send for the *Catalog of National Archives Microfilm Publications* from the National Archives Trust Fund, P.O. Box 100793, Atlanta, Georgia 30384. (As of this writing, this publication costs $8, including a $3 shipping fee.) Your library may also have this catalog; look in your library catalog or ask your reference librarian.

In addition to these repositories, the government stores noncurrent records of government agencies in federal records centers (FRCs) in various locations around the country. The FRC in St. Louis, which specializes in personnel files, contains veterans' records dating as far back as the Spanish-American War. Admission to records in the St. Louis center is restricted to the person covered or to next of kin. To gain access to other federal records, you must have written permission from the agency whose files you wish to examine.

For a brochure on the National Archives, presidential libraries, and federal records storage — *Information About the National Archives for Researchers* — write to Publications Distribution (NECD), National Archives, Room G9, Seventh and Pennsylvania Avenue, N.W., Washington, D.C. 20408; or call 202–501–5235.

Recent Government Papers. Most government files dated before 1960 have been placed in the National Archives. But if the information you want is in government files dated after 1960, you must search in the current files of government agencies. Under the Freedom of Information Act (FOIA) of 1966, most government files are open to the public. To obtain information of this kind, you must write a letter to the Freedom of Information officer affiliated with the government agency that you think holds the files you need and ask for a specific document or information on the subject you are interested in. (If you send your request to the incorrect agency, your letter usually will be forwarded to the correct one.) The more precise you are in specifying the documents you want or their time period, the less time it will take to honor your request. Perhaps you are interested in what the government has done about the problem of acid rain; such papers are probably filed with the Environmental Protection Agency. Or you might be writing a paper on an author who was active in anti-Vietnam demonstrations, like Norman Mailer, and you want to know whether the Federal Bureau of Investigation has a file on him. Write to the FBI, and ask for such information under the FOIA. You will receive an acknowledgment within ten days; if you don't receive the documents, you will be told the status of your request. Use the same process to retrieve papers from any government agency. If the documents you require have a security classification, the agency must decide whether they can be declassified. If they can be declassified, they will be copied and sent to you. The fee for obtaining a document through an FOIA request varies depending on the type and length of the document. The length of time it takes for such a search also varies, so place your request early. You can find the addresses of government agencies in the *United States Government Manual,* which your library should own, or in a District of Columbia telephone book.

A great deal of government information is now available through the Internet and through electronic bulletin boards. A gateway to government information created by the Library of Congress is a good place to find connections to government information. (For more information, see p. 387 of Appendix 1.)

Rhonda Martin's Records Search. Rhonda Martin wanted to find out the background of a legendary figure in her family. Three theories existed: he came to America as a Hessian horse soldier during the American Revolution; he was a Virginian in the Virginia militia during the American Revolution; he arrived as a youth in Pennsylvania from Germany in the 1700s. Martin did her research at the Library of Congress, the National Archives, and the Pennsylvania Archives. At the Library of Congress, she read the rolls of Hessian horse soldiers and the passenger ship lists for 1750 to 1770. No one with the name of her ancestor was listed. From the census records in the National Archives, she discovered where a man by that name lived from 1790, when the first census was taken, until his death in 1823; all of the locations were in Pennsylvania. From the research files of the Daughters of the American Revolution, she learned that a man of the same name had fought in Virginia during the American Revolution but that he had never lived in Pennsylvania. She decided to start from the present and work back. In the Pennsylvania Archives (Harrisburg, Pa.), she located deeds (called indentures) showing that he owned land in Greene County and that he sold "seventeen acres and one hundred and thirty-two perch of land" to his son for $71.20 (a perch equals 30 $\frac{1}{4}$ square yards). In 1798 he paid $1,300 as his glass tax, the first American tax ever levied, based on the number of glass windows in his home. From these and other details, such as names of wife and children, living places, and land purchases, Martin was able to compose a brief biography. He had never lived in Virginia, and the names of his wife and children were different from the names of the wife and children of the Virginia militiaman. Thus she was able to trace the ancestry of those living now back to an indentured servant who had come to the United States when he was seventeen and died in 1823; she was able to prove that the last of the hypotheses was correct.

Museums, Special Collections, and Organizations

Your state or city may have museums, special libraries or organizations with collections of local or historical interest including photographs, maps, diaries, letters, and newspapers. Check your local telephone book. Also consult the *Encyclopedia of Associations* in the reference room of the library. This source organizes associations alphabetically and geographically and includes social service, educational, hobby, government, scientific, cultural, and many other kinds of groups, both national and international. It also lists any publications or library facilities available, along with the organization's areas of concern. For example, it lists the headquarters of the Daughters of the American Revolution (DAR) in Washington, D.C. The DAR Library keeps extensive genealogical records from all states along with a collection of genealogical publications. You can request the DAR's explanatory pamphlet by phoning or writing. George Forte used the *Encyclopedia of Associations* to locate an organization, the Native American Rights Fund (NARF), that issues a monthly newsletter, the *Indian Law Support Center Reporter,* and other publications useful in his research. (For a sample entry from the *Encyclopedia of Associations,* see p. 58.)

Observing, Exploring, and Experimenting

All of us observe, explore, experiment, and draw conclusions on the basis of our findings; these are daily activities. We observe and count the kinds of birds in our backyards; we explore a park or a neighborhood; we experiment with a new recipe. However, we usually do not keep records and put our conclusions into writing. Students in the social sciences, natural sciences, and psychology may want to do these kinds of research in a systematic way. The usual order is identifying the problem, planning a search strategy, collecting and measuring data, analyzing the results, and drawing conclusions.

In doing this kind of research, first formulate a question you want to answer. Can gold be found by panning in local streams? Which grocery chain has the lowest prices? How polluted are local rivers or the air we breathe? How much violence occurs in children's television programs? After deciding on a question, decide on a plan for collecting information to answer it. Then collect your data, analyze it, draw conclusions, and perhaps make recommendations. The result is a scientific paper. (You will find further information on writing a scientific paper in Chapter 12.)

Four Students' Original Research Projects

The following student research projects have used some of the strategies discussed in this chapter.

Sandra Sweitzer observed a prison art class given for the purpose of rehabilitation. Besides observing the members of the class, she interviewed the instructor, the sheriff, and some members of the class. She concluded that the art class had important therapeutic effects on the prisoners; its benefits as a tool for rehabilitation were more difficult to assess. Her paper, in modified form, was published in a local newspaper.

Doris Hill compared prices at three grocery chain stores. She selected ten staple grocery items and checked their prices at these stores periodically for four weeks. She also interviewed patrons at random. After computing her evidence, she discovered much lower average prices at one of the stores. She described the locations and sizes of the stores as well as the varied economic levels of the shoppers in her analysis of the reasons for the difference in prices.

Tom Davis set out to find the location of knapping rocks in his area. *Knapping* is the term used by geologists and anthropologists to refer to the breaking or shaping of rocks. Indians knapped rocks to make implements, but only certain glasslike rocks can be used in this way. Tom studied geological maps from the army map service and other geological evidence to determine possible locations of glassy stones, such as semiglassy quartzite, and then visited the areas to confirm his findings. Besides semiglassy quartzite, he found miscellaneous materials such as crushed stone, quartzite gravel, glassy quartz crystal and chert, and manmade glass. His paper containing his methodology and conclusions also included a geological map of the knapping rocks in his area.

Mark Olin wanted to know whether the five streams in his county were polluted. He collected water samples, grew cultures in petri dishes, and counted and identified the bacteria. After determining that the levels of the bacteria *E. coli* constituted dangerous pollution, he concluded that two of the streams qualified as polluted. Olin then studied maps to find out the source of the pollution. Besides writing his paper, he sent a letter to the county board summarizing his findings.

All four of these projects grew out of the personal interests of the students. They gathered their information carefully and thoroughly and then analyzed it to make it meaningful to them and their readers. If you want to consider publishing your paper, consult Robert A. Day's *How to Write and Publish a Scientific Paper* (Phoenix: Oryx Press, 4th ed. 1994).

EXERCISES

1. Using a tape recorder, interview the oldest member of your family about one of his or her most memorable experiences. Conduct the interview in a professional manner, as a sample of oral history interviewing. Write an account of the interview in your search log, and include the preparations you made, the questions you asked, the reactions of your subject to the interview, what you would do differently next time, and what worked well. Using this information, write a short report for your classmates and instructor on interviewing with a tape recorder.

2. Interview an expert in the profession you wish to enter when you graduate. Ask the person what skills are required for such a position and whether he or she has any suggestions about preparing for this profession. Write a short report on the results of your interview, and offer it to the career counseling office at your college.

3. **FOR PEER RESPONSE**   Choose a partner from your class, and interview each other. Follow the suggestions for interviewing given in this chapter. Your purpose for interviewing will be to find out everything you can about your partner's research project. Take a few minutes to make a list of questions to ask. Make the interview about ten minutes long. After the interview, write down what you have learned. If you have time, check the facts with your partner for accuracy.

4. **FOR THE COMPUTERIZED CLASSROOM**   Divide into groups of three. Design a short questionnaire — four or five questions — to discover the opinions of college students on a topic of current interest, and send your questions by e-mail to your group members. Ask them to suggest improvements based on the guidelines in this chapter and to send their suggestions back to you using e-mail. After revising your questionnaire with help from the suggestions, survey a sample of the student body. Finally, write a one- or two-page report giving the purpose of your survey, the results, and an analysis of the results. Share your results with the class.

PART II

Re-Searching and Writing

C H A P T E R   6

Re-Searching, Developing a Thesis Statement, and Outlining

Re-Searching: Reviewing Your Information

You collect your information in bits and pieces according to what may be available first or what may turn up first. During this stage, you don't know what shape your paper will take. Then when you have collected all of your material, you can re-search it; that is, review it and shape it, much as a sculptor creates a form out of marble or wood. Although the information you collect may come from someone else, the meaning you make from it is your own.

The Researcher's Questions

The first steps in re-searching are to read over your notes and to ask yourself the following questions:

1. What was my purpose in doing this search?
2. Did I realize my goal or did it change?
3. If my goal changed, what is my purpose now?
4. What did I learn from my search?
5. What conclusions can I draw from this knowledge?

Answering these questions will help you to shape and give meaning to all of the material you have collected. In answering questions 1, 2, and 3, you reassess your purpose and relate it to the answer to question 4, what you have learned. The answer to question 4 is a summary of the information you have collected. In answering question 5 you make a generalization or an inference based on the information you have collected; that is, the evidence leads you to an opinion, a judgment, or an evaluation. Making such generalizations is part of everyday life, so you are familiar with the process. For instance, you decide which is the best car for you to buy after looking at several cars, examining their features, checking the prices, and driving them. Or you study the schedule of courses, look up the requirements, weigh your needs and desires, and determine which courses will best suit your needs.

Florence McMullen, a student in an anthropology class, selected as her topic "Teaching anthropology to elementary school students." She answered the re-searching questions in the following way.

1. My purpose was to observe a group of sixth graders enrolled in a class in cultural anthropology and study the educational procedures.
2. I changed my goal and my topic.
3. Instead of concentrating on educational procedures, I decided to study the cultural values of the students in the class.
4. I learned that these students value the following qualities:

   a. Intellectual achievement
   b. Social equality, especially between males and females. However, some traditional behavior patterns still exist (boys and girls tend to sit in separate groups; girls primp and comb their hair in class; boys are noisier and more active).
   c. Contributions of technology to personal comfort (TVs and VCRs, hair dryers, microwave ovens, etc.)
   d. Peace or lack of conflict between individuals and groups

5. I concluded that the cultural values of children have changed in significant ways since I was a child.

Writing a Summary Sentence or Thesis Statement

After you have reviewed your information, you should find it easy to write a sentence or two — sometimes called a thesis statement or argument — that summarizes your paper or states what your paper "proves." If your thesis is still tentative or unproved, you will be working with a hypothesis. In some cases — especially in scientific papers — the hypothesis takes the place of a thesis until more evidence becomes available. Composing such a sentence helps you to find meaning in the information you have collected. Although your summary sentence may change as you write your paper, this statement provides an organizing force for you at the beginning: all parts of your paper must uphold or validate this statement. If you find, as you write, that your material is inconsistent with this statement or irrelevant to it, you can either change your statement to include the new information or discard the new material, leaving your original statement intact.

McMullen's summary statement included her answers to the last two questions. It was both a summary of the information she had found and a conclusion that she had drawn from this information: "In the last twenty years, the changing cultural values of children are shown in the following observed characteristics: respect for learning and intellectual achievement, new perceptions of male/female roles, acceptance of material goods as contributing to the quality of life, and a longing for worldwide peace." Notice that she had discarded as a topic the educational procedures used in this class. Consequently, she would not use any notes she had on this subject.

When you begin to write your paper, the answers to the five questions on page 139 form the framework for your paper. The statement of your purpose and your summary statement are the basis for your introduction; the development of your summary statement forms the body of your paper; and the generalizations you make about your material shape your conclusion. With a good idea of what the beginning, middle, and end of your paper will be, you can write confidently and expeditiously.

Although you are not ready to write yet (you still have to order the details that go into the body of your paper), you may be interested in seeing how McMullen used the answers to these questions in her introduction and conclusion. Here is her introduction.

> I observed a group of sixth graders in a suburban public school. Although I intended at first to record and study the educational procedures used, I became interested in the way the children approached their study topic, cultural anthropology. I realized that they were applying their own cultural values in their study of the cultures of past civilizations. Intrigued by their ethnocentric reactions, I decided to study them in the same way they were studying others. By watching them, I was able to define the cultural values of their (our) society and observe how these values seem to have changed since I was in school.

The following excerpt from McMullen's paper shows how the answer to the last questions formed her conclusion.

> From observing these sixth graders, I conclude that children's cultural values have changed since I was the age of these students. For one thing, they seem to value intellectual pursuits more; they were pleased to be in this special class with an advanced curriculum. When I was in elementary school, children tried to hide any intellectual achievements for fear of teasing or other negative reactions from their peers.

The thesis sentence may appear at the beginning of your paper, in the middle, or at the end. Sometimes it is merely implied. Florence McMullen defines her purpose at the beginning ("to define the cultural values" of the children she observed). Her thesis statement comes at the end ("children's cultural values have changed"). Here are thesis statements from other students' papers:

> Firefighting must be made safer.
> The polygraph can detect lying in most cases.
> The plate tectonics theory explains how earthquakes occur.

Critical Thinking

You were thinking critically as you chose and evaluated your sources, as you took relevant and adequate notes, and as you formulated a summary sentence or thesis statement. That is, you were if you wanted to reach your goal and write a good paper.

Critical thinking includes the following activities.

1. Reviewing your information as a skeptic
2. Questioning your own assumptions as well as the assumptions of those whose information you are relying on
3. Examining and identifying your own biases
4. Analyzing your information carefully and assessing its validity
5. Making sure that your conclusions clearly follow from your information

The case studies that follow illustrate how two different students incorporated critical thinking into their re-search. Your own process will, of course, be different, depending on your topic and the purpose of your paper.

Two Students' Use of Critical Thinking

Janet Fiore began her search by trying to find out how the increased number of women in the workplace has affected the structure of the family. She found that as more women began to work, there were more divorces and more single-parent families. She first concluded that the increase in the proportion of women working outside the home had led to the breakup of the traditional family. But as she looked more closely at her information and examined her assumptions more carefully, she realized that she did not know which factor was cause and which was effect. She had assumed that the entrance of more women into the workplace had led to divorce and single-parent families, but she realized that this assumption reflected a bias. It was true that more women had entered the work force; and it was true that divorce had increased. But there was no evidence that women's working caused divorce. In fact, divorce may have caused women to go to work.

After more study, she decided that probably neither of these cause-and-effect relationships was valid; certainly there was no evidence to point conclusively to either. Instead she decided that a number of cultural factors led to the changes in family composition and family life. She changed the focus of her paper to identify these factors.

When Jason Huang decided to buy a new car, safety was at the top of his list of considerations. He looked first in Consumer Guide's *Automobile Book* (1995) and found helpful data there as well as references to booklets issued by the Insurance Institute for Highway Safety and the Highway Loss Data Institute. He considered all of this information to find out what kind of car would be best and safest for him.

These sources ranked vehicle size at the top of the list — the bigger the car, the better. But he wanted a midsize car, so he would have to ignore that consideration. He decided to check the main safety features to find out what their advantages and disadvantages are and to find out what their specifications should be. He looked at lap and shoulder belts, air bags, side impact protection, head restraints, infant and child seats, and vehicle structure.

- *Lap and shoulder belts* (seatbelt systems). Most cars have a motorized shoulder belt that slides across the body when the car is turned on. The lap belt has to be fastened manually and should fit snugly across the pelvis (not over the abdomen). Some cars still have a nonmotorized belt. The passenger must open the door and step in behind the belt and sit into the seat. It fits across the passenger when the door is closed.

    Advantages: Seatbelts keep the passenger from being thrown against hard surfaces; they are the best protection against death or injury in case of a crash.

    Disadvantages: Many are uncomfortable, and often people don't fasten them. The moving (motorized) belt can get entangled in arms, eyeglasses, and clothing.

- *Air bags.* Air bags inflate in less than one-tenth of a second after a frontal crash. They deflate immediately.

    Advantages: They prevent head and chest injuries and are proven life savers.

    Disadvantages: They can cause injuries if the driver is too close to the steering wheel or if the passenger is not buckled up. Occasionally they inflate when they shouldn't. They can injure a child sitting in the passenger seat.

- *Side impact protection.* All cars now have side guard beams.

    Advantages: These protect occupants when cars crash into trees or poles.

    Disadvantages: They do not protect against side vehicle crashes. Better door padding and side air bags are recommended.

- *Head restraints.* These upward extensions of the front seats are required on all cars.

    Advantages: They keep the head from snapping back during a rear-end crash.

    Disadvantages: Head restraints are not always adjustable to the right height or angle, or they are difficult to adjust.

- *Infant and child seats.* Requirements for children's safety differ from those for adults. Children who are too small for adult safety belts should be fastened into specially built safety seats with straps for each shoulder and another strap between the legs or should be provided with booster cushions so regular safety belts can be used. Infants should be placed in the back seat in a child safety seat facing the rear. Some cars have child safety seats built into the back of the front seat.

    Disadvantage: A deploying air bag on the passenger side can injure a child. Some cars can have cut-off switches installed for air bags to avoid this problem.

After considering all of these safety devices, Huang decided he was well informed about what to look for in his new car. The most important thing was to try out each car to see if the lap and seat belts and the head restraints fit him. He would have to find out whether the motorized or simple manual lap and shoulder belts work best for him. Most cars now have dual air bags, so that would no longer be a choice. And it would be a few years before he would have to consider the problem of child restraints.

Analyzing Arguments

Creative and critical thinking can help you to design and write your paper. In addition, thinking of your research project as the construction of a kind of argument can make it more compelling for you — and your readers. Although the term *argue* is often used to describe what people do when they verbally disagree, rhetorical argument covers a much broader area. In fact, the word *argument* is derived from the Latin word *argumentum* meaning "evidence" or "proof." As Jeanne Fahnestock and Marie Secor point out in *A Rhetoric of Argument* (1990), "all modes of discourse can be subsumed under argumentation." Every well-written essay, research paper, editorial, or book makes an argument; that is, it has a *thesis* (also called a *proposition, controlling idea,* or *claim*) for which evidence or proof is given within the document.

The following section is intended to give you a general understanding of how arguments are constructed and analyzed so you can test the reasoning in your paper and the sources you use. It begins with a description of the two major forms of reasoning: *inductive reasoning* and *deductive reasoning.*

Inductive Reasoning

In this form of reasoning — typically used by scientists and other researchers — one considers particular pieces of evidence and draws general conclusions based on them. For instance, in surveying a representative sample of voters in your township, you might find that 75 percent of those sampled favor passage of a local school levy; thus, you might conclude through inductive reasoning that the levy is likely to pass.

In papers that demonstrate inductive reasoning, writers usually explore a subject or topic they are interested in or state a problem (for example, the causes of and cures for rheumatoid arthritis) without taking a stand. Or they may have a hypothesis or tentative thesis such as, "Agoraphobia, a condition characterized by fear of going outside of the home, can be successfully treated." If the hypothesis is supported, it becomes the thesis. If it is not, the writer states a new thesis based on the evidence.

James Watson and Francis Crick used inductive reasoning in a famous scientific paper presenting the structure for the DNA molecule. In this paper, called a research report, they had to give enough details to be convincing, yet their style was far from what some might call argumentative or contentious. In fact, they opened their report in the journal *Nature* with this modest statement: "We wish to suggest [not *announce* or *assert*] a structure for the salt of deoxyribose nucleic acid (D.N.A.)." They then provided the evidence that proved the truth of their statement. The structure was the double helix. The argument was arrived at through scientific observation, critical thinking, and induction (Crick describes their research process in *What Mad Pursuit* [1988]).

To be convincing, those using inductive reasoning must have collected enough information by themselves (original research) or from believable sources. An argument made by inductive reasoning is not incontrovertibly true; its validity may be challenged. New information might appear that would contradict or invalidate the argument.

Deductive Reasoning

In contrast to inductive reasoning, which moves from particular facts to general statements about those facts, deductive reasoning moves from the general to particular: a writer begins with a conclusion based on induction and then applies it to other situations to draw a further conclusion. Deductive reasoning argues from premises: the *major premise,* which states the conclusion based on induction, the *minor premise,* which makes a statement about a new situation, and the *conclusion,* which connects the assertion in the major premise to the new situation. If the premises are true, the conclusion is necessarily true. Here's an example:

Major premise: All copperhead snakes are poisonous.
Minor premise: The snake that bit Jane was a copperhead.
Conclusion: Jane was bitten by a poisonous snake.

Let's examine the premises. There is scientific evidence that copperhead snakes are poisonous. If the snake that bit Jane has been correctly identified as a copperhead, then the conclusion is true. This structure is called a *syllogism.*

Research papers often demonstrate inductive reasoning or a combination of inductive and deductive reasoning because the writers set out to gather information on a subject they have previously known little about, or they have an idea (a hypothesis) that they wish to test. In this case, the desire to search for new and reliable knowledge is paramount. On the other hand, writers who use deductive reasoning start out with a strongly held belief and usually try to find information that will confirm their view. Such writers have to be careful not to overlook evidence that might contradict their thesis. Of course, their argument will be subject to the scrutiny of their readers. In an article in *College English* (January 1991), Muriel Harris argues that writing centers are a necessary part of a composition program. A syllogism based on her argument can be stated this way.

Major premise: A composition course provided by the English department does not give students adequate instruction in writing.
Minor premise: Writing centers offer benefits not available in the composition classroom, including personalized instruction and the encouragement of independent thinking.
Conclusion: Writing centers are an essential part of college writing instruction and not "unnecessary frills."

For the conclusion to be true, the author has to provide evidence that the major and minor premises are true.

Fallacies

You can use syllogisms like those just described to check the logic in your paper if you have used deductive reasoning. But you must make sure both that the premises are accurate and that the conclusion follows logically. Errors in reasoning are called *fallacies.* Consider this syllogism:

Major premise: Everyone born in the United States is an American citizen.

Minor premise: The person sitting next to me on the plane was born in the United States.

Conclusion: The person sitting next to me on the plane was a U.S. citizen.

The major premise in this syllogism illustrates one of the errors that can lead to faulty reasoning — *ambiguity.* The major premise is ambiguous; it can be construed in more than one way. Although everyone born in the United States is a U.S. citizen at birth, not everyone retains his or her citizenship. Some other fallacies are described below.

Begging the Question. Writers who make this error in reasoning support a conclusion merely by restating it in some other way; they don't introduce new evidence necessary to prove the conclusion. For example:

> The oversight committee should request further hearings in this case because the committee always requests further hearings.

Ignoring Alternatives. Writers who make this type of error suggest that there are only two options when others exist.

> Unless you spend one year in Italy, you will never be a fluent speaker of Italian.

Although spending a year in Italy may lead to proficiency in Italian, there are other ways to become fluent in the language.

Faulty Cause-and-Effect Reasoning (also known as the "post hoc ergo propter hoc" fallacy). Writers who make this logical error assume that because one event followed another the first event caused the second.

> In the year after Jones became director of DataCo, production rose by more than 20 percent. Jones should be commended for increasing production.

That production increased after Jones became director does not necessarily mean that her leadership led to the increased production. If the conclusion in the second sentence is to hold up, the writer needs to offer specific evidence for it.

Hasty Generalizations. When writers make hasty generalizations, they leap to conclusions without providing adequate or representative evidence.

> The trout population in the Hano River has remained steady since 1973. Therefore, Hano County does not need to strengthen its pollution regulations.

The fact that the trout population has not changed does not necessarily mean that Hano County has no other pollution problems that should be addressed by tighter regulations.

Non Sequiturs.   With this type of fallacy, there is no logical connection between the premise or premises and the conclusion; that is, the conclusion does not follow from the premise.

> In college, David had a C average in math; therefore, he will never be a good teacher of any subject.

David's average performance in college math does not necessarily predict how well he will be able to teach any subject.

The Toulmin Model for Analyzing Arguments

The syllogism is a classical device for testing arguments that dates back to the ancient Greeks. More recently, Stephen Toulmin has devised a system that he believes reflects more accurately the actual characteristics of argument (*An Introduction to Reasoning,* 1984). Using this system, with its contemporary vocabulary, you can judge with reasonable accuracy the validity of your conclusions and those of writers whom you use as your authorities. Although the discussion and illustrations given here apply primarily to the main idea or thesis, you can use this system to analyze any other generalization you make, including your concluding summary sentence or sentences or any argument made within your paper.

Claim.   Your first step is to state your *claim.* The claim could also be called your conclusion, argument, proposition, thesis, or recommendation.

> The Pueblo Indians developed an advanced system of astronomical observation.
> Nightmares can be an indication of a serious psychological disorder.

Grounds.   The *grounds* provide the support or evidence for the claim. They may consist of data or the testimony of experts. If the claim is made that radiation can arrest the development of cancer, statistics would be used as grounds.

Warrant.   The *warrant* or *warrants* are assumptions or general beliefs that you and your reader share. They confirm the validity of the grounds and may be stated or unstated. For example, the claim might be made that cholesterol can be reduced by lowering the consumption of certain types of fat. The grounds or supports would include data such as the results of tests conducted at the National Institutes of Health (NIH). The warrants or unstated assumptions of these grounds would be that high cholesterol is harmful and that NIH testing is a reliable source of such data. The writer using these unstated warrants believes that his or her readers would make the same assumptions.

To make assumptions about the reliability of your grounds, you have to be aware of who your readers will be. Besides assuming that the audience will share his or her belief in the reliability of NIH, the writer about cholesterol has to make an assumption that his or her readers have some knowledge of the work done at NIH. Warrants applicable to one reader or group of readers may not persuade others. In addition, the necessary warrants can vary from one discipline or writing situation to another. Articles for popular magazines customarily offer less supporting evidence than, say, articles in a scientific journal. (For more information about considering your audience, see pp. 165–67.)

Backing.   In some cases an additional component of the argument may be required to reinforce the warrant; Toulmin calls this *backing*. You might, for example, give as warrant a source whose reputation for accuracy or reliability is not widely known or accepted. You would then have to give evidence of the source's reliability by citing his or her past connection with a respected institution. If you are providing the results of your own or others' original research as warrants for claims, readers would probably want to know the methodology of the research.

Modal Qualifier.   Toulmin recognized that few arguments are absolutely and unequivocally true. A *modal qualifier* acknowledges the variation in the strength of arguments. If a statement is not true for everyone at all times, you may want to limit it by a qualifier such as *most, usually,* or *probably.* Polls often qualify their statistics or predictions with a statement such as "Accuracy may vary by plus or minus three points."

Rebuttal.   Toulmin's allowance for *rebuttal* recognizes that an argument may have a weakness or questionable aspect. By examining your own argument closely, you may find yourself making a rebuttal or anticipating the rebuttals of your readers. If you were advocating that employers provide child care for their employees' children, some readers might ask, "But shouldn't employees who choose to have children be responsible for their care?" Then you should consider dealing with that question in your paper.

A Sample Analysis of an Argument.   According to Toulmin's system, Jason Huang's conclusion to his paper on automobile safety devices could be analyzed this way:

1. *Claim:* The use of seatbelt systems and air bags in cars provide the most effective and least expensive protection against automobile fatalities.
2. *Grounds:* Tests show that these devices, when properly designed, will save more lives than any other devices.
3. *Warrant: Consumer Guide* (1995) has examined recent models of shoulder and lap belts and air bags and reports that improved designs will raise the usage rate and result in lower mortality rates.
4. *Backing:* Federal crash tests using belted dummies have proved that these devices can save lives.
5. *Modal qualifier:* Although many people still find ways to avoid wearing seatbelts, their use has saved the lives of many who have used them.
6. *Rebuttal:* People should be allowed to choose whether or not to use safety devices, especially air bags. Air bags often inflate at the wrong time; they can injure children; and they have to be replaced after they inflate. Careful driving is the best safety device.

If you carefully analyze your argument this way, you will be able to recognize any flaws before you present it to your readers.

Examining the Validity of the Arguments in Two Sample Papers

Examining the arguments of two of the four sample papers in Chapters 10, 11, and 12 can help you learn how to check the argument in your own paper. One of the four, "Science and Museums Versus Human Dignity" by George Forte, is probably the most easily examined by using deductive reasoning — by reasoning from premises. This syllogism can be constructed:

Major premise: The remains of all human beings should be treated with dignity.
Minor premise: Native Americans are human.
Conclusion: The remains of American Indians should be treated with dignity.

However, there is an inductive element in the paper also. Using inductive reasoning, evidence is observed and a thesis (generalization, conclusion, controlling statement, or claim) is derived. Reasoning from the evidence would have these results:

Observed evidence: Many instances of disturbed and looted Native American graves and of using remains in research without permission have been verified.
Thesis: The remains of Native Americans have not been treated with dignity.

The inductive logic of the paper titled "Gambling: A National Addiction" can be analyzed this way:

> *Evidence:* Statistics show increasing numbers of people gambling. Studies by psychologists analyze and assert the pathological elements of the practice.
>
> *Thesis:* Gambling is a rapidly growing addiction in the United States.

In both of these papers the credibility of the evidence has to be carefully examined. The credentials of the writers as well as of the journals in which their articles were published must be checked; the conclusions they reached from their research need to be validated. These papers, along with the other two, could also be analyzed using the Toulmin method.

Checking Your Thesis

You can check the logic of your own thesis by using one of the methods described above. Of course, your thesis is not final until you finish your paper; you may want to refocus or revise it as you write. You may also find that you need to return to the library for more information or for clarification of information you already have.

Creative Thinking

Although the term *creative writing* is often applied only to fiction and poetry, the writing of creative thinkers can be found in every subject area — from architecture to literary criticism — and in all formats — from professional articles to novels and poems. Creative thinkers write political documents, such as the Declaration of Independence or the American Constitution. Others record their personal observations and thoughts, as Maya Angelou did in *Wouldn't Take Nothing for My Journey Now* (1993), or they write fiction. Scientists often write creatively in areas other than lab reports and scientific articles: Stephen W. Hawking, a theoretical physicist, wrote *A Brief History of Time* (1988) to explain the origin and structure of the universe. Musicians, who usually express their creativity in performing or writing music, also write *about* music: John Cage, innovative composer and musicologist, predicted the development of electronic music in "The Future of Music: Credo" (1958. Rpt. in *Silence*, 1961).

These are well-known creative writers and thinkers. But all of us have creative minds, and we can all be creative thinkers and writers. In fact, at times we all are. Creative thinkers go beyond fulfilling the bare requirements of academic or professional life because they have their own goals. They tend to question what is accepted as true; they like to find solutions to unsolved problems. Thinking creatively often means taking information already known and combining it in a new way or seeing implications that others have overlooked.

David Kuijt's Creative Thinking and Writing

One student, David Kuijt, whose hobby was collecting playing cards, began his research project by studying the history of playing cards. His search took him back to the fourteenth century, to the period just before Gutenberg developed the printing press with movable type. As he read his sources (it was helpful that he could read German), he found some unexpected information: the passion for card playing among guild members — the working people — all over Europe and the problem of supplying cards to players virtually forced the invention of a printing press. The first press used wood blocks.

From that point the movable-type press — Gutenberg's press — was an obvious step. Kuijt argued that that step would not have been taken, at least not as soon, if card playing had not been so popular and if the attempts of rulers to ban card playing had been successful. Previous researchers on the history of playing cards had not examined the history of printing, and researchers on the history of printing had rarely looked at the development of playing cards. Kuijt found it ironic that, if his theory is correct, our technological society owes a considerable debt to the passion of workers for card playing. Kuijt plans to submit his research paper as an article to a magazine on playing cards.

Making an Outline

With your thesis statement as a guide and with a clear idea of the general shape of your paper, you can now turn your attention to the body of the paper. The information you have gathered must be organized logically so that it makes sense to both you and your readers.

You have been using a list of topics and subtopics to guide your search. Now that you have all of your information, you can expand this list if you want to. You can even convert it into a formal outline — that is, an outline with a prescribed logical and syntactical form (explained later in this section). Some people prefer to write using a simple list of topics and subtopics, but others find that designing a formal outline provides further clarification. Whether you use an expanded list or a formal outline, be prepared to alter it as you write your first draft. Your list or outline is your attempt to impose form on the chaos of material that continually exerts its own power. From this tension between form and raw material, your paper takes shape.

Creating a Formal Outline

A formal outline delineates the parts into which your paper is divided as well as the relationship between those parts. It guides you during the writing process, and later, placed at the beginning of your paper or used as the basis for a table of contents, it guides the reader.

If you have been using a computer to record your notes, you'll find it to be especially helpful at this stage. With a program that allows you to view more than one file at once, you can scan your notes from one file, and create your outline in another. Some programs will number and letter your outline headings automatically. But even an unsophisticated program makes it easier to rearrange your headings and subheadings.

At this point you have cards or computer files labeled according to your working outline. Organizing them is the next task. Your computer notes will already be sorted and placed into files with names corresponding to your outline. If you're using cards, sort them into groups that correspond to the outline headings, and read over the notes on the cards. You may find some information that doesn't seem to belong under the existing headings. Jot down or record a brief description (heading) for each of these pieces of information so that it fits into your outline, or discard information that does not belong in your paper (you can expect to have accumulated superfluous material). On the computer you can store such notes in a separate file instead of deleting them so that they are available if you need them later. Now add any new headings to your outline.

In a paper on soil erosion, the following headings and subheadings were part of Joseph Masters's working outline:

Strategies for erosion control
    Agronomic strategies
    Mechanical strategies

As he went through his notes, Masters found information on soil management that did not seem to fit in his outline. After deciding that it belonged under "Strategies for erosion control," he labeled it and added it to his outline:

Strategies for erosion control
    Agronomic strategies
    Mechanical strategies
    Soil management

Your next step is to order the information under each heading in your working outline; as you do this, you may want to change headings and create more subheadings. To make the process easier, read each file or group of cards carefully, and, on a sheet of paper or on the computer, list the specific subject of each note. Then fit these headings into your working outline, changing the wording where necessary and adding subheadings where they fit.

Mavis Olson used a simple working outline as she gathered information for her paper on physical fitness programs in the workplace:

History
Benefits of fitness programs
    Employee benefits
    Employer benefits
Facilities needed
    Space
    Equipment
Setting up a program

After gathering information, she constructed the following summary sentence or thesis and formal outline with additional subheadings.

Summary sentence or thesis: Companies should consider developing physical fitness programs for their employees.

    I. Introduction: History of industry-provided recreation
   II. Objectives of employee fitness programs
       A. To benefit employees
          1. By improving mental and physical health
          2. By reducing boredom, absenteeism, and fatigue
          3. By promoting efficiency
       B. To benefit management
          1. By providing recruitment appeal
          2. By improving employee-employer relations
          3. By lowering organizational health costs
  III. Design of facility
       A. Fitness center design
          1. Architectural layout
          2. Order of construction
          3. Estimated costs
       B. Equipment
          1. Types of exercise equipment
          2. Estimated costs
  IV. Conclusion: The future of fitness programs in the workplace

The Logic of an Outline

An outline organizes the material in your paper into logical divisions. As you sort your cards or rearrange your computer notes, notice how the material helps you to create an outline at the same time that the outline helps you to shape your material. It is a back-and-forth operation. The logic demanded by the structure of the outline helps you to organize your material and provides a way to ensure that you haven't omitted anything important. It also shows you whether your paper will confirm your thesis or argument. If your argument seems weak, you may need to do a little more reading before you begin to write. In outlining the objectives of employee fitness programs, Mavis Olson found that her notes dealt almost completely with employee benefits; she had noted only that management used recreation programs as a recruitment lure. When she constructed her outline containing this information, she saw how unbalanced it was.

II. Objectives of employee fitness programs
    A. To benefit employees
        1. By improving mental and physical health
        2. By reducing boredom, absenteeism, and fatigue
        3. By promoting employee efficiency
    B. To benefit management: by providing recruitment appeal

She had included only one benefit for management. It seemed logical to Olson that management would have to find more benefits to fund such programs. After doing more reading, she found two additional benefits: improving employee-employer relations and lowering organizational health costs. Her thesis now read: Fitness programs benefit both employees and management.

In making an outline, you ensure that you have enough information, you design an orderly presentation for your paper, and you clarify and strengthen your argument. It is this logical structure that makes it easier for your reader to understand what you are trying to convey. Implied in the outline structure are these propositions:

1. *All topics at the same level are of equal, or nearly equal, importance.* All headings numbered with roman numerals, for example, constitute the major divisions of the paper and deserve equal emphasis. Joseph Masters's original outline on soil erosion had these divisions:

    I. Water erosion
       [subheadings]
   II. Wind erosion
       [subheadings]
  III. Strategies for erosion control
      A. Agronomic strategies
         [subheadings]
      B. Mechanical strategies
         [subheadings]
      C. Soil management

As he looked at his notes and outline, he realized that his paper really had two main parts: kinds of erosion (water and wind) and ways of controlling them. To reflect this, he changed his outline by converting two former main headings to subheadings and adding a new main heading to balance "Strategies for erosion control." His outline then looked like this:

    I. Types of erosion
       A. Water erosion
       B. Wind erosion
   II. Strategies for erosion control
       A. Agronomic strategies
       B. Mechanical strategies
       C. Soil management

2. *Each topic, if divided, is split into at least two parts that, at each level, add up to the whole.* Thus, Mavis Olson's outline shows, under "II," two objectives of employee fitness programs. We can assume that her paper will not contain any other objectives and that no other information will appear under this heading. *Note that it is not logical to divide something into one subpart.* If you have only one subtopic under a single heading, no divisions exist, and you should combine the topic and subtopic. Olson's outline first began this way:

    I. Introduction
       A. History and philosophy of industry-provided recreation

She realized that if "A" were the only subdivision, it must be the main heading, so she combined the two.

    I. Introduction: History of industry-provided recreation

Avoid using the labels "Introduction" and "Conclusions" — which mean only "beginning" and "end" — without indicating what they will include. If you use these terms, combine them with a phrase indicating their content, as Olson did. An exception is the scientific paper or report of original research. In such a paper, the opening paragraphs are often labeled "Introduction."

3. *To reflect the relationship among categories in the outline, headings at the same level should have the same grammatical structure.* For example, all of Olson's categories designated by roman numerals are nouns. The "A" and "B" subheadings under "II" are infinitives, and the headings under each of these are prepositional phrases:

   II. Objectives of employee fitness programs
       A. To benefit employees
           1. By improving mental and physical health
           2. By reducing boredom, absenteeism, and fatigue
           3. By promoting employee efficiency
       B. To benefit management
        . . .
  III. Design of facility
      . . .

4. *The outline shows an orderly progression.* In Olson's outline, the main headings seem to progress in the chronological order that would be followed in setting up an employee fitness program. Objectives come first, and then facilities are designed. Her subheadings use either order of importance (II) or chronological order (III). To check your outline for a logical sequence, list the major headings to see whether they are of equal importance and whether they are logically arranged. Then look at each group of subheadings in the same way. Olson had the most difficulty with the order of subheadings under "II. A." Was health more important than efficiency? She decided that from the point of view of the employee it was.

You can see that an outline, besides helping you to organize your paper, helps you clarify the relative importance of its parts. To write an outline, first decide on the major divisions — the main parts into which you intend to divide your paper. After you have decided on your major categories, divide each of them in a similar way. Think arithmetically; make the parts add up to the whole with nothing left over.

The Form of an Outline

Most outlines use alternating numbers and letters along with indentation. Major divisions are indicated by roman numerals; first subdivisions, by capital letters; and second subdivisions, by arabic numerals. Further subdividing is seldom required in papers written for college classes. If you find you need more subheadings, indicate them by small letters, then by arabic numerals in parentheses, and finally by small letters in parentheses. The order should look like this:

I.
   A.
      1.
         a.
           (1)
              (a)

If you glance back at Olson's outline, you'll notice that the period following each roman numeral is aligned. Then each subdivision is indented, with all divisions of the same order arranged in a vertical line and with the letter or number of each subdivision directly under the first letter of the first word in the larger category:

I.
II.
III. Design of facility
   A. Fitness center design
      1. Architectural layout
      2. Order of construction
      3. Estimated costs
   B.

Place a period after each number or letter, but do not put a period after the topics in a topic outline. (You would put periods after the sentences in a sentence outline; see the next section.) Capitalize the first letter of the first word of each topic. Such arrangement and punctuation make your outline easier to read and reinforce its logic.

Other Types of Outlines

Sentence Outlines.   The most common type of outline is, like Olson's, the topic outline, which uses single words or phrases. Sometimes, however, a *sentence outline* is used to define the categories more precisely. To make a sentence outline, you must have your material very clearly in mind. Although such precision is not always possible before writing, creating such an outline does force you to clarify what you want to say. As a result, the actual writing of your paper will be much easier. The following sentence outline helped Farah Farhoumand compose a stronger paper.

Topic: The growing problem of child abuse in the United States
Thesis: Child abuse is a growing problem with diverse causes and remedies.

I. Child abuse is increasing in the United States.
   A. Statistics are difficult to analyze because child abuse is defined differently by different experts.
      1. Some experts define it as severe battering.
      2. Others consider it to be any use of physical force that causes physical injury.
      3. Still others define it as mental as well as physical abuse.
   B. Statistics show that child abuse is increasing.
      1. The Department of Health and Human Services reported that child abuse cases doubled during the last two years.
      2. Large cities, where reporting is more accurate, report dramatic increases in child abuse.
      3. Researchers estimate that the number of reported cases is only a fraction of the real number.
II. Experts differ as to the causes of child abuse.
   A. According to some, the mental and emotional illness of parents causes child abuse.
   B. Others believe that parents' aggression is learned behavior.
   C. Another theory is that child abuse is caused by social, cultural, and economic factors.
   D. A few believe that children with behavioral problems can contribute to their own abuse.
III. Remedies are as varied as the causes.
   A. Recognition of the problem and reporting of cases are essential.

B. Psychologically disturbed parents should be treated.
C. In some cases, children should be separated from their parents and treated.

Decimal Outlines.   The *decimal outline* is often used for whole documents in technical writing because it is easily expanded into many subdivisions. Sometimes almost every paragraph is numbered for easier reference. For example, the heading structure of the *MLA Handbook for Writers of Research Papers* (4th ed., 1995) uses the decimal system. Its index cites numbered divisions and subdivisions instead of page numbers, which makes it easier for readers to locate information. The decimal system also makes it easier to see at a glance the relative importance of a heading. Notice how these systems correspond.

Using numerals and letters   Using decimals
   I. First major topic   1.0
     A. Major subtopic   1.1
       1. Minor subtopic   1.1.1
         a. Subsubtopic   1.1.1.1
         b. Subsubtopic   1.1.1.2
       2. Minor subtopic   1.1.2
     B. Major subtopic   1.2
  II. Second main topic   2.0

Diana Holford used the decimal system in her paper surveying home computers. Here is part of her outline.

1.0 Qualities of a good home computer system
   1.1 Memory
   1.2 Display
   1.3 Upgrading potential
   1.4 Graphics resolution/sound quality
   1.5 Printers
      1.5.1 Laser
      1.5.2 Laser jet
      1.5.3 Dot matrix
   1.6 Keyboard
      1.6.1 Pressure sensitive
      1.6.2 Typewriter
   1.7 Storage
      1.7.1 Floppy disks
      1.7.2 Hard drives
   1.8 Software
      1.8.1 Word processing
      1.8.2 Spreadsheets
      1.8.3 Others
2.0 Six popular computer systems

The Arrangement of Your Notes According to Your Outline

If you add to your outline or if you change its order or wording, be sure that you change the corresponding words or symbols in the upper corner of each note card or in your computer files. Re-sort and re-group the notes according to the outline. You will then be ready to write your paper easily and efficiently.

EXERCISES

1. **FOR YOUR SEARCH LOG** Record the answers to the re-searching questions (see page 139) in your search log.

2. **FOR PEER RESPONSE** Divide into groups, preferably of four or five. Using your search logs, take turns reading aloud to the group the answers to the re-searching questions on page 139. Read slowly. After each reader finishes, the other members of the group should write down what they understand to be the reader's purpose, and then the group should discuss the reader's purpose. Did everyone understand it? If not, what was the difficulty? Can it be clarified?

3. **FOR THE COMPUTERIZED CLASSROOM** Using the Toulmin method of analysis, write down your *claim* and your *grounds*. Send them by e-mail to two of your classmates, and ask them to check your reasoning for fallacies and return their comments to you. Perhaps they will offer a rebuttal. Revise your argument or thesis in the light of their comments.

4. **FOR THE COMPUTERIZED CLASSROOM** Use a syllogism to test the validity of your thesis. E-mail your syllogism to a classmate, and ask him or her to check it for fallacies and then return it to you.

5. Write a progress report describing the status of your research paper. Use memo format and address it to your instructor. Place this heading at the top left margin of your paper:

    To:

    From:

    Date:

    Subject:

Give the following information, using headings:

Your topic and thesis statement

Your updated outline

Work completed. This is the main section of your report. Consult your search log to remind yourself of what you have done. Explain where you are in your process. How much of your research or writing have you finished? What libraries have you visited? What people have you interviewed? What indexes have you used? In what format were they — print, CD-ROM, or online? How many of your sources have you read? *Attach an updated list of sources* (a working bibliography) using the format appropriate to your subject (see Chapters 10, 11, and 12).

Summary. Write a short paragraph summarizing the information you have gathered about your topic up to this point.

Work remaining. Now that you have a reasonably clear idea of the scope of your topic, you should have a better idea of what you have left to do both in terms of the process (such as interviewing and reading journal articles) and the amount and kinds of information needed. Explain in detail what you still need to do.

Evaluation or appraisal. In this section explain problems you may have encountered or findings that have been especially helpful or interesting. Perhaps you have made unexpected discoveries that have broadened the scope or changed the direction of your research.

C H A P T E R   7

Writing Your
First Draft

As you conducted your search, you were satisfying your own curiosity. Now, as you write, you will be satisfying your readers' curiosity. You will also be satisfying the desire we all have at times to tell someone else what we have done, thought, or discovered. If you can maintain the enthusiasm you have when you share information with your best friend, you will automatically eliminate many of the problems that arise in writing a research paper.

Preparing to Write

Preliminary Planning

The Computer as Writing Tool. With a computer you can write and revise your paper easily and efficiently. The ease and speed with which you can draft, revise, and edit a manuscript make procrastination less tempting. And the more features you learn to use, the easier the process becomes. The computer can help you produce a document that is more attractive to your readers and easier for them to read through the use of italics, bold, and special typefaces. (It also can help you check your spelling and usage.) The following guidelines are suitable for most academic papers. However, your instructor may prefer a different format. If you plan to submit your paper for publication, follow the publication's guidelines.

Materials. To create a professional-looking paper, use a laser or ink-jet printer and laser-quality white paper, 8½ by 11 inches, for your final draft. You can use paper of lesser quality for earlier drafts.

PREPARING TO WRITE **163**

Format. You can use these guidelines for academic papers in most disciplines. For formatting variations in academic disciplines see Chapters 10, 11, and 12.

- Leave one-inch margins on all four sides. If you plan to bind your paper, leave an inch and a half on the left.
- Indent paragraphs one-half inch, or five spaces.
- Double-space the entire manuscript including long, indented quotes.
- At the top right corner of each page place a running head ("header") containing an abbreviated title and page number. The header is usually omitted on the first page; your computer will take care of this if you insert the proper command.
- Leave the right margin "ragged" or unjustified. Justified right margins are usually used when there are two or three columns of type on the page. Unless your computer program uses proportional spacing, justified margins create unattractive white "rivers," made up of the spaces between words, down the page.

Type Size. The best type size for most academic papers is 12 points, or perhaps 10 points. You may want to include headings that are slightly larger — 14 or 15 points. In some formats, footnotes or endnotes are set in smaller type — 8 or 9 points.

Typefaces. Most computer programs will give you a choice of several different typefaces (fonts). How will you choose the best one? The typeface you use carries subliminal messages to your readers that can reinforce or detract from your verbal message. It can make your writing easier or more difficult to read.

Typefaces can be classified as either *serif* or *sans serif.* Serifs are the small lines that project from the main lines of letters in some typefaces (for example, the horizontal lines at the top and bottom of I). In general, typefaces with serifs are easier to read because the lines guide the eye horizontally. This book was set in serif type for that reason. On the other hand, sans serif typefaces give a clean, modern look to the page. So if you want your document to have a contemporary, high-tech look, consider using a sans serif typeface such as *Helvetica.* It looks like this:

Helvetica

Helvetica is an especially good choice if you want to use a small type size; it will allow you to fit more information into a smaller space and still have a readable document. (The Internal Revenue Service uses Helvetica for its tax forms and instructions.)

Century Schoolbook, a serif typeface, is often used in textbooks. It doesn't take up as much space as some of the other serif typefaces and is easy to read. *Times New Roman,* also known as *Times Roman,* is a relatively new typeface (first used in 1932). It is commonly used by newspapers because, although it has serifs and has the readability of other serif typefaces, it can still accommodate more words in a smaller space than many other serif typefaces. It may be listed as Times among the choices on your computer. Either of these typefaces, shown below, works well for most academic papers.

Century Schoolbook

Times New Roman

If you want your paper to have a casual, friendly look, you might want to use a typewriter typeface such as *Courier.* Courier is mono-spaced; that is, it uses the same amount of space for each letter, regardless of how much space the letter requires. Unfortunately, Courier may give your paper an amateurish or outdated look because it may remind readers of typewriter text. You probably recognize this example:

`Courier`

A completely different look, one with more personality, is conveyed by *Palatino.* Few writers of academic papers venture to use this somewhat light-hearted typeface. But it might be appropriate for a paper in the arts, such as theater, music, the graphic arts, or dance. Here is an example:

Palatino

For more information on typefaces and document design, see Robert Bringhurst, *The Elements of Typographic Style* (1992) or Tom Lichty, *Design Principles for Desktop Publishers* (1994).

Typewritten Papers. If you do not have access to a computer, you can use a typewriter to produce various drafts of your paper, if this is acceptable to your instructor. You should follow the formatting instructions given above for margins, paragraph indentations, double-spacing, and running heads. Avoid onionskin or erasable paper for your final draft.

Place. Do your composing in a place where you can be free of distractions and, if possible, where you can leave your papers and cards arranged, ready to work on at any time.

Schedule. Review the timetable you constructed as you were planning your search (see Chapter 2). Write down the total time you scheduled for writing and divide it into parts, allowing time for revising and incubating. Take account of your own writing habits: if you revise as you go along, you will take more time on the first draft and probably less time on subsequent drafts. Also use your timetable to help you change any habits that may not benefit your writing. Procrastination often prevents writers from spending as much time as they need on revising. Making a realistic timetable and following it will help you improve your writing procedure and, consequently, your writing.

The following schedule for a ten- to fifteen-page paper provides for three drafts. Your paper may require more. Or you may find that you have two complete drafts with some pages or paragraphs rewritten several times. Make adjustments for your own writing habits. The schedule also includes an incubation period. Many writers have found — perhaps you have too — that their minds work on a problem or a piece of writing even when they aren't giving it their conscious attention. To allow your mind time to do this work is the idea behind scheduling some time for incubation.

> *Writing the first draft:* Focus on getting down all the information you need to make your points clear. Ten to fifteen hours (four or five hours for each writing period).
>
> *Incubation period:* From one to seven days (if you leave your paper for a longer time, you may forget too much).
>
> *Writing the second draft:* Focus on organization and paragraphing. Ten to fifteen hours.
>
> *Incubation period:* Four to twenty-four hours.
>
> *Writing the third draft:* Focus on sentences, words, punctuation, and format. Eight to ten hours.
>
> *Preparing the final draft:* This can take anywhere from one to five hours, depending on whether you will print out your paper or type it from a manuscript.
>
> *Proofreading and photocopying:* Two to four hours.

Try not to rush during the period you have set aside for writing. Writing progresses best when you don't have to feel anxious about finishing; hurried writing is not usually good writing. Of course you will have a deadline to meet. But following your timetable will make it possible for you to have enough time to do your best and meet your deadline too.

Focusing on Your Audience

When you tell a friend about a concert you have attended or a movie you have seen, you use a vocabulary that you know your friend will understand. You include all the background information your friend needs to understand what you are talking about; you use an organizational plan that will make it easy for your friend to follow your explanation; and you use grammatical structures that make your meaning clear.

All these techniques are part of the process of verbal communication that you use daily, whether you are aware of using them or not. In writing your paper, you will want to be sure that you use these techniques with precision and care. Your friends may be able to ask you for clarification; they may know you well enough to understand you even if you are sometimes vague. But you have to assume when you write your paper that your audience will not have the chance to ask you to explain your meaning. Writing a paper takes more planning and more careful execution than talking or writing to a friend. Still, the same desire to tell, the same eagerness to make it possible for your readers to understand you, and your own interest in and enthusiasm for your subject are the most important prerequisites for writing a good paper, just as they are for communicating in any medium.

The main decision you will have to make about your audience is how much knowledge they have about your subject. Will they be familiar with the vocabulary? If your topic is "*Pseudomonas pseudomallei* infections in humans" and you are writing for your microbiology class, you will be able to write such a sentence as "The disease is often mistaken for tuberculosis or mycotic lung infections because of the cavitations on the lungs seen in x-rays" without translating the terms. But if you are writing for your English class, you should either put technical or unfamiliar words in a glossary, define them when you use them, or translate the whole sentence into layperson's terms. How do you decide which of these solutions to use? Here are some guidelines, but they are not hard and fast rules.

1. *Use words that will be understood by your audience, and integrate definitions into your writing when necessary.* For a general audience at the college level, you may be somewhat limited in your ability to discuss highly technical subjects. If you are, don't write

> The disease is often mistaken in x-rays for tuberculosis or mycotic lung infections because of the cavitations on the lungs.

But write

> The pittings or small depressions in the lungs caused by the disease and seen on x-rays often lead to mistaken diagnoses of tuberculosis or parasitic fungus infections.

Obviously, technical language or a higher vocabulary level usually requires fewer words and is often more precise. Therefore, you want to use the highest level that you think your audience can understand. But avoid using technical language just to impress your readers.

Besides suiting your vocabulary to the level of your readers' understanding, you will also have to consider how much they know about your subject and how much they need to know to understand what you are trying to say.

2. *Define words in the text or in a footnote* if you have only four or five words unknown to your audience. You can put each definition in parentheses immediately after the word:

> Sheet erosion(a landslide or mudflow) occurs extremely rapidly and results in greater losses of soil than any other type.

You can put the definition into a sentence that becomes an introduction to the subject:

> A computer network can be thought of as a collection of independent computers. It can include systems as simple as two word processors linked together or as complex as a worldwide system like the Internet, consisting of many computers connected by telephone lines.

Or you can use a content note or footnote:

> A trained analyst examines each photograph for details such as terrain, structures, ground disturbance, discarded material, and signatures.[1]

> ---
> [1]The term *signature* is used to denote a particular pattern, shape, tone, or color that consistently indicates the presence of an object or material in an aerial photograph, even though the object itself may be indistinguishable.

3. *Include a glossary* if you use more than five technical words frequently in your paper (for more suggestions on composing a glossary, see Chapter 9). Do not use words in your glossary that are just as difficult as the word you are defining. Defining *flagella* as "helical protein appendages that allow bacteria to be motile" is probably not going to help your readers.

Establishing Your Own Style and Tone

With your first words you establish a relationship with your readers, much as you do when you introduce yourself personally. The reader gets a sense of you as a person and of the tone you will use in your paper. Your tone may be serious, friendly, humorous, angry, or concerned — just about any emotion or combination of emotions is possible. It's important, though, to be conscious of the tone you are using and to use a tone that fits your subject and the results you want to obtain. Most research papers are serious, but they need not be dull. Whatever your attitude as you write, it will probably assert itself in your writing. A serious but relaxed and friendly attitude usually works well. Humor may work with some subjects, but you have to use it with care; it would not work well, for example, in a paper on the problems of alcoholism or the prevalence of teenage pregnancy.

Sometimes the syntax — the arrangement of words in the sentence — may make your writing hard to understand; write simply, saving complex sentence forms for complex ideas. Notice the following sentences from a paper on the results of environmental impact studies:

> Currently, field tests are being scheduled by the Envionics Corporation to coincide with the receipt of incremental site assessments which will be forwarded from the Environmental Photographic Interpretation Center (EPIC) upon completion.

Fortunately, the writer of this passage realized before she went very far that she was trying too hard to sound authoritative and that the result was unclear writing. By omitting unnecessary use of the passive voice and unneeded words, she composed a much clearer passage:

> The Envionics Corporation will conduct tests for potential hazards as soon as it receives the site assessments now being completed by the Environmental Photographic Interpretation Center (EPIC).

An excessively formal style in which you try to avoid using *I* or *you* can lead to such awkward constructions as the following:

> As has been said, not all of these writers had a political purpose in writing.
>
> As can be seen from Table 2, all cotton grown in the West is now under irrigation.

Instead, you can strengthen your writing by using simple and clear language:

> As I have already pointed out, not all of these writers had a political purpose in writing.
>
> Table 2 shows that all cotton grown in the West is now under irrigation.

Using your own style and writing clearly will help you give your paper unity and coherence. Unity will be reinforced if you are consistent in the verb tense you use. Use the present tense for routine or customary activities.

> Most pregnant girls *learn* about the agency through referral by a church or other organization. The first contact *is* usually *made* by phone call, during which an interview *is set up*.

Use the present tense, too, for references to what is in print or in law:

> Section 104 of the Copyright Law *prohibits* the public performance, for profit, of copyrighted music without permission of the copyright holder.
>
> Ziswiler *points out* that "conservation" applies to animal species, not to individual animals (100).

But use past tense when you are relating a past event, such as an interview:

> Mrs. Rumford *explained* that the adoptive couple must go through one to three years of intense interviewing and observation before they are accepted or rejected as adoptive parents.

Of course, you will be able to make changes when you revise, but you can save yourself time by writing as simply and clearly as you can from the beginning. Start with a style that you feel comfortable with, and you will be able to give your complete attention to what you say rather than to how you say it.

Writing Your Introduction

The first part of a paper is its introduction, but whether you label it as such depends in part on the discipline in which you are writing. Papers in the humanities following the style of the *Modern Language Association* usually do not use a heading. The *Publication Manual of the American Psychological Association* and the *Handbook for Authors of Papers in American Chemical Society Publications* recommend against using Introduction as a heading because the position of the material at the beginning is sufficient. However, Introduction is recommended as a heading in *Scientific Style and Format*, the style manual published by the Council of Biology Editors.

The introduction can be one or several paragraphs long. In it you tell your readers what they need or would like to know about your subject before you begin your specific discussion of it. You might explain your purpose for writing or state the problem you have studied. In writing some papers (especially if you are doing original research), you may want to review published writing on the same subject.

You have already prepared for writing your introduction in Chapter 6 when you answered this question in your search log: "What was my purpose in doing this search?" Here are some other questions you can ask yourself as you think about how to begin your paper:

- How did I happen to get started on this subject?
- What would my reader like to know before I explain what I found?
- What does my reader need to know to understand my paper?
- What am I trying to prove?
- What would my reader like to know about this subject?

Include in your introduction the answers to any of these questions that are relevant to your subject. The answer to the first two questions can provide background or a discussion of the problem you are trying to solve. The answer to the third question may be a brief history of the subject or a summary of what has already been written about it. The answer to the fourth question can be your hypothesis or your thesis statement. You can give your thesis statement in the introduction or in the conclusion at the end of the paper. Often the thesis statement or argument is placed at the end of the introduction. Sometimes the problem or purpose of the study is given.

Beginning with an Anecdote

Lee Atkinson began a paper about the possibility of life on Mars by explaining how he became interested in his subject. Notice that his story leads into the question that he will answer in his paper.

One warm summer day after classes, I made it home just in time to see the noon news. "Viking I has landed and is sending pictures back to earth from Mars," the newscaster said, speaking with the usual deep voice of broadcasters. "Here is the first picture sent back. Notice the can-like object to the left. Scientists say it did not come from Viking."

It looked like a beer can and my mind started whirling. Could there be life on Mars?

Beginning with Background

A paper on the treatments of alcoholism began with some historical background on the use of alcohol.

As a sign of trust and friendship in the early days of civilization, two men would draw their blood and mingle it with each other's. As time passed, alcohol came to be almost as important as blood. It was called "aqua vitae" — "water of life" — partly because it was often safer to drink than water. Trust was established and friendships and agreements were sealed with a cup of wine.

Today alcohol has become a social drink, but for many people social pressures and everyday problems can cause serious drinking problems. These people have a disease called alcoholism. The alcoholic's only hope for recovery is to stop drinking completely. How the alcoholic can do this is the subject of this paper.

Beginning with a Definition

Tom Davis's report resulting from a field exploration for knapping stones began with a definition to help his nonscientific audience — the members of his class — understand his paper. The opening paragraph closed with a statement of the paper's purpose.

Knapping is the art of making cutting tools by the controlled fracturing of stones. Glassy minerals, such as obsidian, chert, or flint (see glossary), are fairly easy to knap because their smooth texture allows us to predict how they will break. A semiglassy mineral, such as quartzite, is much harder to knap because its graininess makes its fractures less predictable. . . . To find the best places for knapping in the area, I first searched the geological literature, including maps, at the U.S. Geological Survey Headquarters. After noting the deposits that are either very large or that were said to contain quartzite cobbles, I knapped cobbles at a site in each deposit. This paper describes the locations of major deposits of knappable stones in the area and the compositions of these deposits. By using the marked map in the appendix, the knapper should be able to locate these sites easily.

Beginning with a Summary

A paper by Maria Sanchez on the problems of health care in the United States began with a question and then stated four answers, which became the four main parts of the paper.

Why is our health care system failing? Those who advocate a national health insurance law have cited four reasons: (1) there are not enough doctors and medical facilities, and those we have are not well distributed; (2) medical services are fragmented and poorly coordinated; (3) many people cannot afford adequate medical care or insurance; and (4) the cost of medical care is rising.

Beginning with a Review of the Literature

Sometimes a writer may want to start with a brief review of what other writers have written on the subject, as Raj Premchand does in a study of Mark Twain's pessimism. In his concluding sentence he states his argument.

> Literary critics have made much ado about Mark Twain's pessimism. What caused it and whether it existed from his early years are questions not yet answered conclusively. On the one hand there are those like DeLancey Ferguson who see him as "a born worrier" (184). Henry Seidel Canby goes to some lengths to explain what he calls Twain's neuroticism (252–54). On the other hand, Bernard De Voto traces his problems to a guilt complex fed by family misfortunes for which he blamed himself (301). But the most likely cause of his problem was, I believe, his feeling of shame for having yielded to the materialism of the Gilded Age.

You can see that an introduction can serve a number of purposes: it can define a word that is crucial to the understanding of the paper; it can state why the writer undertook the study; it can state the purpose of the research; it can briefly outline the body of the paper. In short, the introduction tells readers what they need or would like to know before reading the body of the paper; it introduces them to the subject. Choose the kind of introduction that fits your subject and purpose. You might want to try two or three different kinds to see which works best.

Getting Started without a Plan

If, after trying a number of possibilities for getting started, you still have a blank page in front of you, just begin writing anyway. Start talking on paper or on the computer about your topic as if you were talking to a friend. You can rewrite your introduction later. Or take out your notes and begin writing the body of your paper. You may have a better idea of how you want to write your introduction after you have written some or all of the paper itself.

Using Your Outline and a Computer

Sometimes it's hard to begin writing because the idea of having to begin a long paper can be discouraging. By using your outline and a computer you can combine the advantages of writing without a plan

and the advantages of some structure. Just call up your outline on the computer, and, thinking of each topic in the outline as the heading for a separate paper, begin to write a series of mini-papers. If you expand each heading into a sentence, you will have a thesis sentence for each mini-paper. If you can access more than one file at one time, call up your notes next to your outline and scroll through them as you write. If you can't call up more than one file at once, write from your printed notes or your note cards.

Continue to expand each part of your topic on the outline screen. If you will be using the APA style (see Chapter 11) or the number style (see Chapter 12) when you write your paper, you can leave the headings in place. Later you can turn them into a table of contents if you use one.

This strategy can help you to avoid procrastination. Set a modest goal of the number of topics you want to cover when you sit down at the computer — one you know you can accomplish. Then write at least that much. If you decide you want to write more, of course you can.

Writing the Body of Your Paper

In the body of your paper, you tell what you have discovered about your subject. If you are conducting an original study or experiment, you explain the methods you used as well as the results you obtained. If you are using secondary sources — information from others' studies and experiments — the body is where you give the information you have found. This is where you present the evidence that makes your thesis statement true.

Using Headings

The use of headings within the body varies among disciplines. Papers in the humanities usually do not use headings. If you have done primary research, such as a scientific experiment or a field study in social research, you would present your findings under at least three headings (the introduction would have no heading): Materials and Methods, Results, and Discussion or Conclusions. You can use secondary headings that correspond to your outline. If you are writing a technical report, you will use the headings corresponding to topics and subtopics in your outline. A research paper using secondary sources will usually follow the humanities or technical paper format. In organization, these two are similar, following an outline like those discussed in Chapter 6. (Note that papers citing secondary sources can use any of the three documentation systems illustrated in Chapters 10, 11, and 12.)

Developing Coherence and Unity

Following the outline you have designed before writing your paper (see Chapter 6) will help you to write a paper in which all of the parts are connected logically. Each part should clearly follow the one before it. You should set up expectations for your readers in each part of your paper, which you then fulfill. Each paragraph is a kind of promise that is fulfilled in the next paragraph; each sentence is a promise fulfilled in the succeeding sentence. This linkage creates the feeling of coherence in your paper. Your introduction has already pointed to what you will discuss or prove in the body of your paper. You must now make sure that you follow through.

The sample introductions given earlier in this chapter alert readers to what will follow. Read your introduction over again and see whether it prepares your readers for what you will write in the body of your paper. As you complete the discussion of each subtopic, stop and see whether it moves smoothly and clearly from the preceding topic or subtopic.

Your outline should also provide unity for your paper. You want to make sure that you don't include irrelevant information. If you deviate from your outline as you write, make sure you have a good reason for doing so — perhaps you have left something out of your outline. You'll have a chance to check your first draft for coherence and unity when you revise your paper (see Chapter 8).

Integrating Sources into Your Text

A transformation takes place as you write your paper. The information on your note cards or on your computer, based on the words of a number of writers and speakers plus any information you have collected through your own observation, becomes a unified paper written in your own style and your own words. The paper becomes your message to your readers about the discoveries you have made during your search. The following suggestions may help you to make this transformation. With your notes arranged according to your topics and subtopics on your note cards or your computer screen, read your notes slowly and carefully, one subtopic at a time. When the material in one group of notes becomes part of your thinking — when it is integrated with the rest of your knowledge and experience — you will be ready to write. Then write as if you were passing the information on to your readers. The words should come from what is now in your own mind rather than from the words in your notes. Write as much as you can without looking at your notes; refer to your notes primarily for exact quotations or statistics or to cite your sources of information.

Keeping Your Readers in Mind

Instead of feeling that you are mechanically filling up pages for an assignment, maintain a sense of direct and active communication with your readers as you write. Your sources can become participants in this discussion of your subject; what they have to say is part of the story you are telling. Think of the way you might tell someone about a conversation you have heard on a subject on which several people have disagreed. You will say something like "John said this, but Jim disagreed because.... And Mary didn't agree with either of them. I thought there was some truth in what they all said. . . ." You will want to give a similar sense of a lively discussion on a topic of interest to you and to your readers, as one student, Joan Ostby, did.

For her paper on Hart Crane's poem *The Bridge,* Ostby titled a part of her outline Evaluations. She read over her note cards with this heading and thought about them for a few minutes. There was some ambiguity and disagreement among the critical comments. She looked at her own notes and comments on the poem. She reflected on what had been written by critics about the poem and how she felt about it. When her thinking became clear, she sat down and wrote. She first summarized the views of the critics, quoting from some of them, and then gave her own evaluation. Notice how she varies her introductions of authors and their views.

Quotation with source in parentheses

Combination of paraphrase and quotation with author introducing the sentence

View by another critic: reference in text

Page number identifies source for two previous sentences; reference not needed for each sentence

The reviews of <u>The Bridge</u> are by no means un-
favorable; yet most of the critics seem to
feel that it was a noble effort that did not
quite succeed. It is termed a "magnificent
failure" by some (Horton 142). Allen Tate writes
that <u>The Bridge</u> failed because "a great talent
is engaged upon the problem of stating a position that is fundamentally incapable of definition." As a symbol, the bridge, he believes,
"stands for no well-defined experience" (210).
In <u>Hound and Horn</u> he expresses his disapproval
of the romanticism of the poem (132). Howard
Moss objects also to the symbol of the bridge
because he believes that it remains a static
symbol--even though Crane tries to activate
it. It is, he says, "metaphysical on one hand
and mechanical on the other. It rarely achieves
balance between fact and vision" (42).

Introduction ————— Although these criticisms are probably jus-
to paragraph
giving Ostby's   tified, the poem seems to me to fail because
view
    it lacks integration. The "bridge" itself is
Quotations from ——
the poet being   supposed to be a symbol of unity, connecting
discussed
    the past, present, and future. But the poem as

    a whole does not present that feeling of

    unity. The poetry is not consistently good,

    and the transitions between sections are some-

    times rough. It does not seem, either, that he

Quotations from —— has projected the "absolute ideal" "free from
the poet being
discussed   my own personality" that was his design.

Although she quotes other critics, Ostby maintains control of the ideas expressed. They are merely aids that she uses to tell readers her own view of the poem. (For detailed information on citing sources, see Acknowledging Your Sources, pp. 183–89.)

Keeping Your Readers Informed

The Ostby excerpt illustrates how to combine paraphrases and quotations and at the same time let readers know when they are getting information from sources and when they are getting the writer's own opinions. It also shows how to cite those sources so that parenthetical citations disturb the writing as little as possible. When you can put the name of the author and even the book or article title in the text, you need only the page number in the citation.

Handling Quotations

When you indicate that you are using someone else's language by putting the words in quotation marks, you must make sure that you quote accurately. The spelling of each word and each mark of punctuation must be just as they are in the original. When you make changes in the original to make it fit your own language and style, you must indicate these changes to your reader. The instructions that follow for using quotations from your reading include suggestions on how to show such changes.

1. *Let your own voice dominate.* To keep your own style and tone you will want to use direct quotations sparingly, and, when you do use them, you'll want to integrate them carefully into your paper. If you have followed the suggestion of paraphrasing and summarizing as you read your sources (see Chapter 4) and if you have read each group of notes before starting to write, you should find it easy to use your own

words. However, if you write directly from an article or book, the words of the source may dominate your thoughts and you might write a passage like this:

> "Don't Worry Baby" "became the first pop standard created by Brian Wilson" (Leaf 52). The song was a "staggering, textured tour de force of harmony, dramatic falsetto, and revolving melody. As an expression of teenage yearning and emotional insecurity, it was unsurpassed in the history of rock" (Priess 24).

The voice of the writer in this passage is lost among quotations of little or no significance. There seems to be little purpose in using the words of Leaf; the following paraphrase of the first sentence would work just as well: "'Don't Worry Baby' was Brian Wilson's first pop standard." And the writer does not prepare us for the quotation from Priess nor does she let us know why she is using it. If the writer thought that this was an especially interesting or significant quotation, she could have introduced it this way: "One critic called it 'an expression of teenage yearning and emotional insecurity' and expressed his great enthusiasm for the piece by referring to it as a 'staggering, textured tour de force of harmony, dramatic falsetto, and revolving melody' that was 'unsurpassed in the history of rock.'" This way the passage takes on more of the writer's style, and we hear *her* quoting Priess's words.

2. *Integrate quotations into your paper by introducing the original author.* Work all short quotations into the fabric of your own writing by giving the name of the original author or by identifying the author in some other way, perhaps as an authority. The use of quotation marks is not enough to alert readers to the fact that the words used are not yours. Quotation marks are visual cues, but you need verbal cues as well. Usually, if the words are important enough to be quoted verbatim, the reader wants to know who said them. This passage provides that necessary information:

> Most social learning theorists hold that child abuse is learned behavior. According to Lystad, parents who severely punish their children produce aggressive children who "in turn tend to punish their children more severely" (336).

3. *Integrate quotations by adding words to make the meaning clear or to make the quotations fit grammatically into the rest of the sentence.* Sometimes you will have to omit words of the quotation at the beginning or end or even insert words of your own into the original (see the use of brackets, p. 181). You must make sure, though, that you indicate the changes by punctuation. For example, you can add a word for clarity.

ORIGINAL:
"Orthodoxy, of whatever colour, seems to demand a lifeless, imitative style." (George Orwell, from *Shooting an Elephant and Other Essays*)

WORD ADDED:

"[Political] orthodoxy, of whatever colour, seems to demand a lifeless, imitative style."

Or you might omit words from the beginning of the quotation and change verb tense when necessary.

ORIGINAL:

"And thus, in the days ahead, only the very courageous will be able to take the hard and unpopular decisions necessary for our survival in the struggle with a powerful enemy. . . ." (John F. Kennedy, from *Profiles in Courage*)

INTEGRATED PASSAGE:

Kennedy concluded that "only the very courageous [would] be able to take the hard and unpopular decisions necessary for our survival in the struggle with a powerful enemy. . . ."

4. *Quote only significant or interesting words.* Although the words of someone else intrude on your style, sometimes the words of your source seem the best way to state an idea. Margaret Sharp found these words in her notes; the source was an interview with the manager of an adoption agency.

"Most girls intend to keep their children. It's rare that a girl comes to the agency intending to give up her baby. Those who do are usually older, more mature girls — nineteen or twenty years old. The average age of girls is fifteen years old. Out of 140 cases, we've placed 43 babies."

When the information appeared in her paper, most of the original was paraphrased; only one word was quoted directly.

Associated Catholic Charities took care of 140 young women and their newborn babies last year. Mrs. Rumford explained that most of these "girls" — except for the older ones, the nineteen- or twenty-year-olds — did not have adoption in mind when they came.

It's clear from the context that the word in quotation marks is Mrs. Rumford's. It is the only word that is hers, but the author wanted to report her use of this term to underline the plight of these young women by indicating that they were mere girls. Quoting the whole passage would not have been necessary and would have detracted from the emphasis on one word.

5. *Use long quotations when you want to hear the voice of your source.* The following passage illustrates why you might want to quote a long passage and what the effect is when you do. It also shows how you can prepare your readers for a long quotation. Alice Drake, in her paper on how writers write, wanted to explain how Eudora Welty, the fiction writer, began her writing career. Drake decided that using Welty's writing style would add to the account, so she introduced her and let her tell it in her own words.

> How do great writers start? Is there some sign at the very beginning of what is to come? Eudora Welty, in her biography *One Writer's Beginnings,* described her start this way:
>
> > The earliest story I kept a copy of was, I had thought, sophisticated, for I'd had the inspiration to lay it in Paris. I wrote it on my new typewriter, and its opening sentence was, "Monsieur Boule inserted a delicate dagger into Mademoiselle's left side and departed with a poised immediacy." I'm afraid it was a perfect example of what my father thought "fiction" mostly was (85–86).

Punctuating Quotations

To make your quotations effective and easy to understand, punctuate them carefully. In addition, indicate either by quotation marks (for short quotations) or by indentation (for long quotations) whenever you are borrowing words from someone else.

Introducing Quotations

- Use a comma or a colon to introduce a quotation that can stand alone grammatically: a comma for a short quotation and a colon for a long quotation (see p. 180 for illustrations of long quotations).

  ```
  According to one psychologist, "Child abuse is a phe-
  nomenon of uniform symptoms but of diverse causation"
  (Gil 347).
  ```

- Do not use any introductory punctuation when you integrate the quotation into your own sentence structure.

  ```
  One psychologist has stated that child abuse "is a phe-
  nomenon of uniform symptoms but of diverse causation"
  (Gil 347).
  ```

- Use a colon to introduce a line of poetry or to emphasize a short quotation.

  ```
  A famous soliloquy of Hamlet begins: "To be, or not to
  be: / That is the question."
  ```

Quotation Marks

- Except when you are following guidelines in *Scientific Style and Format* (see Chapter 12), place quotation marks outside commas or periods.

```
"With me," William Faulkner told the students, "a story
usually begins with a single idea or memory or mental
picture."
```

- Place the quotation marks after the quoted material and the period after the citation when you put a citation at the end of a sentence. The citation is considered part of the sentence but not part of the quotation.

```
Lincoln Steffens promoted "the Henry George plan for
the closing up of all the sources of unearned wealth"
(Autobiography 493).
```

- Always place semicolons and colons outside quotation marks except when they are part of the quotation.

```
We meet Lena in the first sentence of Light in August
"sitting beside the road, watching the wagon mount the
hill toward her"; she had come "all the way from Al-
abama a-walking."
```

```
Hotchner writes of Hemingway's "superb skill at in-
struction": Hemingway "guided me every step of the way,
from when we pull up to set the big hook in his mouth
to when we bring him in close to be taken."
```

- Place a question mark inside the quotation marks if the quoted material is a question, outside if the quoted material is part of a sentence that is a question. The following quoted material is a question.

```
According to Young, aphasics can answer the question
"Were you drinking tea?" but cannot tell where they
live.
```

In the next example, the quoted material is not a question; the sentence that contains the quoted material is a question.

```
Do you know who said, "That's one small step for a man,
one giant leap for mankind"?
```

- Use three ellipsis points in addition to a period when an unfinished quotation ends the sentence. Notice the order: ellipsis points, quotation marks, citation, and period. (For further explanation of ellipsis points, see p. 181.)

```
Rubenstein says that "the Consumer Price Index over-
states annual inflation by about 1 percent . . ." (14).
```

Long Quotations

- When quoted material is more than four lines long, indent it ten spaces from the left margin if you're using the author-page style; indent it five spaces for the author-date style. Do not use quotation marks. The right margin remains the same as the rest of the text. If your quotation is only one paragraph or part of a paragraph, don't indent the first word more than the rest. The following quotation begins in the middle of one paragraph and follows with an entire paragraph, the first line of which is indented three additional spaces.

```
As The Great Gatsby closes, Carraway speculates about
Gatsby's death and life:
            I thought of Gatsby's wonder when he first
            picked out the green light at the end of
            Daisy's dock. He had come a long way to this
            blue lawn, and his dream must have seemed so
            close that he could hardly fail to grasp
            it. . . .
            Gatsby believed in the green light, the
            orgiastic future that year by year recedes
            before us.
```

- If a long quotation contains material in quotation marks, enclose that material in double quotation marks.

```
In Tillie Olsen's story "I Stand Here Ironing," the
narrator describes her attempt to "make up" for not
having paid enough attention to her daughter as she was
growing up:
            Now when it is too late (as if she would let
            me hold and comfort her like I do the others)
            I get up and go to her at once at her moan or
            restless stirring. "Are you awake, Emily? Can
            I get you something?"
```

Single Quotation Marks

- Use single quotation marks to enclose a quotation within a quotation.

```
As Hart points out, "Given a problem and the necessary
raw inputs, and 'left alone' to deal with it, our neo-
cortex obligingly will solve it."
```

Brackets

- When you add clarifying words or phrases to a quotation, enclose them in brackets.

      Hamlin Garland admitted that he abandoned polemics
      after "the destruction of the People's party and the
      failure of this novel [A Spoil of Office]."

- Use brackets when you have to add words to make the quotation fit the grammatical structure of your sentence.

      Cooper held that to "encourage the rich to hold real
      estate [was] not desirable" (The Redskins 8).

- Use the Latin word *sic,* which means "thus," in brackets to indicate that your quotation or the spelling of a word is accurate, even though it may appear to be incorrect.

      At the end of Huckleberry Finn, Huck writes that he is
      going "to light out for the Territory" because his Aunt
      Sally is "going to adopt me and sivilize [sic] me."

Ellipsis Points

- Use three ellipsis points (spaced periods) with a space before and after each point to indicate that you have left out part of a quoted passage.

      J. Z. Young maintains that "the important feature of
      brains is . . . the information that they carry" (2).

- When you omit material at the end of a sentence and your quotation appears to be a full sentence, place the period at the end as you normally would, with no space between it and the last word, and then add the three ellipsis points — a total of four points in all.

      According to Time magazine, "the persistent growth of
      euphemism in a language represents a danger to thought
      and action. . . ."

- When you omit a sentence or more in the middle of a passage, use four periods. Be sure that you have a complete sentence both before and after the ellipsis points.

      Faulkner explained in an interview at West Point that
      "every experience of the author affects his writ-
      ing. . . . He has a sort of lumber room in his subcon-
      scious that all this goes into, and none of it is ever
      lost."

Poetry

- When you are quoting more than one line of poetry within a sentence, separate the lines with a virgule or slash (/) and with a space before and after the virgule.

```
To substantiate his view, he quoted Blake's lines: "We
are led to believe in a lie / When we see with not
through the eye."
```

- If you are quoting more than three lines of poetry, begin your quotation on a new line, ten spaces from the left margin, and double-space as you would any other quotation.

```
Ogden Nash is recalled for his witty and sometimes
philosophical poetry:

        I think that I shall never see
        A billboard lovely as a tree.
        Indeed, unless the billboards fall
        I'll never see a tree at all.
```

However, if the lines are unusually long, you may indent them fewer than ten spaces.

- When a poem has unusual spacing or when some of the lines are indented to follow a pattern, follow the spacing of the original.

```
In the concluding verse of "Invictus," William Ernest
Henley enunciated his philosophy of self-determination:
        It matters not how strait the gate,
          How charged with punishments the scroll,
        I am the master of my fate:
          I am the captain of my soul.
```

- Indicate the omission of one or more lines of poetry by typing a line of spaced periods in place of the omitted lines.

```
In his poem "To a Skylark" Shelley addresses the bird
as a being that knows more than humans:
        Teach us, Sprite or Bird,
          What sweet thoughts are thine:
        . . . . . . . . . . . . . . . .
        Teach me half the gladness
          That thy brain must know.
```

Acknowledging Your Sources

When to Acknowledge Your Sources

You must give credit in your paper for ideas or information that belongs to someone else, whether you quote it, summarize it, or paraphrase it. Explaining where you found your material is part of the information about your subject that belongs in your paper. It gives readers a chance to judge its reliability and accuracy and also makes it possible for them to look up more about the subject if they want to. Failure to give the source is literary theft or plagiarism. (For suggestions on avoiding plagiarism, see pp. 112–14 and 189–91.)

But give citations only when they are necessary. Every footnote or endnote number or parenthetical citation disturbs the flow of your writing to some extent. The following suggestions will help you determine when you should cite your source. *Do not cite your source in the following instances:*

1. *Do not cite your source when your information is common knowledge.*

```
Mars was the Roman god of war.

Dwight Eisenhower became president in 1953.
```

Although it may be difficult sometimes to identify what is common knowledge, in most cases you should not have trouble. Any date, like the one given in the example, that can be verified in an encyclopedia, newspaper, or almanac need not be documented, even though many people might not remember it.

2. *Do not cite your source when the information is accepted as true by most people.*

```
Alcoholism impairs the functions of the brain, liver,

stomach, and lungs.
```

This kind of information may be harder to identify. You may know little about the subject you are gathering information on, and everything about it may be new to you. In doing research for a paper on drugs, you may read that most former heroin addicts are unable to stay away from heroin permanently. Is this common knowledge among doctors and heroin users? When you aren't sure whether it's common knowledge, and when your readers are people who are at the same level of knowledge as you and who might question the validity of your information or wonder where you got it, you should document it.

3. *Do not cite your source when the statements or observations are your own.*

```
No one should be locked into full-time custodial care

when alternative means of treatment are available.
```

You should always cite your source in the following instances.

1. *Always cite your source when the information is exclusively the idea or discovery of one person or a group of people.* All direct quotations and most paraphrases and summaries of factual information fit this description.

```
As crime rates rise, more prisoners stay longer in pris-
ons that are already crammed well past their planned ca-
pacity (Jenson 1994).
```

The statement that "more prisoners stay longer" in crowded prisons needs to be documented by citing the person who has the figures to back up this information.

```
In 1981 only 8 percent of architects reported using com-
puters; today nearly all architects use computers in
their work ("Computers" 20).
```

You should give the source of any figures unless you compiled them.

2. *Always cite your source when your readers might like to find out more about the subject.*

```
Administration officials are considering the regulation
of tobacco products as drugs (Burns A3).
```

3. *Always cite your source when your readers might question the accuracy or authenticity of the information.* Ask yourself whether your readers are likely to ask "Where did you find that?" or "Who said that?"

```
One species of mammal becomes extinct each year (Ziswiler
17).
```

4. *Always cite your source when you use a direct quotation of one word or more.*

```
In his later years Lowell called Rousseau "a monstrous
liar" (Letters 466).
```

How to Acknowledge Your Sources

Depending on the documentation style you are using, the sources you cite in your text will appear at the end of your paper either in an alphabetized list titled Works Cited or References or in a numbered list titled Endnotes or Notes. (Footnotes at the bottom of the page to cite references are no longer recommended by any of the major style manuals.) The citations within your text referring to these sources will appear in parentheses or as superscript note numbers. Choose the documentation style preferred by writers in your subject area or by the person or organization you are writing for. Your instructor will be able to tell you what style is required for your paper. The style commonly used by writers in the humanities (English, foreign languages, history, and philosophy) is known as the author-page style and is recommended by the Modern Language Association in the *MLA Handbook for Writers of Research Papers* (1995). Chapter 10 gives detailed guidelines for using this system as well as two sample papers illustrating its use.

The author-date system is favored by writers in the social sciences, biology, earth sciences, and business and is explained in the *Publication Manual of the American Psychological Association* (1994). Details for using this system and a sample paper are given in Chapter 11.

A third major documentation style is the citation-sequence system, preferred by writers in the applied sciences, medical sciences, and engineering and outlined in *Scientific Style and Format,* published by the Council of Biology Editors (1994). The use of this style is explained and a sample paper is provided in Chapter 12.

These three systems — author-page, author-date, and the citation-sequence system — recommend that documentation information be given with-in the paper and a list of references be placed at the end. The following guidelines give some of the most frequent uses of these systems. You will find details in Chapters 10, 11, and 12.

Writers in disciplines such as art, music, theater, religion, and history sometimes use footnotes at the bottom of the page or endnotes following the body along with superscript numbers within the text to refer to the notes. You'll find an explanation of this system together with examples in Appendix 2 (the best-known source of guidelines for this system is the *Chicago Manual of Style* [1993]).

A computer can help you keep track of footnotes and endnotes when you use this system. With the necessary software, your computer will place the correct superscript number in your text when you give the command. Then you can type in your note, either in the text or in a special file. When you are ready, the computer will print the note either at the bottom of the page or at the end of your paper. If you rearrange your notes, your computer will renumber them for you.

When citing sources using any documentation system, be sure to place the citation immediately after the source cited or the information you want to cite; that is, either at the end of the sentence or within it. Do not put a citation at the end of a sentence unless it applies to the whole sentence. If the source is cited within the sentence, place the citation immediately following the relevant information. Note that a citation at the end of a paragraph applies only to the immediately preceding sentence. In this example information within the sentence is cited:

```
According to Sternberg's CRH dysregulation theory,[19] the
amount of CRH produced by a person with rheumatoid arth-
ritis is less than that of a normal person.
```

While you are writing your first draft, include source information so that you will know where the material came from when you write your final draft. No matter what citation system you use in your final draft, give at least the author and page number of every summary, paraphrase, or quotation as you write your first draft.

Author-Page System (MLA Style).   If you use the author-page system of citation, you need to supply the author's last name and the page number of the work in parentheses within the sentence. If the author's name is part of the sentence, place just the page number in parentheses. Readers who want to know the name of the work and the publication facts can look those up in the list of works cited at the end of your paper. Place the parenthetical citation as near as possible to the information you are documenting, either where a pause occurs or at the end of the sentence.

When should you put the author's name in your text and when should you put it in parentheses? To decide the answer, consider the needs of your readers. Here are some suggestions.

1. *If the name of the author is a significant part of the information you are giving, give the name in your text, leaving only the page number for your citation.*

```
According to Van Doren (4), early American fiction writ-
ers were often charged with corrupting public morals.
```

Here the page number, without "page" or "p.," is placed after the name of the author instead of after the information given because a pause occurs after the author's name.

2. *When the information you are giving or the point you are making is more important than the author, place the author's name as well as the page number in the parenthetical citation.*

```
The Alliance adopted the free silver plank in its plat-
form of 1887 (Hicks 132).
```

Note that there is no punctuation between the author and page number and that the period marking the end of the sentence comes after the parenthetical citation.

3. *If you have included more than one work by an author in your list of works cited, you will have to include a brief title in your citation.*

```
As early as 1884, both major parties recognized labor in
their platforms (Destler, American Radicalism 141).
```

4. *If you refer in your text to a whole work, you do not need a parenthetical citation.*

In My Ántonia, Willa Cather allows the narrator to over-
shadow the heroine.

5. *When you have a long quotation set off from the rest of the text, place the citation in parentheses after the punctuation mark at the end of the quotation.* Indent the quotation ten spaces from the left margin.

In The Jungle, Upton Sinclair depicted the horrors of
slaughterhouses in passages like this:

> The fertilizer works of Durham's lay away from
> the rest of the plant. Few visitors ever saw
> them, and the few who did would come out look-
> ing like Dante, of whom the peasants declared
> that he had been into hell. To this part of the
> yards came all the "tankage," and the waste
> products of all sorts; here they dried out the
> bones--and in suffocating cellars where the
> daylight never came you might see men and women
> and children bending over whirling machines and
> sawing bits of bone into all sorts of shapes,
> breathing their lungs full of the fine dust.
> (129)

In the author-page system, you do not put any documentation in footnotes or endnotes. The only notes you might use are content or explanatory notes to explain a point further or to cite other bibliographic sources. If you use these, you put them at the end of the paper before the Works Cited section. In the text place a superscript numeral — like this[1] — to refer your readers to a note at the end of the paper in a section labeled Notes:

[1] See also Schlesinger (717), who points out that
Adams was fascinated with politics throughout his career.

Leave one space between the superscript number and the beginning of the note.

Explanatory or content notes are explained further in Chapter 9; you will find other examples of their use in the sample papers in Chapters 10 and 11.

Author-Date System (APA Style). For those who use the author-date system (writers in the social sciences, biology, business, economics, linguistics, and earth sciences), the date of the information cited, as well as the name of the author, is important and must appear either in your text or in a parenthetical citation. The list of sources appears at the end of the paper arranged in alphabetical order and usually titled References. A few of the most commonly used citations are given here; you'll find others in Chapter 11, along with a sample paper.

As you would want to do with any of these systems, make sure you introduce your source rather than just giving a quotation or paraphrase with a citation at the end.

1. *If you use the author's name as part of your text, place the date in parentheses following the name.*

```
Wellington's study (1994) clearly showed that . . .
```

2. *If the date is important enough to be included in the text, you need no citation unless you are using a direct quotation.* (See number 4.)

```
Wellington's 1994 study showed that . . .
```

3. *If the author's name is not significant to your point in the sentence, you can put both the author and date in the parenthetical citation.*

```
At least one authority (Wellington, 1994) has pointed out
that . . .
```

Note the comma between the author's name and the date.

4. *When you quote directly from someone else's work, you must give a page number.* (Some instructors and some publishers prefer that page numbers be given with each citation.) When the author and the quotation are separated, the date is usually given directly after the name of the author, and the page number follows the quotation.

```
According to Lowe (1979), prison "should be the last al-
ternative" (p. 14).
```

Note that the abbreviation "p." is used with the page number in this system.

5. *With a quotation of more than forty words, indent the whole passage five spaces from the left margin.* If there are any paragraphs within the passage, indent the first line of each paragraph five more spaces.

```
Barlow and Swidner (1983) reported the following results:
    The majority of relationship problems are connected
    with the phobia. This seemed clearly true in the
    first client where the relationship was basically
    very strong. . . . Nevertheless, relationship issues
    improved considerably as phobia improved. This girl
    was referred for further therapy concerning inter-
```

```
personal relationships and career choices following
treatment.
     The second client, on the other hand, came from
a severely disturbed family with constant conflict.
The mother held the family together by trying to ac-
commodate everybody but was hospitalized occasion-
ally for periods of amnesia lasting several days
during times of particularly intense family stress.
(p. 525)
```

Note the location and punctuation of the page number for a long, indented quotation — one space after the final period.

Citation-Sequence System (CBE Style). The citation-sequence system is used by writers in chemistry, physics, mathematics, medicine, and nursing and by some writers in biology. (A few chemistry journals use the author-date system.) With this system, citations start with 1 and are numbered consecutively throughout the paper. Numbers may be placed in parentheses on the line or superscript in typesize one or two points smaller than the typesize of the text. Some writers use a page number with the citation: "1, p 35." If a reference is repeated, its original number is repeated. Items in the list of references at the end of the paper are given in numerical order.

Some writers use a variation of this system: the list of references is numbered in alphabetical order and, consequently, the numbers in the text are not in serial order. For more details on the use of the citation-sequence system and a sample paper, see Chapter 12.

A citation using the citation-sequence system appears this way.

```
Paroxysmal tachycardia occurs more often in young pa-
tients with normal hearts (5).
```

Avoiding Plagiarism

Plagiarism is the use of others' words or ideas without attribution (see Chapter 4 for suggestions on avoiding plagiarism while taking notes). The use of summaries, paraphrases, and quotations from others without citing the source is plagiarism; using verbatim quotations without enclosing them in quotation marks is also plagiarism.

Plagiarism results from a writer's failure to integrate information from sources into his or her own thinking. Such failure often originates in inadequate paraphrasing and summarizing during the note-taking process. Attempts to shorten the process and write directly from sources can also lead to plagiarism. Besides the academic and legal penalties for plagiarism, one of the most unfortunate results is the writer's loss of the pleasure that comes from discovery of knowledge (plagiarism is evidence of the lack of such discovery) and the subsequent pleasure of telling about it.

Plagiarism is usually recognizable because the borrowed material is written in a different style from that of the author of the paper. Sometimes the borrowed material alternates with the writer's words, and distortion and lack of clarity result. Often terms that were explained earlier in the original source are not explained in the paper. Writers involved with their audiences do not write this way. But the writer who uses others' writing instead of his or her own is not concerned primarily with communicating to the reader, and most readers can sense this.

Figure 7.1 is an example of plagiarism in the introduction to a paper. You will find it difficult to understand this passage even though it appears in the beginning of the paper, and you will probably lose interest rather quickly. The plagiarized passages are underlined. Although the writer cites a source, the only citation is given at the end of the last sentence. Therefore, a reader has to conclude that everything but the last sentence is the writer's own. Yet it is obvious that to make such sweeping generalizations about large periods of history, the writer would have had to engage in years of research and would need to produce a book-length work to give the details on which they were based. The scope is beyond a student writer at almost any level. Lack of clarity and coherence are the result of stitching together unexplained generalizations from another writer with a few words of the writer's own.

Plagiarism is a rhetorical as well as an ethical problem. It results from interconnected failures in thinking, note taking, and writing. Here are some suggestions for avoiding plagiarism.

1. Make a schedule when you start work on your paper, and follow it as closely as possible. When you find yourself rushing to meet a deadline, it is easy to get careless and save time by using someone else's words.

2. Choose a topic that you want to learn about and will want to tell others about. If you are genuinely interested in your subject, you will want to use your own words to explain it.

3. Make sure you understand the materials you are reading; if you don't understand them, don't use them in your paper. If you don't comprehend your information, you will have to use someone else's words to explain it.

4. Take notes only after you have integrated your reading into your own thinking. Use paraphrasing and summarizing as much as possible to ensure that the material has become your own.

5. Before you write, review your notes carefully, and make sure you understand how and where they will fit into your paper. If you

FIGURE 7.1 Plagiarism

ORIGINAL

The long epoch from the Second Awakening to the war with Spain was also a century of great tribulation, an "ordeal of faith" for church-going America. . . .

On the intellectual level the new challenges were of two sorts. First, there was a set of specific problems that had to be faced separately: Darwin unquestionably became the nineteenth century's Newton, and his theory of evolution through natural selection became the century's cardinal idea. . . . Accompanying these specific problems was a second and more general challenge: the rise of positivistic naturalism, the cumulative result of modern methods for acquiring knowledge. In every discipline from physics to biblical criticism, myth and error were being dispelled, and the result of this activity was a world view which raised problems of the most fundamental sort. (Sydney E. Ahlstrom, *A Religious History of the American People* [New Haven: Yale University Press, 1972], pp. 763–64)

PLAGIARIZED VERSION

The long epoch from the Second Awakening of 1785 and the war with Spain in 1898 was a century of tribulation and ordeal for religious Americans. During this period, but most notably between the years 1865–1900, many intellectual clergymen created a new Liberal Theology built on the tenets of Darwinism and positivistic naturalism, while the unlettered population remained staunchly conservative based on the orthodoxy of the Puritans.

The intellectuals dealt with two challenges, each of them separately. First, there was Darwin, who had become by 1865 the Newton of the nineteenth century, whose theory of natural selection had become the century's cardinal idea.

The second was a more general challenge: the rise of positivistic naturalism, or the cumulative result of modern methods for acquiring information. In every discipline from physics to biblical exegesis, myth and error were being dispelled, and the resulting world view raised fundamental problems concerning faith and the deterministic principles held by the church (Ahlstrom 763–64).

don't see the connection between your information and your overall purpose, it will be difficult for you to use your own words.

6. Avoid writing directly from your sources. It's difficult not to use the words you see right before you.

If you follow these guidelines, it's unlikely that you will find yourself plagiarizing. Even more important, you will have the pleasure of writing a paper that you yourself will enjoy reading.

Writing Your Conclusion

The last questions you answered in your search log as you finished your re-searching were, "What did I learn from my search?" and "What conclusions can I draw from this knowledge?" If your research was successful, your learning will have changed your thinking in some way; you will see things differently. In the conclusion to your paper, record how your thinking has changed. You shouldn't have to strain to find out what these changes are. These changes in your thinking are what your readers would like to know. The examples that follow show how the thinking of the writers changed and how that thinking was recorded in their conclusions. A conclusion may be only a sentence or two, or it may be several paragraphs.

Often the conclusion states or restates (usually in other words) the paper's thesis. Brian Edwards examined the evidence of global warming and concluded:

> Although environmentalists and the media have been criticized recently for exaggerating the problem posed by the greenhouse effect, global warming remains a serious threat that must be addressed by scientists, policymakers, and citizens.

A conclusion may answer the question posed in the beginning of the paper. Or it may validate or disprove a hypothesis stated earlier. An article by Gary Goertz and Paul F. Diehl ("The Initiation and Termination of Enduring Rivalries: The Impact of Political Shocks," *American Journal of Political Science,* February 1995) concludes in part:

> Enduring rivalries represent a peculiar kind of stability in international relations. We hypothesized that such stability in the international system is not easily disrupted, and a shock is necessary to upset that continuity. . . . Our expectations have largely been confirmed (50).

This kind of conclusion is most often found in an article in a professional journal reporting on original research. Those of you doing original research in the sciences or humanities may start with a hypothesis or perhaps a problem to be analyzed, as the authors of this article did. However, many of you will probably be writing "review papers." That is, you will review reports of original research appearing in professional journals and will base your conclusions on your findings.

A conclusion may summarize. In her paper on the human immunodeficiency virus, Tammatha O'Brien restated the problem, described the progress made, and predicted the outlook for a cure.

> The antibody that will denature HIV remains undiscovered. Although we have completely mapped the genome of this virus, the function of three genes remains unknown. Many aspects of the viral utilization of the host

cell remain unanswered and unexplored. Without these answers the outlook for finding a cure soon appears dim.

A conclusion may recommend change. In a paper on prison overcrowding, Linda Thornberry concluded:

> Long-term incarceration is necessary only for a very small percentage of incorrigible criminals. Nonviolent offenders, especially those serving two years or less, are prime candidates for alternatives to imprisonment. The alternatives that exist should be used in order to avoid prison overcrowding as well as to increase the chances of rehabilitation.

A conclusion may evaluate and predict. Joe Collins made a study of gas-saving devices and concluded:

> The vast majority of devices being marketed as mileage improvers are frauds. Because most of them don't work, it is hard for legitimate devices to gain public acceptance. Some devices that could improve mileage can't get to market because they can't conform to some government regulations.
>
> Any significant breakthroughs in mileage will probably come from the auto makers because they are the only ones with enough capital to invest in massive research and development programs. But in these times of trouble for them, even they may not have the funds without government assistance.

A conclusion fits the paper that it was written for. It grows naturally out of what came before it. If you find yourself thinking, "I'm supposed to write a conclusion, but I don't know what to say," take some time to reread your paper and reflect on it. What do you want your readers to know above everything else? What is the main idea that you would like your readers to remember? What thoughts would you like to leave them with? Tell them as clearly as possible.

Writing the Title

You may already have a working title, but after you have written your first draft you may be able to decide on the final version. Your summary or thesis sentence can help you compose a good title, but it contains more than you need in a title; a thesis sentence includes not only your subject but also what you are going to say about that subject. The title, on the other hand, is not a complete sentence — it doesn't usually have a verb; and it usually gives only the specific subject of your paper, not your conclusions about that subject.

Mavis Olson's summary sentence was "Companies should consider developing physical fitness programs for their employees." She decided on the title "Developing Physical Fitness Programs in the Workplace." The following examples show how thesis statements can become titles:

Thesis sentence: Computer crime can be stopped with expensive secu-
rity programs.
Title: Solving the Problem of Computer Crime
Thesis sentence: The Gilded Age shows Mark Twain's cynical attitude to-
ward democracy.
Title: The Gilded Age: Mark Twain's Comment on Democracy
Thesis sentence: The adoption agency performs an important service
for both the mother and the adopting couple.
Title: The Role of the Adoption Agency
Thesis sentence: The vast majority of devices being marketed as
mileage improvers are frauds.
Title: Getting Taken for a Ride with Gas-Saving Devices

The title can be imaginative, but use humor or cleverness with care.

Writing an Abstract

An abstract or summary is often placed at the beginning of a paper in
the social sciences, in the biological and applied sciences, and in engineering and business. There are two kinds of abstracts, each serving a
different purpose: the descriptive abstract tells what a paper *does;* the
informative abstract tells what a paper *says.* The descriptive abstract describes what the purpose of the paper is and explains how the purpose
is achieved. It talks *about* the paper. The informative abstract, on the
other hand, is a summary — a condensed version of the paper. Most
papers, however, do not have both kinds of abstracts. If you are asked
to write an abstract, be sure you understand what kind it is supposed
to be.

An abstract may be a few sentences long (the descriptive abstract is
usually short), or it may be several paragraphs long. The informative
abstract of a ten- to fifteen-page paper is usually about three-quarters of
a page long. It may appear on the title page single-spaced (if it's short),
on a separate page at the beginning of the paper, or at the end of the
paper.

Descriptive Abstracts

To write a descriptive abstract, read your outline or table of contents
carefully and then convert the outline into cohesive sentences. Notice
the following descriptive abstract; it *describes* what is in the paper and
gives its basic structure.

This paper analyzes the volunteer program at State Museum and relates volunteer tasks to management functions. Specific areas for improvement are
proposed. Finally the role of the volunteer coordinator is discussed, and
recommendations are made for improving volunteer performance.

Informative Abstracts

The informative abstract usually starts with the thesis statement or a summary and then gives details. It, too, should follow the outline or table of contents, but it gives the content of the paper as well as its structure. The following informative abstract was included in a paper titled "The Healing Properties of Herbs."

> Herbalism, the oldest known branch of medicine, has been practiced for centuries in many cultures both to prevent and to cure disease. Despite this extensive use of herbs, past research into their beneficial properties has been limited and results have been contradictory. According to some early studies, herbs cause the human body more harm than good; at the other extreme, researchers have claimed that herbs are wonder drugs that can heal almost any known disease. Recent research in the Western scientific community shows that, when used with the advice of a trained herbalist, herbs can have beneficial effects on the human body.

Abstracts make it possible for readers to find out what your paper is about without reading the whole paper. Some readers in business and government read only the abstract. Readers of journals may read the abstract of an article to find out whether they want to read all of it.

Designing Illustrations

Are you an artist at heart? Do you think putting pictures on paper is one of your talents? Illustrations (sometimes referred to as visuals, visual aids, graphics, or graphic aids) are a visual form of communication that anyone can use to clarify meaning. What we can "see," we tend to understand better — literally as well as symbolically. Illustrations can take the form of tables, graphs, charts, diagrams, photographs, maps, or drawings. They are used most frequently in papers in the social sciences, in earth and applied sciences, and in engineering, but they can be helpful additions to any paper. Tables and graphs help you convey quantitative information at a glance; drawings and diagrams make hard-to-understand ideas and mechanical systems easier to comprehend. If your paper is concerned with history or geography, you can use maps; if literature is your subject, you may want to use photographs, drawings, or tables; if your paper is on a business topic, you may want to use graphs, organization charts, or flow charts. To decide which of these are appropriate for your paper, look for information that can be quantified or visualized.

Tables

Tables present statistical and other information in a readable, understandable way by organizing it into columns and rows. Short, simple tables that can be read as part of the text need not be numbered or titled. Such *informal tables* also need not be framed with ruled lines nor contain internal ruled lines. In her paper on health care, Joyce Lamb first wrote the following sentences:

> We are paying more for medical care now than we ever have before. As a percentage of the gross national product (GNP), health expenditures grew from 9.1 percent in 1980 to 11.9 percent in 1985 and 12.2 percent in 1990 (Jensen 43).

She decided that the figures in the second sentence could be compared more easily if they were in table form, so she changed her paper to read:

> We are spending more of our gross national product (GNP) for medical care now than ever before, as the following figures show (Jensen 43):
>
> | | |
> |---|---|
> | GNP 1980 | 9.1% |
> | GNP 1985 | 11.9% |
> | GNP 1990 | 12.2% |

Formal tables, like informal tables, compare data by aligning them in columns and rows. However, formal tables are not run in with the text, although they should be placed in the text near the passage that refers to them. They are always numbered and titled. In addition, they often contain more statistics and receive more emphasis through the use of horizontal lines and extra space. Formal tables, like other illustrations, can share a page with other text or can occupy a separate page. If you design a table, be sure to label all columns, using parallel grammatical structure, and give the source at the bottom of the table.

Some computer software makes it easy for you to create tables and insert them into your text. Usually, you choose the table-making application and type your data and headings into the cells provided. (With some software, you indicate the number of rows and columns you want before entering your data.) You can then insert borders around your table or between rows and columns. You can also delete or insert rows or columns, sort numerical information, or perform calculations. (For more specific advice on designing and editing tables and other visuals on your computer, consult your software manual.) Figure 7.2 shows an example of a table that was designed on a computer.

If you don't have access to graphics software, you can create your own graphics by using graph paper, charting tape, and transfer rules for tables, and — for bar graphs — shading films, which come on adhesive sheets in a variety of patterns and colors. These materials are usually available in art supply stores.

Graphs

Graphs (sometimes called *charts*) have more pictorial appeal than tables. They frequently show movement — trends or cycles. The three main types are bar graphs, line graphs, and circle or pie graphs. If you have graphics software on your computer, you can easily convert nu-

FIGURE 7.2 Preparing a Table

Table 1. Classes of immunoglobulins

Antibody	Relative amount[a]	Function[b]
IgG	30,000	The most common antibody; serves as a memory antibody for previously encountered antigens
IgA	7,500	Localized to mucous membranes; serves as first line of defense against infection
IgM	2,500	First antibody secreted by maturing B-cells
IgD	100	Acts only as a receptor on B-cells
IgE	1	Responsible for allergic reactions

[a]Source: Adapted from Higgins.[17]
[b]Source: Adapted from Ballston.[21]

merical data to graph form. Usually, you enter your data in table form (see p. 195). Then, using the chart-making functions on your computer, you select the type of graph you want to create — bar, line, or pie chart. The computer will produce the graph and insert it where you want it to appear in your text. You can make bars or pie segments appear in contrasting shades (from white to gray to black) by selecting the appropriate functions. You can also choose different colors for the various elements of your graph if your software and printer allow you to produce color graphics. (Consult your software and printer manuals to find out about the design options that are available.)

Bar graphs enable readers to compare and understand figures quickly and easily. The bars can be vertical or horizontal. In general, vertical bars are used for altitudes and amounts, and horizontal bars for distances or trends, but you do not have to be overly concerned about which type to use as long as you label the items in your graph carefully. If you have graphics capability on your computer, be sure to use it. If not, here are a few guidelines for creating bar graphs.

- Use a scale that shows your data to their best advantage. You may have to experiment a little to find the best increments. Mark the intervals on graph paper, and then draw your bars.
- You do not need grid lines on the final graph unless the bars would be so far away from the figures that the amounts would be hard to determine. You need only tick lines on the side to indicate the amounts.
- Draw bars equidistant from each other, with the width of the spaces less than the width of the bars.

The graph shown in Figure 7.3 was made for a report on soil contamination. In the first two years of gathering samples, no dioxin (polluting substance) was found. Dioxin increased dramatically in the last year (1994). The patterns add interest to the graph and show the contrasts more clearly. This kind of graph is known as a *stacked-bar graph;* it shows cumulative changes over time. The columns in bar graphs can also be grouped to show comparisons (*multiple-bar graphs*). Multiple-bar graphs can compare groups of data (see Figure 7.4).

Line graphs show movement or change, usually over a period of time. The independent variable — the constant measurement or the x-axis, which in the graph in Figure 7.5 is the time interval — is placed horizontally along the base of the graph; and the dependent variable — the one subject to change or the y-axis — is placed vertically. If you are creating a line graph by hand, use points to mark the amounts; the line connecting these points draws the eye along, creating a visual sensation of movement. A line graph can contain one or more lines. If you use more than one line, you have to distinguish the lines by making them broken, dotted, colored, and so on.

Pie or *circle graphs* are useful if you want to show the relation of parts to a whole. The whole, or 100 percent, is represented by the pie, and each slice is a percentage of the whole. This graph is more limited than the bar graph because it is not effective with more than five or six divisions (you can, however, group several small parts in a single slice and

FIGURE 7.3 A Stacked-Bar Graph

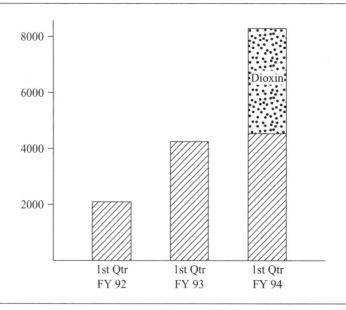

FIGURE 7.4 A Multiple-Bar Graph

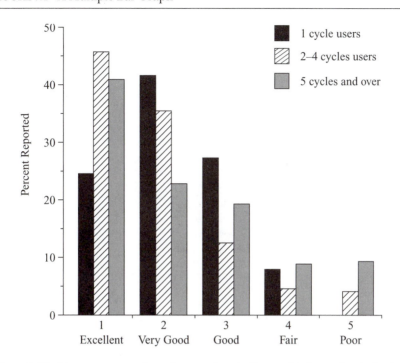

Figure 1. Health status perception of users of anabolic steroids by cycles (episodes). Heavier users (5+ cycles) more often perceive their health as being either excellent or poor. Data from Ysalis (1993, p. 93).

label it "other"). Figure 7.6 shows an example of a pie graph created on a computer.

To construct a pie graph by hand, you will need a compass to draw a circle and a protractor to divide the circumference into segments (3.6 degrees equal 1 percent). Begin at twelve o'clock with the largest segment and proceed around the circle clockwise in descending order of size. In your labels include percentages and, if desired, the absolute quantity.

Drawings and Diagrams

Even simple drawings can help explain complicated structures and movements. In a paper on the Viking spacecraft, Lee Atkinson included the drawing in Figure 7.7 to show how the moon's gravity was used to direct the spacecraft. The drawing illustrates the route of the spacecraft. First directed toward the moon, the spacecraft was drawn into its gravitational pull, which then directed the craft toward Mars.

FIGURE 7.5 A Line Graph

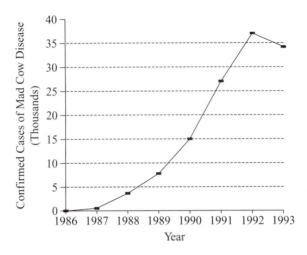

Figure 2. The growth of mad cow (prion) disease from 1986 to 1993. Data from Prusiner p. 54 [19].

FIGURE 7.6 Pie or Circle Graph

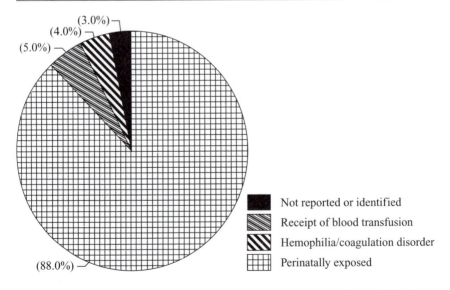

Figure 1. Means of HIV/AIDS transmission in cases reported as of June 1995. Data from Centers for Disease Control and Prevention p. 135 [3].

FIGURE 7.7 A Sample Drawing

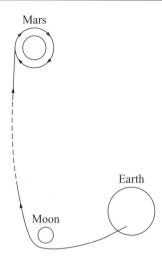

Figure 1. Path of the Viking Spacecraft.

Diagrams are more useful than photographs if you want to show only selected details. Peter DeGress drew the diagram shown in Figure 7.8 to demonstrate the placement of a collector in his design for a solar hot-water heating system.

A *flow chart* shows the stages of a process. You can use boxes to enclose the information for each stage, or you can use diagrams or drawings, as you might if you were to show the operation of a machine. The flow chart by Donna Ellis (Figure 7.9) shows the process of developing a telecommunications device, a process she discussed and evaluated in her paper. In making her report, she indicated the steps in the process, starting with "block diagram" and ending with "prototype testing and qualification." The percentages indicate how much time and money has been expended at each stage of the process. When you have completed the circuit design, you are halfway through the process. If you have graphics software on your computer, you may select "drawing" functions that allow you to create line drawings and geometric figures for flow charts and diagrams.

Making Your Illustrations Part of Your Text

Think of the illustrations in your paper not as elements you add as embellishments but as integral parts of your communication. Introduce and explain your illustrations in your text and then refer your readers to them by number.

FIGURE 7.8 A Sample Diagram

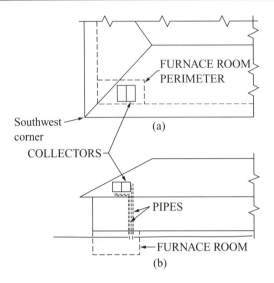

Figure 1. Top (a) and front (b) views of collector placement area.

FIGURE 7.9 A Flow Chart

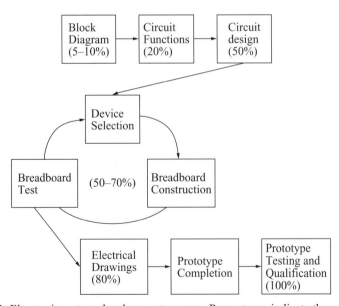

Figure 1. Electronic system development process. Percentages indicate the amount of development completed. Data from P. Korda, RCA Price Operations.

```
U.S. cotton production over the last forty-five years
shows a continuing shift to the West and Southwest, away
from the traditional cotton growing regions of the Delta
and the Southeast (see Figure 5).
```

Or make the reference a part of your sentence.

```
Table 4 shows the dramatic increase in exports of goods
from Japan.
```

If you have three or more illustrations and are using a format with a table of contents (see Chapter 9), you should have a separate page titled List of Illustrations in the front matter of your paper, following the table of contents. If all your illustrations are tables, you can title your page List of Tables; if all are figures, call it List of Figures.

Numbering and Titling Your Illustrations

Illustrations are conventionally classified as either tables or figures. Number each of these types in a separate series using arabic numerals (1, 2, 3, and so on). Tables are usually titled at the top. Figures, which include all other types of illustrations, are usually titled at the bottom. Give the type of illustration first, then the number and the title:

```
Figure 1. Effects of energy sources on muscle contraction.
```

The title should clearly describe the contents of your illustration. Without this guide your readers will have difficulty understanding what the purpose of the table or figure is. In a paper on evaluating computers, titling an illustration "Comparison of computers" tells readers little; but "Retail prices of eight popular personal computers" gives specific information.

Documenting the Sources of Your Illustrations

Documenting sources of illustrations is more complicated than documenting text sources because illustrations consist of both verbal and visual content. You might, for example, borrow the whole of an illustration or just a part; you might borrow statistics that you then arrange in graphic form; or you might use someone else's drawing but modify it in some way. Consistent and complete guidelines are not always provided in style manuals. The system suggested here is adapted for classroom use from the guidelines formulated by Mary C. Hester, Jacquelyn L. Monday, and John I. Snead in "Documenting Illustrations," *Journal of the Society for Technical Communication* (April 1989).

Placement and Format.   Give your source in parentheses after the title of your illustration. (Some writers prefer to give the source in a separate line below the title or at the bottom of the illustration.) Use the parenthetical documentation system you are using in the text of your paper, unless you are using the number system. If you are using the number system, give an abbreviated form of the source: author, and page number and, if your reference list is not in alphabetical order, give the source number in brackets so your readers can easily locate it:

```
(Data from Kirk, p. 32 [5])
```

Be sure to use the same placement and format throughout your paper.

Guidelines.   The following guidelines provide solutions to the six kinds of documentation needs you are likely to have when you include illustrations in your paper: (1) entirely original illustration, (2) original illustration with borrowed data, (3) photocopy, (4) modified photocopy, (5) copied drawing, and (6) altered drawing. APA documentation style (see Chapter 11) is used in the examples, but you should use the style you use in the rest of your document.

1. *Original illustration.* If the statistical or verbal information in your illustration is your own and you have created the illustration as well, you need not give any documentation. However, if you like, you can sign your work within the frame of the illustration, or you can credit yourself in the documentation by giving your name or just typing "by the author."

```
Figure 1. Diagram of pumping station (by Timothy McNair).
Figure 1. Diagram of pumping station (by the author).
```

2. *Original illustration with borrowed data.* If the data are from another source and you have created the visual framework, write "data from . . ." and give the source.

```
Figure 1. Results of treatment when patients control
their own medication for pain (data from Manson, 1988,
p. 24).
```

3. *Photocopy or computer scanning.* If you are using a photocopy or electronically scanned material without changes, write "reproduced from. . . ."

```
Figure 1. The structure of a retrovirus (reproduced from
Benson, 1993, p. 152).
```

4. *Modified photocopy or computer scanning.* If you use a photocopy or computer scanning from your source but modify it (if, for example, you photocopy or scan a map but add coloring or shading), write "adapted from...."

```
Figure 1. Map of North Carolina showing area of Tallulah
Falls formation (adapted from U.S. Geological Survey,
1992, p. 10).
```

5. *Hand-copied drawing.* If you have copied someone else's drawing by hand but have added nothing to it, write "redrawn from...."

```
Figure 1. Nonlinear optical loop mirror (redrawn from
Goodman, 1995, p. 74).
```

6. *Modified hand-copied drawing.* If you have hand-copied a drawing of someone else's and have altered it, write "redrawn and adapted from...."

```
Figure 1. Highest known superconducting temperatures and
the materials used, from 1911 to 1988 (redrawn and
adapted from Hanson, 1989, p. 21).
```

Several kinds of footnote symbols are commonly used in tables and graphs: superscript lowercase letters ([a, b]), superscript numerals ([1, 2]), and symbols such as asterisks and daggers. Most style manuals suggest that you use symbols for illustrative material that are different from the ones you use in your text to avoid confusion. Because any symbols you use in your text are likely to be superscript numerals, you would want to use one of the other systems for your table and figure footnotes. The *MLA Handbook* and APA *Manual* recommend superscript lowercase letters; scientific and technical papers show a variety of symbols.

EXERCISES

1. Choosing from the types of introductions given in this chapter, write two different introductions for your paper. Then select the one you like best. Be prepared to explain your choice to your classmates.

2. Write a profile of the person you see as the typical reader of your paper. It should be about a page long and include descriptions of his or her interests, level of education, knowledge of your paper's subject, and any other pertinent information.

3. Make a table from the following information:

> Maxim Junior College students came last year from three states. But the proportions in the two classes differed. Of first-year students, 28 percent came from North Dakota, 25 percent from South Dakota, and 47 percent from Minnesota. Of second-year students, 17 percent

came from North Dakota, 16 percent from South Dakota, and 67 percent from Minnesota.

4. Construct a multiple-bar graph from the information in Exercise 3.

5. Construct a circle graph from the information in Exercise 3.

6. Using the information you have collected for your research paper, design an illustration that will explain data more clearly than words do. Look for quantifiable data to make tables and graphs. Look for images that might form the basis of drawings or designs.

7. **FOR THE COMPUTERIZED CLASSROOM** Send your classmates your thesis or summary statement by e-mail. Include a list of three possible titles for your paper. Ask for reactions and alternative suggestions. If your class is large, form groups of five and exchange this information.

Revising

I can't write five words but that I change seven.   — Dorothy Parker

I never reread a text until I have finished the first draft. Otherwise it's too discouraging. Also, when you have the whole thing in front of you for the first time, you've forgotten most of it and see it fresh.

— Gore Vidal, novelist

I write my first version in longhand (pencil). Then I do a complete revision, also in longhand. . . . Then I type a third draft on yellow paper. . . . Well, when the yellow draft is finished, I put the manuscript away for a while, a week, a month, sometimes longer. When I take it out again, I read it as coldly as possible, then read it aloud to a friend or two, and decide what changes I want to make and whether or not I want to publish it.   — Truman Capote, novelist and nonfiction writer

I find it easier to discover mistakes or lack of smoothness when I read my paper aloud to myself. That's why I prefer to write and revise my papers when I am all alone. At times I like to read my papers to other people, so I can get an objective opinion about what I have written. It's sometimes easier for another person to hear something wrong than it is for me. I make notes of changes on a hard copy. There I rewrite on the computer.

— Wendy Cohen, student

Revising is a natural and necessary part of the writing process; it is not something that you have to do because you failed to do the first draft properly. It means revisualizing or reseeing your material. Although the amount of change necessary varies from writer to writer and depends on the nature of the project, sometimes extensive changes are necessary. Figure 8.1, a page from Wendy Cohen's first draft, shows part of her revising process. She changed the order, combined and

FIGURE 8.1 Revising the First Draft

combine with first paragraph on next page

Nearly 600,000 of the nearly 1,000,000 teenage females who become pregnant each year elect to complete their pregnancies. /Teenage pregnancy ~~is on the uprise~~ *has been on the rise* since the 1960s and currently ~~results~~ *occurs* in 1/10 of the entire populat~~p~~i*er*on of teen women each year. ~~These women are at high^er risk of death because of their pregnancy and its complications than women between 20-35.~~ Adole~~x~~*s*cents ~~under the age of 14~~ *15 and older* are in danger from complications related to pregnancy ~~and its complications~~ *and at higher risk of death* than women between *the ages of* 20 ~~35~~ *and*. ~~Women between 15 and 19 die 35 percent more frequently than mothers in their early twenties because of complications.~~ *Pregnant* Teenage women ~~who undergo pregnancy~~ *also* deliver low weight babies twice as often as women in their twenties, and ~~experience infant death~~ *their babies die* nearly twice as often as *babies of* mothers in their twenties.

reworded sentences, and added more material. Sometimes revising requires more changes; sometimes, fewer.

All writers develop their own strategies at each stage of the revising process. Students, like professional writers, need to find out what works best for them as well as what does not. "I've always done it this way" doesn't mean that "this way" is the best. Even though you want to produce the best possible paper, you also want to learn a process that you can use for any paper. Trading information on revising practices with your classmates is a good way to pick up ideas that you might want to try.

Preparing to Revise

As you already know from revising short papers, revising can mean that an idea that was only partially developed in an early draft becomes clear; it can mean that new ways of thinking about your subject occur to you; it can mean that you refocus your topic. If you have allowed yourself an incubation period (as suggested in Chapter 7), your mind has unconsciously been at work on your paper. Revising, then, is not so much a matter of correcting what you have already written as it is a second stage of the writing process.

Revising on Paper

If you leave wide margins and keep two or three spaces between the lines, you will be able to rearrange words and sentences easily. If you want to add a whole paragraph, or even a whole page, you can put it after the appropriate page and number it by adding a letter to the page number; for example, the page after page 2 would be page 2a. Make a note on your manuscript to show where page 2a is to be added when you recopy. Or if you want to take a paragraph out and insert it somewhere else, you can cut it out and place it where you want it, using transparent tape or staples.

Revising with a Computer

Revising, or any stage of writing, is physically easier with the use of a computer. You can move parts of a manuscript from one place to another or omit them altogether by pressing a few keys or dragging and clicking a mouse. Such physical ease also benefits writers psychologically; all of us tend to do more of whatever is easier to do. In the revising process, computers are most helpful with the later stages of editing. Software is available to check spelling and definitions, to count the number of words in your sentences, and to point out such structures as passive verbs and trite phrases; but only you can decide whether the changes are necessary.

When planning your revision with a computer, print a copy of your paper before you start so that you can see more of your manuscript at one time. (Many writers believe that it is easier to notice errors in hard copies than in text displayed on a screen.) You can also make notes on your hard copy, or you can even cut and rearrange parts as you would with hand- or typewritten copy before you begin revising the file on your disk.

Following a Plan

Because you are re-viewing your entire paper, it's a good idea to make a plan for revision that focuses first on large elements — the paper's faithfulness to its purpose and to its organization — and then on smaller parts of the paper — paragraphs, sentences, individual words, and documentation. Too much early concern with the structure of sentences and the choice of words can waste your time if the paragraphs containing them are eventually enlarged, shortened, or eliminated altogether.

First Revising Stage:
Focusing on the Whole Paper

Listening to Your Paper

If possible, read your paper twice — once aloud and once silently. If you've written your paper on a computer, work from a printed copy. The first time you read it (or have someone read it to you), assume the role of your audience. Read the title first, as though you were hearing it for the first time, and then read your paper straight through. Just listen to the sound of it and make mental notes of your reactions. You can make notes on paper, too, but don't be distracted right now with details. Do you have enough information? Do you have too much? Is the line of argument clear? Do you find yourself hesitating or stumbling over words or phrases? (These may be places that are difficult to understand.) Does the paper move clearly from one subject to the next and from one paragraph to the next, or do you find yourself trying to figure out your own meaning? Does the tone sound appropriate for the audience, and is it consistently maintained? After hearing your paper, make a note of any changes you might want to make or any places that seemed unclear. You may not want to make these changes, however, until you have completed the second, silent, reading of your paper.

Making an Outline

Now read your paper once more, this time with a pad of paper and pen or pencil in hand. If your computer has this capability, call up your paper in one part of your screen and, in another, open a new file for making an outline. First read your thesis statement or summary sentence so that you have it clearly in mind as you start. Then read one paragraph at a time, and in a few words summarize what each one says. (As an alternative, you can write a summary sentence of each paragraph.) When you finish you will have a rough outline, which you can check against your original outline to see whether it corresponds. Where you find discrepancies, you may be able to see the reasons immediately and make the necessary changes. But it's a good idea to consciously check your paper for each of the following characteristics of a good paper to make sure that your paper contains them.

Check Your Paper's Unity.   Your paper has unity when everything in it is included in your thesis or summary statement. It has unity when every idea in your outline fits within your thesis statement. If you find in your outline something outside the scope of your original concept, you will have to either broaden your topic or eliminate the idea that doesn't fit. If your summary statement is "Sex education programs in the schools have benefited teenage students," your outline should show only those benefits. However, if according to your outline, you have included some negative results and some needed improvements, you have more in your paper than you planned for. If you want to keep the negative results but show overall benefits, you should reword your summary statement to read: "Although sex education programs in the schools need some improvement, they have already resulted in important benefits to teenagers."

Check Your Paper's Organization. Make sure the order of your outline is logical. Try to identify the order: Have you used chronological order? Comparison and contrast? Order of importance? Order of size (large to small or small to large)? Or have you proceeded from problems to solutions? From causes to effects? From the general to the specific? Other kinds of order are possible, as well as combinations. After identifying the order you have used, make sure you have followed it throughout your paper. Also check the order of subheadings. If your summary sentence is "Although sex education in schools needs improvement, it has already resulted in substantial benefits for teenagers," you may have the following main headings:

Benefits of sex education in schools
    Reduction of the number of teenage pregnancies
    Other benefits
Some problems of sex education programs
Suggested reforms of current sex education programs

You have to decide whether this is the best order. You have three main topics: benefits, problems, and reforms. If benefits are most important, as indicated by the fact that you put them in your main clause in your summary statement, then you have a most-to-least-important organization. You also have chronological order: you start with current benefits, move to analysis of problems, and then suggest what can be done in the future.

Check Your Paper's Reasoning. Is your thesis clear? Does everything in your paper support your thesis or your claim? Test its logic by composing a syllogism that fits your argument, or analyze your paper according to the Toulmin model for analyzing arguments (see Chapter 6). Have you adequate grounds for your claim? What warrants do you base your grounds on? Are they shared by your readers? If you are arguing, as one student did, that "the courts have been inconsistent in their decisions on cases involving affirmative action," you would have to cite the court cases, and possibly the statistics on the number of such cases, to prove your statement. One of your warrants would be that affirmative action is a desirable goal.

Check Your Paper's Coherence. The links between points in your outline should be clear; the reader shouldn't be surprised when you shift to another subject. Such shifts or transitions are often prominently marked by the repetition of key words; by the use of transitional words such as *therefore, however, before,* and *for example;* or by the use of headings. Sometimes, however, transitions are more subtle; a time sequence, for example, may be enough to provide coherence between parts. Sometimes the visual break itself between sections or paragraphs is sufficient. If you add transitional words or phrases just because you think you should, rather than because logic or sense demands them, you may tell your readers what they already know. A common example is the use of *In conclusion* at the beginning of a concluding paragraph that obviously sums up what you have said. Putting yourself in the place of your readers will help you to discover where coherence is lacking.

First-Stage Revising Process: Student Examples

Wendy Cohen's Process: Limiting the Scope of the Paper. Wendy Cohen started with what seemed to be a manageable topic: the care of pregnant women. After doing some preliminary reading, she had five main headings to help her direct her research:

1. Misconceptions and myths about pregnancy
2. Day-to-day care
3. Common problems
4. Problems of high-risk pregnant women
5. Diseases of pregnancy

She read eagerly and extensively because she was very interested in her subject. When she reached her deadline for ending her search for information, she knew she had a lot of material, but she didn't realize how much until she began to write it down. When she finished, she had more than forty pages. Because she knew that revision in itself would be a sizable job, she decided that she could not meet her deadline unless she limited the scope of her paper.

First, Cohen made a detailed outline — a map to see where she was. Under "Day-to-day care" she listed "Nutrition, Effect of emotional health, Work, Sleep, Sex, Exercise, Clothing, and Travel." Under "Diseases of pregnancy," she listed "Rubella, Syphilis, Herpes, Gonorrhea, Rh disease, Diabetes, and Anemia." She seemed to be on her way to writing a book, but she didn't have time to write one. She had to leave out something, but she didn't know what. In fact, she didn't really want to leave out anything; she wanted all the work she had done to show up on the pages of her paper. But Cohen finally decided to be realistic and limit her paper to the parts of her subject that she was most interested in — that is, to the care of women who were most likely to have problems in pregnancy and the diseases that caused some of those problems. She excluded the first three headings in her first outline. This was the final outline of her paper:

I. The importance of the prenatal period to mother and child [the introduction]
II. The risks of teenage pregnancy
III. The risks of pregnancy for women over thirty-five years of age
IV. The dangers of disease during pregnancy
  A. Rubella
  B. Toxemia — preeclampsia
  C. Rh disease
  D. Venereal disease
V. Recommended uses of drugs and vaccines in high-risk pregnancies

Cohen was now ready to write a second draft based on this outline. Because she had done so much research on her subject and knew it so well, she was able to write her second draft easily and confidently. By revising each section as she went along, she was able to complete her paper in three complete drafts — the minimum number for most writers.

Jacinta Cepeda's Process: Shaping and Focusing the Paper. Jacinta Cepeda wrote a paper on the criminal justice system. Her summary sentence was "The criminal justice system — consisting of law enforcement, judicial process, and corrections — does not adequately control crime." This was her working outline:

I. Law enforcement
II. The judicial process
  A. Attorneys
  B. Courts
III. Corrections
IV. Evaluation

After completing the first draft of her paper, she reread it paragraph by paragraph and made the following informal outline:

I. The police department
  A. Lack of emphasis on law enforcement
  B. Lack of sufficient staff and budget
II. The adversary system
  A. Use of inexperienced public defenders
  B. The greed of private lawyers
III. The courts
  A. Delayed hearings
  B. Inequities in sentencing

C. Full dockets
D. Overuse of plea-bargaining
IV. Correctional systems
A. Overcrowded prisons
B. Lack of sufficient staffing
C. Lack of meaningful work
D. Denial of simple amenities in order to punish
V. Lack of help for victims
VI. Evaluation and solutions

With her new outline in hand, she checked her paper for the following characteristics.

Unity. Here she noticed a problem. Heading V, "Lack of help for victims," did not fit into her summary statement. Her concern for victims had developed as she wrote her paper. At the beginning she had written:

> According to James Campbell, criminal justice means "effectively controlling the increasing levels of deviant behavior in a manner consistent with our ideas of fair and humane treatment" (11). As a crime-controlling agent, our current criminal justice system does not work.

However, near the end of the paper she had written:

> Protection of victims should be a main concern of the justice system. Criminals have more rights than the victims. That is not justice! The offenders should pay restitution to the victims. The victims are the neglected ones, not the criminals.

Cepeda found that she had shifted the focus of her topic as she wrote — a common occurrence in writing a first draft. In the beginning she was writing about justice for criminals, and at the end she was writing about justice for victims. She had to decide whether she wanted to broaden the focus of her paper to include justice for both criminals and victims or to leave out an issue she felt strongly about — the rights of victims. Before making this decision, she thought she would wait until she had checked *all* four points.

Organization. Cepeda next checked the organization of her paper. It followed the chronological order of handling criminal cases — arrest, trial, and imprisonment. Each point she made fit into this order, except for one — "Overuse of plea-bargaining" under heading III. She began her discussion of plea-bargaining with this sentence: "The prosecuting and defense attorneys should not use plea-bargaining as freely as they do." She needed to move this idea to the section on the adversary system.

Reasoning. The issue of reasoning coincided with her unity problem. Her statement "Criminals have more rights than victims" was vehement and heartfelt, but she had given no evidence to prove it. In fact, she realized she would have trouble proving such a sweeping generalization. To add more details here would require more research and would change the whole focus of her paper; she would have to leave out much of what she had already written. Reluctantly, she decided to stay with the original design of her paper and leave out the section on lack of help for victims.

Coherence. Transitions occur between all elements of a paper — between sections, between paragraphs, and between sentences. Cepeda was looking now for transitions between sections. She had three major transition points: (a) between number I, "The police department," and number II, "The adversary system"; (b) between number II, "The adversary system," and number III, "The courts"; and (c) between number III, "The courts," and number IV, "Correctional systems." Major divisions of a paper are often like minipapers; hence, you can achieve a transitional effect by indicating the completion of the discussion of one subject and by using wording that looks forward to the next section or paragraph. Or the new section can look back by using a word or phrase that connects the two and shows their relationship.

Cepeda looked at her transitional sentences. This is the way sections II and III began (the transitional words are italicized):

> The adversary system *also* needs to be modified.

> The courts are *also* in need of radical changes.

In addition, she used the word *also* as a transitional word within sections: "The judges *also* create inequities within the court system." The transition to section IV had no transitional words at all:

> There are many faults with the current system of corrections.

She needed some variety in her transitional words as well as different language to show the relationships between these sections. She changed the transition between sections II and III to the following sentence:

> Although improvement in the adversary system would help to improve the justice system, changes in the courts are needed even more.

Then Cepeda rewrote the transition between sections III and IV (between the courts and correctional systems) in this way:

> If these suggestions were followed, the improvement within the judicial process would be noticed within a year.

Thus she ended the section on the judicial process with an evaluation and a recommendation. The beginning of the section on correctional systems looked back at the first two sections and then focused on its own theme — corrections:

> However, the problems within police departments and the judicial process seem relatively easy to solve when compared with the problems of changing the offenders.

She was now ready for the second stage of revising.

Second Revising Stage: Focusing on Parts of the Paper

Checking Paragraphs

Read each paragraph in your paper to make sure it is integrated, unified, complete, and coherent. The following examples show how students have rewritten paragraphs to improve them.

Improve Integration of Sources.   Whether you summarize, paraphrase, quote, or use your own ideas, your writing should flow as though it came from one source — you. Your writing will be integrated if you make the information you collect part of your thinking rather than just a transfer from cards or articles. Here is a passage from the first draft of a paper on alcoholism.

> Studies have shown that family behavior patterns are often important in the transmission of alcoholism from parent to child. Some of these patterns are parental conflict about drinking, parental disagreement about drinking practices, and parental abuse of alcohol (3, p. 42). Scientists have claimed that problem drinking among males can be predicted just by looking at their age, socioeconomic class, ethnic origin, and religious affiliation (4, p. 163).

In rereading his paper, the writer noticed that the sentence beginning "Scientists have claimed" moved away from the subject of family behavior patterns and even contradicted what he had written in the first two sentences about family patterns as a primary cause of alcoholism. He had gotten the information for the first two sentences from one source and the information for the last sentence from another, and he hadn't integrated them. He rewrote the paragraph to show the relationship between these ideas and to clarify them. He also combined the first two sentences, with this result:

> In transmitting alcoholism from parent to child, such familial behavior patterns as parental conflict about drinking, parental disagreement about drinking practices, and parental abuse of alcohol have been important (3, p. 42). However, some scientists believe that alcoholism is more of a social

phenomenon and claim to be able to predict problem drinking among males just by looking at their age, socioeconomic class, ethnic origin, and religious affiliation (4, p. 163).

Keep the Paragraph Unified. The writer of a paragraph makes a promise to readers to explain something. Usually this promise is made in the first sentence (often called a *topic sentence*). Readers expect that everything in the paragraph will help to carry out the promise so that the paragraph will be unified. When the writer fails, readers are disappointed and confused. The following paragraph makes a clear promise but doesn't keep it.

> The real task for society as a whole is to develop incentives that will be more attractive to teenagers than having babies. Many people feel that teaching their child to say no to sex is the solution to the problem, but it is not. Saying no is an important part of solving the problem but not the solution in itself. According to Noel, parents must help teenage girls develop more self-confidence and improve their ability to make their own decisions (92). If they learn these skills, they are not as likely to succumb to peer pressure, not only in sexual matters but in other areas of their lives. Dr. Marion Howard, director of a teen services program, recommends the following guidelines for parents (Noel 94):
>
> Learn to listen.
> Try to avoid judging the child.
> [Etc.]

This paragraph promises to talk about the responsibility of society in dealing with the problem of teenage pregnancy. But it shifts to the problem of peer pressure and suggests ways for parents to help their child make decisions. The subject of this paragraph is really how improvement in the relationship between parents and child can help the child withstand the peer pressure that leads to pregnancy. This writer rewrote the beginning of the paragraph to make the promise match the content.

> As part of the solution to the problem of teenage pregnancy, professionals have suggested educating the parents so that they can communicate better with their children (Noel 92). Many parents feel that teaching their child to say no to sex is the solution to the problem; but, although saying no is part of the solution, it is not the solution itself. According to Noel, parents must help teenage girls develop more self-confidence and improve their ability to make their own decisions (92). If they learn these skills, they are not as likely to succumb to peer pressure, not only in sexual matters but in other areas of their lives. Dr. Marion Howard, director of a teen services program, recommends the following guidelines for parents (Noel 94):
>
> Learn to listen.
> Try to avoid judging the child.
> [Etc.]

Now the paragraph is unified around the idea of what parents can do about this problem.

Sometimes the writer introduces an irrelevant idea into the middle of a paragraph.

> Since most of a prisoner's complaints are aired in prison disciplinary hearings, the organization of such hearings is interesting to examine. *In a correctional institution, administrators normally have several forms of enforcing discipline, such as the withdrawal of privileges afforded the average inmate. More severe discipline such as isolated confinement can be instituted for serious offenses.* In 1973 the Supreme Court determined that the state must provide twenty-four hours' written notice of charges, that prisoners have the right to call witnesses, and that an impartial body be chosen to consider the case. But prisoners are not allowed to cross-examine witnesses and there is no provision for legal counsel.

The italicized sentences introduce the idea of how administrators enforce discipline and do not belong in this paragraph, which is about the organization of disciplinary hearings. The reasons for calling such hearings should be discussed in an earlier paragraph.

Include Enough Information.   If a paragraph leaves unanswered questions in readers' minds, more information is probably needed. The first draft of a paper on subliminal advertising contained the following paragraph:

> As a result of Vance Packard's book *The Hidden Persuaders,* six state legislatures and the U.S. House of Representatives introduced legislation to ban subliminal techniques. In the 1960s, public discussion on the subject virtually disappeared; the proposed legislation was never enacted.

It was not the book but what Packard said in his book that led to the legislation. Readers are likely to wonder what that was. The writer rewrote the paragraph this way:

> As a result of Vance Packard's accusations in *The Hidden Persuaders* that advertisers practice the "psychoseduction" of consumers and "play on our subconscious," six state legislatures and the U.S. House of Representatives considered legislative action to ban subliminal techniques.

Make the Paragraph Coherent.   When a paragraph has coherence, each sentence fulfills the promise of the preceding sentence and in turn predicts what will follow. Thus each sentence is a link in the chain of sentences that forms the paragraph. This linkage allows readers to understand you easily and quickly. But when you set up readers' expectations and then don't fulfill them, the result is confusion. Readers may be able to sort out the order, but it will take some time. And they shouldn't have to do your job. A paragraph is like a conversation between the writer and readers, with the readers making mental responses or asking questions after each sentence and the writer setting up those responses or questions and then answering them.

In the following coherent paragraph, the reader's mental response is given in brackets so that you can see how each sentence satisfies the issue raised in the previous one:

> The main reason for the computer industry's vulnerability to security problems is that businesses do not want to spend money. [Reader: How does that encourage security problems?] The necessary precautions are not being taken for a system whose usefulness relies heavily on security. [Reader: What precautions are not taken?] Businesses must have auditing systems and effective user-identification methods to monitor and control who is using their system. [What else?] They must keep backup files to replace those that are erased and altered. [Anything else?] Finally, they must be willing to prosecute those who breach security, instead of refusing for fear of bad publicity. [The word *finally* signals the end of the paragraph.]

Because the expectation set up by each sentence is fulfilled by the succeeding sentence, readers can read the paragraph quickly, without confusion.

Checking Sentences and Words

Use Computer Editing Software.   A number of software packages are available to help you revise your paper. They can help you find such problems as overuse of linking verbs or passive voice, repetition of words or phrases, redundant expressions, and clichés. They can count the number of words in sentences; if you find too many short sentences or too many long ones, you can rewrite some of them. Computers can help you find errors in spelling, capitalization, and punctuation. You can also consult electronic dictionaries for meanings of words if you have the necessary software. But the computer has limitations; *you* have to decide whether to make any changes. Passive voice and linking verbs are frequently useful; and the computer can't distinguish words that are spelled correctly but are inappropriate in context such as *affect* for *effect* or *their* for *they're*. Still, editing software can be helpful.

Even if you don't use a computer, you should read your paper once again, focusing on the sound and meaning of the sentences. When a sentence seems unclear or when it does not flow easily and naturally, you may be able to see the problem immediately and correct it. But if you have trouble identifying the source of the difficulty, the following suggestions will help you improve your writing.

You'll notice that your sentences may need attention in more than one place because a breakdown in one place often causes breakdowns in others. A sentence with major problems needs more than the change of a word or two; it needs complete rewriting. Sometimes, too, your sentences may be free of errors but still need improvement.

The following suggestions show how you can improve the strength, unity, and coherence of your sentences by using strong verbs, by structuring your sentences for emphasis and clarity, and by eliminating unnecessary words.

Use Strong Verbs.   Writing conveys the energy of the writer, just as the voice conveys the energy of a speaker. And, just as you find your mind wandering from the words of a speaker who is dull or monotonous, you soon lose interest in reading sentences that lack vitality and strength.

Verbs generate energy for your sentences and give your sentences the life that keeps your readers reading. If you use too many weak verbs, such as verbs in the passive voice *(was written)* or linking verbs (forms of the verb *to be* such as *is, are, was,* and *were*), you make your writing lifeless and dull. You can use editing software to find such verbs for you, but you still have to decide whether they are the best choices. In general, you should use the passive voice only when the receiver of the action is more important than the doer or when you don't know who the doer is. Linking verbs are useful, of course, but avoid overusing them. The following examples show problem sentences (with problem spots italicized) that students found in their papers, along with analyses and revised versions.

> **FIRST VERSION:**   A decision *was made* by the president to begin the bombing at once.
>
> **REVISION:**   The president decided to begin the bombing at once.

Was made is in the passive voice. The real action in the sentence has been weakened by putting it in the form of a noun — *decision.* To improve this sentence, the writer put the main action of the sentence into a verb form — *decide.*

> **FIRST VERSION:**   The adversary system *is in need* of improvement.
>
> **REVISION:**   The adversary system needs improvement.

The linking verb *is* undermines the vitality of this sentence. Using the noun *need* instead of the verb form further weakens the sentence.

Revise Sentences That Are Too Long.   The meaning of your sentences is conveyed partly by their structure. A sentence that is too long can become monotonous and fail to emphasize anything. But counting the number of words in a sentence won't tell you whether a sentence is too long. A sentence is too long when it lacks a central, emphatic idea or when the connections between words become so unclear that readers can't follow the meaning to the end.

One remedy for a long, unwieldy sentence is to divide it, as the following example shows.

FIRST VERSION: According to Alvin Bronstein, the executive director of the ACLU's National Prison Project, "prisons were instituted in a Jacksonian hope that human improvement was possible if a criminal's unfortunate upbringing could be overcome in an antiseptic and healthy setting," but obviously today's prisons do not meet such standards.

REVISION: According to Alvin Bronstein, the executive director of the ACLU's National Prison Project, "prisons were instituted in a Jacksonian hope that human improvement was possible if a criminal's unfortunate upbringing could be overcome in an antiseptic and healthy setting" (19). Obviously today's prisons do not meet such standards.

None of the ideas in the first version stands out. To emphasize the last part of the sentence, the writer put it into a short simple sentence of its own. The contrast with the longer preceding sentence makes both sentences more effective.

Another remedy for a long sentence is to shorten it.

FIRST VERSION: Perhaps a reason for young immigrants from such nations as Poland and the former Soviet Union being perceived — and perhaps stereotyped — as the new "model minority" is that more and more of them are arriving in America and earning prizes and awards in U.S. academic institutions.

REVISION: As growing numbers of immigrants from Poland and the former Soviet Union earn academic prizes in U.S. schools, Eastern European students are increasingly becoming stereotyped as the new "model minority."

The revised version is tighter and it emphasizes the key information of the sentence — that Eastern Europeans are increasingly being perceived as the new "model minority."

Combine Short Sentences by Using Subordination. A short, simple sentence is emphatic; it highlights one idea. When you have too many short sentences together, you are telling your readers that all the ideas in them are of equal importance. You are failing to show readers the relative importance of ideas and the relationships between those ideas, thus leaving them to figure out the relationships on their own. In addition, groups of short sentences usually repeat the same pattern (subject, verb, object) and repeat words, especially pronouns. Although, with care, use of one or two short sentences can be effective, too many of them make your writing monotonous and lifeless. Signs of sentences that might be improved by combining are successive short sentences, sentences that repeat words, and sentences that begin with pronouns. Notice the repetition of the same word (or a pronoun that refers to that word) at the beginning of each of the following sentences.

FIRST VERSION: The first law was known as the "28-hour law." It protected livestock shipped by rail. It stated that cattle had to be exercised in pens if their journey was to be longer than twenty-eight hours.

REVISION: The first law, passed in 1906 and known as the "28-hour law," protected livestock shipped by rail and required that cattle be exercised in pens if their trip was longer than 28 hours.

In the first version the word *law* and the pronoun *it* referring to *law* begin each sentence. In his revision the writer put the ideas he believed to be less important into subordinate (less important) structures. His revision is clearer and stronger.

Use Coordination to Show Equal Relationships.   Sometimes you want to show the equality of ideas: you want to coordinate rather than subordinate ideas. Joining two or three clauses of the same kind can be effective, as the following example illustrates.

FIRST VERSION: Many people believe that a child's sexual values develop slowly from observation, imitation, and guidance at home. Teaching sex education in school would only be a waste of time and money because attitudes, values, and outlooks are already established at home.

REVISION: Many people believe that a child's sexual values develop slowly from observation, imitation, and guidance at home and that teaching sex education in school would waste time and money.

In the first version, some of the ideas in the two sentences are almost the same, so some can be eliminated. Since it seems clear that the second sentence is also part of what "many people feel," the writer combined and coordinated them.

Use Parallelism for Emphasis.   Parallelism is a form of coordination that uses repetition of structures and words for emphasis. The writer sets up a pattern that gains its effectiveness from building to a climax, like Lincoln's conclusion to the Gettysburg Address: "that government of the people, by the people, and for the people, shall not perish from the earth." Here three prepositional phrases are linked, and the word *people* is repeated. In Julius Caesar's famous statement about conquering Gaul (France) — "I came, I saw, I conquered" — three short clauses beginning with *I* build from the simple "I came" to the strong "I conquered." Use parallelism to create such emphasis when you can.

Problems can arise when you set up the pattern and do not follow it through. You must continue with the structure you started with (such as prepositional phrase, subordinate clause, noun, or adjective), and you must repeat the word, when there is one, that signals the parallelism. These structures usually are joined with coordinating conjunctions such as *and* or *but*. The examples show how a sentence can be strengthened by parallelism and how to remedy faulty parallelism.

FIRST VERSION: In the remedial reading clinic he learned *how to* coordinate his eye movements, *how to* scan for information, and *how* frequent reviewing for key ideas helps.

REVISION: In the remedial reading clinic he learned how to coordinate his eye movements, how to scan for information, and how to review for key ideas.

In the first version, *how to* is repeated twice, and *how* is used once. The revision changes the final *how* clause to a clause beginning with *how to*.

FIRST VERSION: Other advantages of the aircraft include day or night operation in all types of weather, continued operation for eleven hours and twice as long if refueled in flight, and if systems malfunction, its computer switches all operations to backup computer circuits.

REVISION: In addition, the aircraft can operate day or night in all types of weather, can fly for eleven hours (twice as long if refueled in flight), and, if systems malfunction, can switch to backup computer circuits.

A long, complicated sentence like the first version needs the clarifying force of parallelism. First notice the use of a noun *(operation)* instead of a verb to carry the action in the first two elements and the use of a weak verb, *include*. In revising, the writer used strong verbs *(operate, fly, switch)*. This example lends itself to more than one solution; the writer's choice depends to a great extent on what comes before and after this sentence.

Eliminate Unnecessary Words. Make every word count. When you add unnecessary words, you make your readers, who have to read them and disregard them, do your work for you.

FIRST VERSION: This illustration shows the financial impact *with respect to* FY95 salaries.

REVISION: This illustration shows the financial impact *of* FY95 salaries.

With respect to is one of many phrases, such as *with regard to* and *at this point in time,* that can be shortened to one or two words.

Avoid Needless Repetition of Words. You can repeat words effectively for emphasis, but when you don't want to emphasize, the repetition is irritating. Needless repetition of words in successive sentences usually means that the sentences can be combined.

FIRST VERSION: They have fur that is a dense coat of underfur covered by longer guard hairs. This fur is shiny and varies in color from black to dark brown but may also have white-tipped hairs scattered throughout.

REVISION: Their dense, shiny coat of underfur, covered by longer guard hairs, varies from black to dark brown with scattered white-tipped hairs.

In the first version, the words *fur* and *is* are repeated, and the main verbs *(is)* are weak linking verbs. Note also the unneeded phrase *in color*. If you read these sentences aloud, you will hear their deadness. In her revision the writer located the subject of the sentences and the main action word and then built a sentence around them. The subject is *coat of underfur*, and the main action word is *varies*. These form the core of the revised sentence.

Avoid Using Jargon.   Jargon is the language of a particular group, usually a professional group. Doctors, lawyers, teachers, computer programmers, truck drivers, musicians, and baseball players all use jargon among themselves. Jargon is the shorthand that makes it possible for the members of these groups to communicate easily with each other. But jargon is also a way to show who belongs to the group and who doesn't. In the effort to prove membership, writers often use awkward constructions and unclear language. Overuse of the passive voice and linking verbs is common. Student writers can easily slip into using this jargon as they read the sources used in writing their papers. In your paper you should use specialized terms only when clarity demands that you do and not to show that you know the language of a certain group. Now is the time to change any jargon you have used to plain English, as the following example illustrates.

FIRST VERSION: Experiments similar to those performed on *nonhuman animals* have *yielded congruent* results with humans.

REVISION: Experiments similar to those performed on *nonhuman animals* have *shown the same* results with humans.

The writer simplified the phrase *yielded congruent*.

Correcting Faulty Connections

Just as sections of your paper and paragraphs must be coherent, the parts of a sentence must be clearly connected. Each word in a sentence must link up with some word or words so that the sentence will read smoothly and make sense. The basic linkage is between subject and predicate or verb. Secondary linkages are between nouns and verbs, adjectives and nouns, and pronouns and nouns. Making these links correctly helps your readers understand your sentences more easily.

Make Subjects and Verbs Agree in Number.   The subject determines whether a verb is singular or plural. Most writers don't have trouble when the subject and verb are next to each other *(Jack is my brother)*, but when the subject and verb are separated by a phrase or clause, it's easy to lose track.

FIRST VERSION: Many experts believe that specific *instructions* to prepare youngsters for the many responsibilities of marriage *is needed* now more than ever before.

REVISION: Many experts believe that specific *instructions* to prepare youngsters for the responsibilities of marriage *are needed* now more than ever before.

In the first version, the subject *instructions* is separated from the verb *is needed* by several words. Although the word *marriage* comes immediately before the verb, the writer had to find the real subject and make the verb agree with it.

Connect Participles with Nouns or Pronouns. Participles are verb forms used as adjectives and therefore must modify a noun. When the link between participle and noun is broken, a participle is said to be "dangling."

FIRST VERSION: After *studying* this definition, a *discrepancy* is immediately recognized.

REVISION: After *studying* this definition, *I* immediately recognized a problem.

When a participle (a verb form) appears in a phrase at the beginning of a sentence, readers expect it to modify or connect with the first noun in the main clause; that noun will explain who or what is doing the action. In the first version, *studying* is linked with *discrepancy,* a link that doesn't make sense. In the revision, the subject *I* links up with the participle *studying.* Note that the change results in another improvement: the verb becomes active *(recognized)* instead of passive *(is recognized).*

FIRST VERSION: So far, I am ahead of my research *deadline, making* the rest of my schedule relatively free of pressure.

REVISION: Because I am ahead of my research deadline, the rest of my schedule will be relatively free of pressure.

When the participial phrase comes at the end of a sentence, readers expect it to connect with the nearest noun. But in the first version, *making* seems to connect with the whole idea in the first clause. It's clearer to have a participle refer to a single word or to rewrite the sentence completely, as the writer did in the revision.

Make Pronouns Agree in Number with the Nouns They Refer To. Because a pronoun represents a noun, it should be the same number (and also the same gender, if that's relevant) as the noun it's representing. The following examples show lack of such agreement.

FIRST VERSION: A *child* needs to be educated beginning at birth; teaching should not have to be delayed until *they* enter school.

REVISION: *Children* need to be educated beginning at birth; teaching should not have to be delayed until *they* enter school.

In the first version, the pronoun *they* refers back to *child,* but *they* is plural and *child* is singular. Either the noun or the pronoun could have been changed, and the writer chose to make the noun plural.

FIRST VERSION: The serious *runner* may alter *his or her* lifestyle considerably because *he or she* begins to center *his or her* life on running. *One* must abstain from doing many things that *one* previously did.

REVISION: Serious *runners* may alter *their* lifestyles considerably because *they* begin to center *their* lives on running. *They* must abstain from doing many things *they* previously did.

His or her and *he or she* are used in the first version to avoid sexism, but the repetition becomes awkward. To avoid this awkwardness, the writer shifted to *one* in the second sentence. The best solution here is to use the plural for both noun and pronouns.

Make Pronoun Reference Clear.   Since pronouns are substitutes for nouns, readers must know which nouns the pronouns are replacing.

FIRST VERSION: Industrial recreation is a growing career opportunity. Because of *this,* I would like to learn more about *it.*

REVISION: Because *industrial recreation* offers many career opportunities, I would like to learn more about *it.*

In the first version, what does *this* refer to? What does *it* refer to? Industrial recreation? A career opportunity? Note that combining these sentences eliminates extra words and sharpens the meaning by subordinating the less important idea.

Maintaining Consistency

Keep the Same Perspective throughout a Sentence.   Avoid shifting the perspective of a sentence or group of sentences by changing the pronoun from first person (*I* or *we*) to second person (*you*) or to third person (*he, she,* or *it*) when referring to the same person or group.

FIRST VERSION: Many *people* lease cars because, compared to financing, the payments are much lower. The only drawback is that at the end of the leasing term *you* do not own the car.

REVISION: Many *people* lease cars because, compared to financing, the payments are much lower. The only drawback is that at the end of the leasing term *they* do not own the car.

The first version mixes a noun in the third person, *people,* with a pronoun in the second person, *you.* In the revision, both the noun and pronoun are in the third person.

Keep the Same Point of View throughout Your Paper.   Most research papers are written primarily in the third person. Although the use of the first person *(I)* is no longer forbidden, as it once was, you do not want to overwhelm your readers with constant use of *I* and especially with the overuse of *I feel* or *I think.* You also want to avoid using *we* as a polite form of *I.* But if you have conducted an experiment, for example, it is appropriate to use the first person in explaining it. James Watson and Francis Crick begin their article announcing their discovery of the structure of DNA with these words: "We wish to suggest a structure for the salt of deoxyribose nucleic acid (D.N.A.)." They continue to use *we* freely throughout the article.

If you are writing instructions, you should use the second person *(you).* Research papers are rarely how-to papers, but if you have written such a paper, make sure that you have not shifted from *you* to *one* or *they.*

Keep the Tense Consistent.   If you are talking about past events, use the past tense; if you are talking about the present, use the present tense. When you are referring to the contents of one of your written sources, use the present tense: "Young *concludes* that . . ." because what the writer has put into print still exists.

> **FIRST VERSION:**   The defendants *appealed* the decision, but the Court of Appeals *affirmed.* The Supreme Court, however, *reverses* the decision and *holds* that double-celling *does* not violate the Eighth Amendment.

> **REVISION:**   The defendants *appealed* the decision, but the Court of Appeals *affirmed.* The Supreme Court, however, *reversed* the decision and *held* that double-celling *does* not violate the Eighth Amendment.

In the first version, the verbs in the first sentence are placed in the past tense, but the first two verbs in the second sentence shift to the present tense. The third verb, *does,* is correctly in the present tense because it expresses something that is still true. The revision puts all verbs except the last in the past tense.

Changing Incorrect or Confusing Punctuation

Punctuation is part of the structure and meaning of your sentences. Periods and question marks define sentences. Internal marks of punctuation such as commas and semicolons are crucial to the meaning and the sound within the sentence: they are not just decorative symbols. Try reading the following sentence using the marks of punctuation as sound clues. As you will gradually discover, the sound suggested by the punctuation doesn't fit the meaning.

> Although these definitions include groups such as the Hell's Angels, who operate nationwide, engage in illegal activities and use violence to enforce their rules; and other organized outlaw groups, this paper will deal with the best-known organized criminal group, the Mafia.

Punctuated this way it is clearer:

> Although these definitions include groups such as the Hell's Angels — an organization that operates nationwide, engages in illegal activities, and uses violence to enforce its rules — and other organized outlaw groups, this paper will deal only with the best-known organized criminal group: the Mafia.

Sometimes problems occur with a short sentence. Try to read this sentence aloud.

> His death was not the end however it was the beginning of a new medical era.

Now read these two versions of the sentence aloud to hear the difference.

> His death was not the end, however; it was the beginning of a new medical era.

> His death was not the end; however, it was the beginning of a new medical era.

(*Note:* The second version could be improved by dropping the *however.*) The meaning changes with the punctuation. If you don't let your readers know, they will have to punctuate the sentence themselves.

When you construct your sentences, use the marks of punctuation as carefully as you do your words. You will find detailed suggestions about punctuation in Chapter 9.

Focusing on Documentation

Check your documentation to make sure it is correct and complete. If you use the number system, you may have to renumber your parenthetical citations and the order of your references after you revise your paper. Detailed documentation conventions are given in Chapter 10 (author-page system), Chapter 11 (author-date system), and Chapter 12 (citation-sequence system).

EXERCISES

1. Find two examples of passive voice in your paper, and change the verbs to active voice. After observing the difference in effect, decide which voice you want to use.

2. Find two or three sentences in your paper that you think might sound better if they were combined. Decide first which idea is the most important. Then combine the sentences, putting the most important idea into the main clause and the other ideas into subordinate clauses or phrases. Assess the results, and decide whether you made the best decision.

3. Rewrite the same sentences you worked with in Exercise 2, putting another idea in the main clause. Decide which version is best.

4. Read the sample paper "Science and Museums versus Human Dignity: Problems in Implementing the Native American Graves Repatriation Act" in Chapter 10. Test its logic by putting the author's reasoning into syllogistic form. Are the premises true? Does the conclusion follow logically? Or analyze it according to the Toulmin model for analyzing an argument. (See Chapter 6 for a discussion of syllogisms and the Toulmin method.) Discuss the results with your classmates.

5. **FOR YOUR SEARCH LOG**   Record your revising process in your search log. Evaluate your process, and decide how you could make it more efficient.

6. **FOR PEER RESPONSE**   Form groups or three or four with your classmates, and read the first few pages of your paper to the other members of the group; or have another member of the group read from your paper to you. Read slowly. When you have finished, ask each member of the group to write a sentence summarizing what you have read. Read and compare the results, and then decide whether what you have said in your paper is clear.

7. **FOR PEER RESPONSE**   Find a classroom partner. Interview each other about your revising processes (see the excerpts by the professional and student writers at the beginning of this chapter). If you have time, discuss the whole writing process starting with the first draft. When you have finished, report your discoveries to the class. Then, as a group, evaluate the most common revising practices, and decide which ones might be improved.

8. **FOR THE COMPUTERIZED CLASSROOM**   Bring a disk containing your paper to the computer lab, and set up a network with a group of classmates. After you put the first pages of your papers on the network, read them and write online (or on paper) what you believe the thesis of each paper is. Members of the group then will learn how clear and focused their first page is. If there is time, repeat the exercise with the last page of each person's paper, and comment on the accuracy and effectiveness of each conclusion.

CHAPTER 9

Preparing Your Final Copy

After revising your first draft (following the suggestions in Chapter 8), you are now ready to complete your paper. Four steps remain:

1. Revising to correct spelling, grammar, and mechanics
2. Preparing preliminary elements (*front matter*)
3. Preparing supplemental elements (*back matter*)
4. Preparing and proofreading the final copy

Making Your Final Revision

After the extensive revision of your first draft, your copy may be so messy that you will have trouble reading it, especially if you have revised it by hand and haven't entered the changes into a computer. You will need a clean copy so that you can concentrate on details. First check your documentation to make sure you have the correct authors and page numbers. Then, with the help of the suggestions on the following pages, check spelling, grammar, and such mechanical elements as capitalization, abbreviations, and numbers.

Spelling and Usage

Spelling

Pay special attention to the correct spelling of homophones — words that sound the same but have different spellings and meanings (*their, there; led, lead; to, too, two; effect, affect*). Your computer's spellchecker is no help in finding misuses of such words. If you are a chronic misspeller, your task will be easier if you have a list of words you frequently misspell to guide you (if you don't have such a list now, think of keeping one in the future). Reading your paper aloud will also help you to find misspellings. Consult a computer or print dictionary for any spellings you are uncertain of. If you are tempted to think that spelling is not important because your readers can figure out what you mean, remember that your readers should not have to assume a responsibility that is yours. Besides, such careless errors will cause your readers to question your reliability in other parts of your paper.

Word Usage

Use words accurately and idiomatically. Select the right preposition; words such as *by, for, in,* and *on* can be troublesome because their meanings are not easily defined and because dialects vary in their use of these words. Eliminate unnecessary words: use *off,* not *off of; result,* not *end result; green,* not *green in color.* Avoid vague words: instead of "I was involved in developing a database . . . ," write "I developed . . ." or "I assisted in developing. . . ." When you aren't sure which word to use, consult a handbook or dictionary.

Mechanics

Abbreviations

The use of abbreviations varies according to the style you are using. Here are some general guidelines for use of abbreviations in your text. For illustrations of abbreviations with a specific style of documentation, see the sample paper in the chapter discussing the style you are using (Chapters 10, 11, 12).

Use abbreviations in the text of your paper in the following situations:

- When the abbreviation is commonly used as a word itself: A.D. *200* or AD *200* (anno Domini, in the year of the Lord, or since the beginning of the Christian era); *a.m., p.m.* or A.M., P.M. (*ante meridiem,* before noon; *post meridiem,* after noon); *IQ* (intelligence quotient); *UN* or *U.N.* (United Nations).
- After spelling out the complete term the first time it is used and giving the abbreviation. This convention applies especially to terms that may be frequently used in your text: *Rapid Deployment Force (RDF); Department of Transportation (DOT); miles per hour (mph).*
- For personal and professional titles: *George Brown, Ph.D.* (or *PhD*); *Mark Stevens, Jr.; Prof. Julia Lawson.*

- In technical or scientific writing for units of measurement when they are accompanied by numerical values (usually without punctuation): *20 mm* (millimeters), *50 l* (liters).

Note: A recent dictionary may list abbreviations in alphabetical order as it does words, or it may present a list of abbreviations in a separate section. Such a list will also indicate whether the abbreviation should contain periods.

Do not abbreviate the following elements in the text of your paper.

- Latin terms, except when they are used in parenthetical material: *for example,* not *e.g.; that is,* not *i.e.; and so forth,* not *etc.; versus* or *against,* not *vs.*
- Personal titles preceding the surname only: *Governor Glendening;* but *Gov. Parris Glendening.*
- Names of countries, states, counties, cities, and the like: *the United States; Annapolis, Maryland* (in addresses in correspondence use abbreviations).
- Geographical words such as *street, avenue, drive, road,* and the like (remember to capitalize them when they are part of a name): *Rodeo Drive, Lorcom Lane.*

Capitalization

When you capitalize a word, you give it special distinction. To preserve this distinction, capitalize as sparingly as possible. You already know that the first letter of a sentence is capitalized, including the first letter of a quotation that is a complete sentence. Listed here are other frequent instances of capitalization (but note that documentation systems often follow different capitalization conventions).

Capitalize the following elements in the text of your paper.

- The first, last, and all principal words of book titles. Do not capitalize articles (*a, an,* and *the*), prepositions (such as *in, by, of, before*), and coordinating conjunctions (such as *and, or, but, nor, for*), unless they are the first or last words of a title: "He was reading *Of Time and the River.*" Note that the divisions of a book or literary work are not always capitalized when referred to in the text: *preface, introduction, appendix, chapter 4, act 1, stanza 3.*
- Periodical, journal, and newspaper titles. Do not capitalize the introductory definite article: the *National Review,* the *New Yorker.*
- Most derivatives of proper names: *Freudian slip;* but *china doll, roman numerals.*
- Regions of the country: *Hemingway and Fitzgerald both grew up in the Middle West;* but not directions such as north, south, east, and west: *Americans went west in large numbers during the gold rush.*

- Titles preceding personal names: *Prof. Rosabeth March;* but not titles following names: *Rosabeth March, professor of history.*
- Titles of college courses: *He taught History of the American Revolution;* but not names of subjects unless they are proper nouns: *She changed her major from French to biology.*

Documentation

Check your parenthetical or endnote documentation carefully against your note cards or note files to make sure authors, titles, and page numbers are correct. Details about documentation are given in Chapters 10, 11, and 12.

Numbers

For the use of numbers in parenthetical citations, see Chapter 7. For the use of numbers in reference lists, see the chapter discussing the documentation system you are using (Chapter 10, 11, or 12); the list of references or works cited at the end of each sample paper illustrates the principles of that system. The conventions or style for numbers within the text varies from one discipline to another and even from one organization to another. Newspapers, businesses, and government agencies often have their own conventions. Conventions used by the three main academic divisions — humanities, social sciences, and applied sciences — are given here for the most common situations.

Numbers in the Humanities and Social Sciences. As a general rule, use words for whole numbers from one through nine and numerals for all other numbers (unless your instructor has another preference). However, when a number over nine occurs at the beginning of a sentence, spell out the number. If a sentence begins with a number requiring several words, it's best to recast the sentence:

FIRST VERSION: 1,039 new employees were hired during the past week.

REVISION: During the past week, 1,039 new employees were hired.

Use numerals for the following elements.

- Numbers over nine: *29, 138, 2,986.*
- Dates: *June 19, 1950.*
- Street addresses, decimals, fractions, percentages, and times of day: *312 Perkins Lane, $20.18, 3-1/2, 5%, 8 a.m.*
- A series of numbers: *8 days, 4 hours, and 30 minutes.*
- References to pages and other parts of literary works: *page 42, chapter 3, act 1, lines 295–98.*

Use a combination of words and numerals for the following.

- Large numbers: *3.2 billion.*
- Consecutive modifying numbers: *three 2-way radios.*

Note: A comma is usually placed in large figures after every third digit counting from the right: *2,098* and *3,229,894.* Exceptions are address numbers: *2100 Vacation Lane;* four-digit years: *1995;* and page numbers: *page 2389.*

Numbers in the Earth and Applied Sciences.   There is wide disparity in style and format among the sciences, partly because of the different kinds of measurements that are used in the various branches of science. The most commonly used conventions for numbers (given here) should be adequate for most college papers. If you wish to publish your paper, you should follow the style of the publication you plan to send your manuscript to.

As a general rule, use numerals for anything that can be counted or measured. However, use words when numbers begin sentences or when two separate numbers are adjacent in a sentence. Note the following distinctive uses of numbers in science papers.

- Numbers with four digits have no punctuation and no spaces: *3597.*
- Numbers over four digits contain a space between each group of three, beginning with the decimal point and going in either direction: *14 583.36* and *500 243 489.*
- A number preceding a unit of measurement is given in numerals: *3 mm.*
- Dates are written without punctuation: *9 June 1993; 12 May.* Months should be written out in the text, but in tables and graphs they should be abbreviated using the first three letters (*9 Jun 1993; 12 May*).
- Time is usually expressed in the twenty-four-hour system: *0830* and *2259.*
- Measurements are given in the metric system, and the decimal system is usually used instead of fractions (except in equations).

Punctuation

Punctuation is a matter of convention. If we are to talk to each other on paper, we must agree on what these marks mean or what sounds they create in pitch and rhythm. For example, if you know the different sounds created by the use of a comma and a semicolon, you will be able to hear the difference in meaning between the following sentences:

> I am not passing judgment on the conduct of the war, rather I wish to explain the reasons for continuing it.

> I am not passing judgment on the conduct of the war; rather I wish to explain the reasons for continuing it.

Notice that as you read the first sentence, your voice dropped only a little after *war* because you were expecting an added-on phrase, perhaps like the pattern in this sentence: "Let's go by train, rather than by plane." However, as you read the second sentence, your voice probably dropped more after *war*, and there was a greater pause because of the signal given by the semicolon; then you moved on to the second clause of the sentence. In contrast, the first sentence misled you. You may have had to read part of the second clause of the sentence before you realized that the comma did not signal the addition of a minor sentence structure, such as a phrase. If so, you had to quickly reread the sentence in order to understand it. Writers must follow the conventions of punctuation to avoid confusing readers.

The following guidelines are intended to help you understand how marks of punctuation are used to create sound and meaning. But because these guidelines are attempts to describe what experienced writers do most of the time, they cannot make allowances for all of the variations that are possible. Therefore, your ultimate objective should be to develop a sense of how marks of punctuation make your sentences sound, so that instead of consulting a rule when you punctuate, you can listen to the meaning the punctuation gives to your sentence.

Apostrophe.   Use an apostrophe

- To form the possessive: *the boat's rudder* (singular); *the boats' rudders* (plural); *Mr. Jones's house* (singular ending in *s*). *Note:* Do not use an apostrophe in the possessive pronouns *its, hers,* or *theirs: The house lost its roof in the storm.*
- To indicate omitted letters in a contraction: *can't, it's* (meaning *cannot* and *it is*). Be sure to place the apostrophe where the omission occurs. *Note:* An occasional contraction in a research paper can be the right word choice, but too many contractions detract from the serious tone that you want to maintain throughout your paper.

Brackets.   Use brackets

- To insert explanatory material or editorial comment into a quotation: *James Fenimore Cooper wrote, "The class to which he [the gentleman] belongs is the natural repository . . . of the principles of a country."*
- To enclose *sic,* a Latin word meaning *thus,* placed after an error in a quotation to indicate that the error was in the original: *He wrote that "Though President Crater [sic] is admired today, his administration was marred by numerous errors."*

Other uses of brackets with quotations are discussed in Chapter 7.

Colon.   Use a colon

- To introduce items in a series when the words introducing the series form a complete clause: *A business letter must have the following parts: return address, inside address, greeting, body, and complimentary close.*

Notice that the word before the colon (*parts*) identifies the kind of items that will be listed. Notice, too, that a significant pause follows the word just before the colon. If you incorrectly use a colon between a verb and its object or between a preposition and its object, you cause an unnecessary break in your sentence: *The courses offered in literature included: Eighteenth-Century Poets, Victorian Novel, and American Short Story.* A colon here causes an undesirable break between the two main parts of the sentence — the verb and its objects.

- To separate titles from subtitles: *Eight American Authors: A Review of Research and Criticism.*
- To separate two main clauses when the second explains the first: *I knew the man who answered the door: he was my father.*

For use of the colon with quotations, see Chapter 7.

Comma.   Insert a comma

- After a long introductory clause or phrase: *Because he has fought for a lost cause, he serves as a symbol for Adam's ancestors.*
- Before *and, but, or, for, nor, so,* and *yet* (coordinating conjunctions) when they connect two independent clauses (clauses that can stand alone as sentences): *Hospital costs have risen 170 percent, and physicians' fees have risen 60 percent.*
- Between coordinate adjectives: *The long, dry, dusty climb up the canyon wall exhausted the hikers.*
- After words introducing or following direct quotations: *"Most people favor presidential primaries," he reported.*

For use of the comma with quotations, see Chapter 7.

Use a pair of commas

- To separate clauses or phrases that are not essential to the meaning of the sentence (nonrestrictive elements): *The idea of property rights, especially the rights to possession of land, can be traced to Locke.* But do not use commas to set off elements of a sentence that are essential to its meaning (restrictive elements): *The two candidates who received the most votes ran in the run-off election.*
- To set off a contrasting phrase: *Carson City, not Reno, is the capital of Nevada.*

Dashes.   You can use dashes

- To indicate an interruption or a shift in direction at the end of a sentence: *The president restrained his anger until the end of the meeting — well, almost until the end.*
- In pairs to set off words and phrases from the rest of the sentence. Dashes differ from comma pairs and parentheses, which deemphasize what they enclose, by emphasizing the words they set off: *He had one reservation — and it was a big one — about the decisions they had to make.*

Note: When typing dashes, use two hyphens with no space before or after. You can create a real dash (called an em dash) if you are using a computer. (Refer to your software manual for instructions.)

Ellipsis Points.   Insert ellipsis points (spaced dots)

- To indicate an omission in a quotation: *Thoreau wrote in* Walden: *"It would be some advantage to live a primitive and frontier life . . . if only to learn what are the gross necessaries. . . ."* When words are omitted at the end of a sentence and the remaining words form a complete sentence, four dots are used — a period and the three ellipsis points. Unless confusion would result from not using them, ellipsis points are usually not needed when words are omitted at the beginning of a quotation or when the quoted words are clearly not a sentence: *John Kennedy called courage "that most admirable of human virtues."*

Other uses of ellipsis points are explained in Chapter 7.

Hyphen.   Insert a hyphen

- To divide a word at the end of a line. (Computers will divide words automatically.) Avoid breaking a word at all, if possible. When necessary, divide a word between syllables: *syl-lables.* Use your dictionary if you are in doubt. Do not leave one letter alone at the end of a line: *a-lone.* Do not leave only one or two letters to begin a new line: *lone-ly.*
- To join words: *self-evident.* Divide hyphenated words only at the hyphen: not *self-ev-ident.* It's not always easy to tell when a word should be written as a compound (*per-cent*), as one word (*percent*), or as two words (*per cent*) because some words that used to be two words are now hyphenated or written as one. (*Percent* is now the most common spelling.) Your dictionary can help you. However, you should join words with a hyphen in the following cases:
    1. When an adjective created by joining two or more words precedes the noun it modifies, as in the following examples: a noun and participle (*death-defying leap*); a phrase of three or more words (*a once-in-a-lifetime chance*). But do not hyphenate two modifiers when the first is an adverb ending in *-ly: a heavily wooded site.*
    2. When a noun is created from a verb and an adverb: *My car needs a tune-up.* Do not use a hyphen when a verb is followed by an adverb: *The mechanic agreed to tune up my car.*

Parentheses.   Use parentheses to separate less important information from the rest of the sentence so that the flow of the sentence is disrupted as little as possible, as in the following circumstances.

- When citing sources in your text: *(Adams 105).*
- When adding explanatory material: *He was elected president of the OAS (Organization of American States).*

- When enclosing figures or letters that introduce sequential elements: *Leasing a car has three advantages over buying: (1) you need only a small down payment; (2) you can buy the car at a depreciated price at the end of the leasing term; and (3) your insurance premiums are lower. Note:* This use of numbers to introduce the clauses signals their beginning and emphasizes them. But the numbers also interrupt the flow of the sentence, so use them sparingly.

Period.   Use a period

- At the end of a sentence that makes a statement. In a sentence ending with a quotation, even if it is only a single word, always place the period *before* the quotation marks: *He closed his concert with Beethoven's "Moonlight Sonata."*
- In most abbreviations: *Ms., p.m.* Omit periods in abbreviations of some organizations known better by their initials: *UN, IRS, NBC. Note:* Writers in earth and applied sciences do not usually use periods after abbreviations: *Mary Cole, PhD; 8 am; Prof John Sims.*
- After numbers or letters introducing items in a list when these are stacked, as in an outline:

  A. To benefit employees

     1. By improving mental health

Parentheses usually enclose numbers used to itemize elements within a sentence: *He made the following decisions: (1) to . . . and (2) to. . . .*

Question Mark.   Use a question mark

- After a direct question: *What causes soil erosion?* Do not use a question mark after an indirect question: *He wanted to find out what causes inflation.* Place the question mark within quotation marks when the quotation is a question: *I couldn't answer the question "Who wrote* Rabbit, Run *?"* Place the question mark outside the quotation marks when the whole sentence is a question: *When are you going to say "I quit"?*

Quotation Marks.   Use double quotation marks

- To enclose direct quotations: *"Who are you, anyway?" he demanded.*
- To enclose titles of short pieces (poems, short stories, articles, parts of books, short pieces of music, and speeches).

Use single quotation marks

- To enclose quoted words within another quotation: *The speaker began: "Ladies and gentlemen, let us recall Patrick Henry's words 'Give me liberty or give me death.'"*

Punctuation of quotations in the text of your paper is discussed fully in Chapter 7.

Semicolon.   Insert a semicolon

- Between two independent clauses not linked by a coordinating conjunction. Remember that *however* and *therefore* can't take the place of coordinating conjunctions; therefore (as in this sentence), a semicolon is needed when either introduces the second independent clause.
- When two independent clauses linked by a coordinating conjunction contain internal punctuation: *The politician of the earlier novels was controlled by the money of the businessman — he was a hireling; but here he has become a big businessman himself.*
- Between items in a series when there are commas within the terms: *The following cities recorded temperatures below zero for the period studied: Butte, Montana; Bismarck, North Dakota; Boise, Idaho; and Escanaba, Michigan.*

For use of the semicolon with quotations, see Chapter 7.

Slash (or Virgule).   Use the slash

- To indicate the end of a line of poetry when it is run in with the text: *Hamlet's speech beginning "O, that this too too sullied flesh would melt, / Thaw, and resolve itself into a dew!" is often cited as an indication of his despair.*
- To indicate a choice: *The best sellers in recent months have been in science fiction and/or romance.* The use of the slash in *and/or* can easily be overdone; usually you should use either *and* or *or.* Sometimes it is better to repeat *or: I may decide to major in science or math or both.*
- To separate the numerator from the denominator in a fraction: *2/3.*

Note: There is no space before or after the slash except when it is used to separate lines of poetry run in to your text.

Italics (Underlining).   Underlining in typewritten copy appears as italics in print. Because most computers now allow you to create italics, you may want to use italics instead of underlining in your papers. Use underlining instead of italics if you are working on a typewriter, if your paper will be typeset, or if this is your instructor's preference. Use italics or underlining

- To indicate titles of separate publications, such as books, plays, newspapers, pamphlets, and periodicals, as well as nonprint titles, such as the names of television and radio programs, records, films, musical compositions, paintings, sculpture, ships, and planes.
- To distinguish words being discussed from words that are part of the text: *He doesn't seem to know what <u>monophobia</u> means.*
- To show emphasis: *"I said I did <u>not</u> want to go."*

- To distinguish foreign words not yet anglicized: *He explained to the class the use of the <u>deus ex machina</u> in Greek and Roman plays.* Words that have been anglicized shouldn't be italicized or underlined: *The main item on the menu was quiche.* If you are in doubt, consult your dictionary.

Front Matter

Title Page

A short paper (up to ten pages) does not usually need a separate title page. If your paper is longer, if it is a technical report, if it has front matter, or if your instructor prefers, use a title page. It should contain, on separate lines, the title of your paper, your name, the instructor's name, the course title, and the date. Although you can use any attractive format, the most common and probably the easiest is centering these items beginning a little above the middle of the page. Only the first letter of each important word of the title should be capitalized; the words should not be underlined. If your title is long, use two lines and divide it where a pause seems natural (see the title page of the sample paper on page 276).

If you do not use a title page, leave a one-inch margin at the top of the first page and then place your name, the name of the professor, the course title, and the date in the upper left corner, using double-spacing. After another double-space, center the title; then double-space and begin your text (see the sample paper on page 298).

Abstract

Place your abstract on a separate page with the heading Abstract centered. Capitalize only the first letter of the heading (unless you are writing a technical report, in which case you would usually capitalize all letters). Double-space your abstract (see Chapter 7 for an explanation of writing an abstract).

Table of Contents

A table of contents (TOC) is often part of a technical report or a research paper prepared for education, business, or government organizations or for private research groups. Each audience may have different interests and needs. Employees or the public may want to learn what research has been done at an institution; managers may want a general view of the research on the subject presented in the report; experts may want to find out the details of a research project. The table of contents, which is really an outline in a different format, provides readers with a detailed summary of the report as well as page numbers, so that readers can locate specific subjects quickly and easily. The headings used in the TOC make reading and understanding the text of the report easier.

You can easily transfer the headings and subheadings of your outline to the TOC, although you don't need to include any subheadings below the third level. Every heading or subheading that you list in your TOC must appear word for word as in the report. The numbers or letters that you use with the headings in your outline are usually not included in the TOC; instead, typography or indenting indicates the different levels of headings. (For suggestions on typography in headings, see Chapter 11.) If you do include numbers and letters with the headings in the body of your paper, they should also appear in the TOC.

You can prepare the TOC after typing the final copy of your paper so that you can insert the correct page numbers. An alternative is to type it at the beginning and insert the page numbers later. (Note that the front matter can be numbered with lowercase roman numerals if you choose to do it this way. However, if you use the APA or social sciences style, front matter should be numbered with arabic numerals starting with the title page.)

Although the order, contents, and typography of a formal report can vary, the form for the table of contents described here will be acceptable in most cases. If possible, confirm this form with the person for whom you are writing the report.

See page 360 for an example of a table of contents in a research paper. (*Note:* If you do not include a TOC, your title page will be the first page and your abstract the second.)

List of Illustrations

If your paper includes both figures and tables (any graphic that is not a table is considered and labeled a figure), combine them in one list called List of Illustrations or simply Illustrations and subdivide that list into parts labeled Figures and Tables. If you have only one kind, title it accordingly — List of Figures or List of Tables. A list of three or fewer illustrations can be placed on the same page as the table of contents, just below the contents. If you have more, list them on a separate page following the TOC.

Outline

An introductory outline is optional. You do not need an outline if you have either an abstract or a table of contents. If your instructor wishes you to submit an outline, place the word Outline at the center of the page as your heading. (See Chapter 6 for guidelines for the spacing and punctuation of outlines.) The outline you prepared for your first revision (see Chapter 8) will probably need no changes; however, if you have made changes in the order or content of your text, adjust your outline to reflect them. Proofread it carefully to ensure that the headings are parallel and that the mechanics (capitalization, punctuation, and use of numbers and symbols) are correct.

Back Matter

Appendixes

The appendix or appendixes contain information that isn't necessary to the body of your paper and may be difficult to integrate into your text but that is important and helpful to your readers. Any of the following might appear in an appendix: sample questionnaires, maps, worksheets for feasibility studies, excerpts from documents, interview questions, correspondence, photocopies of documents, details of an experiment, lengthy tables or lists of statistics. An appendix is useless, however, unless readers know it's there; when you are discussing a point amplified in an appendix, refer to it: (*see appendix, p. 19*). Place the appendixes after the reference list. You may number them as a continuation of your text (with arabic numerals) or, if appendixes are the last section of your paper, you may use a separate numbering system consisting of capital letters to identify the main groups of information and arabic numerals to identify the separate items of those groups; for example, A1, A2 (for two questionnaires used) and B1, B2 (for statistics and calculations based on the questionnaires). Each appendix should also be titled. Peter DeGress included worksheets in the appendix of his feasibility study on solar heating (see Figure 9.1).

Content or Explanatory Notes

Writers who use in-text documentation rather than endnotes may still use content or explanatory notes to amplify or explain information they have given in the text. You can use content notes to cite further sources of information on a subject, to give details or statistics that may be interesting but are not essential to your paper, to explain procedures you have used, to acknowledge contrary evidence, or to mention the names of those persons or organizations that provided you with special help. Such notes should be used sparingly; if the information is not important enough to be included in your text, you may not need it at all.

If you use a content note, type a superscript number in the text ([1])

FIGURE 9.1   A Sample Appendix

Appendix 1.   Project Data Sheet.

WORKSHEET A — PROJECT DATA

PROJECT   *Drain Down DHW System*

Location *Washington, D.C.* Latitude	= *40°*

Building Heating and/or (Hot Water Load)

Design Heat Loss Rate, q_d	= *N/A* Btu/h
Winter Design Temperature (97-1/2%), t_w	= *N/A* °F
Average Hot Water Consumption (may vary on a monthly basis)	= *60* gal/day
Average Cold Water Supply (main) Temp., t_m	= *55* °F
Hot Water Supply Temp., t_s	= *140* °F

to refer readers to the note. (If you are using superscript numbers for citing sources, use superscript lowercase letters for content notes. In the list of notes place the corresponding letters on the line with the text.) Content notes may be positioned in any of the following places, depending on the citation style you are using.

- In the author-page and the citation-sequence styles, notes are placed on a page titled Notes, following the body of the manuscript.
- In the author-date style, notes are placed at the bottom of the page on which the superscript number is given (see the example in the sample paper on p. 331 in Chapter 11). If the paper is to be published, notes should be placed on a separate page entitled Footnotes following the references and appendices.

It's likely that any of these styles will be acceptable in a college class unless your instructor has an alternative preference. When placing notes on a separate page, center the title (Notes, Footnotes, or Endnotes) on the page following the text. Double-space before beginning the first note. Indent the number for each note five spaces, and raise it one half-space above the line. Double-space throughout — both within entries and between entries. A content note for the author-page and citation-sequence styles would look like this (for the author-date style, do not leave a space after the superscript number):

^{1} However, in his introduction to the American edition of <u>Fabian Essays</u>, Bellamy states that he favored not
only government ownership of the productive mechanism but
also equal distribution of the product.

Footnotes or Endnotes

Most writers find it easier to document their papers by putting brief citations in parentheses or by using superscript numbers within the text and a list of references at the end. Some writers, however, especially those in the humanities, prefer to use footnotes or endnotes either with or without a separate list of references. This system of documentation is explained in Appendix 2.

Glossary

If you are writing a technical or scientific paper for an audience that includes nonexperts, you will probably need a glossary — a list of technical or scientific words and their definitions. Two or three technical words can easily be defined within your paper by putting each definition in parentheses following the term. But too many of these will clutter your paper and can annoy those readers who are already familiar with the terms.

In compiling a glossary, you will have to assess carefully the knowledge of your audience to decide which words or terms to include. Then you will have to define those terms — that is, translate them into words that your audience will understand. The first time you use a word defined in your glossary, highlight it with italics or underlining, boldface type, or capital letters. Then refer your reader to the glossary in a footnote or in parentheses:

An asthmatic reaction always includes a <u>bronchospasm</u> in
the lower respiratory tract (underlined terms are defined
in the glossary).

Many glossaries consist entirely of nouns and their definitions, but glossaries may also contain verbs, adjectives, and adverbs. Each definition should be cast in the same part of speech as the word being defined. In other words, if the word being defined is a noun, the definition should begin with a noun giving the class to which the item belongs and a qualifying clause or phrase; if it is a verb, the definition should consist of an infinitive with possibly a modifying clause or phrase; if it is an adjective, it should be defined with an adjective or perhaps an adjectival phrase. The following examples illustrate incorrect and correct ways to define terms.

DEFINING A NOUN

Incorrect: software: computer programs. [Incomplete.]
Correct: software: programs used to direct the operation of computers.

DEFINING AN ADJECTIVE

Incorrect: panchromatic: imagery in all colors. [*Panchromatic* is an adjective; *imagery* is a noun.]
Correct: panchromatic: sensitive to light of all colors.

DEFINING A VERB

Incorrect: digitize: the process of converting measured data into digits readable by computer. [*Digitize* is a verb and *process* is a noun.]
Correct: digitize: to translate measured data into digits readable by a computer.

Definitions in a glossary can be brief because the reader has the advantage of seeing the word in context, which further defines it. Avoid using such unnecessary phrases as "a word that means" or "a term that is used to." Definitions in a glossary can also be complete sentences, but most consist of phrases. The two structures should not be mixed.

The glossary is usually placed before the list of references. Figure 9.2 shows an excerpt from a glossary for a report comparing two computer programs.

FIGURE 9.2 Excerpt from a Glossary

GLOSSARY

add-in board: an electronic component that provides additional functions to the computer system.

compiler: a computer program that converts programs written in a high-level language into a code that is understandable to a computer.

database: a comprehensive collection of related data organized for access electronically.

hard disk: a rigid disk coated with magnetic material on which information can be stored.

modem: an electronic device that makes it possible to transmit data to or from computers by telephone.

List of References

At the end of your paper, on a separate page, place the list of the sources you have cited. You can label this list Works Cited (used by writers following the author-page system) or References (used by those following either the author-year system or the citation-sequence system). These lists contain only the works cited in the text of your paper. An additional list titled Bibliography may include background sources or works recommended for further reading.

Your list of references should include all sources: books, articles, chapters of books, pamphlets, unpublished writing, and nonprint sources, such as radio and television programs, paintings, and computer databases. Chapter 10 explains the author-page reference system; Chapter 11, the author-date system; and Chapter 12, the citation-sequence system.

Preparing Your Final Copy

Your final copy will usually contain these elements in the following order. (Remember that your paper may not contain all of these and that some styles of documentation may recommend a different order of elements.) Consult your instructor for the elements needed in your paper.

Front matter (or preliminary elements)
  Title page (explained in this chapter, p. 240)
  Abstract (see Chapter 7, p. 194)
  Table of contents (explained in this chapter, p. 240)
  List of illustrations (explained in this chapter, p. 241)
  Outline (see Chapter 6, p. 152)
Text of your paper
Back matter (or supplementary elements)
  Content notes (explained in this chapter, p. 242)
  Endnotes (explained in Appendix 2, p. 244)
  Glossary (explained in this chapter, p. 244)
  List of references (see Chapter 10, 11, or 12 for the appropriate documentation style)
  Bibliography
  Acknowledgements. If you wish, you can mention sources of help or information you have received.
  Appendixes (explained in this chapter, p. 242)

A preface is usually unnecessary in a college paper. If you want to acknowledge special help, use a content note. If someone has provided you with information orally, use the proper citation format for your documentation style.

Computer Help

As you prepare your final copy, use your computer to help you complete the following formatting tasks.

- Number your pages.
- Insert a header in the upper right corner containing your last name or a shortened title and the page number.
- Set the margins you want, usually an inch on all four sides — 1½ inches on the left if you will be binding your paper. Also adjust the right margin so that it's justified or unjustified (ragged right). Most writers prefer a ragged right margin for this kind of document because it promotes easier reading and eliminates the awkward spacing of words that sometimes results with justified margins.
- Set the spacing to double-space.
- Set paragraph indentation to five spaces or one-half inch.
- Select a suitable type size. The best type size for a paper like this is 10- or 12-point.
- Select a suitable typeface. Avoid exotic typefaces such as those in outline or shadow, or any of the script typefaces. Choose one of the commonly used typefaces with serifs (small cross strokes at the top or bottom of the letters) such as Times New Roman or Schoolbook; these are easy for the eye to follow. However, if you want a cleaner, more high-tech or modern look, use a typeface without serifs (sans serif) such as Helvetica.

Software is available to format your notes, your parenthetical documentation, and your reference lists according to the documentation system you are using.

Materials

Use 8½-by-11-inch white paper of good quality. Use a laser printer for a professional-looking, easy-to-read manuscript. Print on only one side of the paper. If you type your paper, use a fresh ribbon.

Format

Margins vary according to the documentation format you are using. Please see details in the chapter illustrating your format — Chapter 10, 11, or 12. Double-space the text of your paper, including indented quotations. Indent the first line of each paragraph five spaces. Number pages consecutively throughout the paper, using arabic numerals without punctuation (use lowercase roman numerals for front matter). Place numbers in the upper right corner. (The number of the first page, however, may appear at the bottom of the page if you use citation-sequence system.) Page headings vary according to the documentation system you are using.

Proofreading and Duplicating

After your paper has been printed or typed, read it again. Read it aloud, if possible, to force yourself to slow down and recognize typographical and spelling errors. If you have lengthy tables or other groups of figures in your paper, try to find a friend to check your figures as you read them aloud. You might want to mark your changes on a hard copy first, then transfer the changes to your computer file. Make corrections on the typewriter by using correction tape or white correction fluid.

Be sure to make a photocopy of your paper for yourself before handing it in. You may be able to submit a good-quality photocopy of your paper, but check with your instructor before doing so. Also, don't forget to save a copy on your disk with both a hard copy and an on-disk copy so you will have extra insurance against loss.

Cover and Binding

Most short student papers need no special cover or binding. Adding a blank sheet of paper before the title page and after the final page helps keep your paper neat. You can secure the pages with a paper clip in the upper left corner. However, if you are writing a formal report or a long paper, you may want to use a cover. Use a lightweight cardboard cover that will lie flat when it's opened. Fasten a label on the cover on which you have typed your name and the title of your paper. Avoid plastic covers with removable spines; they often fall apart when opened.

EXERCISES

1. **FOR YOUR SEARCH LOG** As your last entry in your search log, record your final thoughts on this project. What have you learned about your subject that is important to you? What have you learned about the process of writing a paper that you will be able to use when you write future papers? What parts of your process will you repeat? How will you improve your process next time?

2. **FOR PEER RESPONSE** In this exercise you will proofread a classmate's finished paper. Proofreading is different from editing. When you proofread, you will look only for minor errors in spelling and typing and for small punctuation errors. If you are proofreading the day the paper is due, it is too late to make larger changes. For this exercise, exchange papers with the person next to you, or follow the directions of your instructor for redistributing papers.

FOR READERS   Use a pencil and write lightly so you do not mar the appearance of the paper.

a. Write your last name in the top right corner of the first page.

b. Read your classmate's paper carefully and slowly. Focus on individual words. Do not read primarily for meaning, as you normally do, because such reading causes you to read words in groups and to see the words and spelling that you expect to see. When you find an error or an omission, put a light pencil mark in the margin. *Do not make any changes in the paper.*

c. Confer with the writer and explain your findings. The writer may not agree with you. It is up to the writer to decide whether to make the changes you suggest.

FOR WRITERS

a. Note the comments of your reader and decide what changes you want to make.

b. If the paper is to be handed in during class, make changes neatly and only with dark ink. Write extra words above the line and use a caret (**∧**) to show where they should be inserted. Draw a line through words to be omitted. Insert the correct punctuation.

c. Erase your reader's pencil marks.

d. If there are too many errors, or if there are major errors, recopy your paper (with your instructor's permission).

PART III

Writing Papers across the Curriculum

DOCUMENTATION SYSTEMS

C H A P T E R   10

Writing a Paper
in the Humanities:
The Author-Page Style

The suggestions for format and documentation given here and in the sample papers that follow use the guidelines recommended in the *MLA Handbook for Writers of Research Papers* (4th ed., 1995). Parenthetical citations are given in the text of the papers, and a list of works cited is placed at the end.

Parts of the Manuscript

A paper in the humanities usually emphasizes the text of the paper itself. Therefore, most papers have only two parts: the text and the list of works cited. However, the following list shows the possible elements of such a paper. Your instructor will help you decide how many of these you need.

Title page (optional)
Outline (optional)
Text of paper
Content notes
Works cited

Format

Title Page

You do not need a title page with your paper unless you include an outline at the beginning of the paper. If you do use a title page, center the following information on the page, using a separate line for each element: the title of the paper, your name, instructor, course name, and date. Capitalize the first word, the last word, and all important words in your title. Do not underline, italicize, or use other punctuation marks unless your title contains a quotation or another title (1). Use a colon to separate the title from the subtitle (2).

(1)   Critics' Changing Views of <u>Troilus and Cressida</u>

(2)   "In the Beginning":

         A Discussion of Metaphors in the Creation Story

Use spacing between the elements on the title page to make the page attractive.

Margins and Spacing

Leave one-inch margins on all sides of the text, including the top and bottom. Indent paragraphs five spaces or one-half inch. Use double-spacing in the text; in all long quotations, which should be indented ten spaces or one inch from the left margin; and in all other parts of your paper including the outline, the works cited section, and notes, if you use them.

Page Numbers

Place page numbers half an inch from the top of the page and one inch from the right. Use arabic numerals without punctuation. Number all pages (except the title page if you include one) and place your last name before each number beginning with page 1 to identify your paper in case pages are separated. If you use a title page and outline, number the pages of the outline with small roman numerals, starting with page ii (the title page is counted as page i but is not numbered).

Headings

Papers in the humanities usually do not have headings within the text. You should have a heading at the beginning of each of these parts of your paper: the outline (if you have one), the text (which is headed by the title), notes, and works cited. Start each of these on a new page and center the title one inch from the top of the page. Capitalize the first letter of each word; do not underline or use other marks of punctuation.

Outline

If you include an outline, it should come after your title page. Center the heading Outline one inch below the top of the page. Double-space and begin your outline. (See Chapter 6 for the format of outlines.)

First Page

If your paper does not have a title page, place your name, instructor's name, course title, and date (double-spaced) in the upper left corner on the first page half an inch below your last name and the page number and one inch from the top. Double-space and center the title of your paper. Then double-space and begin your text.

If you are using a title page, you need repeat only the title of your paper on the first page of the text (see pp. 276, 279). Place it one inch below the top of the page (half an inch below your last name and the page number). Double-space and begin your text.

Content Notes

Content notes can be used in addition to parenthetical documentation to explain something not important enough to interrupt your text. You may not need to include them, but if you do, avoid lengthy discussions and limit them to brief explanations or bibliographic comments. Use the same format as for endnotes (see Chapter 9).

Documentation

Parenthetical Citation

Give the sources of your information in parentheses as close as possible to the material you are documenting — at a natural pause or at the end of a sentence. Your parenthetical citation must give enough information to identify a source in your list of works cited; it must also give the page number on which you found the information. The sample papers in this chapter show how these citations are used.

The following examples illustrate the most common types of parenthetical references.

ENTIRE WORK

You might refer in your text to a whole work; in that case you wouldn't need a parenthetical citation. Be sure to include the name of the author in your text also.

```
In The Politics of Non-Violent Action, Sharp outlines the
long history of successful nonviolent struggle.
```

WORK BY ONE AUTHOR

If you use the author's name as part of your sentence, put only the page number in parentheses.

```
Wyman mentions that German miners in the sixteenth cen-
tury used dowsing to find silver, copper, and lead (47).
```

If you give neither the name nor the page number in the sentence, then you must give both in parentheses with no punctuation between them.

```
German miners in the sixteenth century used dowsing to
find silver, copper, and lead (Wyman 47).
```

Follow the same format for citing the work of an editor, a translator, or compiler. Do not include abbreviations indicating the role of a person: *Smith, ed.* This role will be identified in the list of works cited.

TWO OR MORE WORKS BY THE SAME AUTHOR

If you have included more than one work by an author in your list of works cited, you must include a brief title in your text or in your parenthetical citation.

```
In fact, Adams admitted that he unwittingly benefited
from corrupt political practices (Education 49).
```

The complete title of the book cited is *The Education of Henry Adams.* Note that there is no punctuation between the title and the page number.

If you name both the author and the work in your text, you need only the page number in parentheses.

```
In fact, Adams admitted in his Education that he unwit-
tingly benefited from corrupt political practices (49).
```

If you name neither the author nor the title in the text, include both in the parenthetical citation. Note that a comma separates the author from the title.

```
He unwittingly benefited from corrupt political practices
(Adams, Education 49).
```

WORK BY TWO OR THREE AUTHORS

If your source has two or three authors, cite all of them either in your text or in parentheses, as you would a single author.

```
As Friedman and McLaughlin point out, a poem is "a mirror
of the conventions . . . of the period in which it was
written" (3).
```

```
A poem is "a mirror of the conventions . . . of the
period in which it was written" (Friedman and McLaugh-
lin 3).
```

WORK BY MORE THAN THREE AUTHORS

If your source has more than three authors, give the name of the first author listed in Works Cited, followed by *et al.,* the Latin abbreviation for *et alii,* meaning "and others." There is no punctuation between the name of the first author and the abbreviation.

```
According to Spiller et al., America was the embodiment
of a long-held European dream (192).
```

```
America was the embodiment of a long-held European dream
(Spiller et al. 192).
```

If you prefer, you may give the last names of all authors.

CORPORATE AUTHOR

Give the name of a corporate author (government agency, association, or research organization) in the text or in a parenthetical reference, as you would with a personal author. If the group is known by its abbreviation, give the abbreviation in parentheses with the first citation and then use just the abbreviation in all of the subsequent citations. For example:

```
In a recent study of freshman writing, the National Coun-
cil of Teachers of English (NCTE) found that students
think of revising as nothing more than correcting grammar
and punctuation (58).
```

The subsequent reference:

```
The study recommended that . . . (NCTE 92).
```

When the name of a corporate author is long, it is probably best to include it in the text rather than interrupt the text with a long parenthetical reference.

WORK WITHOUT AN AUTHOR

Give in your citation enough of the title to enable your readers to find it in your list of works cited; usually one, two, or three words are enough (including the first word or two of the title as it is listed in Works Cited). For a pamphlet entitled *Marriages of the Dead:*

```
The ceremonial life is not open to everyone (Marriages
71).
```

If you include the title in your sentence, put the page number in the parenthetical reference.

> In <u>Marriages of the Dead</u> the reader is warned that the
> ceremonial life is not open to everyone (71).

MULTIVOLUME WORK

In citing one volume of a multivolume work, use the following format. Note that the volume number is followed by a colon and then by the page number.

> Cardenal tells the group that "in the Old Testament the
> messianic era had often been described as an epoch of
> great abundance of wine" (1: 154).

If you include the author's name in the parenthetical reference, use the following format. Do not use a comma between the author and the volume number.

> "In the Old Testament the messianic era had often been
> described as an epoch of great abundance of wine" (Carde-
> nal 1: 154).

The next two examples show how to cite an entire volume. A comma separates the author's name from the abbreviation for volume.

> Volume 1 gradually introduces the Solentiname group
> through their interpretations of the stories (Cardenal).

> The Solentiname group is gradually introduced through
> their interpretations of the stories (Cardenal, vol. 1).

If you have included only one volume of a multivolume work in your list of works cited, you do not need the volume number in parenthetical citations.

INDIRECT SOURCE

It is best to cite the original source, but if that source is unavailable to you, use the abbreviation *qtd. in* for "quoted in" to indicate that you have used an indirect source for the information.

> Dodd ascertained that in 1814 "there were 1,733 croppers
> in Leeds, all in full employment" (qtd. in Thompson 551).

You can include a content note giving the full publication information for the original source, as cited in the indirect source.

TWO OR MORE WORKS BY DIFFERENT AUTHORS IN THE SAME CITATION

When citing two or more authors within the same parentheses, cite each author as you normally would but separate the citations with semi-colons.

```
It was generally believed that the soldiers acted under a
solemn oath and that disobedience to the general's orders
was punished with death (Carroll 67-70; Lee and Hammonds
261-65).
```

If the citation is long, it is better not to put it in parentheses. Instead, include it in the text or put the whole reference in a content note.

Literary Works. For literary prose works that are published in different editions, give the page number first, followed by a semicolon, and then include other identifying information such as book or chapter (328; bk. 3). For classic poems and plays, omit the page number and include the act, scene, or line in the parenthetical reference. This information will enable readers to find the material in different editions.

When you use the title of a literary work several times in your text, write it out the first time and give its abbreviation in parentheses. You can use the abbreviation you find in your source or create your own from the first letters of the main words: *The Winter's Tale* (WT).

NOVEL OR OTHER LONG PROSE WORK

In parentheses give the page number, followed by a semicolon, and then the additional information, abbreviated.

```
In Babbitt, Sinclair Lewis portrays a businessman who was
"no more conscious of his children than of the buttons on
his coat-sleeves" (227; ch. 18).
```

VERSE PLAY

Omit page numbers; instead, include the act, scene, and line numbers, with the divisions separated by periods. Use arabic numerals rather than roman numerals unless your instructor asks you to do otherwise.

```
In Hamlet's famous lines about acting, he says that the
purpose of playing is "to hold, as 'twere, the mirror up
to nature" (Hamlet 3.2.23).
```

Or you can include the title of the play in your text.

```
According to Shakespeare in Hamlet, the purpose of the
theater is "to hold, as 'twere, the mirror up to nature"
(3.2.23).
```

POETRY

Do not use the abbreviations *l.* or *ll.* for "lines" because these can be confused with numbers. Include identifying information (book, canto, or part) followed by the line numbers in a parenthetical citation.

```
Tennyson's In Memoriam reveals his cautious optimism: "I
can but trust that good shall fall / At last . . ."
(44.14-15).
```

If you are citing only lines, use the word *line* or *lines* in your first reference and in subsequent references cite the numbers only, as in these two examples from Edgar Allan Poe's "Annabel Lee." The first reference:

```
"That the wind came out of the cloud, chilling / And
killing my Annabel Lee" (lines 25-26).
```

The subsequent reference:

```
"In her tomb by the side of the sea" (41).
```

ONE-PAGE ARTICLES AND WORKS ARRANGED ALPHABETICALLY

In citing a one-page article from a periodical or an article from a work arranged alphabetically (an encyclopedia or a dictionary, for example), include the author's name in the text or in a parenthetical reference and omit the page number. If an encyclopedia or dictionary article is long, give the page number.

```
"Although folk belief accepts the skills of dowsers,
their successes in finding water are no more frequent
than those gained by other methods" (Middleton).
```

If the article is not signed, include a brief title in the text or in a parenthetical citation.

```
He was almost forty years old before his first volume of
poetry was published ("Frost").
```

List of Works Cited

The Works Cited page follows the content notes, if there are any. Center the heading one inch from the top of the page. Number the page consecutively with the other pages. Arrange the entries alphabetically according to the last name of the author or, if no author is given, by the first word in the title, except for *A, An,* or *The.* Use italics for titles. If your computer printer does not reproduce italic clearly, or if you are using a typewriter, underline titles. Arrange the information for each entry in this order (omitting items that do not apply): author's name, title of part of book, title of book, name of editor or translator, edition, number of volumes, series name, place of publication, name of publisher, and date of publication. This information is usually found on the title and copyright pages. If the publisher or publication date is not given, use the abbreviation *n.p.* or *n.d.* in its place.

Begin the first line of each entry at the left margin and indent all other lines five spaces. Double-space throughout — between items and between lines in each item.

Books. Here are examples of the most commonly used entries.

ONE AUTHOR

The last name of the author is first, with periods after the author's name, the title, and the date. The title is underlined. A colon follows the place of publication, and a comma is placed after the publisher.

```
Faulkner, William. A Fable. New York: Random, 1954.
```

Note the abbreviation of the publisher's name. Give only as much as is needed to identify the complete name.

TWO OR MORE BOOKS BY THE SAME AUTHOR

Put the titles in alphabetical order. For each work following the first, use three hyphens instead of the author's name.

```
McMillan, Terry. Disappearing Acts. New York: Pocket
     Books, 1989.

---. Waiting to Exhale. New York: Viking, 1992.
```

Note: If the author is one of several authors of a work, do not use three hyphens; use the whole name.

TWO AUTHORS

The last name of the first author is first; the second author's name is in regular order. Give the names in the order in which they appear on the title page.

```
Kaufer, David S., and Kathleen M. Carley. Communication
     at a Distance: The Influence of Print on Sociocul-
     tural Organization and Change. Hillsdale: Erlbaum,
     1993.
```

THREE AUTHORS

Engst, Adam C., Corwin S. Low, and William Dickson. <u>In-</u>
<u>ternet Explorer Kit for Macintosh</u>. Indianapolis:
Hayden, 1994.

MORE THAN THREE AUTHORS

Note the comma between the first author and the abbreviation *et al.*
because the order of the name has been reversed. (Also, note that *UP*
is an acceptable abbreviation for *University Press.*)

Flower, Linda, et al. <u>Reading to Write: Exploring a Cog-</u>
<u>nitive and Social Process</u>. New York: Oxford UP,
1990.

CORPORATE AUTHOR

Juran Institute. <u>Quality Improvement Pocketguide</u>. Wilton:
Juran, 1992.

GOVERNMENT PUBLICATIONS

When the name of the author is not known, give the government
agency as author. Then give the title of the publication, identifying information such as bill or document numbers, and publication information (place, publisher, and date).

United States. Cong. Senate. <u>Hearing Before the Committee</u>
<u>on Indian Affairs</u>. 103rd Cong., 1st sess. S. Hrg.
103-98. Washington: GPO, 1993.

This is a Senate document. Like most government documents, it was
published by the Government Printing Office (GPO). Other types of
congressional publications are House documents (H. Doc. 976), bills
(S 45; HR 52), resolutions (S. Res. 101; H. Res. 45), and reports
(S. Rept. 32; H. Rept. 3).

When the name of the author is known, follow the format for a book
or periodical (see "Periodicals," p. 267).

Hile, Joseph P. "Proposed Exemption of Required Label
Statements on Food Containers with Separate Lids."
Dept. of Health and Human Services. Food and Drug
Administration. 21 CFR Part 101. <u>Federal Register</u> 50
(249): 52937-38.

For references to the *Congressional Record,* you need only the abbreviated title of the publication, date, and page numbers.

Cong. Rec. 6 Dec. 1985: S17128.

Note: House and Senate sections are paged separately, so be sure to give the identifying letter (H or S).

TWO OR MORE PUBLICATIONS BY THE SAME GOVERNMENT AGENCY

For consecutive works by the same government agency, in entries following the first entry use three hyphens and a period in place of the government and agency names common to the initial entry. In the following example, the two sets of hyphens replace "United States" and "Cong."

United States. Cong. House. Subcommittee on General Oversight and Investigations of the Committee on Interior and Insular Affairs. The Destruction of
America's Architectural Heritage: Looting and Van-
dalism of Indian Archaeological Sites in the Four
Corners States of the Southwest. 100th Cong., 2nd
sess. Washington: GPO, 1988.

---.---. Senate. Select Committee on Indian Affairs.
Hearing on the Native American Museum Claims
Commission Act. 100th Cong., 2nd sess. Washington:
GPO, 1988.

Four sets of hyphens replace "United States," "Cong.," "House," and the name of the committee.

United States. Cong. House. Committee on Energy and Com-
merce. Subcommittee on Health and the Environment.
Acid Rain Control Proposals. 101st Cong., 1st sess.
Washington: GPO, 1989.

---.---.---.---. Subcommittee on Energy and Power. Acid
Rain Oversight. 100th Cong., 2nd sess. Washington:
GPO, 1989.

ANONYMOUS AUTHOR

When the author's name is not given on the title page, the entry begins with the title of the book.

Solid for Mulhooly. New York: Carleton, 1881.

PSEUDONYMOUS AUTHOR

The author's real name is placed in brackets.

```
Premchand [Dhanpat Rai]. The Gift of a Cow. Bloomington:
    Indiana UP, 1936.
```

EDITOR OF AN ANTHOLOGY

```
Logan, Shirley Wilson, ed. With Pen and Voice: A Critical
    Anthology of Nineteenth-Century African-American
    Women. Carbondale: Southern Illinois UP, 1995.
```

EDITOR

If the focus of your paper is on the work or its author, cite the author first.

```
Bishop, Elizabeth. The Collected Prose. Ed. Robert
    Giroux. Farrar, 1994.
```

If your paper emphasizes the editor or the edition used, cite the editor first.

```
Giroux, Robert, ed. The Collected Prose. By Elizabeth
    Bishop. Farrar, 1994.
```

TRANSLATOR

If the focus of your paper is on the work or its author, cite the author first.

```
Flaubert, Gustave. Madame Bovary. Trans. Paul de Man. New
    York: Norton, 1965.
```

If your paper emphasizes the translation used, cite the translator first.

```
de Man, Paul, trans. Madame Bovary. By Gustave Flaubert.
    New York: Norton, 1965.
```

WORK IN A SERIES

After the author and title of the individual work, include the series name and number, if any, and a period. Do not underline the name of the series or enclose it in quotation marks.

```
Meinert, Charles W. Time Shortened Degrees. ERIC/Higher
    Education Research Rept. 8. Washington: American
    Assn. for Higher Educ., 1974.
```

WORK IN SEVERAL VOLUMES

Use this format to cite one volume when each volume has a separate title:

```
Skidelsky, Robert. The Economist as Saviour 1920-1937.
     Vol. 2 of John Maynard Keynes: A Biography. New
     York: Viking, 1994. 2 vols.
```

Use this format if all volumes are listed under one title:

```
Morison, Samuel Eliot, and Henry Steele Commager. The
     Growth of the American Republic. 2 vols. New York:
     Oxford UP, 1941.
```

WORK IN A COLLECTION OF WRITINGS BY THE SAME AUTHOR

For an essay, short story, or poem, place the title of the work in quotation marks and include the page numbers on which it appears in the collection.

```
Orwell, George. "Shooting an Elephant." A Collection of
     Essays. Garden City: Anchor-Doubleday, 1954. 154-62.
```

WORK IN A COLLECTION OF WRITINGS BY DIFFERENT AUTHORS

Besides the title of the work and page numbers, also identify the collection's editor as given on the title page of the book.

```
Hearn, Lafcadio. "Mosquitoes." Mentor Book of Modern
     Asian Literature. Ed. Dorothy Blair Shimer. New
     York: NAL, 1969. 236-38.
```

For a novel or play, underline or italicize the title of the work.

```
Rizal, Jose. Noli me Tangere. Mentor Book of Modern Asian
     Literature. Ed. Dorothy Blair Shimer. New York: NAL,
     1969. 251-74.
```

In citing a work in a collection of previously published pieces, give the complete information for the original publication if you can and then add *Rpt. in* (for "reprinted in"), and give publication information for the collection.

```
Oates, Joyce Carol. "Where Are You Going, Where Have You
     Been?" The Wheel of Love. New York: Vanguard, 1970.
     Rpt. in The Story and Its Writer. 4th ed. Ed. Ann
     Charters. Boston: Bedford, 1995. 1009-21.
```

Cross-references: If you are citing two or more works from the same collection, you can list the entire collection in one entry and then list individual works by referring to the collection. Give the author and title of the piece, followed by the last name of the collection's editor and the page number of the individual piece.

```
Swansea, Charlene, and Barbara Campbell, eds. Love Sto-
    ries by New Women. Charlotte: Red Clay, 1978.
Thompson, Jean. "The People of Color." Swansea and Camp-
    bell 11-30.
Vreuls, Diane. "The Seller of Watches." Swansea and Camp-
    bell 141-49.
```

INTRODUCTION, PREFACE, FOREWORD, OR AFTERWORD

Use the format in the following example if you are citing only the introduction, preface, foreword, or afterword. If the author of that element is also the author of the book, give only the last name of the author after "By." If you are citing the whole book, use the regular author format and omit the citation for the introduction, preface, foreword, or afterword and the page numbers.

```
White, Edmund. Introduction. The Selected Writings of
    Jean Genet. Ed. White. New York: Ecco, 1993. vi-xvi.
```

REVISED EDITION

Use the designation given in the book on the title page or the copyright page: *Rev. ed., 1st ed., 1985 ed.*

```
Gibaldi, Joseph. MLA Handbook for Writers of Research Pa-
    pers. 4th ed. New York: MLA, 1995.
```

REPRINT OF OLDER EDITION

Give the date of the original edition before the publication information of the edition you're using.

```
Pater, Walter. Marius the Epicurean. 1885. London:
    Macmillan, 1927.
```

PUBLISHER'S IMPRINT

Give the name of the imprint followed by a hyphen and the name of the publisher.

```
Kostof, Spiro. The City Shaped: Urban Patterns and Mean-
    ings Through History. Boston: Bulfinch-Little,
    Brown, 1993.
```

THE BIBLE

No bibliographic listing is necessary if you use the King James version and if your reference is to chapters or verses in the Bible. Give the book, chapter, and verse citation parenthetically in your text: (John 5.3–6). Abbreviate parenthetical references to books of the Bible when they contain five or more letters (Gen. for Genesis, Chron. for Chronicles). Spell them in full in the text. If your reference is to commentary or notes in a particular edition of the King James version or to another translation, give bibliographic information as you would for any book. Use this format for other editions or other translations of the Bible.

The New English Bible. New York: Oxford UP, 1972.

Encyclopedias and Dictionaries.   For encyclopedias, dictionaries, and similar reference works that are regularly updated and reissued, you do not need to supply the editor, publisher, or place of publication. Give the author's name first if the article is signed. If only the author's initials are given, find the full name in the list of authors. Give the title of the article, the name of the reference work, and the edition. Volume and page numbers are unnecessary when the work is arranged alphabetically.

UNSIGNED ARTICLE

"Pornography." The New Encyclopaedia Britannica:

    Micropaedia. 1995 ed.

Note the British spelling of the title.

SIGNED ARTICLE

Bender, Paul. "Obscenity." Encyclopedia Americana.

    1996 ed.

Periodicals.   For all periodicals, you will need to supply the author's name, the title of the article, and the name of the publication. For professional journals you will also need the volume number (and sometimes the issue number), year of publication, and inclusive page numbers. For magazines, which are usually published weekly, biweekly, or monthly, you will need the complete date, instead of volume and issue numbers, as well as the page numbers.

ARTICLE IN JOURNAL WITH CONTINUOUS PAGINATION

Most professional journals use continuous pagination throughout the year. That is, the second and subsequent issues do not begin with page 1 but with the page number that follows the last page number of the previous issue. When issues are bound yearly, the continuous pagination provides easy reference. In your citation, give volume number, year, and inclusive page numbers.

> Wells, Susan. "Women Write Science: The Case of Hannah
> Longshore." <u>College English</u> 58 (1996): 176-91.

ARTICLE IN JOURNAL WITH SEPARATE PAGINATION

The issue number (7 in the example) appears after the volume number (42 in the example) so that the article can be located when the issues are bound. An alternative is to add the month or season in parentheses before the year: 42 (Sept. 1995). When a journal uses only an issue number, put the issue number in place of the volume number.

> Turner, John R. "Online Use Raises New Ethical Issues."
> <u>STC Intercom</u> 42.7 (Sept. 1995): 5.

SIGNED ARTICLE IN WEEKLY MAGAZINE

Give the complete date, beginning with the day, and abbreviate all months except May, June, and July.

> Brodkey, Harold. "This Wild Darkness: Personal History."
> <u>New Yorker</u> 5 Feb. 1996: 52-53.

SIGNED ARTICLE IN MONTHLY MAGAZINE

> Edelson, Mat. "Can the New Medicine Cure You?" <u>Washing-</u>
> <u>tonian</u> Feb. 1996: 69-76.

UNSIGNED ARTICLE IN MAGAZINE

Alphabetize according to the first word of the title, not including *A, An,* or *The.*

> "Smithsonian 25 Years." <u>Smithsonian</u> Apr. 1995: 28-40.

SIGNED, TITLED REVIEW

> Bernstein, Jeremy. "Eye on the Prize." Rev. of <u>A Mind Al-</u>
> <u>ways in Motion: The Autobiography of Emilio Segrè</u>,
> by Emilio Segrè. <u>New York Review of Books</u> 24 Mar.
> 1994: 19-22.

PUBLISHED INTERVIEW

> Sacks, Oliver. Interview. "The Man Who Mistook His Wife
> for a What?" <u>Psychology Today</u> May-June 1995: 29+.

Add the interviewer's name, if known ("Interview with . . ."). When pages are not consecutive in a newspaper or magazine article, give the first page number and a plus sign.

Newspaper Articles. For the author's name and article title, use the same format as for other periodicals. In giving the name of the newspaper, omit any introductory article. Then give the day, month, year, and page numbers, including the section number if each section starts with 1. If an edition appears on the masthead, show it before the page number.

SIGNED ARTICLE

Estrich, Susan. "When the Center Does Not Hold." <u>St.</u>
    <u>Louis Post Dispatch</u> 28 Jan. 1996: B3.

Note: The *New York Times* numbers its pages differently, depending on the day of the week. From Monday through Friday, it publishes articles in four separately numbered sections — *A, B, C,* and *D.* The following article appeared on Wednesday. If an edition is named on the masthead, add it after the date.

Van Natta, Don, Jr. "Judge Finds Wit Tested by Criti-
    cism." <u>New York Times</u> 7 Feb. 1996: B1.

All Sunday editions are divided into several separately numbered sections. In the works-cited list give the section number, followed by the page number.

Talbott, Strobe. "Terms of Engagement." <u>New York Times</u> 4
    Feb. 1996, sec. 4: 13.

In Saturday editions, the pages are numbered consecutively from the first page to the last.

Gilpin, Kenneth. "Mattel Ends Bid to Merge with Hasbro."
    <u>New York Times</u> 3 Feb. 1996: 35.

UNSIGNED ARTICLE

"High Stakes in Bridgeport: Two Proposals for Casinos."
    <u>New York Times</u> 25 Sept. 1995: B7.

SIGNED EDITORIAL

Fiedler, Tom. "Reflections on the Military, the Media."
    Editorial. <u>Miami Herald</u> 26 May 1996: 3L.

UNSIGNED EDITORIAL

"A Parent's Choice." Editorial. <u>Wall Street Journal</u> 1
    Feb. 1996: A18.

LETTER TO THE EDITOR

Tomazic, Stephanie. Letter. "Good Reasons to Leave the
    '50s in Mothballs." <u>Cleveland Plain Dealer</u>. 28 Jan.
    1996: 40.

Other Written Sources. Here are some examples of citations for
other written sources.

UNPUBLISHED DISSERTATION

Childress, Ronald. "Fear in the Art and Life of Henry
    James." Diss. U of Maryland, 1993.

For a published dissertation, use the same format as you would for a
book.

MANUSCRIPT OR TYPESCRIPT

The order should be author, description of material (or a title if it
has one), form of material (*ms.* for manuscript, *ts.* for typescript), identifying number and name of institution, if any, and location. This example cites privately owned and stored papers.

Ostby, Vivian. Journal, ms. Private papers. Arlington, VA.

PAMPHLET

<u>Literature and Drama</u>. Princeton: Films for the Humanities
    & Sciences, 1996.

PUBLISHED PROCEEDINGS OF A CONFERENCE

Hendler, James, ed. <u>Artificial Intelligence Planning Sys-</u>
    <u>tems</u>. Proc. of First International Conference, Amer-
    ican Association of Artificial Intelligence, June
    15-17, 1992, College Park, MD. San Mateo: Kaufmann,
    1992.

LEGAL DOCUMENT

Legal citations are varied. For documents not illustrated here, see *A
Uniform System of Citation* published by the Harvard Law Review Association (16th ed, 1996). In referring to the United States Code, give the

title number, US Code or USC, section number, and date. Alphabetize under "US Code."

```
29 US Code. Sec. 65. 1976.
```

For court cases, give the name of the case, volume, name and page of the report cited, name of the court that decided the case, and year. The following case, for example, was decided by the U.S. Court of Appeals for the District of Columbia in 1965. It can be found in volume 350 of the *Federal Reporter*, second series, page 445.

```
Williams v. Walker-Thomas Furniture Co. 350 F 2d 445. DC
     Cir. Ct. 1965.
```

PERSONAL LETTER OR E-MAIL

```
Earnest, Dorothy. Letter to the author. 21 July 1995.

Rubin, David. E-mail to the author. 5 Feb. 1996.
```

Nonprint Sources.   In your research some of your sources may not be in printed form. Here are examples of bibliographic entries for nonprint sources.

ART IN A MUSEUM

```
Bernini, Gianlorenzo. Neptune and Triton. Victoria and
     Albert Museum, London.
```

REPRODUCTION IN A BOOK OR PERIODICAL

Give the artist's name, title of the painting, the owner (institution or person), and the location, followed by publication information and page number.

```
Matisse, Henri. Les deux soeurs. The William D. Lippitt
     Memorial Collection. Denver Art Museum. Henri Ma-
     tisse: The Early Years in Nice 1916-1930. By Jack
     Cowart and Dominique Fourcade. New York: Abrams,
     1986. 74.
```

INTERVIEW

In person:

```
Van Valkenburgh, Willard. President, Federal Investment
     Co. Personal interview. 12 Oct. 1995.
```

By telephone:

```
Ebb, Carmel. Telephone interview. 2 July 1994.
```

FILM

For a film give the title, director, and any other information you wish to include, such as writer, producer, and performers. Conclude with the distributor and year.

```
Sense and Sensibility. Screenplay by Emma Thompson. Dir.
      Ang Lee. Perf. Thompson, Alan Rickman, Kate Winslet,
      and Hugh Grant. Sony, 1995.
```

If you are citing a person connected with the film, give that name first.

```
Thompson, Emma, screenwriter. Sense and Sensibility. Dir.
      Ang Lee. Perf. Thompson, Alan Rickman, Kate Winslet,
      and Hugh Grant. Sony, 1995.
```

LECTURE

At a professional conference:

```
Royster, Jacqueline Jones. "When the First Voice You Hear
      Is Not Your Own." Address. Opening General Sess.
      Conf. on Coll. Composition and Communication. Wash-
      ington. 23 Mar. 1995.
```

PERFORMANCE

For a play, opera, ballet, or concert, give the same information you would give for a film. Begin with the name of the performance or the person you are citing and conclude with the place and date of the performance.

```
Moon Over Buffalo. By Ken Ludwig. Dir. Tom Moore. Perf.
      Carol Burnett. Martin Beck Theater, New York. 1 Jan.
      1996.
```

MUSICAL PERFORMANCE

```
Ein Deutsches Requiem. By Johannes Brahms. Dir. René
      Clausen. Perf. Concordia College Alumni Choir.
      Carnegie Hall, New York. 30 May 1994.
```

If you wish to cite the composer or performance of a particular person, put his or her name first.

Brahms, Johannes. <u>Ein Deutsches Requiem</u>. Dir. René
  Clausen. Perf. Concordia College Alumni Choir.
  Carnegie Hall, New York. 30 May 1994.

DANCE PERFORMANCE

To cite the company, put its name first. To cite the music, put it first.

New York City Ballet. <u>Swan Lake</u>, <u>Firebird</u>, and <u>Afternoon</u>
  <u>of a Faun</u>. New York State Theatre, New York. 31 Jan.
  1996.
<u>Fancy Free</u>. By Leonard Bernstein. Chor. Jerome Robbins
  with John Gardner and Ricardo Bustamante. Cond. Jack
  Everly. American Ballet Theatre. John F. Kennedy
  Center for the Performing Arts, Washington. 27 Mar.
  1990.

If you are citing the choreographer or the performance of a particular person, begin with that person's name.

SOUND RECORDING

Give the name of the person you are citing; the title of the record, tape, or CD; artists if you wish; manufacturer; catalog number; and year of issue (if unknown, use *n.d.*). After the name of a cited orchestra conductor, give the name of the orchestra. In the following entry, the date of recording is given in addition to the much later date of issue.

Ellington, Duke, cond. Duke Ellington Orch. <u>Duke Elling-</u>
  <u>ton at Fargo, 1940</u>. Rec. 7 Nov. 1940. Book-of-the-
  Month Records, 30-5622-F, 1978.

TELEVISION OR RADIO PROGRAM

Give the title of the program, actors' or other pertinent names (if appropriate), network, local station and city, and broadcast date.

<u>Iwo Jima: Red Blood, Black Sand</u>. PBS. WETA, Washington.
  16 Feb. 1996.

VIDEOTAPE

Cite videocassettes, videodiscs, or filmstrips like films. Give the medium before the name of the distributor.

<u>Winds of Change: A Matter of Choice</u>. Speakers Hattie
    Kauffman and N. Scott Momaday. Wisconsin Public
    Television. Videocassette. PBS Video, 1990.

MUSICAL COMPOSITION

Give the composer's name, title (underlined only if identified by name,
such as the *Moonlight Sonata*) or form, number, key, and opus number.
Here the sonata cited is not identified by name, and it has no number.

Beethoven, Ludwig van. Violin sonata in A major, op. 12.

Electronic Sources.   When documenting electronic sources, provide
any information that would help readers find the original source. Because electronic sources may be updated periodically, you should usually include the date of access.

CD-ROMS

A CD-ROM may be issued once, like a book, or updated regularly.
When referring to a regularly updated CD-ROM, include the year (and
month, if available) of electronic publication, as in the following example. If the source originally appeared in print, include the publication date and inclusive pages.

Ephland, John. "What Is Swing?" <u>Down Beat</u> May 1995: 6.
    <u>InfoTrac: General Periodical Index</u>. CD-ROM. Informa-
    tion Access. June 1995.

Handle single-issue CD-ROMS like books.

<u>Street Atlas USA</u>. CD-ROM. Freeport: DeLorme Mapping, 1995.

ONLINE DATABASES

When citing online material, include the designation *online* and the
name of the computer service or network. If the material has a print
counterpart, include standard publication information for the print
source. This example shows an entry for a scholarly journal that numbers each issue from page 1: "24" is the volume number, "5" is the issue
number, and "5–11" are the page numbers. *BRS* is the computer service. Note that the entry concludes with the date of access.

Swanson, David B., et al. "Performance-based Assessment:
    Lessons from the Health Professions." <u>Educational
    Researcher</u> 24.5 (1995): 5-11. <u>ERIC</u>. Online. BRS. 12
    Apr. 1996.

If an online source doesn't have a print counterpart, include the author's name (if provided), title and date of the work, and name of the
database (underlined or italicized). You should also include the desig-

nation *online,* the name of the computer service or network, and date of retrieval.

If you retrieved a source through the Internet, specify this medium in your Works Cited entry. You may also include the electronic address of the source, as in the following example.

```
Montgomery, Lucy Maud. Anne of Green Gables. Online.
    Project Gutenberg. Internet. 4 Dec. 1994. Available
    FTP: uiarchive.cso.uiuc.edu/pub/etext/gutenberg/
    etext92/anne11.txt
```

POSTING TO AN ELECTRONIC BULLETIN BOARD OR NEWSGROUP

Use the designation *Online posting* and describe the forum, including, for instance, the name of the newsgroup. When documenting correspondence in the Usenet network, include the designation *Usenet.* Conclude the entry with the date on which you accessed the information.

```
Smito, Rich. "Re: Galaxy Formation Theories." 12 Nov.
    1995. Online posting. Newsgroup sci.astro. Usenet.
    20 Nov. 1995.
```

SOFTWARE

```
MAPEXPERT. Computer software. Microsoft, 1993. PC-DOS
    2.0, Windows, 386SX, CD-ROM.
```

Two Sample Research Papers Using the Author-Page Style

The author-page system of documentation used in the following two papers is recommended in the *MLA Handbook for Writers of Research Papers* (4th ed., 1995). This system is used by writers in literature and other disciplines in the humanities. In the author-page system, brief parenthetical citations in the text refer to a list of works cited, which is placed at the end of the paper. In the first paper, on the progress of a law requiring the return of Native American remains, the writer provides a title page because he includes a formal outline with the paper. In the second paper, a literary research paper on the feminism of Elizabeth Bishop, the text begins on page 1, following a brief heading and the title of the paper.

Notice that both of these papers make an argument — stated in the thesis — that is carefully structured and supported. Annotations of both of these papers point out their argumentative features. For more advice on developing arguments, see pp. 144–51.

If you are hand-ing in an outline with your paper, include a title page. Center the title of your paper (not underlined or enclosed in quota-tion marks) and type your name, your instructor's name, the course name, and the date below it. If you are not hand-ing in an outline, type all identifying information on the first page of the text. (See the sample paper on Elizabeth Bishop in this chapter.)

Science and Museums Versus Human Dignity:

Problems in Implementing

the Native American Graves Protection

and Repatriation Act of 1990

by

George Forte

Professor Eunice Miller

English 231

12 December 1996

Forte ii

Outline

Thesis: Native Americans, in efforts to return remains and artifacts to the appropriate tribes, have pushed for passage of the Native American Graves Protection and Repatriation Act of 1990. Although passage of this law was an important step in restoring justice, a number of obstacles--practical, financial, and political--have kept it from being carried out in full. However, museums must be more efficient in complying with its requirements. In addition, the government must provide adequate funding for the inventory and return of sacred objects.

I. History of disregard for Native American ancestral remains and sacred objects

   A. Exhuming of Native American graves and artifacts by archaeologists and anthropologists for study

   B. Display and selling of Native American religious objects and remains by private collectors

   C. Failure to apply laws prohibiting desecration of graves to those of Native Americans

   D. Tendency of other Americans to regard Native Americans as nonhuman

   E. Destruction of grave sites and destruction of remains and sacred objects

Outline follows title page and begins on p. ii (title page is counted but not numbered). Last name used before page number for identification.

Thesis states what the paper attempts to prove.

Topic outline shows structure of support for argument in thesis. You could also use a sentence outline.

Forte iii

II. Passage of the Native American Graves
Protection and Repatriation Act of
1990

III. Problems in implementing the law
A. Difficulty in making cultural iden-
tification
B. High cost to museums and Indian
tribes
C. Inadequate funding by Congress
D. Delay of museums and scientists in
complying with the law

IV. The future of NAGPRA

Forte 1

Science and Museums Versus Human Dignity:

Problems in Implementing the Native American

Graves Protection and Repatriation Act of 1990

The words "rest in peace" appear on many
tombstones in the United States. But the
skeletal remains of thousands of Native Americans[1] are not resting in peace. They have been
dug up from graves by archaeologists and anthropologists,[2] who have examined and studied
them, and by relic hunters, who have sold
them. They have been collected from battle-
fields by soldiers and have ended up as cu-
rios; skulls have been fancied as candle-
holders. They have been picked up from fields
by farmers, and they have surfaced during the
excavations for roads and dams.

In addition to human remains, Native
American artifacts of all kinds--from weapons
and religious objects to the pipes and pots of
everyday use--have been found. These have
often ended up in public or private museums,
where they are displayed or studied, or in the
possession of private collectors, who have
sold some of them for thousands of dollars at
collectors' shows (Arden 392).

It is not surprising, then, that Native
Americans have felt angry and hurt. Douglas
Preston, a former writer and editor at the
American Museum of History in New York, supports them. He believes that Native Americans
still feel the injustice of losing their land
and that the looting of their graves and the
keeping of their ancestors' remains is just

Text page numbers begin with 1, preceded by last name.

Center title: double space to text.

Superscript numbers refer to content notes giving additional information at end of paper.

Writer starts paper with background information.

Citation appears at the end of the sentence, before the period.

Forte 2

Author's name is in text, so only page number appears in citation.

one more aspect of this conquest (67).

Native Americans, with considerable jus-
tification, view as racist the interest of museums and curio collectors in the remains and
religious objects of their ancestors. In efforts to oppose this racism and return remains
and artifacts to the appropriate tribes, they
pushed for passage of the Native American
Graves Protection and Repatriation Act of

Thesis statement.

1990. Although passage of this law was an important step in restoring justice, a number of
obstacles--practical, financial, and politi-
cal--have kept it from being carried out in
full. To make the law work, museums must be
more efficient in complying with its requirements. In addition, the government must provide adequate funding for the inventory and
return of sacred objects.

Most states have laws prohibiting desecration of graves, but these laws have not
generally been applied to Indian graves.
Walker Echo-Hawk, staff attorney for the Native American Rights Fund, describes the pre-
vailing attitude of Americans this way: "You
desecrate a white grave and you end up sitting
in prison. But desecrate an Indian grave, and
you get a Ph.D." (Brower 43). Another Native
American, Suzan Shown Harjo, executive director of the National Congress of American Indi-

*Writer quotes au-
thorities to back
his assertion.*

ans, agrees: "It comes down to whether Indians
are human. . . . The fact that the Smithsonian

*Quotation shorter
than three lines is
integrated into the
text.*

has 19,000 of our people is one of the last
vestiges of colonialism, dehumanization, and

Forte 3

racism against our people" (Molotsky A14).

Many historians would agree with them.
When the European explorers and conquerors
came to this country, the morality of appro-
priating native lands was debated by philosophers and theologians. One of the doctrines
supporting the rights of conquest in this
country held that the Indians were barbarians
and heathens and that "By divine law the
Christian imperial nations were superior and
had the right to dominion and rule over non-
Christian inhabitants and their territories"
(Parker 3).

Writer provides evidence of racist attitudes and behaviors toward Native Americans.

Paraphrase, summary, and quotation combined.

All of the arguments of Europeans justifying the taking of Indian lands led to the
same comforting conclusion--that, as Timothy
Christian, dean of law at the University of
Atlanta puts it, "European occupation was law-
ful according to the law of nations" (ix).
But, he adds, "the law of nations . . . was
little more than a self-serving crystalliza-
tion of state practice." The crux of the matter is that the colonists did not regard
Native Americans as human: "As subhumans they
were incapable of possessing rights--legal,
natural, or divine" (xiii).

Writer paraphrases source as a transition between two quotations.

This attitude that Native Americans were
less than human persisted long past colonial
days. One of the most gruesome examples of
this subhuman treatment occurred in the American Museum of Natural History in New York in
1896. The explorer Robert F. Peary brought six
Eskimos from Greenland to visit New York.

Writer uses an example to support his assertion.

Forte 4

Franz Boas, an anthropologist, and his col-
league Aleš Hrdlička wanted to study them and
arranged to house them on the museum's fifth
floor. The Eskimos had colds when they came,
and because of their lack of immunity, four of
them developed tuberculosis and died. Preston
tells what happened next:

> Hrdlička and Boas quickly went to
> work. Here was a splendid, unparal-
> leled opportunity to add postmortem
> data to their Eskimo file. Hrdlička
> directed that all four be macerated,
> boiled, and reduced to skeletons at
> the College of Physicians and Sur-
> geons of Columbia University. He
> then installed the skeletons in the
> museum's collection, where he could
> study them at leisure. (71)

The interests of three main groups--muse-
ums, scientists (archaeologists and anthropologists), and private collectors--have
conflicted with the interests of Native Americans. Among these three groups the interests
of the museums and the scientists are closely
allied: the scientists, who want to study the
remains, have depended on the museums to house
the items; and the museums have depended on
the scientists to provide them with material
to display and information to explain the dis-
plays to the public. Scientists have claimed
that they need museum holdings to study past
cultures and gather medical information; for
example, they have discovered traces of cer-

Writer summarizes arguments of museums and scientists.

Forte 5

tain proteins that remain in human bones many
years after death. By analyzing these they believe they will be able to track the spread
and evolution of certain diseases and perhaps
help wipe them out (Preston 72). Of course,
they haven't dug up other Americans' bones to
study them.

The collectors, on the other hand, have
been private individuals who view the artifacts and remains as the property of the owners of the land where they were found. They
believe they are entitled to dig on private
land when they have obtained permission from
the landowner. Many of them, like the scientists and museums, think of themselves as pre-
servers of the articles they have collected.
Although some may be sincere in their declara-
tions of respect, most of them seem to be primarily interested in profit. One clay pipe in
the shape of a human head brought a collector
$4,500 (Arden 376). Scientists, who call col-
lectors "looters," complain that collectors
destroy historical evidence by digging without
care and without making records of what they
find and where they find it. George Stuart of
the National Geographic gives an example of
the damage they have done:

> In New Mexico virtually every site
> of the Mimbres--a people of the
> Mogollon culture--has been wrecked
> by looters seeking their delicately
> painted black-on-white bowls. In
> North Carolina the strata of 7,000

*Writer uses a tran-
sition to discuss
interests of collec-
tors.*

*Writer opposes col-
lectors, using ex-
amples.*

*No indentation
for first line of a
quotation that
does not begin a
paragraph in the
source.*

Forte 6

years of human occupation lie in a
jumble, destroyed in a matter of
days by seekers of a few "col-
lectible" stone spearpoints and
scrapers.

As an archaeologist I deplore
the ongoing destruction, for my profession literally depends on the excavation of in situ material--remains
of the past in the precise place
where they were left by those who
made and used them. The artifact out
of context is, for the most part, of
as little use as the beached plank
of a wrecked ship. (393)

More support for opposition to collectors.

Perhaps the most notorious of these digs
occurred on Slack Farm in Kentucky. In 1987,
ten men paid a farmer $10,000 to open more
than 650 gravesites on his farm to collect
bones and artifacts presumably for resale to
collectors (Arden 381). Because the disturbing
of graves is against the law in Kentucky,
these men were charged with "desecration of a
venerated object" (Arden 378). But the damage
had been done.

For their part, the museums say they have
an important role in public education. Dr.
William Boyd, president of the Field Museum of
Natural History in Chicago, explained his view
of the controversy in a radio interview (Indian Artifacts II):

I don't think we should view this
debate as only one between Native

Forte 7

Americans [on one side] and insensi-
tive faceless museums on the other
because what is involved here is the
enlightenment and understanding of
millions of Americans who come each
year to museums to be educated and
to learn about each other.

Brackets set off words added to clarify a quotation.

Anthropologists and archaeologists see museum
holdings as their "database" (Preston 67).
These scientists, like the museums, see themselves as <u>preservers</u> of the Native American
culture, not destroyers of it; they believe
their work to be beneficial not only to the
general public but to Native Americans themselves. Yet, for the most part, they have
viewed these remains impersonally. A book by
two Missouri archaeologists (Chapman and Chapman) illustrates the scientific attitude in
1983. In their book, <u>Indians and Archaeology</u>
<u>of Missouri</u>, they give directions for collect-
ing and digging for artifacts. They advise new
archaeologists to find a map of the area they
want to survey, locate the house nearest the
area, and secure permission from the owner to
do a survey. The authors explain what to look
for in the way of artifacts, how and where to
dig, and how to record items they collect
(144).

Arguments of scientists revisited.

Summary of source.

Though they caution archaeologists to
keep careful records, they make no mention of
consulting living Native Americans (the last
tribes living in Missouri moved to Kansas and
Oklahoma in 1823 and ceded their land to the

Writer interprets evidence; he doesn't just report it.

Forte 8

United States) (117). The authors don't say
whether any archaeologists in Missouri have
tried to make any connections with these
tribes. They weren't thinking in those terms
at all. It's hard to imagine them digging up
the graves of other Americans' ancestors in
this cold, objective way.

But the views of museums and scientists
have been gradually changing under pressure
from Native Americans to have laws passed that
would require the return of burial remains

Writer provides ex-
amples of chang-
ing views of
museums and
scientists.

and artifacts. Many museums--among them the
Smithsonian Institution, the Museum of the
American Indian in New York, and Stanford University (Brower 41)--began to move toward
repatriation in the late 1980s. The University
of South Dakota returned remains of Sioux in
their possession to be reburied at Wounded
Knee, where more than 200 Sioux were massacred
by US cavalry (Brower 44). A few states have
passed laws requiring the return of human
remains.

The archaeologists, too, have begun to
soften their position somewhat. Cheryl Ann
Munson spoke on the subject of Native American
museum claims on behalf of the Society for
American Archaeology in 1988 at the Hearings
of the Senate Select Committee on Indian Affairs. She recommended that remains be re-
turned--but only if they have no scientific
value or if "direct lineal relationships" can
be established (64). In all other cases, she
said, they should be kept and disputes should

Forte 9

be "resolved on a case-by-case basis" (63-64). Like the museum officials, society members did not want a law passed requiring the return of all remains. Such a law would diminish their control over these objects.

Not surprisingly, Native Americans were not satisfied with these concessions. They wanted the protection of a law requiring repatriation--a law that would cover both private and public institutions as well as individuals. And they finally got such a law. The Native American Graves Protection and Repatriation Act (Pub. L. 101-601), or NAGPRA, was passed on January 23, 1990. It requires that Native American remains and funerary objects be returned to the appropriate tribes and tribal organizations.

Transition to discussion of law described in thesis.

The passage of this law was a significant step forward for Native Americans, but more difficult problems lay ahead. To implement the provisions of the bill, museums were required to inventory the skeletal remains and artifacts and publish the list in the Federal Register. Indian tribes and tribal groups would then ascertain whether they were culturally affiliated with any of the items. If such affiliation could be established, tribes could claim them. Museums had five years from the date of the bill's passage to complete their inventories ("NAGPRA News" 27). After publication of the inventories, tribes that qualified would have thirty days to reply to the museum. This protocol proved to be more difficult than

Writer sets up discussion of problems with the law.

Short title used to cite work with no author.

Forte 10

it seemed at first.

Writer sets up explanations with "first" in this paragraph and "second" in the next.

The first problem was money. Early inventories of museum holdings indicated "millions of sacred objects and ancestral remains" to be relocated (Allen 2). It was costing museums a great deal of money to identify and catalog relevant items. Because relocation of the items by Indian tribes would also be expensive, the U.S. government made money available through grants. The money provided was far less than what was needed, however. For a joint tribal-museum request of $10 million for 1994-1995, Congress appropriated only $2.3 million (Allen 2).

The second problem was the difficulty of making cultural identification so that the items could be restored to the related tribe. When such difficulties arose, available information was turned over to the Secretary of the Interior, who consulted with the NAGPRA Review Committee; the committee then decided what to do with the remains.

Writer uses question as transition to the current status of the issue.

What is the current state of the implementation of NAGPRA? A congressional hearing on this question was held before the Committee on Indian Affairs on 6 December 1995, five years after the passage of the bill. In opening the hearings, Senator Daniel K. Inouye, vice chairman, reported that "more than 2,700 Native American human remains, nearly 123,000 associated funerary objects, 16 objects of cultural patrimony, and 212 sacred objects" had been repatriated since the passage of the

Forte 11

bill (2). That was the good news.

The bad news was that museums had fallen far behind in repatriating remains they held. A native Hawaiian organization had brought a lawsuit against a museum for "failing to expeditiously return Native Human Remains" and for "conducting additional scientific research on the remains" (Inouye 2). The legal question involved was "whether native human remains have standing under the law" (3), a question with many ramifications. It was a prime example of the conflict between the rights of museums to conduct research on human remains and the desires of Native Americans with claims to those remains to keep and protect them. The court found that NAGPRA "does not prevent museums or federal agencies from conducting additional scientific studies or research on human remains, except after completion of the initial inventory" (6). Senator Inouye of Hawaii suggested that Native Americans might want to have Congress pass a law prohibiting such actions (2).

The next area of contention was the fact that museums had not completed their inventories within the time specified in the law. Katherine H. Stevenson (associate director of Cultural Resource Stewardship and Partnerships in the Department of the Interior) reported at the December 6 hearing of the Committee on Indian Affairs that a number of museums had not completed their inventories and had applied for extensions. She explained that, for the

Writer describes more problems in implementing the law.

Forte 12

completed inventories, the next step was now
under way: "the protracted and potentially
contentious consultation process to verify
their [Indian tribes'] rights to particular
Native American human remains, funerary objects, sacred objects, and objects of cultural
patrimony" (7). She alluded to "disputes" between Native American groups and museums and
stated that these were "expected to increase."
"Civil penalty regulations" would have to be
issued, she said, to ensure compliance (7).

Complaints by tribal members against the
failure of museums to comply with NAGPRA per-
vade the remaining testimony before the committee. One of the strongest statements was
issued by Jesse Taken Alive, chair of the
Standing Rock Sioux Tribe. After thanking the
Senate Committee on Indian Affairs for conducting the hearing and also thanking the sen-
ators from North Dakota for their help, Jesse
Taken Alive said he would "speak plainly," and
he did: "We are not satisfied with the limited
level of input and representation given to
tribes throughout the regulatory process" (2).
He continued: "NAGPRA, if nothing else, is a
series of compromises between Native nations
and the science and museum industries" (2).

One of the main complaints was the lack
of grant money to enable museums to conduct
inventories and to enable the tribes to repatriate human remains and cultural items.

Meanwhile, disputes between museums and
tribes were said to be increasing along with

*Writer presents
counterviews of
Native Americans.*

*Calls for more reg-
ulations described.*

Forte 13

demands for publication of new regulations so
that these disputes could be properly adjudi-
cated. A particularly sore point was the ex-
clusion of the Smithsonian Institution from
the requirements of NAGPRA. Although the
Smithsonian had been actively involved in
repatriation, the law did not require it to
adhere to the regulations set forth in NAGPRA
for other museums. A new law would have to be
passed to bring it into complete compliance.

Other points of contention and uncer-
tainty were the museums' disposal of unidentified and unclaimed remains--mostly ancient--
and the continued study of some of them. Scientists pointed out that because they could
learn a great deal from them, continued study
should be allowed. Native Americans asserted
that because these remains were culturally
related to them, they should be able to
reinter them according to native religious
rites.

Museums weighed in with a positive report
on the progress of restoring remains and artifacts to Native Americans. Dan L. Monroe, a
past president of the American Association of
Museums and director of the Peabody Essex Museum, offered this testimony at the 6 December
hearing:

*Positive report
given . . .*

> While implementation has not been
> without significant challenges and
> difficulties, and while it is too
> soon to give any comprehensive,
> long-term assessment of the impact

Forte 14

of NAGPRA, to date the Act has
largely succeeded in realizing Congressional objectives. (7)

. . . and then re-
futed by another
source.

But Jesse Taken Alive was not happy with
the amount of progress that had been made. He
complained that the long-promised regulations
called for under NAGPRA have never been issued. "We feel certain," he said, "that if it
were <u>native</u> people who were passing laws and
writing regulatory language so that <u>you</u> could
repatriate <u>your</u> relatives' bodies and sacred
things from <u>us</u> and <u>our</u> museums, you would feel
the same way" (3). He suggested a solution at
the hearing:

New solution de-
scribed.

We propose that this Committee direct the NAGPRA Review Committee to
consult with regional coalitions of
tribal NAGPRA representatives to re-
work the proposed regulations, send
a copy of their final draft to all
tribal governments for their review
and comment, thus providing balance
to a legal document that will finally represent the interests of our
indigenous nations. (8)

He ended in a conciliatory tone:

Honored members of the Committee, we
have today witnessed another step
toward improving the government-to-
government relations between our Nations and the United States. By
holding today's hearing, you have
given us something we have struggled

> for for nearly two years: today we
> have been heard. . . . We thank you
> for what you have done to make this
> historic and precedental law do what
> it was intended to do: open the door
> to the Spirit World, one final time,
> for our loved ones, and begin the
> healing process by returning the sa-
> cred things we need to revitalize
> our Nations. (8-9)

So the problems persist. According to
Monroe, "At its heart, this issue involves
rights of scientific inquiry versus Native
American religious rights" (6): cowboys and
Indians twentieth-century style. Although much
progress has been made, more needs to be done,
especially to return unidentified and unclaimed remains. The solution depends in part
on the willingness of Congress to appropriate
the necessary funds. It also depends on the
willingness of scientists and museums to respect the rights of Native Americans.

Writer concludes by emphasizing the need for more action.

Forte 16

Content notes are placed at the end of the paper and before the list of works cited.

Leave a space between the superscript number and the beginning of the note.

Notes

[1] The term <u>Native Americans</u> refers to those indigenous peoples living in what is now the United States, including Alaska and Hawaii. Following the definitions given in Senate Bill 1980, the Native American Grave Protection and Repatriation Act, the word <u>Indian</u> is used here to refer to a member of an Indian tribe--a group of Native Americans joined by organization or common lineage in the United States. The term <u>Alaska Native</u>, though not used in this paper, is defined in the bill as an Eskimo, Aleut, or Alaska Indian. Similarly, the term <u>Native Hawaiian</u> is defined as a descendant of those living in Hawaii before the coming of the Europeans in 1778.

The number is indented five spaces; the rest of the note is flush left.

[2] Anthropologists study people, especially their social relationships and customs. Archaeologists study and interpret ancient cultures by means of artifacts and other remains often found through excavation. Archaeologists studying Native American culture are usually trained in anthropology as well as archaeology.

Forte 17

Works Cited

Allen, W. Ron. Statement to the Senate Committee on Indian Affairs. US 103rd Cong.,
2nd sess. 6 Dec. 1995. Ts. Senate Committee on Indian Affairs, Washington.

Arden, Harvey. "Who Owns Our Past?" National
Geographic Mar. 1989: 376-93.

Boyd, William. Interview with Rebecca Clay.
Indian Artifacts II. Natl. Public Radio.
WAMU, Washington. 30 July 1990.

Brower, Montgomery. "Walter Echo-Hawk Fights
for His People's Right to Rest in Peace--
Not in Museums." People 4 Sept. 1989:
42-44.

Chapman, Carl H., and Eleanor F. Chapman. Indians and Archaeology of Missouri. Columbia: Missouri UP, 1983.

Christian Timothy J. Introduction. The Law of
Nations and the New World. By L.C. Green
and Olive P. Dickason. Edmonton: Alberta
UP, 1989. vii-xiii.

Inouye, Sen. Daniel K. Introductory Statement.
Oversight Hearing on Implementation of
the Native American Graves Protection
and Repatriation Act. Pub. L. 101-601.
6 Dec. 1995. Ts. Senate Committee on Indian Affairs, Washington.

Molotsky, Irvin. "Smithsonian to Give Up Indian Remains." New York Times 1 Sept.
1989, natl. ed.: A14.

Monroe, Dan L., witness. United States. Cong.
Senate. Committee on Indian Affairs.
Hearing on Implementation of the Native

Typescript material.

Sources arranged alphabetically by authors' last names.

First line is flush left; rest of citation is indented five spaces or a half-inch.

Weekly magazine.

Book.

Testimony.

American Graves Protection and Repatriation Act. 103rd Cong., 2nd sess. 6 Dec.
1995. Ts. Senate Committee on Indian Affairs, Washington.

Munson, Cheryl Ann, witness. United States.
Cong. Senate. Select Committee on Indian
Affairs. Hearing on the Native American
Museum Claims Commission Act. 100th
Cong., 2nd sess. Washington: GPO, 1988.

Anonymous article listed alphabetically by title.

"NAGPRA News: Implementing the Native American
Graves Protection and Repatriation Act."
Federal Archeology Spring 1995: 27.

Parker, Linda S. Native American Estate: The
Struggle over Indian and Hawaiian Lands.
Honolulu: U of Hawaii P, 1989.

Preston, Douglas J. "Skeletons in Our Museums'
Closets." Harper's Feb. 1989: 66-75.

Stevenson, Katherine H., witness. United
States. Cong. Senate. Committee on In-
dian Affairs. Hearing on Status and Im-
plementation of the Native American
Graves Protection and Repatriation Act.
103rd Cong., 2nd sess. 6 Dec. 1995. Ts.
Senate Committee on Indian Affairs,
Washington.

Monthly magazine.

Stuart, George E. "The Battle to Save Our
Past." National Geographic Mar. 1989:
392-93.

Taken Alive, Jesse, witness. United States.
Cong. Senate. Committee on Indian Affairs. Hearing on Status and Implementation of the Native American Graves
Protection and Repatriation Act. 103rd

Forte 19

Cong., 2nd sess. 6 Dec. 1995. Ts. Senate Committee on Indian Affairs, 1995.

United States. Cong. <u>Native American Graves
Protection and Repatriation Act</u>. 101st
Cong., 2nd sess. Pub. L. 101-601. Wash-
ington: GPO, 1990.

---. ---. Senate. Select Committee on Indian
Affairs. <u>Hearing on the Native American
Museum Claims Commission Act</u>. 100th
Cong., 2nd sess. Washington: GPO, 1988.

*Consecutive govern-
ment publications.*

Grimaldi 1

Rachel Grimaldi

Professor Diaz

English 210

15 March 199-

Attitudes toward Feminism in the Poetry

of Elizabeth Bishop

Although her poetry received the Pulitzer Prize and the National Book Award, Elizabeth Bishop was looked upon by some of her contemporaries as merely an excellent woman poet; her friend and mentor Robert Lowell called her poetry "the best written by a woman in the twentieth century" (78). Bishop, feeling that such categorization was condescending and that it deprived her of being compared with male poets, refused to let her poetry be printed in anthologies of women's poetry, a decision that seemed to some to be antifeminist. Yet late in her career, she remarked, "I've always considered myself a strong feminist" ("Art" 80). Not surprisingly, then, critics looking for precise depictions of gender roles have found her poetry hard to classify (Blasing 265). But her attitude toward feminism, as exhibited in her poetry, actually anticipates that of current-day feminists who oppose "difference feminism"--that is, the assumption that women are socially, culturally, and morally different from men (Pollitt 42-62). Bishop did not see the need to distinguish women's art from the art of men.

Throughout most of her career (from the 1920s until her death in 1979), Bishop re-

Writer provides background for Bishop's attitudes.

Short title used to cite one of several works by the same author.

Paper's key argument stated in thesis.

Grimaldi 2

sisted categorization by gender. The fact that people consistently grouped her work with that of other contemporary women poets particularly bothered her. As Lorrie Goldensohn notes, Bishop criticized confessional, autobiographical poets like Sylvia Plath and participated in "common rejection of what was perceived as an unwanted feminizing of the arts" (69). She deplored any overemphasis on the personal that might lead to the trivialization of poetry.

Bishop's refusal to associate herself with contemporary female poets has been cited by C. K. Doreski as evidence that her poems have nothing to do with feminism, and he therefore dismisses feminist approaches to Bishop's work as "misreadings" (xii). But her attitude toward feminism is much more complex than Doreski suggests. She felt that the segregating of women and men leads to the stereotyping of roles--for example, to the belief that women are more emotional than intellectual. Her poetry reflects these views. She often casts traditional female images in a negative light (Diehl 101). In her poem "The Riverman," the adventurous protagonist (the artist figure) is a man fleeing from his domestic wife who brews him "stinking teas" that he throw[s] out, "behind her back" (Complete Poems 106). Bishop's poem turns the common figure of the mermaid (typically female) into a Riverman who has escaped to an underwater world. In one stanza of the poem, in which the Riverman longs for a "virgin" mirror

Grimaldi 3

Lines of poetry in-
dicated by slashes.

to see his true self, he finds only "spoiled"
mirrors--"spoiled, that is, for anything / but
the girls to look at their mouths in, / to examine their teeth and smiles" (107). Here
Bishop seems to be criticizing domestic women
who act in a stereotypical, superficial manner
and instead aligns herself with the more "am-
bitious" and "serious" man.

Her classic, semiautobiographical poem
"In the Waiting Room" offers perhaps the best
example of her attitudes toward women and femininity. In this poem, the protagonist appears
to be the poet as a child ("Elizabeth"), awakening to the realization that she is female.
As she looks at <u>National Geographic</u>, Elizabeth
feels both admiration for the naked women's
bodies and repulsion at their defomed "necks
wound round and round with wire" and their
"horrifying breasts" (159). Even more dis-
tressing to the poet is that these deformed
women also submit their babies to a similar
torture to make their heads pointed. The poem
details the horrifying moment when Elizabeth
realizes "you are one of them. / Why should
you be one, too?" (160). In both "The
Riverman" and "In the Waiting Room," Bishop

Writer qualifies
Bishop's attitudes.

does not seem to be criticizing all women, but
rather women who participate in their own op-
pression or who accept society's stereotypes
about how they should look and act.

Many of her poems deal with a theme that
has often accompanied feminism throughout our
century--a criticism of patriarchy, or social

Grimaldi 4

domination by men. Bishop first wrote the poem "Roosters" in response to Nazi fascism during World War II, but critics such as Joanne Feit Diehl (101) and Bonnie Costello (136) have read this poem as a critique of "male arrogance and female submission" with a "subtheme of militarism." In the poem, the speaker asks roosters a question that many feminists have asked of patriarchal men: "what right have you to give / commands and tell us how to live?" (Complete Poems 36). These belligerent roosters do not face any direct female resistance, however, and are instead admired by their "rustling wives" despite the fact that the wives "lead hens' lives / of being courted and despised" (35). In 1977, Bishop said of "Roosters," "I suddenly realized it sounded like a feminist tract, which it wasn't meant to sound like at all to begin with. So you never know how things are going to get changed around for you by the times" (Starbuck 19).

The linking of patriarchy and aggression occurs again in "Brazil, January 1, 1502." In that poem, she points out the hypocrisy and treachery of Spanish explorers who set out to rape Indian women "directly after [Catholic] Mass" (92). Both "Roosters" and "Brazil" contain a common feminist theme: the victims of aggressive men are usually women.

Writer summarizes poems' ideas as they apply to feminism.

Bishop's work sometimes focuses on domesticity and celebrates activities common to women's lives. Because she wrote "quiet" poems based on observation rather than action, her

Feminine aspects of Bishop's poems explored.

Grimaldi 6

poetry often was criticized by male reviewers
who perceived it as too feminine. In the
Kenyon Review, Alvarez calls Bishop's powers
of observation "little more than an obscure
fussiness" with a "finicky air"; he prefers a
more masculine style, in which the "languge
makes you jump to [the] meaning" (321).

In response to such negative appraisals
of Bishop, Alicia Ostriker sees this reticent,
quiet quality of Bishop's poetry as typical of
women's poetry, with its "long tradition of
feminine self-effacement and disguise" and its
poetics of female intimacy (70). Domestic,
"feminine" themes appear also in such poems as
"Faustina, or Rock Roses," which details a
visit to an old woman on her deathbed, and
"The Shampoo," in which the central action is
the washing of a woman's graying hair. In a
rare public statement in 1978, Bishop said
"women's experiences are much more limited,
but that does not really matter--there is
Emily Dickinson, as one always says. You just
have to make do with what you have after all"
("Elizabeth Bishop Speaks About Her Poetry"
1).

While some of her poems make art out of
the small moments of women's lives, others go
even further to celebrate femininity as a mystical force of nature. In "The Moose," a bus-
load of passengers confronts the wonder of a
female moose:

*Quotation longer
than four lines in-
dented ten spaces
and double-
spaced.*

> Taking her time,
> she looks the bus over,

> grand, otherworldly.
> Why, why do we feel
> (we all feel) this sweet
> sensation of joy? (169)

The moose, which is visible by moonlight, imparts a sense of the sublime in nature and a "sweet sensation of joy" to those in the bus who are watching. Throughout Bishop's work, moonlight is a common metaphor for freedom and creativity. In "The Riverman," the speaker escapes from his real-world wife to rendezvous underwater with the female moon spirit, Luandinha. Whereas real women are sometimes portrayed negatively in Bishop's poetry to show their status in society, female spirits of nature are celebrated as crucial forces against repression, stagnation, and a "patriarchal urge to master nature" (Costello 127).

Although she doesn't write often from a lesbian point of view, Bishop, a lesbian herself, uses the knowledge of being an outsider to question gender conventions. Diehl argues that her poems offer "a map of language where sexual identity yields to a fluidity of gender that does away with rigid heterosexist categories" (92). Many of the characters in Bishop's poetry serve as examples of the ambiguity of gender categories. In "Arrival at Santos," Miss Breen, an actual person who accompanied Bishop to Brazil, is described as "about seventy, / a retired police lieutenant, six feet tall, / with beautiful bright blue eyes and a kind expression" (89). Bishop highlights this woman's androgynous qualities to show that real people do not fit into rigid gender categories. Her poem "Exchanging Hats" demonstrates that gender is a cultural category that one can try on like a hat, as the poem's "unfunny uncles" don ladies' hats and "anandrous aunts" put on "yachtsmen's caps" (200). Focusing on the poem's line "costume and custom are complex." Costello points out that the poem "expresses the radical instability and inauthenticity of all cultural roles" such as gender (148). Bishop doesn't think that women or men are innately different mentally or that either sex is necessarily superior, and her poetry tries to undermine the cultural system that classifies "masculine" and "feminine" behaviors. Even though she doesn't always sympathize with all women, Bishop seems feminist in her basic refusal of stereotypes; and more particularly she appears to be a 1990s feminist who understands that gender roles are learned and not innate.

The most interesting characters of her poetry are not strictly men or women but rather misfits who don't seem to fit into either gender role. Costello notes that "her misfits are of both sexes" (128), but they seem even more genderless than Costello suggests. Although the Riverman is technically a man, when he enters the underwater world, he is a cross between human and fish; and he seems to have erotic encounters with both the

Writer offers original interpretation of poem.

Writer furthers her argument about Bishop's feminism.

Grimaldi 9

male Dolphin and the female Luandinha. Because the merman figure journeys under the water, he can escape the gender conventions that govern on the surface--on land.

"The Man-Moth," Bishop's most brilliant exploration of the hybrid misfit who sees the world differently, seems very much like Bishop herself. Living below the surface of the earth, he identifies with the moon, which "looks rather different to him" (4); he thinks it is a hole in the sky. Like a lesbian trying to fit into a heterosexual culture, the Man-Moth tries "to push his small head through that round clean opening / and be forced through . . . although / he fails, of course, and falls back scared but quite unhurt" (14). The creature's special power is his perspective, his alterd vision. Bishop, as Man-Moth, did not fit into gender categories or accepted poetic categories, but her experience enabled her to see the folly of the categories themselves.

As the women's liberation or feminist movement evolved in the 1970s, Bishop became more sympathetic to its cause. In a letter in 1979 (the year of her death), she told friends that patronizing reviewers "brought her feminist facet uppermost" (qtd. in Lombardi 2). In 1977 Bishop explained her earlier refusal to be in collections of women's poetry this way: "I felt it was a lot of nonsense, separating the sexes. I suppose this feeling came from

Qtd. in ("quoted in") *indicates that statement came from secondary source.*

Grimaldi 8

feminist principles, perhaps stronger than I
was aware of" (Starbuck 21). In fact, Bishop's
attitudes toward gender anticipated those of
contemporary feminists who see a danger in
rigid distinctions between male and female
roles--distinctions that, according to Katha
Pollitt, continue to remain popular: "Indeed,
although the media like to caricature feminism
as denying the existence of sexual differences, for the women's movement and its opponents alike 'difference' is where the action
is" (43-44). She continues, "The truth is,
there is only one culture . . ." (58). To Pollitt and feminists who share her views, playing up the differences between men and women
is not insignificant--not merely a matter of
preference; rather it has real economic and
political consequences. She writes:

> The biggest problem with . . . ac-
> counts of gender difference is that
> they credit the differences they
> find to universal features of male
> and female development rather than
> to the economic and social positions
> that men and women hold, or to the
> actual power differences between in-
> dividual men and women. (48)

Critics who ignore the relationship of
Bishop's poetry to the development of feminism
are missing an important focus of her art. At
first she positioned herself against the
women's liberation movement and against some

Writer ties Bishop into current feminism.

Writer introduces long quotation by summarizing the point.

Ellipsis points indicate that something was omitted from the original.

Conclusion emphasizes the ways in which Bishop was a feminist and her significance to feminism.

Grimaldi 9

of the other women writers of her time; then
she realized that she was a feminist who re-
sisted social divisions solely on the basis of
gender. While some of her poetry experiments
with a celebration of women for their special,
mystical qualities (common to "first-stage"
feminism), the large body of her poems focuses
on a criticism of gender stereotypes and of
the cultural system that keeps them in place.
Although most of Bishop's work was published
between 1949 and 1976, her ideas are echoed in
the current feminist thought of the 1990s.
Elizabeth Bishop was a feminist ahead of her
time.

Grimaldi 10

List of Works Cited, alphabetically arranged, begins new page.

Works Cited

Alvarez, A. "Imagism and Poetesses." <u>The Kenyon Review</u> 19 (Spring 1957): 321.

Bishop, Elizabeth. "The Art of Poetry XXVII." <u>The Paris Review</u> 80 (1981): 56-83.

Three hyphens followed by a period indicate second and third works by same author.

---. <u>The Complete Poems, 1927-1979</u>. New York: Farrar, 1983.

---. "Elizabeth Bishop Speaks about Her Poetry." <u>New Paper</u> 4 (June 1978): 1-2.

Blasing, Mutlu Konuk, "From Gender to Genre and Back: Elizabeth Bishop and 'The Moose,'" <u>American Literary History</u> 6 (Summer 1992): 265-86.

Work in an edited anthology.

Costello, Bonnie. "Attractive Mortality." <u>Elizabeth Bishop: The Geography of Gender</u>. Ed. Marilyn May Lombardi. Charlottesville: U of Virginia P, 1993. 127-52.

Diehl, Joanne Feit. <u>Women Poets and the American Sublime</u>. Bloomington: Indiana UP, 1990.

Book.

Doreski, C. K. <u>Elizabeth Bishop: The Restraints of Language</u>. New York: Oxford UP, 1993.

Goldensohn, Lorrie. <u>Elizabeth Bishop: The Biography of a Poetry</u>. New York: Columbia UP, 1992.

Lombardi, Marilyn May. "Prologue: 'Another Way of Seeing.'" <u>Elizabeth Bishop: The Geography of Gender</u>. Charlottesville: U of Virginia P, 1993. 1-13.

Book with an author and editor.

Lowell, Robert. <u>Collected Prose</u>. Ed. Robert Giroux. New York: Farrar, 1987.

Grimaldi 11

Ostriker, Alicia. <u>Stealing the Language: The
    Emergence of Women's Poetry in America</u>.
    Boston: Beacon, 1986.

Pollitt, Katha. <u>Reasonable Creatures: Essays on
    Women and Feminism</u>. New York: Knopf,
    1994.

Starbuck, George. "Interview with Elizabeth
    Bishop." <u>Ploughshares</u> 3 (1977): 11-29.

*Published inter-
view.*

Writing a Paper in the Social Sciences: The Author-Date Style

Many writers in anthropology, biology, business, education, economics, psychology, political science, and other social sciences follow the system of documentation known as the APA or author-date style, explained in the *Publication Manual of the American Psychological Association* (4th ed., 1994). These writers give the author and date in the text because this information is important to readers. Because the APA *Manual* applies primarily to manuscripts that will be submitted for publication, not to college papers or dissertations, many of the suggestions, such as margins and spacing, are designed for the convenience of editors and typesetters; the authors suggest that students adapt these to their use. Therefore, the following guidelines give priority to the needs of student writers of "final-copy" manuscripts in these disciplines. If you plan to publish your article in a journal, you will find most of these guidelines compatible with your purpose; however, for some formatting details, you should consult the APA *Manual*. David Han's paper in this chapter uses the APA style.

Parts of the Manuscript

FOR ORIGINAL RESEARCH PAPERS	FOR THEORETICAL OR REVIEW PAPERS
Title page	Title page
Abstract	Abstract
Table of contents	Table of contents
List of tables and figures	List of tables and figures
Introduction	Introduction

FOR ORIGINAL RESEARCH PAPERS (CONT.)	FOR THEORETICAL OR REVIEW PAPERS (CONT.)
Method ⎫ Results ⎬ Discussion ⎭	Body with headings
Content notes, if used	Content notes, if used
References	References
Appendixes	Appendixes

Consult your instructor for the parts that you need for your paper. For example, you may not need a title page, table of contents, or appendixes. (Most of you will be writing a review paper.) Use extra spacing to improve readability, especially before and after headings.

Format

Title Page

On the title page place the title of your paper, your name, and any other information your instructor prefers, such as course title and number, instructor's name, and date. Center your title on the page, capitalizing the first letter of all important words; don't underline the title or place it in quotation marks. Type your name three to four lines below the title. Place each of the other items on a separate line below near the bottom of the page; double-space between items. If your instructor requests it, place the first two or three words of the title and an arabic numeral 1 in the upper right corner, and number succeeding pages consecutively with arabic numerals. (Note that the next page should be numbered as page 2, even if no number is placed on the title page.) Some instructors may require lowercase roman numerals on preliminary pages.

Margins and Spacing

Leave margins of one inch on all sides. Double-space throughout the manuscript including the abstract and long indented quotations. The reference list may be single-spaced within entries (double-space between them) if you will not be submitting your paper for publication. Indent the first word of each paragraph five spaces or a half-inch. Indent long quotations (more than forty words) five spaces from the left margin. For long quotations of more than one paragraph, indent the first line of subsequent paragraphs five additional spaces.

Page Numbers

Use arabic numbers for all pages, beginning with the title page. Place the number in the upper right corner, one inch from the top and one inch from the side. Place a shortened form of your title five spaces to the left of the page number. Your computer should be able to place this running head on each page automatically. If you have front matter such as a table of contents and an abstract, you may want to use lowercase roman numerals on preliminary pages.

Abstract

The abstract is a one-paragraph summary of your paper: an appropriate length is from 100 to 125 words for a primary research paper, from 75 to 100 words for a review or theoretical paper. It gives the purpose and content of your paper but does not evaluate or comment on the content. For more information on writing abstracts, see Chapter 7.

Place the title Abstract at the center of the page two lines below the shortened title and page number. Unlike other paragraphs, the text of the abstract begins at the left margin.

Headings

Headings serve the purpose of an outline. Most papers contain two or three levels of headings. For clarity, you should make these headings typographically distinct. For two levels, use the following format for a theoretical paper. If you are using a typewriter or submitting manuscript for publication, underline headings as shown below. If you're using a computer, substitute italics for underlining.

Water Erosion
[Level one, centered]

<u>Rainsplash Erosion</u>
[Level two, at left margin and underlined or italicized]

A two-level heading system for a primary research paper would look like this:

Method
[Level one]

<u>Procedure</u>
[Level two]

If you have three levels of headings, use this system for theoretical papers.

Production
[Level one, centered]

<u>Cost and Efficiency</u>
[Level two, at left margin and underlined or italicized]

   <u>Larger areas in production</u>.
   [Level three, indented five spaces and underlined or italicized;
   initial capital letter only; text follows on same line]

For a primary source paper, the headings would be Method at level one, Observation at level two, and Setting at level three.

First Page of Text

Type the shortened title and the page number 3 in the upper right corner of the page. Center the full title two to four spaces below the page number, capitalizing the first letter of each important word. Double-space and begin typing the text.

Introduction

The first paragraphs of the paper introduce readers to the problem being studied, the reasons for the study, and previous work done and literature written on the subject. It may also summarize the research that was done for this particular study. The APA *Manual* recommends that the introduction have no label or heading because its position shows that it is an introduction, but a heading is used in some journals. Chapter 7 gives several examples of introductions.

Content Notes

Content notes provide supplementary information not essential to the main text of the paper; they should be used sparingly. They are placed on a separate page following the body of the paper. Superscript numbers should be placed in the text after the material to be footnoted. Use the heading Footnotes at the top of the page two lines below the shortened title and the page number; double-space and begin with the superscript number of the first footnote. Indent the first line of each footnote five spaces, and double-space between lines.

Documentation

Parenthetical Citation

To indicate the source of the information you use, give the author and the year of publication either as part of your text or in parentheses as near as possible to the cited information. Some writers also include the page number: (Jones, 1993, p. 36). Page numbers must be given with quotations.

WORK BY ONE AUTHOR

If you use the author's name as part of your sentence, place only the date of publication in parentheses.

```
Olson (1994) first reported the results in a recent
study.
```

If you give both date and author in your sentence, you do not need a citation.

```
In a 1994 study at Stanford, Olson addressed this prob-
lem.
```

If you give neither in your sentence, you must give both in parentheses.

```
A recent study at Stanford (Olson, 1994) addressed this
problem.
```

WORK BY TWO AUTHORS

Give the names of both authors every time the work is cited.

```
Barlow and Seidner (1993) contend that . . .
```

WORK BY THREE, FOUR, OR FIVE AUTHORS

Give the names of all authors the first time the work is cited. When the names are given in parentheses, use an ampersand (*&*) instead of *and*.

In later citations, give only the name of the first author, followed by *et al.*

```
According to Hewitt, Smith, and Larson (1995) . . .
Recent research (Hewitt, Smith, & Larson, 1995) has shown
. . .
The researchers (Hewitt et al., 1995) further hypothe-
sized . . .
```

WORK BY SIX OR MORE AUTHORS

Give only the last name of the first author followed by *et al.* A work written by Wilson, Miles, James, Wylie, Masters, and Flower would be cited as follows:

```
According to Wilson et al. (1994) . . .
A recent study of phobics (Wilson et al., 1994) showed
. . .
```

CORPORATE AUTHOR

Give the full name of a corporate author (government agency, association, or research organization) each time it occurs in the text. However, if the group is well known by its abbreviation, give its abbreviation with the first citation and use the abbreviation in subsequent references.

```
In a television series on mental health (National Broad-
casting Company [NBC], 1991) . . .
In the first of its series, NBC (1991) . . .
Schizophrenia was shown (NBC, 1991) . . .
```

WORK WITHOUT AN AUTHOR

In your citation give enough of the title to enable your readers to find it in your reference list; usually two or three words are enough. For example, an article titled "Power Conflict in Groups" would be cited as: ("Power Conflict," 1989).

TWO OR MORE AUTHORS WITH SAME LAST NAME

If you have used as sources two or more authors with the same last name, you must give their initials each time you refer to their work.

```
According to C. R. Lewis (1992), and L. M. Lewis (1995)
. . .
```

TWO OR MORE WORKS BY THE SAME AUTHOR

Give the name followed by the dates of the works.

```
Research shows (Jones, 1989, 1994) . . .
```

If the works were published in the same year, use the alphabetical suffixes you assign to the works in the reference list.

```
(Mill, 1988a, 1988b)
```

TWO OR MORE WORKS BY DIFFERENT AUTHORS

When citing two or more authors within the same parentheses, give them in alphabetical order and separate the entries with semicolons.

```
(Jones, 1993; Logan & Marsh, 1989)
```

PART OF A SOURCE

You may want to cite a page, chapter, illustration, or other specific part of a source. When you use a quotation, you must always give the page number.

```
(Rogers & Martin, 1995, chap. 4)
(see Figure 4 in Lorenzo, 1996, p. 45)
```

PERSONAL COMMUNICATION

When you refer to letters, interviews, or telephone or electronic communications, give the citation in your text only. Don't include it in your reference list because it cannot be found by anyone else. Give the initials as well as the last name.

According to J. R. Davis (personal communication, March
4, 1994) . . .

LEGAL DOCUMENTS

For court cases mentioned in the text, give the name of the case,
italicized or underlined, and the date in parentheses.

United States v. Castillo (1975)

If the reference is a parenthetical citation, the entire reference is in
parentheses.

(United States v. Castillo, 1975)

For statutes, give the name of the act and year.

Equal Employment Opportunity Act (1972)

or

Equal Employment Opportunity Act of 1972

For other kinds of legal citations, see C. Edward Good, *Citing and Typing the Law* (3rd ed., 1992).

Reference List

Type the shortened title and the page number at the top right of the
page, skip a line, and center the heading References.

If you are writing for publication, double-space within and between
entries, but if you're writing a final-copy paper (the usual college paper),
you can save space by single-spacing within items. Always double-space
between items.

Arrange references in alphabetical order according to the last name
of the first author. If more than one reference is by the same author,
give the author's name each time and arrange the entries in chronological order of publication.

Flavell, J. H. (1963).
Flavell, J. H. (1977).

If you have entries with the same first author and different second or
third authors, the entry with one author precedes multiple-author entries. Then arrange entries alphabetically in order of the subsequent
authors.

Leakey, R. E. F. (1976).
Leakey, R. E. F., & Lewin, R. (1977).
Leakey, R. E. F., & Walker, A. C. (1976).

When two works by the same author are published in the same year, arrange the works alphabetically by title and distinguish them by using lowercase letters — a, b, c — after the date.

```
Chomsky, N. (1976a).
Chomsky, N. (1976b).
```

The next sections illustrate formats for references appropriate for most college papers using the author-date system. In the examples given here, titles of books, journals, and other lengthy works are underlined. Use italics instead of underlining if you are working on a computer and not submitting your manuscript for publication (in the latter case you would use underlining). The examples here also appear with "hanging indents"; that is, each line after the first is indented five spaces. If you are submitting a manuscript for publication, you should not use hanging indents; rather, you should indent only the first line of each reference. The journal publishing your work will then convert the standard indents to hanging indents. You'll find an example of a reference list at the end of David Han's paper (p. 343).

Books. Here are some examples of entries for books in the APA author-date system.

ONE AUTHOR

Give last name of author first, followed by initials only. The date of publication (in parentheses) is followed by a period. Italicize or underline the title of the book, and capitalize only the first letter in the first word of the title as well as the first letter of the subtitle, if any. Give the city of publication and, if necessary for clarity, the state or country. Use a short title of the publishing company as long as it's intelligible, but give names of university presses in full. Keep the words *Books* and *Press*.

```
Walker, M. B. (1992). The psychology of gambling. New
     York: Pergamon Press.
```

TWO OR MORE AUTHORS

Include all names, no matter how many. (Note that in-text citations use a different format with multiple authors.) Use commas to separate all names; use an ampersand (*&*) instead of *and* before the last name. Invert all authors' names.

```
Reuven, B., & Brenner, G. A. (1990). Gambling and specu-
     lation: A theory, history, and a future of some
     human decisions. Cambridge: Cambridge University
     Press.
```

CORPORATE AUTHOR

Alphabetize corporate authors by the first significant word. When the author and publisher are the same, use *Author* for the name of the publisher.

National Broadcasting Company. (1954). <u>Why sales come in</u>
    <u>curves.</u> New York: Author.

BOOK WITHOUT AN AUTHOR OR EDITOR

Alphabetize a book with no author by the first significant word in the title; in this case, *uniform*.

<u>A uniform system of citation.</u> (1986). Cambridge, MA: Har-
    vard Law Review Association.

REVISED EDITION

McIlwain, H. (1972). <u>Biochemistry and the central nervous</u>
    <u>system</u> (Rev. ed.). New York: Churchill.

ONE VOLUME IN MULTIVOLUME WORK

Use the U.S. Postal Service abbreviation for the state when the location of the city is not well known or when it might be confused with another city of the same name.

Stouffer, S. A., Suchman, E. A., DeVinney, L. C., Star,
    S. A., & Williams, R. M., Jr. (1949). <u>Studies in so-</u>
    <u>cial psychology in World War II: Vol. 1. The Ameri-</u>
    <u>can soldier: Adjustment during army life.</u> Manhattan,
    KS: Military Affairs/Aerospace Historian.

ENGLISH TRANSLATION OF A BOOK

Bringuier, J. (1980). <u>Conversations with Jean Piaget</u>
    (B. M. Gulati, Trans.). Chicago: University of
    Chicago Press. (Original work published 1977)

In your text, use this citation: (Bringuier, 1977/1980).

CHAPTER OR ARTICLE IN EDITED BOOK

Do not invert the editor's name when it is not in the author position.

Rosenthal, R. J. (1987). The psychodynamics of pathologi-
    cal gambling: A review of the literature. In T. Gal-
    ski (Ed.), <u>The handbook of pathological gambling</u>
    (pp. 41-70). Springfield, IL: Thomas.

Periodicals.　Use the following formats for periodical articles in a reference list.

JOURNAL ARTICLE: ONE AUTHOR

For the article title, capitalize only the first word, any proper nouns, and the first word of the subtitle, if any. Do not italicize or underline the title, and do not put it in quotation marks. For the periodical title, capitalize the first letter of each main word and italicize or underline the title; also italicize or underline the volume number and follow it with a comma; give beginning and ending page numbers for the article. Use *p.* or *pp.* before page numbers in references to magazine and newspaper articles but not in references to journal articles.

Brotsky, S. (1968). Classic conditioning of the galvanic
　　　skin response to verbal concepts. Journal of Experi-
　　　mental Psychology, 70, 244-253.

When a journal is paginated by volume instead of by issue, you don't have to include the issue number.

JOURNAL ARTICLE: TWO AUTHORS

Give last names of both authors first; use an ampersand (*&*) between them.

Barlow, D. H., & Seidner, A. L. (1983). Treatment of ado-
　　　lescent agoraphobics: Effects on parent-adolescent
　　　relations. Behavioral Research and Therapy, 21,
　　　519-525.

JOURNAL ARTICLE: THREE OR MORE AUTHORS

Give names of all authors in the list of references regardless of how many there are; use an ampersand before the last name. Italicize or underline the volume number and follow it with a comma. In the text, however, when there are more than five authors, give only the name of the first, followed by *et al.* (not underlined or italicized).

Telch, M. J., Tearnan, B. H., & Taylor, C. B. (1983). An-
　　　tidepressant medication in the treatment of agora-
　　　phobia: A critical review. Behavioral Research and
　　　Therapy, 21, 505-516.

ARTICLE IN JOURNAL PAGINATED BY ISSUE

Place the number of the issue in parentheses after the volume number without a space between them.

Andreason, N. C., O'Leary, D. S., Cizaldo, T., Arndt, S., Rezai, K., Watkins, L., Boles Ponto, L. L., & Hichwa, R. D. (1995). Remembering the past: Two facets of episodic memory explored with positron emission tomography. American Journal of Psychiatry 152(11), 1578-1583.

MAGAZINE ARTICLE

Place the month after the year; for a weekly magazine include the day of the month. Give the volume number.

McAuliffe, K. (1995, September). Elephant seals, the champion divers of the deep. Smithsonian, 26, 45-56.

SIGNED NEWSPAPER ARTICLE

Give the year first, followed by the month and day. Give the section number, if any, followed by a page number. Place a comma between numbers when pages are discontinuous.

Sack, K. (1995, September 30). Gambling fuels Louisiana voter anger. The New York Times, p. A16.

UNSIGNED NEWSPAPER ARTICLE

When an article has no author, alphabetize the entry by the first significant word of the title.

High stakes in Bridgeport: A Smithsonian chronology. (1995, September 25). The Washington Post, p. H5.

NEWSPAPER ARTICLE WITH DISCONTINUOUS PAGES

Separate page numbers with a comma.

Sawyer, K. (1996, January 18). Two planets discovered that might sustain life: Bodies orbit stars in Big Dipper, Virgo. The Washington Post, pp. A1, A22.

LETTER TO THE EDITOR

For a letter to the editor in any publication, place identification in brackets after the title.

Sales, T. (1995, September). Thinking about mind [Letter to the editor]. Scientific American, 268, 12.

Other Printed Material.   Here are some examples of references for other kinds of printed material.

TECHNICAL OR RESEARCH REPORT

Give identifying information or the report number in parentheses following the title of the report.

> Congressional Budget Office. (1982). <u>Financing social</u>
>   <u>security: Issues and options for the long run</u> (S/N
>   052-070-05787-4). Washington, DC: U.S. Government
>   Printing Office.
>
> Trivett, D. A. (1975). <u>Academic credit for prior off-</u>
>   <u>campus learning</u> (ERIC/Higher Education Research Re-
>   port No. 2). Washington, DC: American Association
>   for Higher Education.

LEGAL DOCUMENT

This court case was decided by the U.S. Court of Appeals for the District of Columbia in 1965. It can be found in volume 350 of the *Federal Reporter,* second series, page 445.

> Williams v. Walker-Thomas Furniture Co., 350 F.2d 445
>   (DC Cir. 1965).

The following statute was codified in title 29 of the *United States Code* in section 65. For legal references, use the symbol for *section* (§) if you have it on your computer or typewriter. If you don't, abbreviate it: *Sec.*

> Occupational Safety and Health Act, 29 U.S.C. § 65 (1976).

PAMPHLET OR BROCHURE WITH NO DATE

Follow the same format as that for listing books. If no date is given, put *n.d.* in parentheses. In brackets identify the work as a pamphlet or brochure.

> National Institute of Mental Health. (n.d.). <u>Depression:</u>
>   <u>What you need to know</u> [Brochure]. Rockville, MD:
>   U.S. Department of Health and Human Services.

PROCEEDINGS OF A MEETING

> Petersen, J. (1988). Editing out your blind spots. In
>   J. Leathersich (Ed.), <u>Proceedings: 35th ITCC</u> (pp.

31-33). Philadelphia: Society for Technical Communication.

UNPUBLISHED MANUSCRIPT

Meyer, P. (1974). Assessing life/work experience: A ra-
tionale for faculty-based models. Unpublished manuscript, Florida International University, Miami.

Electronic Media.

CD-ROM ABSTRACT

Jaeger, R. M. (1995). Setting performance standards
through two-stage judgmental policy capturing [CD-
ROM]. Applied Measurement in Education, 8(1), 15-40.
Abstract from: ERIC Document Reproduction Service:
ERIC Item: EJ 504 356

ONLINE SOURCES

If a source is available in both print and online forms, use the print
form if possible.

E-MAIL (PERSONAL COMMUNICATION)

Communication conducted through e-mail and electronic discussion groups should not be included in the reference list because it is
not retrievable by the reader. Instead, provide the citation in the text
in parentheses. Give the name of the author of the information, the
type of communication, and the date. The following examples show
how to cite this information when the name is included as part of the
sentence and when it is not.

Denise Walker (personal communication, E-mail, March 23,
1995) described the research being done at her university.

Elementary classroom teachers are facing unexpected challenges today (Matthew Ivers, personal communication,
E-mail, June 3, 1996).

ONLINE JOURNAL ARTICLE

Use the same format as you would for a print article, providing
source, location, and date, if available. Add sufficient information to
retrieve the article (that is, give the pathway).

Berlin, J. (1995, October 31). A gargantuan retrospective
        [7 paragraphs]. basilisk [On-line serial], 1(1).
        Available:http://swerve.basilisk.com/c/cinMA_
        967.html

Do not put a period after the path because extra punctuation may con-
fuse the computer.

Audiovisual Media.

TELEVISION BROADCAST

Crystal, L. (Executive Producer). (1996, March 12). News
        Hour with Jim Lehrer. New York and Washington, DC:
        Public Broadcasting Service.

FILM

Tiana [Thi Thanh Nga] (Producer & Director). (1993). From
        Hollywood to Hanoi [Documentary film]. New York:
        Friendship Bridge Productions.

CASSETTE RECORDING

Brinkley, D. (Speaker). (1995). David Brinkley: A memoir
        [Cassette recording]. New York: Random House Audio
        Books.

If the recording has a number, give that in parentheses (instead of
brackets) after the medium: (Cassette Recording No. xxxxxx).

VIDEOTAPE

Kauffman, H., & Momaday, N. S. (Speakers). (1990). Winds
        of change: A matter of choices [Videotape]. Madison:
        Wisconsin Public Television. (Available from PBS
        Home Video 800-344-3337.)

Sample Research Paper
Using the Author-Date Style

In the following paper David Han has used the author-date system recommended in the *Publication Manual of the American Psychological Association,* a style guide used by writers in psychology and other social
sciences. The APA guidelines can be modified to conform to your department's or instructor's requirements. For example, words are un-

derlined in your paper that would be italicized in print. However, if you have access to a computer that can create italics, you may choose to italicize titles of books and other long works. If you use a typewriter, or if your instructor prefers that you do not use italics, underline material instead.

Gambling: A National Addiction

Title, writer's name, affiliation, and any other information specified by instructor.

by David Han

Double space — Professor Enid Gustafson
English 485
Lakeland College
May 10, 1996

Short title with page number on each page.

Abstract (on separate page, double-spaced, with first line flush left) provides a brief overview.

                    Abstract

Many people gamble as a form of entertainment,
but others are addicted to it. U.S. gambling
has increased because opportunities have increased: governments and private groups have
organized lotteries to pay debts or raise
money for charity, and more casinos have
opened. Proliferating gambling opportunities
have resulted in markedly more pathological
gamblers. These gamblers use gambling to satisfy an addiction and typically go through
three stages: winning, losing, and desperation. Recognition of addiction usually occurs
in the desperation phase. Treatment and rehabilitation are similar to those for other addictive behaviors. The primary sources of help
are Gamblers Anonymous and psychiatric therapy. Meanwhile increasing opportunities for
gambling are likely to aggravate the problem.

The Growth of Gambling

More Americans are gambling than ever before. The American Psychiatric Association
(1994) estimates that 1% to 3% of adults are
pathological gamblers. And they are losing
more money--$35 billion gambling legally in
1993 (Montgomery, 1995). At the same time,
there are more opportunities for gambling,
which has become "the fastest growing industry
in America" (Johnson, 1995, p. A1). More Americans went to casinos in 1993 than went to
major league baseball parks (Hirshey, 1994).
It's hard to tell, of course, which comes
first--demand or supply. As more people
gamble, more gambling opportunities are made
available; and vice versa. Gambling casinos
and government-sponsored lotteries have increased as more and more states (now 48) have
made gambling legal (Bujold, Ladouceur, Sylvain, & Boisvert, 1994).

Some states offer lottery games with
multimillion-dollar prizes. Casinos provide
resort-like atmospheres where a lot or a little
can be wagered on a variety of games. Cities,
such as Bridgeport, Connecticut ("High Stakes
in Bridgeport," 1995), are building casinos to
raise needed revenue. Iowa had no lottery in
1985. Now 90% of Iowans gamble in 10 big casinos; 5.4% of these gamblers have a gambling
problem (Johnson, 1995). Gambling is also connected with crime. In 1993, 15,000 arrests
were made in the United States for gambling

First-level heading format.

Newspaper section letter and page provided for direct quotation.

Names of all authors are given in the first reference.

Short title used for a work with no author.

Gambling   4

offenses (U.S. Bureau of the Census, 1995).
See Appendix for gambling arrests by age. Statistics like these prompted William Safire
(1995), in an op-ed column in The New York
Times, to call gambling "the new evil empire"
(p. A27).

Gambling is not limited to large estab-
lishments. It is sponsored in cities and small
towns by small charity casino operators including local fire departments and religious
groups. Besides the legal betting opportunities, illegal betting also flourishes because
of lack of enforcement of gambling laws (Rosecrance, 1988).

*Author's name ap-
pears in parenthe-
ses because it's not
in first part of sen-
tence.*

Gambling has increased on college campuses, too, as student bookmakers have prolif-
erated (Nakamura & Asher, 1995). Although
gambling by athletes and coaches is forbidden
by the National Collegiate Athletic Association, gambling by other students is governed
only by state laws. However, enforcing state
laws on a college campus can be difficult
(Nakamura & Asher, 1995). Gambling has even
moved into high schools. In Nutley, New Jer-
sey, three high school students forced a 14-
year-old student into a car, drove him to a
nearby city and dumped him; he was being punished for failing to pay a $500 gambling debt
(Russakoff, 1995). Betting is increasing even

Thesis statement.

though most gamblers lose money. But gamblers
always think they are going to win. Gambling
is rapidly becoming a national addiction.

Gambling   5

Types of Gamblers

Analysis of the gambler's personality goes back at least as far as Dostoevsky, who based his short novel The Gambler (1866) on a time in his life when he developed a passion for roulette. Custer and Milt (1985) have identified six types of gamblers:

1. Casual social gamblers. They enjoy the social and entertainment aspects of gambling. They may play cards with friends for small stakes, or they may take an occasional trip to Atlantic City or Las Vegas. Gambling is only one of many activities they enjoy.

2. Serious social gamblers. When casual gamblers begin to gamble more regularly at more than one type of game, their status is upgraded to "serious." Gambling is the primary source of pleasure and entertainment for them.

3. Antisocial-personality gamblers. Gambling is only one of their antisocial acts. They are willing to make money by using marked cards, loaded dice, or any other dishonest method.

4. Relief and escape gamblers. They use gambling to relieve feelings of boredom, frustration, and anxiety. Disputes with a spouse, workplace difficulties, loss of a job--these can lead to gambling as a way to escape.

5. Professional gamblers. For them, gambling is a business; they study all aspects of it and play to win.

First-level heading format.

Numbered list flush left; boldface type used to highlight categories.

Writer provides specific examples.

6. <u>Pathological gamblers.</u> They no longer have rational control over their gambling habits.

Transition to more specific information on pathological gambling.

Some gamblers remain casual social gamblers; others, however, become more and more involved in gambling until they reach the level of pathological gamblers.

The Pathological Gambler

Although some individuals, sponsoring groups, and governments welcome gambling as an opportunity for additional income, it comes with a heavy price--a corresponding increase in the number of pathological or compulsive

Publication date placed close to author's name.

gamblers. Custer (1987) estimates that almost 2% of adults in the United States, or 4 million people, are pathological gamblers.

When Volberg and Steadman (1992) divided pathological gamblers into groups based on income, they found that those with higher incomes tend to be white men, whereas those in lower income brackets are more likely to be nonwhite and female. Higher-income gamblers tend to gamble more frequently with deleterious effects on their personal relationships. The majority of pathological gamblers are members of this higher-income group.

Second-level heading.

<u>Compulsive or Pathological?</u>

Researchers differ on the best terminology to describe this condition. The terms <u>compulsive</u> and <u>pathological</u> are often used

Superscript number refers to content note, below.

interchangeably. Rosecrance (1988),[1] however, is not happy with either term. He writes:

Although the term <u>compulsive</u> (or its sci-

entific counterpart, <u>pathological</u>) is widely
used and accepted in reference to gambling, it
does not describe adequately the behavior pattern it seeks to define. <u>Compulsive</u> and <u>patho-
logical</u> connote psychological aberrations that
are not found in the majority of troubled gamblers. <u>Problem gambling</u> is a more accurate
term, and is defined as the losing of excessive amounts of money through gambling.
(p. 117)

However, the term <u>problem gambling</u> has not
been generally adopted. And, according to
Walker (1992b), "the term 'compulsive gambling' has also been abandoned by most [so-
cial] agencies, although it is still used by
Gamblers Anonymous and is still widely accepted as descriptively accurate by the general population" (p. 170). He goes on to trace
the evolution of these concepts from "a disorder of impulse control [compulsive gambling]"
(p. 171) to addiction in editions of the American Psychiatric Association's <u>Diagnostic and
Statistical Manual of Mental Disorders</u> from
1980 to the most recent, the fourth edition,
in 1994. This latest edition (known as <u>DSM-IV</u>)
views pathological gambling as similar to substance dependency.

    Although the differences between these

----

[1]See Rosecrance (1988, pp. 106-120) for a
lengthy discussion of the terms <u>compulsive</u> and
<u>pathological</u> as applied to gambling.

Quotation of more than 40 words is indented five spaces from the left margin and double-spaced. Page numbers given for direct quotations.

Your instructor may prefer that you place footnotes on a separate page at the end of your paper.

Gambling   8

Writer offers —
and explains —
contrasting views.

terms may seem subtle to the nonexpert, those who use the term <u>pathological</u> stress that gambling is more than just a behavioral prob- lem--that it is a medical problem as well. In other words, the gambler, like the alcoholic, may experience negative physical effects upon withdrawal.

The belief that gambling is an addic- tion--that it has both physiological and psy- chological components--is widespread. Galski (1987) believes that, besides behavioral dif- ferences, there may be actual physical differ- ences between gamblers and nongamblers because he has frequently noticed learning disabili- ties and attention disorders among gamblers. He suggests "the possibility that cortical dysfunctioning may play a role in pathological gambling" (pp. 133-134). Bujold et al. (1994) also continue to view gambling as pathological and gamblers as in need of treatment.

It's not likely that this controversy over terminology will be settled soon. But clearly the majority of experts on this sub- ject favor the term recommended in <u>DSM-IV:</u> <u>pathological gambling.</u> Therefore, that term is used here.

<u>Diagnosing Pathological Gambling</u>

A number of tests have been designed and administered in an attempt to measure and identify the characteristics of pathological gamblers (see Galski, 1987, pp. 130-132). Custer and Milt (1985) identify the following

Gambling   9

personality traits as being typical:

- a sensitive ego unable to withstand rejection
- impulsiveness
- a tendency to be overanxious and de-
  pressed
- a high level of energy, fueled by excitement and risk
- a need for instant gratification
- a low tolerance for frustration

People with these traits are candidates for
becoming pathological gamblers if the right
circumstances present themselves. Diagnostic
criteria are listed in Table 1 (p. 10).

Stages of Gambling

Gamblers are likely to go through several
stages before pathology develops (Custer &
Milt, 1985). For those who have trouble making
friends, gambling may start primarily as a social activity--an opportunity to be with other
people. Gamblers begin by betting small
amounts on card games or poker. Then they
start to bet larger sums, and winning brings
social status in addition to financial gain.
This stage inevitably leads at some point to
losing money--large sums of it. Finally,
gamblers have no control over the urge to
gamble; they bet more and more money each time
in a futile attempt to recoup their losses.
They have reached the desperation stage, even
borrowing or stealing money for gambling. Ultimately, gamblers may lose their job, their

List is introduced with a complete sentence.

Bulleted list highlights traits.

Reference to table in text.

Writer traces stages of problem.

Table gives diagnostic criteria in more detail.

Table 1. <u>Criteria for Diagnosing Pathological Gambling</u> (taken from American Psychiatric Association, 1994, p. 618)

A. Persistent and recurrent maladaptive gambling behavior as indicated by five (or more) of the following:

  (1) is preoccupied with gambling (e.g., preoccupied with reliving past gambling experiences, handicapping or planning the next venture, or thinking of ways to get money with which to gamble)

  (2) needs to gamble with increasing amounts of money in order to achieve the desired excitement

  (3) has repeated unsuccessful efforts to control, cut back, or stop gambling

  (4) is restless or irritable when attempting to cut down or stop gambling

  (5) gambles as a way of escaping from problems or of relieving a dysphoric mood (e.g., feelings of helplessness, guilt, anxiety, depression)

  (6) after losing money gambling, often returns another day to get even ("chasing" one's losses)

  (7) lies to family members, therapist, or others to conceal the extent of involvement with gambling

  (8) has committed illegal acts such as forgery, fraud, theft, or embezzlement to finance gambling

  (9) has jeopardized or lost a significant relationship, job, or educational or career opportunity because of gambling

  (10) relies on others to provide money to relieve a desperate financial situation caused by gambling

B. The gambling behavior is not better accounted for by a manic episode.

---

property, and their spouse (Bujold et al.,
1994). Thoughts of suicide are common, and
some do commit suicide.

Causes

Of course not all people gamble, nor do
all those who gamble become addicts. Why do
some people gamble excessively when figures
show that most people lose? Some psychologists
believe that gambling addiction (a compulsion
or pathology) has cognitive origins; others
believe that it has behavioral origins.

Cognitive origins of pathological gambling. Although it is true that gambling increases when opportunities increase, some
people do not gamble no matter how great the
opportunity. The obvious reason given by gamblers is "to make money." However, most habit-
ual gamblers lose money over time, so they
must have other reasons. These reasons often
vary according to the kind of gambling engaged
in. Those who gamble at horse races, baseball,
and other sports claim they do it for the excitement. Others find it an enjoyable social
activity. But pathological gamblers abandon
normal modes of reasoning; they refuse to recognize that the outcome is controlled by ran-
domizing devices such as roulette wheels, dice,
cards, and the drawing of lots. Some attribute
their winning--even of lotteries--to skill
rather than chance (Walker, 1992a, p. 84)

Clearly, many gamblers do not think ra-
tionally. Walker describes lottery ticket buy-
ers who believe they have come close to winning

Third-level heading.

Letters after dates identify two works published by same author in the same year.

when the number of their ticket is close to the winning number. Such "near-wins" encourage gamblers to try again and again. Even failure to win can entrap gamblers; they believe that, if they haven't won, the odds are that they will be lucky. Walker (1992b) explored motivation in a group of slot machine players. The results of his study, "consistent with earlier work which showed high levels of irrational thinking in artificial gambling games" (p. 245), have led him to support (somewhat tentatively) a cognitive theory of gambling motivation.

If gambling excessively is irrational, what causes people to abandon their ability to reason? Walker (1992b), while acknowledging that an attempt to connect gambling with personality traits is risky, suggests that three personality traits may predispose a person to gamble: "extroversion, locus of control [gamblers profess to believe they are in control; some actually claim that they know which numbers are more likely to win or lose in a lottery], and sensation-seeking" (p. 94). However, Walker admits that the hard evidence is not there--that results of studies showing a connection between personality traits and gambling have been inconclusive.

A study by Carlton and Goldstein (1987) showed brain activity in gamblers similar to that of those diagnosed with attention deficit disorder. Although the authors admit their study is preliminary, results suggest that

Brackets enclose material not in original.

there may be physiological reasons for gamblers' irrationality.

Behavioral origins of pathological gambling. A number of writers on pathological gambling (e.g., Bujold et al., 1994; Jacobs, 1987) have commented on the self-harming behavior of many gamblers. Not only do they gamble excessively, they exhibit other compulsive behavior such as "compulsive use of tobacco, and often of coffee, talk, and food" (McCormick & Taber, 1987, p. 21). They have trouble maintaining relationships because of their lack of empathy and their aggressive behavior. In fact, most of the literature discusses the behavior of compulsive gamblers. It is not surprising, therefore, that the main treatment these writers suggest is altering behavior.

According to McCormick and Taber (1987), pathological gamblers exhibit both obsessive and compulsive behavior. In their view, these gamblers think about gambling much of the time. Eventually, so much effort is required to maintain the habit that the enjoyment of gambling diminishes and is replaced by anxieties about where to get more money to pay off debts and gamble more. Pathological gamblers will often concede that they have a problem, but instead of trying to correct it, they use it as an excuse to keep gambling. Although they find gambling stressful, they find that not gambling is even more stressful.

Gambling   14

Psychologists are generally aware of their lack of definitive information on causes of pathological gambling. Many if not most of them, like Volberg and Steadman (1992), cite the need for further study to determine the source of this growing problem.

Treatment

The two main sources of treatment for gamblers are membership in Gamblers Anonymous and counseling by a psychotherapist. Gamblers Anonymous, modeled after Alcoholics Anonymous, approaches gambling as a disease that can be treated but never cured. It counsels gamblers to be constantly vigilant against relapse

General categories of treatment established.

(Walker, 1992b). Counseling may take place with the gambler alone, with a spouse, or in a group setting; frequently, individual and group therapy are combined. Group or individual therapy aims to change the behavior of the gambler.

Gamblers Anonymous

Gamblers Anonymous held its first meeting in 1957. Those who join must first answer the following 20 questions about the effects of gambling on their lives (Sharing Recovery, 1984, pp. 61-62):

1. Did you ever lose time from work due to gambling?

2. Has gambling ever made your home life unhappy?

3. Did gambling affect your reputation?

4. Have you ever felt remorse after gambling?

5. Did you ever gamble to get money with
   which to pay debts or otherwise solve
   financial difficulties?

6. Did gambling cause a decrease in your
   ambition or efficiency?

7. After losing did you feel you must
   return as soon as possible to win
   back your losses?

8. After a win did you have a strong
   urge to return and win more?

9. Did you often gamble until your last
   dollar was gone?

10. Did you ever borrow to finance your
    gambling?

11. Have you ever sold any real or per-
    sonal property to finance gambling?

12. Were you reluctant to use "gambling
    money" for normal expenditures?

13. Did gambling make you careless of the
    welfare of your family?

14. Did you ever gamble longer than you
    had planned?

15. Have you ever gambled to escape worry
    or trouble?

16. Have you ever committed, or consid-
    ered committing, an illegal act to
    finance gambling?

17. Did gambling cause you to have diffi-
    culty in sleeping?

18. Do arguments, disappointments, or frus-
    trations create within you an urge
    to gamble?

19. Did you ever have an urge to celebrate any good fortune by a few hours
of gambling?

20. Have you ever considered self-destruc-
tion as a result of your gambling?

Anyone who answers yes to seven or more of
these is considered in need of help and is ad-
mitted to the group (Walker, 1992b, p. 191).
There are no membership fees.

Gamblers Anonymous advocates a 12-step
program similar to that of Alcoholics Anonymous. Here is how the program works. Every
week a group of men and women, known as a fel-
lowship, gathers to share experiences,
strengths, and hope (Sharing Recovery, 1984).
Recovery depends on regular attendance at
group meetings; gamblers are expected to attend meetings for the rest of their lives. It
is difficult to measure the success of this
strategy because those who stop going to meetings cannot be counted as either successes or
failures. There is also a difference of opinion among experts as to whether total abstinence is necessary (as in the case of
alcoholics) or whether moderate social gambling is possible.

Therapy Programs

The goals of most professional treatment
programs, like those of Gamblers Anonymous,
are abstinence from gambling and repayment of
gambling debts (Volberg & Steadman, 1992). But
because these treatment programs usually re-

quire payment whereas Gamblers Anonymous is
free, lower-income gamblers are less likely to
choose this kind of help. For those who do,
payment of debts may be a difficult, if not
impossible, goal. Also, those at the lower end
of the economic scale may be more likely to
see gambling as a way to improve their economic status. Clearly, the economic status of
the gambler is a crucial element in treatment
and recovery.

Problems with treatment options explored.

Because gambling is often used as a way
of coping with stress (Bujold et al., 1994),
psychotherapy programs attempt to provide alternative coping strategies. They also help to
dispel the characteristic delusion that gamblers can predict or control the outcome of
the game. In other words, they deal with both
cognitive and behavioral aspects. Besides providing treatment for existing problems, some
programs include education in how to resist
relapse. Members learn how to develop self-
control and make changes in their lifestyle
(Bujold et al., 1994).

Help for College Students

Separate issue set off with its own heading.

Treatment at the college level is a
little different. Counseling centers are usually prepared to help students who have gambling problems, but often students don't
acknowledge such problems. Even if they do,
they usually don't show up for help until they
have faced serious consequences of gambling,
such as poor grades or a deteriorating rela-

tionship. Some colleges are planning to
incorporate advice against gambling into
orientation programs conducted by students
(Nakamura & Asher, 1995).

Prognosis

*Conclusion reiter-
ates problem and
looks toward the
future.*

    Clearly, many people are struggling with
addiction to gambling. Meanwhile, the social
and monetary pressures on pathological gamblers are increasing. Gambling has become more
and more acceptable among all classes of society, including the previously exempt middle
class. Government-sponsored lotteries continue
to proliferate. Religious and other private
groups continue to sponsor gambling in the
name of charity. It's likely that these trends
will continue. As these groups collect money,
pathological gamblers and their families will
be reaping the results: family disruption,
possible bankruptcy, and bills for treatment,
or worse. Will there be governmental regulation of gambling? That's possible; there is
already some regulation. But as with alcohol
and other addictive substances, it finally is
up to gamblers to regulate themselves. At
least one gambling researcher maintains an op-
timistic view: "In time, the vast majority of
American gamblers will learn to gamble respon-
sibly" (Rosecrance, 1988, p. 169). Want to
bet?

References

American Psychiatric Association. (1994). Diagnostic and statistical manual of mental
disorders [DSM-IV] (4th ed.). Washington,
DC: American Psychiatric Association.

Bujold, A., Ladouceur, R., Sylvain, C., &
Boisvert, J. (1994). Treatment of pathological gamblers: An experimental study.
Journal of Behavioral Therapy and Experimental Psychiatry, 25, 275-282.

Carlton, P. L., & Goldstein, L. (1987). Physiological determinants of pathological
gambling. In T. Galski (Ed.), The handbook of pathological gambling (pp. 111-
122). Springfield, IL: Thomas.

Custer, R. F. (1987). The diagnosis and scope
of pathological gambling. In T. Galski
(Ed.), The handbook of pathological gambling (pp. 3-7). Springfield, IL: Thomas.

Custer, R., & Milt, H. (1985). When luck runs
out: Help for compulsive gamblers and
their families. New York: Facts on File.

Galski, T. (1987). Psychological testing of
pathological gamblers: Research, uses,
and new directions. In T. Galski (Ed.),
The handbook of pathological gambling
(pp. 123-145). Springfield, IL: Thomas.

High stakes in Bridgeport: Two proposals for
casinos. (1995, September 25). The New
York Times, p. B7.

Hirshey, G. (1995). Gambling nation. In Ri-
conda, A. (Ed.), Gambling (pp. 43-69).

*Only works cited
in text are listed as
references. Give
last names first,
followed by ini-
tials.*

*Work in an an-
thology.*

*Newspaper article
with no author
given.*

Gambling   20

New York: Wilson. (Reprinted from The New
York Times Magazine, July 17, 1994, pp.
35-61.)

Jacobs, D. F. (1987). A general theory of ad-
dictions: Application to treatment and
rehabilitation planning for pathological
gamblers. In T. Galski (Ed.), The handbook of pathological gambling (pp. 169-
194). Springfield, IL: Thomas.

Signed newspaper article with section letter.

Johnson, D. (1995, September 25). More casinos, more players who bet until they lose
all. The New York Times, pp. A1, A10.

McCormick, R. A., & Taber, J. I. (1987). The
pathological gambler: Salient personality
variables. In T. Galski (Ed.), The handbook of pathological gambling (pp. 9-39).
Springfield, IL: Thomas.

Montgomery, D. (1995, April 30). Mr. Chips:
Folks lost $31 million last year in
Prince George's County casinos. The Wash-
ington Post, pp. F1, F4.

Nakamura, D., & Asher, M. (1995, May 14). At
Maryland, all bets aren't off: Student
gambling mirrors national trend. The
Washington Post, pp. D1, D6.

Book.

Rosecrance, J. (1988). Gambling without guilt:
The legitimation of an American pastime.
Pacific Grove, CA: Brooks/Cole.

Russakoff, D. (1995, April 12). Sports betting
rings moving into schools. The Washington
Post, p. A3.

Safire, W. (1995, September 28). New evil empire. The New York Times, p. A27.

Gambling   21

Sharing recovery through Gamblers Anonymous.
        (1984). Los Angeles: Gamblers Anonymous
        Publishing.

U.S. Bureau of the Census. (1995). Statistical
        abstract of the United States: 1995
        (115th ed.). Washington, DC: Reference
        Press.

Volberg, R. A., & Steadman, H. J. (1992). Ac-
        curately depicting pathological gamblers:
        Policy and treatment implications. Jour-
        nal of Gambling Studies, 8, 401-412.

Walker, M. B. (1992a). Irrational thinking
        among slot machine players. Journal of
        Gambling Studies, 8, 245-261.

Walker, M. B. (1992b). The psychology of gam-
        bling. New York: Pergamon.

Book with no author.

Article from journal paginated by volume.

Gambling   22

Appendix

Percentage of Persons Arrested for Gambling
in the U.S. by Age: 1993
(data from U.S. Bureau of the Census, p. 207).

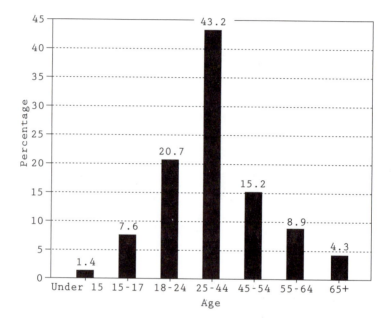

Writing a Paper in
Science or Technology:
The Citation-Sequence
and Name-Year Systems

Those writing scientific or technical papers use a variety of styles to cite and document sources. Three typical styles are described in *Scientific Style and Format: The CBE Manual for Authors, Editors, and Publishers* (6th ed., 1994). These three styles — the citation-sequence, name-year, and alphabet-number methods — are described later in this chapter, following a review of the elements of scientific and technical papers.

Parts of the Manuscript

The elements of scientific or technical papers vary according to their contents and the purpose for which they are written. Most follow one of three formats outlined here. The first format (the research report) describes the results of original research; it also requires library research to survey and describe previous related original research. The second type of paper, usually called a review paper or review article, surveys the original research on a scientific or technical subject, evaluates the results, and may suggest the likely directions of future research. Scholarly journals in the sciences and technology publish these two types of papers. The pages of both are numbered with arabic numerals starting with page 1.

The third type, the technical report or monograph, is a thorough scholarly examination and analysis of a subject. It is usually longer than the first two types; and the author, in addition to offering background information based on library research, often presents a strong viewpoint or argument. The format is the same as that for a book. It has front matter: a title page, abstract, and table of contents with all but the title page numbered with small roman numerals (the title page is counted but not numbered); page 1 begins with the introduction. This type of paper may be published separately, although sometimes it is part of an anthology. The sample paper on page 358 illustrates the format of a monograph, but your instructor may prefer that you use one of the other formats. If you plan to publish, consider which of these three types is most appropriate and check the requirements of the journal you plan to submit your article to. (For further information on publishing, see Robert A. Day's *How to Write and Publish a Scientific Paper* [Oryx, 1994] and Herbert B. Michaelson's *How to Write and Publish Engineering Papers and Reports* [Oryx, 1990]).

Here, in brief, are three possible formats for your paper, based on these three types. Consult your instructor about the parts you will need in your paper.

FOR RESEARCH REPORTS	FOR REVIEW PAPERS	FOR TECHNICAL REPORTS/MONOGRAPHS
Title page	Title page	Title page
Abstract	Abstract	Abstract
Introduction	Introduction	Table of contents
Subjects, materials, and method	Headings, as needed	List of illustrations (optional)
Results	Text	Headings, as needed
Discussion		Text
References	References	References
Tables	Tables	Tables
Glossary (optional)	Glossary (optional)	Glossary (optional)
Appendix (optional)	Appendix (optional)	Appendix (optional)

Format

Title Page

On the title page put the title, your name, and any other identifying information you and your instructor might wish, such as instructor's name, course number, and date. The title page doesn't usually carry a number but is always counted. If you plan to publish, you may be required to put a running head, a brief form of the paper's title, on the title page as well as on other pages. Some instructors prefer title, abstract, and beginning of text on page 1.

Margins and Spacing

Type your manuscript on 8½-by-11-inch paper. Use double-spacing throughout. Leave margins of one inch on all sides of the page. Indent each paragraph five spaces. Leave right margins unjustified.

Page Numbers

Number all pages consecutively with arabic numerals beginning with the title page, unless you use front matter other than the abstract (see next paragraph). Place the page number in the upper right corner. If you have only a title page and an abstract, count the title page as page 1 and number the abstract page 2; your text then begins on page 3.

When you have front matter and a table of contents, number all pages before the beginning of the text with small roman numerals (ii, iii, etc.). You do not need to place a number on the title page, but you should count it in the numbering. A running head, a brief form of the title placed before the page number, is sometimes used for papers written for publication so that initial evaluators won't be able to identify the author. Such headings are helpful in any paper because pages may be misplaced. In a college paper, however, you can place your last name instead of the title before the page number.

Abstract

Place your abstract on a separate page and number it as you would any other page. Abstracts should be concise; usually they are between 125 and 250 words. If your paper is based on your own research, give your objectives; the methods, materials, and techniques you have used; and any hypotheses you are testing. If your paper is based on library research, explain your purpose, the problem studied, or questions being explored. Use abbreviations and symbols sparingly. Do not include specific data that would require documentation. The abstract should be understandable without the rest of your paper. (See Chapter 7 for more information on writing an abstract.)

Illustrations

You may include a list of illustrations in the front part of a technical report if you have more than three or four. Illustrations for a report submitted for publication should be grouped at the end of the manuscript. In a college paper they should be placed in the text near their text reference.

You should identify the source of your information at the bottom of each illustration. If information for a figure comes from several sources, put a superscript lowercase letter after the data cited and give the sources in corresponding footnotes at the bottom of the figure. Superscript letters are used instead of numbers to avoid confusion with the numbers in the illustration. (See Chapter 7 for more information on designing illustrations.)

Headings

To help your readers grasp the structure and content of your paper and to make your paper more visually attractive, use headings derived from your outline. Two or three levels of headings are common. Under a heading you should have at least two subheadings if you have any. Avoid using the heading Introduction for your first section. Also, avoid breaking up your text with too many headings. For a typical college paper, two levels will probably be adequate.

Each level of heading should be somewhat different typographically and should have a different placement. Here is a common format:

USES OF ACUPUNCTURE
[Level one, capitals or small capitals, centered, or upper- and lowercase, boldface]

Chronic Conditions
[Level two, upper- and lowercase, italics or underlined, set at left margin]

Musculoskeletal System Problems.

[Level three, underlined upper- and lowercase or italic small capitals, run in at the beginning of a paragraph]

First Page

Place the page number and running head in the upper right corner at least one-half inch from the top of the page. Double-space twice and type the title of your paper, centered, in capital letters. Double-space and begin your introduction.

Introduction

The introduction usually doesn't have a heading; its place in the paper is self-explanatory. You should make clear here what your purpose is or what problem you are studying or trying to solve. However, avoid writing "My purpose in this paper is. . . ." If you are doing original research, you should briefly review the relevant writing on the subject so that your readers know the background of your study.

Explanatory Notes

Use endnotes sparingly to add explanatory material when its inclusion in the text would be disruptive. Place a superscript symbol such as an asterisk, dagger, or lowercase letter (a, b, c) in a typesize one or two points smaller, after the material to be explained and place a corresponding superscript symbol at the end of the paper to introduce the note. Indent the first line of each note five spaces or a half-inch.

Documentation

Those who publish their writing in technical and scientific journals (writers in chemistry, physics, biology, mathematics, engineering, medicine, nursing, and computer science) use a variety of styles to cite sources and document them in a References list at the end of the paper. Many of these writers follow the recommendations in *Scientific Style and Format: The CBE Manual for Authors, Editors, and Publishers* (6th ed., 1994) by the Council of Biology Editors. This manual recommends either the citation-sequence (C-S) system or the name-year (N-Y) system. In the C-S system, sources are cited with a number in the text that refers to a list of bibliographic entries, numbered in order of citation, at the end of the paper; in the N-Y system, sources are cited with name and date of publication. Full bibliographic information is provided in an alphabetical list at the end of the paper. However, since many writers in technology and science use the alphabet-number (A-N) system, the CBE manual also explains that system: users of the A-N system cite sources by numbers referring to a numbered alphabetical list at the end of the paper. Each of these systems is explained here briefly.

Citation-Sequence (C-S) System

If you use the C-S system, list and number your sources in the order of their citation in your text. (In later references to a source you've already cited, use the original reference number.) Place superscript numbers (or numbers in parentheses) immediately following the words in the sentence to which they refer or at the end of a sentence if they apply to the whole sentence. If you give the author's name in the sentence, you will probably want to place the number of the reference immediately after it. Do not place a number at the end of a paragraph and expect the reader to know that it applies to more than the last sentence. Place both superscript and parenthetical numbers before all marks of punctuation.

The superscript reference numbers in the text should be in a typesize one or two points smaller than the rest of the text. Assign numbers to sources in the order in which you cite them, and place them in the reference list in that order at the end of the paper. Title your list References, References Cited, or Works Cited. The following examples show two ways you might cite the information from your first source.

CITATION IN TEXT

For a citation referring to the information in the whole sentence:

```
Gross motor movements such as crawling, walking, and run-
ning are attained before fine motor movements such as
writing and object manipulation¹.
```

For a citation referring to just the author:

```
According to Gabbard¹, gross motor movements such as
crawling, walking, and running are attained before fine
motor movements such as writing and object manipulation.
```

CITATION IN LIST OF REFERENCES

```
1. Gabbard CP. Lifelong motor development. 2nd ed.
   Dubuque (IA): Brown & Benchmark; 1996. 458 p.
```

The following examples show how to list other sources in your reference list if you are using the C-S style. You can adapt them to the N-Y and A-N formats.

Books.   All authors' names should be reversed, and initials should be used instead of first and middle names (do not separate last names and first and middle initials with a comma). Titles are not underlined or italicized. Capitalize only the first word of titles; the first word of subtitles should be lowercased. Conclude with city, state or country if needed for clarity, publisher, date, and the number of pages in the book.

BOOK WITH ONE AUTHOR

```
2. Weil A. Spontaneous healing. New York: Knopf; 1995.
   309 p.
```

For a book with a subtitle:

```
3. Crick F. The astonishing hypothesis: the scientific
   search for the soul. New York: Scribner's; 1994.
   317 p.
```

BOOK WITH TWO OR MORE AUTHORS

```
4. Reynolds JF, Mair DC, Fischer PC. Writing and reading
   mental health records. Newbury Park (CA): Sage; 1992.
   109 p.
```

Give the names of all authors up to ten. If there are more than ten authors, write "and others."

BOOK WITH AN EDITOR

5. Bowen EC, Schneller BE, editors. Writing about science. New York: Oxford U Pr; 1991. 371 p.

CHAPTER OR SELECTION IN AN EDITED ANTHOLOGY

6. Weiner N. Moral problems of a scientist: the atomic bomb 1942. In: Bowen EC, Schneller BE, editors. Writing about science. 2nd ed. New York: Oxford Univ Pr; 1991. p 161-77.

CORPORATE AUTHOR

7. GAF Materials Corporation. Ruberoid® modified bitumen roofing application and specifications. Wayne (NJ): GAF; 1994. 83 p.

ELECTRONIC BOOK

8. THE WHOLE BRAIN ATLAS [monograph online]. Boston: Brigham and Women's Hospital, Harvard Medical School; 1995 [updated 1995 Aug]. Available from: Harvard Medical School via the INTERNET. Accessed 1995 Nov 19.

Periodicals. Capitalize only the first word of the article title (don't capitalize the first word of a subtitle) and all important words of journal titles. Single-word journal titles are not abbreviated (e.g., Nature); most titles are abbreviated by dropping the last few letters of a word, leaving only enough information to make it identifiable (e.g., J for "Journal" or Assoc for "Association"). Single-syllable words in journal titles are usually not abbreviated. If you don't know the accepted abbreviation of a journal, write out the title. Note that journal titles are not italicized or underlined.

ARTICLE IN JOURNAL WITH CONTINUOUS PAGINATION

9. Bosley DS. Collaborative partnerships: academia and industry working together. Tech Com 1995;42:611-19.

ARTICLE IN JOURNAL PAGINATED BY ISSUE

10. Kostelnick C. Supra-textual design: the visual rhetoric of whole documents. Tech Com Quarterly 1996 winter; 5(1):9-33.

MAGAZINE ARTICLE

11. Royte E. 'Let the bones talk' is the watchword for scientist-sleuths. Smithsonian 1996 May:83-90.

NEWSPAPER ARTICLE

12. Kolata G. Thou shalt reduce salt intake: true? false? choose your study. New York Times 1996 May 2;Sect A:11(col 1).

NEWSPAPER ARTICLE IN SPECIAL SECTION

13. Colburn D. Glaucoma: what you don't know could hurt you. Washington Post 1996 May 21;Health: 10.

ELECTRONIC JOURNAL ARTICLE

14. Strasberg YF, Strasberg MS. Gallbladder surgery. On-line Forecast [serial online] 1996 Jan. Available from: http://ada.judds.com via the INTERNET. Accessed 17 Apr 1996.

Other Sources.

MONOGRAPH

15. Hahn TE. The Alexandria canal: its history and preservation. Morgantown (WV): WV Univ Pr; 1992. 76 p.

CONFERENCE PROCEEDINGS

16. [Anonymous]. 37th International Technical Communications Conference; 1990 May 20-23; Santa Clara, CA. Washington: Society for Technical Communication; 1990. [various pagings].

Name-Year (N-Y) System

If you use the N-Y system, cite sources in the text by giving the author's name followed by the year of publication. If you name the author in the sentence, include just the year in parentheses. In the reference list, list authors' names in alphabetical order followed by the year of publication. For sources with multiple authors, cite the authors in your text by giving only the first name followed by "and others" and the date.

CITATION

Gross motor movements such as crawling, walking, and running are attained before fine motor movements such as
writing and object manipulation (Gabbard 1992).

or

According to Gabbard (1992), gross motor movements such
as crawling, walking, and running are attained before
fine motor movements such as writing and object manipulation.

If you give both name and year in the text there is no need for an in-text citation.

In his 1992 study, Gabbard points out that gross motor
movements such as crawling, walking, and running are attained before fine motor movements such as writing and
object manipulation.

REFERENCES USING THE N-Y SYSTEM

Gabbard CP. 1992. Lifelong motor development. 2nd ed.
Dubuque (IA): Brown & Benchmark. 458 p.

Obarzanek E, Velletri PA, Cutler JA. 1996. Dietary protein and blood pressure. JAMA 275(20):1549-56.

Roger M. 1989. Perinatal infection. In: Kaslow RA, Francis DP, editors. The epidemiology of AIDS: expression, occurrence, and control of HIV-1 infection.
New York: Oxford Univ Pr; 231-41.

Alphabet-Number (A-N) System

The Alphabet-Number (A-N) system is a popular citation system. If you use it, arrange the reference list alphabetically and number the entries. Cite references in the text by number. Format entries like those in the N-Y system.

REFERENCES USING THE A-N SYSTEM

1. Gabbard CP. 1992. Lifelong motor development. 2nd ed. Dubuque (IA): Brown & Benchmark. 458 p.

2. Obarzanek E, Velletri PA, Cutler JA. 1996. Dietary protein and blood pressure. JAMA 275(20):1549-56.

3. Roger M. 1989. Perinatal infection. In: Kaslow RA, Francis DP, editors. The epidemiology of AIDS: expression, occurrence, and control of HIV-1 infection. New York: Oxford Univ Pr. p 231-41.

Choosing Your Documentation System

Each of the three systems described above has its advantages and disadvantages. Using one of the number systems makes it easier to give several sources in one citation. The citation-sequence system is often preferred to the alphabet-number system because the latter requires a separation of numbers, according to the alphabetical order ([2,4,3,8,9,1]). The sequential numbering of the C-S system saves space ([2-4,7-9]). On the other hand, with the A-N system the order of names in the reference list does not change even when, during revision, the order of blocks of text may be changed.

The N-Y system also does not require reordering or renumbering of the reference list if the order of citations changes or if new names are added during the writing of the paper. And it provides immediate information for the reader (the author's name and date of publication). However, when several sources are cited in one place, the list of names and dates can create a long interruption in the text of the paper.

Use the citation style that works best for you. If you plan to publish, follow the style of the journal you submit your manuscript to. The following sample paper uses the C-S format — the one preferred by the CBE manual and by the *American Medical Association Manual of Style* (8th ed., 1989).

Bibliography

You may want to provide your readers with a list of sources that you used for background information but didn't cite specifically in your paper. This list appears with the heading Bibliography after the list of references.

Sample Research Paper
Using the Citation-Sequence System

Melanie Reynolds, the author of the following scientific paper, uses the citation-sequence style of documentation described above. With this style, references are numbered in the order in which they are mentioned in the text, and the list of references at the end of the paper is then arranged in numerical order. When a source is referred to more than once in the text, the original number assigned to it is repeated.

Although the subject of the paper — environmental tobacco smoke (ETS) — and many of the sources cited are technical, Reynolds translated technical terms into language understandable to a general, rather than a primarily professional, audience. She also used extensive evidence to advance her argument for stronger measures against secondhand smoke.

CBE style calls for a title page that is not numbered but counted as part of the text.

The Effects of Environmental
Tobacco Smoke
by
Melanie Reynolds

Professor, course, and date provided.

Professor Andrea McCuen
Anatomy 281
May 10, 1996

Effects of ETS ii

ABSTRACT

Tobacco, found growing in the Americas by Columbus, was soon grown and smoked around the world. Cigarettes, a later American invention, came to be the most popular way to satisfy the addiction to nicotine. The accompanying health hazards of smoking--primarily lung cancer and heart disease--did not seem to affect sales negatively.

Awareness of the health problems caused by environmental tobacco smoke (ETS) came much later. Exposure to ETS in the workplace, in public buildings, or at home can result in a number of health problems: lung cancer, emphysema, and heart disease for adults, and asthma and SIDS for children.

Recently, smoking policies have been introduced that limit the secondhand smoke levels in public buildings, schools, and workplaces. Enforcing these regulations is expected to reduce ETS-caused health problems in adults. It will be more difficult to eliminate the health problems children face in the home, but parent education and awareness may diminish even these. Ultimately, tobacco should be declared an illegal substance.

Use small roman numerals for any front matter and arabic numbers for all pages in the body of the text.

An information abstract summarizes the paper's contents. Complete details and statistics are not included.

Table of contents (required only for books and monographs) based on text headings. First-level headings are typed flush left; second-level headings are indented.

Effects of ETS iii

CONTENTS

Effects of ETS 1

Our atmosphere--the air we breathe--is full of pollutants; some are natural, and some are produced by humans. President Truman (in office from 1945-1952) was the first federal official to direct the attention of the US government to the problems of pollution. In 1955, Congress passed the Air Pollution Control Act.[1]

Superscript number refers to first item in References.

It was a beginning. Other laws were passed, but they were aimed only at cleaning up outdoor air. Eventually attention turned to the indoor environment and particularly to the pollution caused by smoking--to environmental tobacco smoke (ETS)[a].

Superscript letters distinguish citations of content notes from citations of numbered references.

ETS consists of a mixture of mainstream smoke (MS)[b], and, to a lesser extent, sidestream smoke (SS). This mixture contains thousands of constituents, including respiratory irritants, toxins, and carcinogens. Until recently, most people were concerned only about the health of smokers. Now, however, as evidence of the dangers of ETS increases, the welfare of those who do not smoke is being considered, and smoking is being eliminated in workplaces and public places. The effect of ETS on children in the home, however, has not received the attention it deserves.

Introduction sets up problems of ETS and provides a summary statement.

HISTORY OF SMOKING IN AMERICA

First-level heading centered.

When Columbus arrived in America, he found Native Americans cultivating tobacco and using it for smoking, chewing, and snuffing. It was also being cultivated in Brazil, Central America, and Mexico[2]. Tobacco seeds soon

Historical information traces origins of tobacco use.

Effects of ETS 2

were taken to Spain, Portugal, and Rome, where tobacco was grown and used for its supposed medicinal purposes. Sir John Hawkins, the naval hero, introduced it to England in 1565, and it quickly spread to all parts of the world. It became a profitable export crop in the colonies after 1612.

Objections to the use of tobacco arose early. James I of England (1603-1625) taxed tobacco imports and criticized its use in <u>A Counterblast to Tobacco</u>. Tobacco users were punished in Russia and Turkey. However, these efforts had little effect[2]. In the United States, tobacco was smoked in cigars and pipes until after the Civil War, when cigarettes were introduced. Then tobacco consumption exploded: people began to use it extensively in almost every part of the world.

Early objections to tobacco smoke described; colorful quotation provided.

Nonsmokers have complained about tobacco smoke since smoking began. Goethe, (1749-1832), the German poet and scientist, complained about ETS, even though he didn't call it that: "Smokers pollute the air far and wide and asphyxiate every respectable individual who cannot smoke in self-defence. Who can enter the room of a smoker without feeling nausea?"[3].

Over the years, especially in the second half of this century, tobacco companies have marketed numerous brands of cigarettes, both to entice people to smoke and to satisfy the needs of those who are already smoking. Much of the advertising, like the ads featuring Joe

Effects of ETS 3

Camel, has seemed designed to lure young people to smoke. The millions of smokers in this country have responded by paying billions of dollars to appease their habit.

EARLY RESEARCH ON THE EFFECTS OF SMOKING

The reasons behind the desire to smoke range from the desire for social acceptance to the satisfaction of a powerful physical need created by the chemical ingredients in the cigarette. At first, people were unaware of the serious physical effects of smoking; they were aware only of the resulting bad breath, smelly clothes and hair, raspy voice, cough, and yellow-stained teeth and fingers.

Early research focused on the harmful effects of smoking on smokers. Nonsmokers, of course, could see and smell cigarette smoke but gave no thought to its effects on them. Most people did not realize that this second-hand smoke was just as deadly to nonsmokers as it was to smokers. Recently, however, research has begun to focus on the hazards for nonsmokers. In 1986, Surgeon General C. Everett Koop issued a report, The Health Consequences of Involuntary Smoking[4], that alerted Americans to a growing problem: secondhand smoke has caused health problems, such as lung cancer, emphysema, and heart disease, among those who do not smoke. And in 1992, ETS was classified by the US Environmental Protection Agency (EPA) as a human carcinogen. In fact, research funded by the tobacco companies themselves and leaked to the public by a former tobacco com-

Author describes how ETS's effects on nonsmokers came to light. (Her summary anticipates later details.)

At first, acronym is spelled out and followed by its abbreviation; the abbreviation is used from then on.

Effects of ETS 4

pany officer showed that sidestream smoke is carcinogenic[5].

CONSTITUENTS OF SECONDHAND SMOKE

Tobacco smoke is a complex aerosol, consisting of liquid particles dispersed in a gas medium. Each liquid particle, from 0.2 to 1.0 microns in length, is composed of at least thousands of inorganic and organic chemicals consisting of respiratory irritants, toxins, mutagens, and carcinogens[6].

The type of tobacco, the physical design of the cigarette, and the smoker's puffing characteristics all affect the composition of the smoke[7]. Temperatures at the butt end of the cigarette reach only 30°C, whereas those at the burning end near 900°C. This high temperature of combustion helps generate the many chemicals in cigarette smoke[8].

Author provides scientific details that show why secondhand smoke is so harmful.

Because of the temperature of combustion and the filtration by the cigarette, most of the gas and liquid particulate components of cigarette smoke are found in greater concentrations in sidestream smoke than in mainstream smoke[8]. The following carcinogens have been identified as having increased concentrations in sidestream smoke: 2-naphthylamine, aniline, and benzo(a)pyrene. The list of other irritants and dangerous chemicals found in cigarette smoke is a long one: glycoproteins, formaldehyde, ammonia, nitrogen oxides, hydrogen cyanide, carbon dioxide, carbon monoxide, N-nitrosamines, and nicotine, the main chemical that causes addiction to cigarettes[6].

Effects of ETS 5

HEALTH PROBLEMS CAUSED BY SECONDHAND SMOKE

The irritants in secondhand smoke cause problems in the mucous membranes of the nose, throat, lower respiratory tract, and the eyes[4]. Respiratory tract symptoms such as itching, cough, and sore throat are common, as are reddening and itching in the eyes. Glycoproteins, found in tobacco smoke (including sidestream smoke), can cause allergies and the formation of blood clots[5]. Many adults also experience reduced lung function and chest discomfort as the result of ETS[9].

Health problems caused by ETS described in more detail.

In addition, ETS produces dangerous long-term effects. Diseases such as lung cancer and heart disease are major threats to nonsmokers that need to be addressed.

Author provides transition to two major health threats of ETS.

Lung Cancer

Second-level heading flush left.

The first disease to be connected with mainstream smoking was lung cancer. Lung cancer from passive smoking occurs because much higher levels of carbon monoxide and carbon dioxide are generated during smoldering of sidestream smoke than during puff-drawing of filtered mainstream smoke[4]. Furthermore, 4 to 10 times more nitrogen oxide is released in sidestream smoke than is inhaled in mainstream smoke. Most of the particulates from these toxic chemicals are smaller than $1\mu m$. This small size allows for penetration into the smallest airways in the lungs[4]. Once in the lungs, many of the secondhand smoke particles begin to express their toxic and carcinogenic effects.

Effects of ETS 6

Of course, smokers have a much higher
risk of lung cancer than nonsmokers who inhale
secondhand smoke. But the malignant effects of
secondhand smoke on nonsmokers are still cause
for alarm. A British study[10] concluded that nonsmokers living with smokers have a 35 percent
greater risk of lung cancer than nonsmokers
who live with nonsmokers. In fact, according
to the study, secondhand smoke is responsible
for the deaths of 3000 of the 110,000 Americans who succumb to cancer each year.

Heart Disease

In their 1995 article, Glantz and Parmley[11] explain the relationship between passive
smoking and heart disease. They point out that
the detrimental effects of tobacco smoke on
the cardiovascular system are responsible for
37,000 of the 53,000 total ETS-related deaths
resulting from heart disease. In fact, according to Boyle[12], passive smoking is "the third
leading preventable cause of death, after active smoking and alcohol".

When nonsmokers inhale secondhand smoke,
their blood's ability to deliver oxygen to the
myocardium (heart tissue) is reduced. The carbon monoxide in secondhand smoke competes with
oxygen for binding sites on red blood cells,
thus displacing and consequently inhibiting
normal oxygen delivery to the heart[11]. Many
children of smoking parents exhibit raised
levels of 2,3-DPG, an enzyme that compensates
for oxygen deprivation by facilitating the
oxygen unloading by red blood cells. Ulti-

Effects of ETS 7

mately, Glanz and Parmley found, passive smoking reduces oxygen delivery to the heart from the blood; it also reduces the heart's ability to effectively use the oxygen it does receive[10].

Author clarifies study's findings.

HEALTH EFFECTS ON CHILDREN

The developing lungs of children are more vulnerable to the toxins in cigarette smoke than are those of adults[13]. Yet children are exposed to secondhand smoke almost everywhere, and they have few choices as to where they go or whom they must be with. Former Surgeon General Joycelyn Elders pointed out that 9,000,000 children under the age of 5 are exposed daily in their homes to secondhand smoke; 800,000 are exposed at school or in their child-care centers; and many others breathe smoke-polluted air in automobiles, shopping malls, and restaurants[14]. Three groups of investigators from the Harvard School of Public Health have agreed that children exposed to parental smoking exhibit decreased lung function into adulthood, the effects of which are irreversible[15].

Author explains why ETS poses special risks for children.

According to a 1995 EPA report[16], exposure to secondhand smoke causes 300,000 lower respiratory tract infections annually, including pneumonia and bronchitis in children under 18 months of age. These infections, the effects of exposure to parental smoking, result in 15,000 unnecessary hospitalizations yearly[16].

Statistics provide compelling support for author's point.

The Third National Health and Nutrition

Examination Survey (NHANES III), conducted
from 1988 to 1991, resulted in this startling
statistic: "For ages 2 months to 11 years, the
prevalence of reported ETS exposure at home
was 43 percent"[16].

Children may be affected even before
their birth by the smoking habits of their
mothers. Figure 1 (p. 9) shows that the babies
of mothers who smoke during pregnancy are more
likely to have below-average weight at the
time of birth[17]. Low birthweight can affect
the chance of survival or the susceptibility
to disease.

Asthma and sudden infant death syndrome
are two major childhood diseases linked to
secondhand smoke.

Asthma

Young children's lungs are especially
vulnerable to the toxic chemicals in smoke.
Some 8000 to 26,000 of nonasthmatic children
develop asthma each year[18]. Children under 5
who are exposed to maternal smoking are 2.1
times more likely to develop asthma than children who are not exposed to such conditions[19].
For children already asthmatic, secondhand
smoke exposure increases the number of occur-
rences and the severity of symptoms for between 200,000 and 1,000,000 of them every
year[20]. Their asthmatic condition will stay
with these children for the rest of their
lives

SIDS

The number 1 cause of death for infants

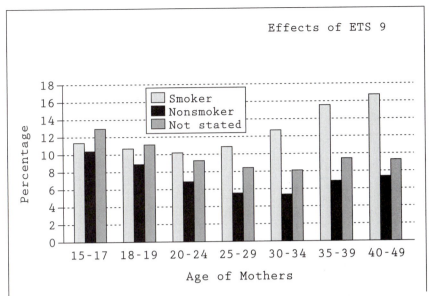

Effects of ETS 9

Figure 1   Percentage of babies with low birthweight by age and smoking status of mother: 1992
(data from US Bureau of the Census[17] p 83)

*Source of informa-
tion identified at
bottom of illustra-
tion.*

between the age of 1 month and 1 year is sudden infant death syndrome (SIDS)--'the sudden,
unexpected death of an apparently healthy infant'[21]. It's clear that exposure to secondhand smoke causes many of these deaths because
Skolnick[18] found that the babies of smoking
mothers are 3 times more likely to die of SIDS
than those infants not exposed to smoke. Secondhand smoke has greater amounts of ammonia,
benzene, carbon monoxide, nicotine, and carcinogens such as 2-naphthylamine than does
mainstream smoke, so children of smoking mothers are especially vulnerable[21]. In addition,
even though breast feeding usually protects
children against many childhood illnesses

Effects of ETS 10

because of the nutrients provided by the
mother, those infants who were breast fed by
smoking mothers were more likely to die of
SIDS[21].

CURRENT REGULATIONS

In January 1993, the Environmental Protection Agency published an assessment of the
respiratory health effects of ETS[20]. Based on
the scientific evidence collected, the EPA
concluded that secondhand smoke "belongs in
the category of compounds classified as Group
A (known human) carcinogens" and that widespread exposure to secondhand smoke in the
United States presents a serious and substantial public health risk. The report concludes
that secondhand smoke is responsible for 3000
lung cancer deaths per year and that 2200 of
these are the result of exposure outside of
the home[22]. The American Heart Association,
the American Lung Association, and the American Cancer Society all agree that ETS should
be treated as an "environmental toxin" and

*Author tells how
problems with ETS
have culminated
in major legisla-
tion.*

that it should be banned from the workplace
and other public places[18]. On the basis of
this evidence the Smoke-Free Environment Act
of 1993 was passed.

*Key provisions of
the law described.*

The Smoke-Free Environment Act provides
smoking restrictions to protect nonsmokers
from involuntary exposure to secondhand smoke.
Such restrictions apply to indoor environ-
ments, specifically any building regularly entered by 10 or more persons at least 1 day per

Effects of ETS 11

week, including shopping malls and federal, state, and local government buildings[23]. This act essentially provides comprehensive protection to all persons, including children, workers, and the general public--except in their homes. Many preschool children, of course, spend virtually all their time at home.

OPPOSITION TO SMOKE-FREE REGULATIONS

The EPA declaration of secondhand smoke as a Class A carcinogen, in a class with asbestos, benzene, and radon, ignited a debate over the rights of smokers versus nonsmokers[24]. For years, opponents of smoking restrictions have refuted the scientific evidence presented by the EPA that secondhand smoke carries carcinogenic elements. The Tobacco Institute, the main lobbying group for powerful tobacco companies such as Philip Morris and R.J. Reynolds, has been the major opponent of smoking restrictions--even though the Institute's own research (which it attempted to keep secret) showed that passive smoking is harmful[5].

Author introduces — and refutes — opponents to tobacco restrictions.

However, the credibility of the tobacco companies is beginning to erode. In an issue of JAMA devoted primarily to the problems caused by smoking and the attempts by the tobacco companies to cover up these problems (19 July 1995), Barnes and others[5] reveal the existence of internal documents resulting from research Brown and Williamson Tobacco Corporation (B&W) conducted on sidestream smoking.

Effects of ETS 12

They charge that B&W hid and falsified its research when it found that the results were un-
favorable. They received some of the papers
from an anonymous source[c]; some came from a
former BAT (British American Tobacco Company)
officer. The information they gathered makes
clear that ETS is very harmful to the health
of nonsmokers.

*Block quotations
indented five
spaces.*

> The tobacco industry's strategy re-
> garding passive smoking has been remark-
> ably similar to its strategy regarding
> active smoking. It has privately con-
> ducted internal research, at least some
> of which has supported the conclusion
> that passive smoking is dangerous to
> health, while it has publicly denied
> that the hazards have been proven.
> Healthy Buildings International, a com-
> pany that has testified at over 100 congres-
> sional hearings that secondhand smoke is not a
> health threat in properly ventilated build-
> ings, was investigated for falsifying data on
> the risks of secondhand smoke while at the
> same time concealing that it works for the To-
> bacco Institute[25]. Barnes and others also
> point out the duplicity of the tobacco compa-
> nies[5].

CONCLUSION

It is astonishing that it took so long
for the harmful effects of secondhand smoke to
be recognized. Since the first report on these
hazards in 1986, other research has followed
showing that secondhand smoke is a very dan-

Effects of ETS 13

gerous compound. Finally, measures are being
taken to prevent many of these poisons from
harming the public. The Smoke-Free Environment
Act of 1993 provided the strict regulations
that must be implemented and enforced to help
keep the air clean. It is unlikely that we
will ever breathe totally unpolluted air, but
restrictions on smoking will ensure that the
air we breathe in the future will be considerably less harmful than the air we have
breathed in the past. Smokers themselves have
become more aware of the harm they can cause
nonsmokers and are noticeably more careful.

Author summarizes her findings and discusses the current state of the issue.

Some progress has been made, but the news
is not all good. The editors of JAMA[26] (April
1996) state that whereas the number of smokers
declined for 25 years before leveling off between 1990 to 1993 at about 25 percent, smoking has increased among 8th, 10th, and 12th-
grade students. In the same issue, Pirkle and
others[27] explain the results of their study on
ETS. They found evidence of cotinine (the
harmful element of nicotine) in a high proportion of the people tested--both smokers and
nonsmokers.

Obviously, more needs to be done. Further
restrictions on smoking in public places
should be implemented, but the ultimate goal
should be the elimination of tobacco products.
For years, this multibillion dollar industry
has provided money to political parties and
individuals in exchange for leniency in making
laws against smoking. In a 1995 editorial in

Author has built up evidence to make an argument for the banning of tobacco products.

Effects of ETS 14

<u>JAMA</u>[28], officials of the American Medical As-
sociation outline steps they think should be
taken. They conclude with these words:

*Powerful quota-
tion supports au-
thor's argument.*

> In summary, the evidence is unequiv-
> ocal--the US public has been duped by the
> tobacco industry. No right-thinking indi-
> vidual can ignore the evidence. We should
> all be outraged, and we should force the
> removal of this scourge from our nation
> and by so doing set an example for the
> world. . . .

*Paper ends on
forceful note.*

Politicians must stop accepting money
from tobacco companies. Instead, they should
classify smoking tobacco as an illegal substance because of its carcinogenic and toxic
chemicals. Secondhand smoke would then no
longer be a problem, and millions of American
lives would be saved. I believe this will happen. I just don't know when.

Effects of ETS 15

NOTES

Content notes precede references.

a. Other terms used for ETS include <u>secondhand</u> <u>smoke</u> and <u>ambient smoke</u>. The inhaling of smoke by nonsmokers is often referred to as <u>involuntary smoking</u> or <u>passive smoking</u>.

b. Mainstream smoke is smoke inhaled by the smoker and then exhaled. Sidestream smoke comes from the burning end of a cigarette.

c. The anonymous source (the person who collected the damaging papers, smuggled them out of the offices of the Brown and Williamson Tobacco Corporation, and then leaked the information) was revealed in a <u>Washington Post</u> story on 23 June 1996[29]. He is Merrell Williams, hired as a paralegal by a Louisville law firm to secretly collect the information from the tobacco company, the law firm's client. The law firm, anticipating possible lawsuits by cigarette smokers, was planning to use the information Williams gathered to build a defense.

Begin new page, center heading, and double-space throughout.

All authors' names reversed. No commas separate last names and initials.

Encyclopedia article.

Introduction to a book.

Government agency report.

Only first word of journal articles (and book titles) capitalized.

Book titles not underlined or italicized.

Published proceedings of a symposium.

REFERENCES

1. Spengler JD, Samet JM. A perspective on indoor and outdoor air pollution. In: Samet JM, Spengler JD, editors. Indoor air pollution: a health perspective. Baltimore: Johns Hopkins Univ Pr; 1991. p 1-29.

2. Moore EL. Tobacco. Vol. 26. Encyclopedia Americana; 1996.

3. Shephard RJ. The risks of passive smoking. New York: Oxford Univ Pr; 1982. Introduction; p 9-11.

4. US Department of Health and Human Services. The health consequences of involuntary smoking. A report of the surgeon general. Washington: USGPO; 1986. DHHS, PHS Publication (CDC) 87-8398.

5. Barnes DE, Hanauer P, Slade J, Bero LA, Glantz SA. Environmental tobacco smoke: the Brown and Williamson documents. JAMA 1995;274(3):248-53.

6. Douville JA. Active and passive smoking hazards in the workplace. New York: Van Nostrand Reinhold; 1990. 221 p.

7. Eatough DJ, Hansen LD, Lewis EA. The chemical characterization of environmental tobacco smoke. In: Ecobichon DJ, Wu JM, editors. Environmental tobacco smoke. Proceedings of the international symposium at McGill University; 1989 Nov 3-4; Lexington (MA): Lexington Books; 1990. p 3-39.

8. Guerin MR, Jenkins RA, Tomkins BA. The chemistry of environmental tobacco smoke: composition and measurement. Chelsea (MI):

Effects of ETS 17

Lewis; 1992. 330 p.

9. Browner CB. Environmental tobacco smoke: EPA's report. EPA 1993;19(4):18-19.

10. Wald NJ, Nanchahal K, Thompson SG. Does breathing other people's tobacco smoke cause lung cancer? British Med J 1986;293(6556):1217.

Journal names abbreviated.

11. Glantz SA, Parmley WW. Passive smoking and heart disease. JAMA 1995;273(13):1047-53.

Volume and issue numbers provided for journal article.

12. Boyle P. The hazards of passive--and active--smoking. New England J of Med 1993;328(23):1708-9.

13. Raloff J. Threat from passive smoke upgraded. Science News 1994;145(24):373.

14. United States Cong. Senate. Surgeon General M. J. Elders speaking for smoke-free environment act of 1993. 103rd Cong., 2nd Sess. S. Doc. 1680 (1994). USGPO.

Congressional testimony.

15. Marino G. Parents' smoking damages their kids' lungs. Science News 1994;146(1):5.

16. Nelson H. USA:EPA passive smoking report. Lancet 1994;340(8815):360-1.

17. US Bureau of the Census. Statistical abstract of the United States. 115th ed. Washington: US Bureau of the Census; 1995. 1045 p.

18. [Anonymous]. Draft report on health effects of passive smoking made available. EPA J 1992;18(3):45.

Anonymous article.

19. Skolnick A. First AHA statement on tobacco and children. JAMA 1994;272(11):841.

20. [Anonymous]. Secondhand smoke designated a known human carcinogen. EPA J 1993; 19(2):5.

Effects of ETS 18

21. Klonoff-Cohen HS, Wiley KJ. The effect of passive smoking and tobacco exposure through breast milk on sudden infant death syndrome. JAMA 1995;273(1):795-8.

22. Stone R. Study implicates secondhand smoke. Science 1994;264(5155):30.

23. Brahams D. Passive smoking. Lancet 1993;341(8844):525-26.

24. Hecht SS, Hoffmann D. A tobacco-specific lung carcinogen in the urine of men exposed to cigarette smoke. New England J of Med 1993;329(21):1543-6.

25. Hall CW. US probing firm that studied secondhand smoke. Washington Post 1996 Feb 16;Sect D:1(col 1).

26. [Anonymous]. Editorial. JAMA 1996;275 (16):1281-84.

27. Pirkle JL, Flegal KM, Bernert JT, Brody DJ, Etzel RA, Maurer KR. Exposure of the US population to environmental tobacco smoke: the third national health and nutrition examination survey, 1988 to 1991. JAMA 1996;275(16):1233-40.

28. Todd JS, Drummond R, McAfee RE, Bristow LR, Painter JT, Reardon TR, Johnson DH, Corlin RF, Coble YD, Dickey NW, and others. The Brown and Williamson documents: where do we go from here? [editorial]. JAMA 1995;274(3):256-58.

29. Leiby R. Smoking gun. Washington Post 1996 June 23;Sect F:1(col 2).

Section, page, and column numbers provided for newspaper articles.

Editorial.

Multiple authors.

A P P E N D I X   1

Annotated List
of References

This guide to reference sources can help you plan your research by offering a list of reference books, indexes, and current journals in the disciplines. From this list you should be able to design a plan of action for your research. Some items in this list may not be available in your library, and there may be some useful resources available locally that aren't listed here. You may want to supplement the sources here by going over your research plan with a reference librarian or your instructor.

The first section covers general sources of information—sources that are useful in a variety of situations and that every researcher should know about. The next section lists resources that are useful generally in the humanities, social sciences, and sciences followed by resources in specific academic disciplines. Internet resources are indicated for most disciplines, more as illustrations of what are likely to be available than as recommendations. The Internet is a mercurial place where sites change frequently and new resources are added daily.

Availability of reference books and indexes in electronic format is shown, though you will have to determine which ones you have access to. The same index, for example, could be available through an off-campus computer connected to the college's PAC (public access catalog), a computer tape or CD-ROM running on the campus network, a local area network (LAN), or at a single computer workstation in the library. In some cases, libraries may be able to search a particular index only through an expensive database service and may charge for searches performed by librarians. Check with a librarian for the best way to access the indexes you need for your research.

The annotations given here should help you make choices among reference tools, but you will also need to consult the front pages of reference books or the help screens or user manuals of electronic resources to find out how to use the resource and what abbreviations are employed in the text.

Brief Contents of Appendix

General Sources

Guides to Reference Works

The American Library Association Guide to Information Access. New York: Random House, 1994.

> A current guide that covers online catalogs, CD-ROM indexes, and Internet resources in a general way, then surveys thirty-six areas — such as film, literature, and history — listing guides to reference books, print and electronic indexes, government agencies, and associations for each. Includes academic topics but also covers subjects such as automobiles and parenting.

Sheehy, Eugene P. *Guide to Reference Books.* 10th ed. Chicago: American Library Association, 1986. With supplements.

> Identifies reference books in all formats published all over the world. Covers general reference works (such as national bibliographies published in various countries) as well as reference books for disciplines. Under the topic Economics, for example, there are descriptions under the subheadings Economic Conditions, Economic Development, Accounting, Advertising and Public Relations, and so on. This is one of the best and most complete bibliographies of reference books, but many of the items listed are available only in large research libraries. The supplements include many electronic resources.

Walford, A. J. *Walford's Guide to Reference Material.* 6th ed. London: Library Association, 1991–1994.

> An international guide to reference books, with a British emphasis. Volume 1 covers science and technology; volume 2 covers social sciences, history, religion, and philosophy; volume 3 covers general sources, languages and literature, and the arts. As in Sheehy, entries are annotated.

Catalogs and Directories

Books in Print. New York: Bowker, 1948–. Annually, with supplements.

> A list of books currently available from publishers and distributors, including scholarly and trade books, paperbacks, and children's books. Searchable by author, title, or subject. The print version includes a directory of

publishers' addresses. *Books in Print Plus* on CD-ROM includes brief reviews for many of the books. This is a good place to search for currently available books on any topic.

Directory of Electronic Journals, Newsletters, and Academic Discussion Lists. Washington, DC: Association of Research Libraries, 1991–. Annually.

A useful resource guide to materials available through the Internet for the serious researcher. Includes information on how to subscribe or join a discussion list and gives detailed descriptions, distribution information, and electronic sites.

Gale Directory of Databases. Detroit: Gale, 1993–. Annually.

Covers databases available online, on CD-ROM, or in other electronic formats. Detailed descriptions are included, as are indexes by subject, title, vendor, and producer. Available in electronic format.

Gale Directory of Publications and Broadcast Media. Detroit: Gale, 1990–. Annually, with supplements.

Covers magazines, newspapers, and journals, as well as radio, television, and cable stations. The arrangement is geographic. It includes indexes. Subscription and advertising information are also provided.

Katz, William. *Magazines for Libraries.* 8th ed. New York: Bowker, 1995.

A selective, annotated list of recommended periodicals arranged by subject. The annotations evaluate the periodical in terms of approach, audience, and importance to its field. This is an excellent place to check a given periodical's reputation and find out whether a popular or news publication has a known political or social bias. New editions are published every few years.

Ulrich's International Periodicals Directory. New York: Bowker, 1932–. Annually, with supplements.

A listing of over 145,000 periodicals and series from all over the world, arranged by subject and with indexes. It includes annuals, continuations, conference proceedings, and other series published at least once every three years. In addition to listing basic bibliographic information, addresses of editors and publishers, and prices, it sometimes includes very brief descriptive statements. One of the most useful features of *Ulrich's* is the inclusion of information on where a given periodical is indexed. Also available in electronic format.

WorldCat (Online). Available through the OCLC FirstSearch service.

A user-friendly version of the OCLC database, a catalog of bibliographic records from libraries around the world. It lists close to 30 million books, videos, periodicals, and recordings, and is updated daily. It is searchable by author, title, or subject, and searches can be refined by limiting publication year, language, and format. This is an excellent place to start if you need a comprehensive bibliography and are searching, for example, for every edition of every book written by a given author. If your library does not have FirstSearch access, you may still be able to search the OCLC database through a public terminal or by arrangement with a librarian.

Indexes to Periodicals

Your library probably has access to one or more of the following indexes in print, microtext, or electronic format. These are particularly good resources if your topic is likely to be covered in periodicals.

General Periodicals Index. San Mateo, CA: Information Access, 1985–. Monthly.

Sometimes called *InfoTrac,* this electronic database of 1,100 magazines and newspapers includes abstracts for some of the indexed articles. A companion index, *Academic Index,* covers many popular magazines as well as major journals in the disciplines. Another version, *Expanded Academic Index,* is an in-depth interdisciplinary index to the literature of academic disciplines that covers around 1,000 magazines and journals.

New York Times Index. New York: New York Times, 1851–. Semimonthly.

Even if you don't read the original newspaper stories, this remarkable index can give you a detailed grasp of the chronology of events. It tends to place references under fairly broad headings; then it arranges news stories chronologically, giving not only the exact citation of the date, page, and column of the story but a short summary of each cited story. Many libraries keep a microfilm copy of the newspaper, and some have a full-text computerized version of the index.

NewsBank. New Canaan, CT: NewsBank, 1982–. Monthly.

A newspaper index available in various formats. Some libraries subscribe to a CD-ROM version that comes with full text of a locally prominent newspaper. Other libraries have an index coupled with microfiche newspaper files, covering articles from over 100 U.S. newspapers.

Nexis/Lexis (Online). Mead Data Central. Daily updates.

Nexis covers newswires and newspapers from around the world, generally from the mid-1980s to the present, and is updated daily. Many of the resources covered are presented in full text. *Lexis* contains full text of U.S. laws — both state and national — and legal information sources.

Periodical Abstracts OnDisc. Ann Arbor, MI: University Microfilms International, 1986–. Monthly.

An index to popular periodicals with abstracts. More than one version is available, covering from 500 to 1,500 publications, depending on which version your library subscribes to.

Readers' Guide to Periodical Literature. New York: Wilson, 1900–. Semimonthly.

A venerable and high-quality index to selected popular magazines, available in print and electronic versions. One electronic version, *Readers' Guide Abstracts,* includes brief descriptions of about 60,000 articles a year.

Indexes to Special Materials

The following indexes cover materials not based on subject matter but on the format or type of publication — book reviews in all fields, doctoral dissertations, government documents, and so on. They overlap somewhat with other indexes and bibliographies. For example, the articles you would find about a person in the *Biography Index* might also turn up in a search of the *Readers' Guide to Periodical Literature,* and an essay covered in the *Essay and General Literature Index* might also turn up in a search of the *MLA International Bibliography.*

American Statistics Index. See entry under Statistical Sources.

Bibliographic Index: A Cumulative Bibliography of Bibliographies. New York: Wilson, 1938–. Three times a year.

An alphabetical subject index to books and articles that includes bibliographies listing more than fifty items. This is a good place to gather sources for a substantial literature review.

Biography Index: A Cumulative Index to Biographical Material in Books and Magazines. See entry under Biographical Sources.

Book Review Digest. New York: Wilson, 1905–. Monthly.

A handy guide to book reviews published in popular periodicals and trade publications such as *Library Journal* and *Publishers Weekly.* Excerpts from reviews are included, as are notes about how long each review is, making it handy if you are looking for more substantial analysis. This is a particularly good source if you want to know how a book was received at the time it was published. Available in electronic format.

Book Review Index. Detroit: Gale, 1965–. Bimonthly.

This index covers more publications than *Book Review Digest* and tends to include more scholarly journals as well as other publications. It does not include excerpts. This is a good choice if you are looking for reviews that appear in fairly specialized periodicals. Available in electronic format.

Combined Retrospective Index to Book Reviews in Scholarly Journals, 1886–1974. Detroit: Gale, 1979–1982.

For book reviews published in academic journals in the past, this index, covering over 450 journals, is invaluable. This is a good choice if you want to find out how a scholarly book was received at its time of publication.

Congressional Information Service. *CIS Index to Publications of the United States Congress.* See entry under Government Documents.

Dissertation Abstracts. Ann Arbor, MI: University Microfilms International, 1938–. Monthly.

Abstracts of doctoral dissertations written in the United States and Canada, arranged in general subject categories. Dissertations are often impossible to borrow through interlibrary loan, but University Microfilm sells copies. Available in electronic format.

Essay and General Literature Index. New York: Wilson, 1900–. Semiannual.

This index recognizes that many essays and articles are published in books. It indexes by author and subject those items published in collections that are not covered in many indexes. It is particularly useful for works in the arts and humanities. Available in electronic format.

Monthly Catalog of United States Government Publications. See entry under Government Documents.

Statistical Reference Index. See entry under Statistical Sources.

News and Current Events Sources

Clarinet. Internet. Availability varies.

This news service posts hourly updates of news stories from Associated Press and Reuters. Institutions subscribe to the service and provide access through the Internet, generally in the form of newsgroups. Ask your library or academic computing department whether it's available and how to access it. Commercial online services such as Compuserve and America Online offer similar current news to their subscribers.

CQ Researcher. Washington, DC: Congressional Quarterly, 1991–. Weekly.
A looseleaf collection of overviews of current and controversial issues. Multiple viewpoints and statistical information are presented for each topic, followed by an annotated bibliography. Indexes make it easy to find relevant overviews. Formerly called *Editorial Research Reports* (1924–1990).

Editorials on File. New York: Facts on File, 1970–. Semimonthly.
A looseleaf compendium of editorials published in U.S. and Canadian newspapers, with commentary. Indexes, cumulated quarterly and annually, make it possible to find editorials by subject matter.

Facts on File. New York: Facts on File, 1940–. Weekly.
A digest of world news, organized by broad topic. Indexes are published twice monthly and are cumulated. This is a handy place to find news facts quickly; its age makes it useful for subjects from World War II on.

Historic Documents. Washington, DC: Congressional Quarterly,1972–. Annually.
A chronological presentation of speeches, reports, court decisions, and other public documents often not published anywhere else. Some of the documents are not printed in their entirety. Most have some contextual information about source and significance.

Biographical Sources

American Men and Women of Science. See entry under Science and Technology.

Biographic and Genealogical Master Index. Detroit: Gale, 1980–. Annually.
An index to biographical information in reference books and an invaluable shortcut when you are looking for biographical information. It now covers biographical sources for about three million people. Available in CD-ROM.

Biography Index: A Cumulative Index to Biographical Material in Books and Magazines. New York: Wilson,1947–. Quarterly.
An index to English language books and articles. Includes memoirs, biographies, obituaries, magazine profiles, children's books, and an index organized by profession. It is a useful supplement to biographical reference books. Available in electronic format.

Current Biography. New York: Wilson,1940–. Monthly, with annual cumulations.
Contains lengthy biographical sketches of men and women currently in the news. Entries include references to additional sources of information. Each issue has an index classified by profession and obituaries.

Dictionary of American Biography. 11 vols., with index and supplements. New York: Scribner's, 1928–1937.
Consists of long scholarly articles about American men and women who were not living at the time the *Dictionary* was published. Bibliographies are included at the end of each entry. Indexes are arranged by place of birth, college, and profession. A British equivalent is called the *Dictionary of National Biography.*

Dictionary of Scientific Biography. See entry under Science and Technology.

Notable American Women, 1607–1950: A Biographical Dictionary. 3 vols. Cambridge: Belknap–Harvard University Press, 1971.
Presents scholarly articles (patterned after the *Dictionary of American Biography*) about American women living between 1607 and 1950 who made con-

tributions to American society. Articles include bibliographies. Volume 3 lists names by profession. *Notable American Women: The Modern Period* (Cambridge, Mass.: Belknap–Harvard University Press, 1980) gives biographical sketches for American women who died between 1951 and 1975.

Who's Who in America. Chicago: Marquis Who's Who, 1899–. Biennially.
The standard biographical dictionary on living Americans. Biographical information is given in concise form. Besides *Who's Who in America,* a number of more specific biographical dictionaries, such as *Who's Who in the Midwest, Who's Who in American Politics, Who's Who among Black Americans,* and *Who's Who in France,* focus on a particular geographic area or group. A British equivalent is called simply *Who's Who.*

Government Documents

American Statistics Index. See entry under Statistical Sources.

Congressional Information Service. *CIS Index to Publications of the United States Congress.* Washington, DC: CIS, 1970–. Monthly.
A detailed index to congressional hearings, reports, special publications, documents, and so on, with abstracts. The annual cumulation is titled *CIS Annual,* which includes legislative histories of laws enacted during the year. Available in electronic format under various names, including *CIS* and *Congressional Masterfile.*

Congressional Record. Washington, DC: Government Printing Office, 1873–. Daily while Congress is in session.
The official record of congressional proceedings and debates. Does not include the text of bills but does have congressional speeches, debates, and votes. An index to the publication comes out regularly. Available online through the *THOMAS* Internet site. See entry for *THOMAS* under Political Science and Government.

Monthly Catalog of United States Government Publications. Washington, DC: Government Printing Office, 1895–. Monthly.
A long-running index to publications by federal government agencies and Congress, arranged by issuing agency and indexed by author, title, subject, and series, or report number. Includes the Superintendent of Documents classification number, used by many libraries to shelve documents. Available in electronic format under various names, including *Marchive GPO CAT/PAC, Government Publications Index,* and *Government Documents Catalog Service.*

Foreign Relations of the United States. Diplomatic Papers. Washington, DC: Government Printing Office,1862–. Annually.
A collection of correspondence, memos, treaties, and messages from presidents and diplomats. In many cases volumes are devoted to a specific region or country.

Guide to U.S. Government Publications. Ed. John L. Andriot. McLean, VA: Documents Index, 1973–.
Annual annotated two-part guide to government materials. Part 1 contains series and periodicals published by U.S. government agencies, and part 2 lists the Superintendent of Documents classification numbers issued to date.

Library of Congress. Marvel Gopher. Internet. Available at gopher.marvel.loc.gov

Library of Congress. World Wide Web Home Page. Internet. Available at http://lcweb.loc.gov

A great deal of government information is now available through the Internet and through electronic bulletin boards. The gateway to government information created by the Library of Congress is a good place to find connections to many government information sources. In addition to connections to a multitude of government agencies, the Library of Congress provides online exhibits and connections to its vast catalog.

Public Papers of the Presidents of the United States. Washington, DC: Office of the Federal Register, 1958–. Annually.

Includes the public messages, speeches, and statements of U.S. presidents; updated by the *Weekly Compilation of Presidential Documents.*

United States Government Manual. Washington, DC: Government Printing Office, 1973–. Annually.

A guide to the agencies of government and their relationship to one another. With organization charts, indexes, and contact names and numbers.

United States. Supreme Court. *United States Reports.* Washington, DC: Government Printing Office, 1754–.

Presents the texts of Supreme Court decisions in chronological order. As decisions are made, they are published in separate pamphlets, called "slip decisions," and are later cumulated.

Statistical Sources

Statistical handbooks are published for a wide variety of topics: the aging population, children, women, Native Americans, and so on. Many countries publish compendia of national statistics, and international organizations, such as the United Nations and its subgroups or the International Monetary Fund, issue statistics relating to a variety of countries. Some of the most frequently used statistical sources are given below, but a librarian can guide you to more specific sources for your topic.

American Statistics Index. Washington, DC: Congressional Information Service, 1973–. Monthly.

Indexes statistics in government documents by subject, name, categories, agencies, and so on, giving full bibliographic information and Superintendent of Documents number. Some libraries have a microfiche set of the documents referred to in the index. Available in electronic format.

Bureau of the Census Gopher. Internet. Available at gopher.census.gov

Bureau of the Census World Wide Web Home Page. Internet. Available at http://www.census.gov

The Census gopher site includes many tables of census information relating to population, economics, and social issues. Offerings on the World Wide Web include current country information, complete with maps.

The Gallup Poll. Wilmington, DE: Scholarly Resources, 1972–. Annually.

Summarizes data from Gallup opinion polls taken from 1935 to the present. Updated by a monthly publication, *The Gallup Report.*

National Trade Data Bank (NTDB). CD-ROM. Washington, DC: Department of Commerce, 1990–. Monthly.

A CD-ROM series that includes a mass of information, much of it statistical, relating to international trade. A related CD-ROM series is the *National Economic, Social, and Environmental Data Book (NESE),* which covers domestic markets, small business, and environmental issues relating to business.

Statistical Reference Index. Washington, DC: Congressional Information Service, 1980–. Monthly.

An index to statistics from sources other than the federal government, including associations, organizations, state governments, and publications. Indexed by subject, name, and category. Some libraries have all of the source documents on microfiche.

United States Department of Commerce, Bureau of the Census. *Statistical Abstract of the United States.* Washington, DC: GPO. Annually.

Summarizes statistical information on economic, social, and political subjects for the United States. Some international statistics are also included. Statistics are grouped by general subject, such as foreign commerce and aid or agriculture, and include a detailed index. Each graph or table has a citation to the government document from which it was taken. Available on CD-ROM.

Sources in
General Disciplinary Groups

Humanities

Arts and Humanities Citation Index (AHCI). Philadelphia: Institute for Scientific Information,1978–. Bimonthly, with annual cumulations.

A multidisciplinary index composed of three separate indexes to about 1,300 periodicals in the arts and humanities: the *Source Index, Citation Index,* and *Permuterm Subject Index.* For format and directions for use, see the discussion of the *Social Sciences Citation Index,* chapter 3. Available in electronic format.

Blazek, Ron, and Elizabeth S. Versa. *The Humanities: A Selective Guide to Information Sources.* 3rd ed. Littleton, CO: Libraries Unlimited, 1988.

A guide to the literature of the humanities covering information sources in philosophy and religion, visual arts, performing arts, and language and literature. For each subject, a chapter explains how to obtain information in that field and a chapter lists the major reference works and periodicals. Evaluative annotations that explain coverage, arrangements, and most appropriate use accompany each citation.

Current Contents: Arts and Humanities. Philadelphia: Institute for Scientific Information, 1979–. Weekly.

A weekly compilation of the tables of contents of more than 1,300 humanities periodicals arranged in eight general subject categories. This publication provides the most current access to the content of these journals through a title key word (subject) index and an author index. Available in electronic format.

Dictionary of the History of Ideas: Studies of Selected Pivotal Ideas. New York: Scribner's, 1973–1974.

A multivolume set covering topics in intellectual history, using an interdisciplinary approach. Articles are long and scholarly and include useful bibliographies. Emphasizes Western intellectual history. Includes an index.

Humanities Index. New York: Wilson, 1974–. Quarterly, with annual cumulations. Supersedes *Social Sciences and Humanities Index,* (1965–1974) and *International Index to Periodicals,* (1907–1965).

Provides access by subject and author to more than 290 core periodicals in the classics, archaeology, language, literature and literary criticism, folklore, religion and philosophy, area studies, history, theater, and film. Book reviews are included alphabetically by author in a separate listing at the end of the volume. Available in electronic format.

Social Sciences

Current Contents: Social and Behavioral Sciences. Philadelphia: Institute for Scientific Information, 1974–. Weekly.

A compilation of the tables of contents of more than 1,300 social and behavioral science periodicals arranged by thirteen subject disciplines. Provides the most current access to the contents of these journals through a title key word (subject) index and an author index. Available in electronic format.

International Encyclopedia of the Social Sciences. Ed. David L. Sills. 18 vols. New York: Macmillan, 1968.

Contains signed scholarly articles on the concepts, methods, major persons, and theories in anthropology and psychiatry, sociology, and statistics. Articles are arranged alphabetically by topic with additional access provided by a detailed index (volume 17) and cross-references. Each article has a bibliography of references. Volume 18 (1980) provides a biographical supplement. This encyclopedia updates but does not replace the classic *Encyclopedia of the Social Sciences* (New York: Macmillan, 1930–1935). Though you won't find current developments covered here, you will gain an authoritative and bibliographically rich grounding in the traditions of the social sciences.

PAIS International in Print. New York: Public Affairs Information Service, 1991–. Monthly.

A continuation of the long-running Public Affairs Information Service Bulletin (1915–1990) merged with the *Foreign Language Index* (1972–1990). Covers books, articles, and government documents relating to political, social, and economic affairs. Available in electronic format.

The Social Science Encyclopedia. London: Routledge, 1985.

A one-volume survey of the social sciences, with over 700 articles on disciplines, issues, theories, and significant figures, all with good introductory bibliographies.

Social Sciences Citation Index (SSCI). Philadelphia: Institute for Scientific Information, 1969–. Bimonthly, with annual cumulations.

Indexes more than 1,400 periodicals in the behavioral and social sciences. Following the same plan as ISI's other citation indexes, this index has three separate ways of finding information in the indexed periodicals: the Citation Index, Source Index, and Permuterm Index. (See *Social Sciences Citation Index,* chapter 3.) Available in electronic format.

Social Sciences Index. New York: Wilson, 1974–. Quarterly, with annual cumulations. Supersedes *Social Sciences and Humanities Index* (1965–1974) and *International Index to Periodicals* (1907–1965).

Provides access by subject and author to the major English-language periodicals in political science, sociology, economics, anthropology, psychology, planning and public affairs, environmental sciences, law, criminology, and behavioral sciences. Book reviews are listed alphabetically by author at the end of each volume. Available in electronic format.

Webb, William H., and Associates. *Sources of Information in the Social Sciences: A Guide to the Literature.* 3rd ed. Chicago: American Library Association, 1986.

The standard guide to the social sciences, with sections on social science literature in general, history, geography, economics, business administration, sociology, anthropology, psychology, education, and political science. For each discipline there is an essay reviewing the basic works and methodologies in that field and an annotated guide to abstracts, periodicals, current and retrospective bibliographies, dictionaries, handbooks, and other reference works.

Science and Technology

American Men and Women of Science: Physical and Behavioral Sciences. Ed. Jaques Cattell Press. 19th ed. 8 vols. New York: Bowker, 1995.

A biographical directory of more than 130,000 living American scientists. Arranged alphabetically, the entries include data on age, educational background, professional experience and memberships, mailing address, and area of research. Behavioral and social scientists were included in the first thirteen editions. Available in electronic format. A new edition appears about every three years.

Chen, Ching-Chih. 2nd ed. *Scientific and Technical Information.* Cambridge, MA: MIT Press, 1987.

An annotated guide to reference books in all areas of science and technology except medicine. The book is arranged by type of reference book (dictionaries, handbooks, abstracts) and by subject within each category.

Current Contents: Life Sciences. Philadelphia: Institute for Scientific Information, 1958–. Weekly.

A weekly compilation of the tables of contents of more than 1,100 life science periodicals arranged in eleven subject groups. This publication provides current access to the contents of these journals by subject (through a title key word index) and by author. ISI publishes similar publications in other areas of science: *Current Contents: Agriculture, Biology and Environmental Sciences; Current Contents: Physical, Chemical, and Earth Sciences; Current Contents: Engineering, Technology and Applied Sciences;* and *Current Contents: Clinical Practice.* Available in electronic format.

Dictionary of Scientific Biography. 18 vols. New York: Scribner's 1970–1980. With supplements.

Like the *Dictionary of American Biography,* this multivolume set gives lengthy and scholarly biographies of deceased scientists. Their technical contributions are clearly discussed, and thorough bibliographies of primary and secondary sources are appended. One of the supplementary volumes includes surveys of science in ancient civilizations.

General Science Index. New York: Wilson, 1978–. Quarterly, with annual cumulations.

Provides subject access to approximately 110 core science periodicals in the fields of biology, medicine, environmental science, mathematics, chemistry, geology, astronomy, meteorology, physics, and general science. Includes a separate listing of book reviews arranged alphabetically by author. Available in electronic format.

McGraw-Hill Dictionary of Scientific and Technical Terms. 5th ed. New York: McGraw-Hill, 1994.

Designed to supplement general dictionaries by providing brief and up-to-date definitions of specialized scientific and technical words. Line drawings illustrate some of the definitions. *The McGraw-Hill Science and Technical Reference Set,* a multimedia CD-ROM, combines the dictionary with a concise encyclopedia of science and technology.

McGraw-Hill Encyclopedia of Science and Technology. 7th ed. 20 vols. New York: McGraw-Hill, 1992.

Covers all areas of science and technology, including medicine. With emphasis on recent advances, the articles include both broad surveys as well as discussions of more specific, technical concepts. Articles are arranged alphabetically by topic with cross-references to the text and bibliographies included for most articles. Volume 20, the Index, includes both an analytical index (every concept, person, and term) and a topical index (grouping all articles under seventy-eight general subject headings). The encyclopedia is updated by the *McGraw-Hill Yearbook of Science and Technology.*

Science Citation Index (SCI). Philadelphia: Institute for Scientific Information, 1955–. Bimonthly, with annual cumulations.

Indexes more than 1,000 periodicals and monographic serials in science, technology, medicine, agriculture, and the behavioral sciences. It does not include book reviews except those published in *Science* and *Nature.* It follows the same plan as ISI's other indexes. (See *Social Sciences Citation Index,* chapter 3.) Available in electronic format.

Sources in
Specific Academic Disciplines

Accounting. *See* Business, Accounting, and Economics.

Agriculture. *See* Biology and Agriculture.

Anthropology and Archaeology

Abstracts in Anthropology. Farmingdale, NY: Baywood, 1970–. Semi-quarterly.
Consists of abstracts in the fields of archaeology, cultural and physical anthropology, and linguistics; the abstracts are grouped in a classified arrangement, with author and subject indexes.

Atlas of World Cultures: A Geographic Guide to Ethnographic Literature. Newbury Park, CA: Sage, 1989.
An ethnic atlas with bibliography, based on the documents collected in the *Human Relations Area Files.* Forty maps locate 3,500 cultural groups; over 1,200 ethnographic studies are listed for the groups.

The Cambridge Encyclopedia of Archaeology. Ed. Andrew Sherratt. New York: Cambridge University Press, 1980.
Instead of being arranged alphabetically by subject, the chapters are arranged in three groups. Chapters 1–7 deal with the development of modern archaeology. Chapters 8–61 cover different archaeological periods and regions. The final chapters discuss methodology and provide a chronological atlas. A bibliography, organized by the chapter divisions, and a detailed subject index conclude the volume.

Encyclopedia of World Cultures. Boston: Hall, 1991–.
This set, based on the documents found in the *Human Relations Area Files,* covers over 1,500 cultural groups, summarizing information on their history, cultural relations, economy, kinship, family and marriage practices, religion, and cultural expression. A remarkable and very useful work.

Heizer, Robert F., et al. *Archaeology: A Bibliographical Guide to the Basic Literature.* New York: Garland, 1980.
A guide to the literature on the history and methodology of archaeology. The final chapter lists bibliographies, dictionaries, and atlases. The detailed table of contents provides access by subject, and an author index is included.

Human Relations Area Files (HRAF). New Haven, CT: Human Relations Area Files. Ongoing.
A collection of data on cultural groups, including books, articles, manuscripts, and translations into English of foreign materials, arranged by culture and available in some large libraries on microfiche. A selection of HRAF data is available on the CD-ROM series *Cross-Cultural CD.*

Kibbee, Josephine Z. *Cultural Anthropology: A Guide to Reference and Information Sources.* Englewood, CO: Libraries Unlimited, 1991.
A handbook for the researcher in cultural anthropology, including information on library resources and how best to use them for research in this area.

The World Wide Web Virtual Library: Anthropology. Internet. Available at http://www.usc.edu/dept/v-lib/anthropology.html.
A good place to start an exploration of the Web, providing several interactive programs that combine hyper-linked texts with graphics and a large list of connections to other anthropological resources.

JOURNALS

American Anthropologist. Washington, DC: American Anthropology Association, 1888–. Quarterly.

Contains scholarly articles and research reports covering all areas of anthropology. The Commentaries section provides a forum for discussion of previous research; the journal contains an extensive bibliography of book and film reviews arranged by subject.

American Journal of Archaeology. Bryn Mawr: Archaeological Institute of America, 1885–. Quarterly.

Publishes research articles on the archaeology and art history of the Mediterranean region with some articles on neighboring areas. It also includes notes, grant information, and book reviews.

Anthropological Quarterly. Washington, DC: Catholic University of America Press, 1928–. Quarterly.

Contains three or four scholarly articles per issue as well as lengthy book reviews.

Archaeology. Boston: Archaeological Institute of America, 1948–. Bimonthly.

Intended for lay readers as well as scholars, articles report results of archaeological research in all regions of the world. It includes book reviews and information on exhibitions, new books, tours, and excavations.

Art and Architecture

Art Index. New York: Wilson, 1929–. Quarterly, with annual cumulations.

An index by author and subject to approximately 200 international periodicals, yearbooks, and museum bulletins on art and related subjects, such as aesthetics, design, film, and photography. Available in electronic format.

Bibliography of the History of Art (BHA). Santa Monica: CA: J. Paul Getty Trust, 1991–. Quarterly.

Covers art from prehistory to the present. Arranged in broad categories, listing citations and abstracts for books, articles, exhibition catalogs, dissertations, and so on. Indexes provide access by subject and author. Formerly published as two series, *Répertoire international de la littérature de l'art (RILA)* and *Répertoire d'art et d'archéologie (RAA)*. Available in electronic format.

Contemporary Artists. 3rd ed. Chicago: St. James, 1989.

A biographical guide to artists and their works, with lengthy bibliographies. Includes a number of plates.

Ehresmann, Donald. *Fine Arts. A Bibliographic Guide to Basic Reference Works, Histories, and Handbooks.* 3rd ed. Littleton, CO: Libraries Unlimited, 1990.

An annotated guide to the literature of painting, sculpture, and architecture. The first part covers bibliographies, library catalogs, indexes, and dictionaries as well as references on iconography. The second part provides references to histories and handbooks on historic periods in a chronological arrangement. An author/title/subject index is included for the whole volume.

Encyclopedia of World Art. 15 vols., with supplements. New York: McGraw-Hill, 1968.

Presents lengthy articles arranged alphabetically on concepts, artists, periods, and geographic regions. Each article is signed and gives a bibliography of further references. Volume 15 is an index to the rest of the volumes.

Hall, James. *Dictionary of Subjects and Symbols in Art.* Rev. ed. New York: Harper & Row, 1979.

A dictionary of persons, picture titles, objects, and symbolism in Christian and Classical art.

Information Sources in Architecture. Ed. Valerie J. Bradfield. London: Butterworths, 1983.

Designed for the researcher and professional architect, the book covers information sources for each step of the construction process. Contributed chapters cover libraries, information retrieval techniques, trade literature, government publications, design, and office management. Includes an index.

Jones, Lois Swan. *Art Research Methods and Resources: A Guide to Finding Art Information.* 3rd ed. Dubuque: Kendall/Hunt, 1990.

An introduction and detailed guide to researching art for both students and specialists. More than 19,000 citations are given, with detailed listings of periodicals, databases, and sources for iconographic research.

Oxford Dictionary of Art. Oxford: Oxford University Press, 1988.

A handy guide to ideas, people, works, and movements in the arts. For country surveys, see the older *Oxford Companion to Art* (1970).

Web Museum. Internet. Available at http://sunsite.unc.edu/wm/.

Provides a French connection to virtual art museums around the world, with tours, exhibits, and beautiful graphics (such as pages from illuminated manuscripts). A showcase of the ways in which Internet can convey more than text.

JOURNALS

Art Bulletin. New York: College Art Association of America, 1912–. Quarterly.

Prints scholarly articles about art and art history, often grouped by related subjects, with each issue covering several topics. The articles include research notes and lengthy book reviews.

Art in America. New York: Art in America, 1913–. Monthly.

Consists of review articles and commentary on art and artists of all historical periods. The emphasis is on contemporary American art, but non-American work is also covered. It also publishes book reviews and reviews of exhibitions.

Art Journal. New York: College Art Association of America, 1941–. Quarterly.

Includes scholarly articles on art and artists from all countries and periods as well as book reviews and museum news.

Burlington Magazine. London: Burlington Magazine Publications, 1903–. Monthly.

Publishes two or three scholarly articles per issue on individual artists, works of art, schools, and periods of art history. It also contains short research articles, extended book reviews, and exhibition reviews.

Journal of the Society of Architectural Historians. Philadelphia: Society of Architectural Historians. 1940–. Quarterly.

Publishes architectural criticism, book reviews, and articles on architectural history.

Progressive Architecture. Stamford, CT: Reinhold, 1920–. Monthly.

Covers the international scene in architecture with emphasis on the United States. It is written for the professional and deals with all aspects of architecture, with two special sections each month, one of design and one of building technology.

Astronomy and Space Science

Astronomy and Astrophysics Abstracts. New York: Springer-Verlag, 1969–. Semi-annually.
A classified subject index with international coverage of astronomy and astrophysics. Each volume includes a subject and author index.

The Cambridge Encyclopedia of Astronomy. Ed. Simon Milton. New York: Crown, 1977.
A broad-based survey of astronomy prepared by astronomers, intended for both amateurs and professionals. It includes an index and a star atlas.

Encyclopedia of Astronomy and Astrophysics. San Diego: Academic, 1989.
An alphabetical compilation of articles on major topics in the field, giving long signed essays, suitable for a broad audience, but fairly technical. Each essay is accompanied by a glossary and bibliography.

Facts on File Dictionary of Astronomy. 2nd ed. New York: Facts on File, 1985.
A handy guide to the language used in astronomy, with over 2,300 technical definitions.

International Aerospace Abstracts. Phillipsburg, NJ: American Institute of Aeronautics and Astronautics,1961–. Semimonthly.
An index to published literature in periodicals and books, meeting papers, and conference proceedings in space sciences and aeronautics. It includes separate indexes by subject, author, contract number, meeting paper and report number, and accession number. Semiannual and annual cumulations. Available in electronic format under the name *Aerospace Database.*

International Encyclopedia of Astronomy. New York: Orion, 1987.
Around 2,500 short articles, with several longer ones, on topics such as the "big bang" and pulsars. Includes many biographical entries.

National Aeronautics and Space Administration (NASA) Home Page. Internet. Available at http://www.gsfc.nasa.gov/NASA_homepage.html.
Includes current information on shuttle launches, NASA policy and planning information, an online atlas of Mars, and a "hot topics" news service.

Seal, Robert A. *A Guide to the Literature of Astronomy.* Littleton, CO: Libraries Unlimited, 1977.
An introduction to the literature of astronomy.

JOURNALS

Astronomy and Aeronomics. New York: American Institute of Aeronautics and Astronautics, 1932–. Eleven issues per year.
Covers recent trends and developments in space flight, hydronautics, and rocketry.

Astrophysical Journal. Chicago: University of Chicago Press, 1895–. Semi-monthly.
Reports original observations and research at national and academic institutions. Each issue comes in two parts: part 1 contains full-length research papers and part 2 contains shorter reports.

Aviation Week and Space Technology. New York: McGraw-Hill, 1916–. Weekly.
Covers current trends and events affecting scientific as well as business aspects of aviation and aerospace. It also contains occasional in-depth reports and some directory-type information.

Sky and Telescope. Cambridge, MA: Sky, 1941–. Monthly.
Publishes popular and semitechnical articles on all aspects of astronomy. It includes a celestial calendar, sky chart, and news notes.

Biology and Agriculture

AGRICOLA. Beltsville, MD: U.S. National Agriculture Library, 1970–. Monthly.
The most complete database of agricultural information, covering all aspects of the discipline. Includes records from the *Bibliography of Agriculture* and the catalog of the National Agriculture Library, with 90 percent of the 2.5 million records referring to articles, the rest to books and other publications.

Bibliography of Bioethics. Detroit: Gale, 1975–. Annually.
A subject index to magazine and newspaper articles, audiovisual materials, books, and government documents in bioethics. The subject headings used are listed in the thesaurus in volume 1; each volume also contains an author and title index. Available in electronic format.

Biological Abstracts. Philadelphia: BioSciences Information Service, 1926–. Semimonthly, with semiannual cumulations.
Covers international research literature in all the life sciences except clinical medicine. Five indexes provide access to the abstracts: author, subject, generic (organism name), biosystematic, and concept. The subject index lists key words from the titles of the articles. The concept index indexes the articles by one of 500 major concepts. Available in electronic format, under the names *BIOSIS, BIOSIS Previews,* or *BIOSIS Express.*

CSA Life Sciences Collection. Bethesda, MD: Cambridge Scientific Abstracts, 1987–. Quarterly.
A database of abstracting journals, including those on animal behavior, biochemistry, ecology, endocrinology, entomology, marine biology, microbiology, neuroscience, virology, and AIDS research. The CD-ROM version of this database is called *Compact Cambridge Life Sciences.*

Encyclopedia of Bioethics. Ed. Warren T. Reich. 4 vols. New York: Macmillan/ Free Press, 1978.
Contains lengthy scholarly articles on moral and ethical aspects of the life sciences, such as euthanasia, drug use, ethical use of technology, and behavior control. Extensive cross-references and bibliographies are included. Too dated to include latest controversies but still of value for its excellent coverage of general issues.

Encyclopedia of Human Biology. 8 vols. San Diego: Academic, 1991.
Over 600 lengthy articles on all sorts of topics relating to human biology — behavior, biochemistry, immunology, genetics, pharmacology, etc. The final volume includes a general index.

Guide to Sources on Agricultural and Biological Research. Ed. J. Richard Blanchard and Lois Farrell. Berkeley: University of California Press, 1980.

An annotated guide to research tools in agriculture and the life sciences. The introduction explains the communication process used in science. Following a chapter on general information sources in the life sciences, chapters describe reference works in the plant sciences, animal sciences, physical sciences, food sciences and nutrition, environmental sciences, and the relevant social sciences. The final chapter discusses computerized databases.

Human Genome Project Gopher. Internet. Available at gopher.hgmp.mrc.ac.uk.
One of several interrelated sites for information on the Human Genome Project. Includes information on searching the Genome Data Base, discussion of related projects, and connections to research sources elsewhere.

Information Sources in the Life Sciences. 3rd ed. London: Butterworths, 1987.
A guide to a variety of resources (including databases) in areas such as genetics, zoology, and ecology.

Tootill, Elizabeth. *The Facts on File Dictionary of Biology.* Rev. ed. New York: Facts on File, 1988.
Gives brief definitions of biological terms, concepts, processes, and descriptions of organisms. Diagrams and charts illustrate such concepts as the carbon cycle and the geological time scale.

JOURNALS

American Journal of Botany. Columbus, OH: Botanical Society of America, 1914–. Ten issues per year.
Presents original research articles in all areas of botany, including economic botany and paleobotany.

American Zoologist. Thousand Oaks, CA: American Society of Zoologists, 1961–. Quarterly.
Includes original research and review articles as well as symposium papers on specific zoological topics. It also contains information on the society and occasional book reviews.

BioScience. Arlington, VA: American Institute of Biological Sciences, 1950–. Monthly.
Covers the entire range of current topics in biology and is suitable for both specialists and lay readers.

Business, Accounting, and Economics

ABI/Inform. UMI/Data Courier, 1970–. Updated weekly.
A database that indexes and abstracts more than 800 international periodicals in business and management. Available in electronic format. The *ABI/Inform Research Edition* CD-ROM indexes some 900 business periodicals, while the *ABI/Inform Express Edition* CD-ROM covers only around 100.

Accounting and Tax Index. Ann Arbor, MI: University Microfilms International, 1992–. Quarterly.
A detailed index to specialized publications in accounting and taxation. Previously published as *Accountant's Index* (1923–1991). Available in electronic format.

Business Periodicals Index. New York: Wilson, 1958–. Monthly.

    An index to nearly 300 English language business periodicals. Available in electronic format.

Daniells, Lorna M. *Business Information Sources.* 3rd ed. Berkeley: University of California Press, 1993.

    The first eight chapters cover business reference sources, bibliographies, indexes and abstracts, directories, statistical sources, investment sources, and data on current business and economic trends. The second part of the book discusses management resources in accounting, information systems, banking, insurance, marketing, personnel management, and related fields. The last chapter lists important reference books for a small office library. Entries are annotated and a subject, author, and title index is included.

Disclosure. Bethesda, MD: Disclosure, 1977–. Weekly.

    A database of financial and management information on 12,000 publicly held companies.

Edgar. Internet. Available at gopher.town.hall.org or http://www.town.hall.org.

    An experimental database of 10K reports filed with the Securities and Exchange Commission by publicly owned corporations. Instructions for downloading texts from the project's FTP site are included. Because it is experimental, users are cautioned that formats and protocols will change without warning.

The Encyclopedia of Management. Ed. Carl Heyel. 3rd ed. New York: Van Nostrand Reinhold, 1982.

    Contains signed articles on management concepts and techniques, accounting, labor relations, and related subjects. Most articles give additional sources of information; an outline of core subject readings can be used to guide a reading program.

Journal of Economic Literature. Nashville: American Economic Association, 1963–. Quarterly.

    Each issue includes an annotated list of new books, classified by subject, a subject index of articles in current periodicals with abstracts for the most significant articles, and tables of contents for current economics journals. Critical book reviews are at the beginning of each volume. Available in electronic format under the names *Economic Literature Index* and *EconLit.*

The New Palgrave: A Dictionary of Economics. 4 vols. London: Macmillan, 1987.

    A fully revised work based on the venerable *Palgrave's Dictionary of Political Economy,* giving detailed and scholarly analyses of economic theories and issues. Includes biographical information on prominent economists.

The New Palgrave Dictionary of Money and Finance. 3 vols. New York: Stockton, 1992.

    Includes over 1,000 entries, some brief definitions of terms (such as *Ginnie Maes*) and others longer explorations of theory and history of monetary economics, finance, and banking.

Predicasts F & S Index United States. Cleveland: Predicasts, 1968–. Monthly, with quarterly and annual cumulations.

    A good index to use when looking for current information about U.S. companies and industries. The index covers more than 750 business, industrial, and financial periodicals. It is divided into two sections: the white pages list articles by company name, and the colored pages are arranged by seven-digit industry codes and by basic economic indicators. Major articles are designated with a black dot. Available in electronic format, some versions offering full-text articles.

Rosenberg, Jerry M. *Dictionary of Business and Management.* 2nd ed. New York: Wiley, 1983.

Contains brief definitions for more than 10,000 terms. Appendixes include tables for forms of measurement and interest, a list of graduate programs in business and management, and a summary of major economic events in U.S. history.

Wall Street Journal Index. New York: Dow Jones, 1958–. Monthly, with annual cumulations.

Indexes the final eastern edition of the *Wall Street Journal* and *Barron's* (since 1981). The index to *Barron's* (the green pages at the end of the volume) includes entries by subject and corporate name; the rest of the index is divided into two sections: general and corporate. Entries give a citation and brief summary of the contents of each article. Available in electronic format.

JOURNALS

American Economic Review. Nashville: American Economic Association, 1911–. Quarterly.

Includes lengthy articles and short papers on economic topics as well as commentary and notes.

Harvard Business Review. Cambridge: Harvard University, 1922–. Bimonthly.

Contains articles on management issues, problems, and theories. Ideas for Action section has brief articles reporting developments and trends. Occasional book reviews are included.

Journal of Accountancy. New York: American Institute of Certified Public Accountants, 1905–. Monthly.

Provides three or four major articles per issue discussing issues, developments, and practical applications in accounting, as well as brief news reports, professional news, book reports, and brief notes on articles of interest in other periodicals.

Journal of Business. Chicago: University of Chicago Press, 1928–. Quarterly.

Contains empirical and theoretical studies of business and economics topics; lists of books received; and news of appointments, grants, retirements, and dissertations.

Quarterly Journal of Economics. New York: Wiley, 1886–. Quarterly.

A highly regarded journal, and the oldest English-language journal of economics. Articles are geared to economists, professors, and students and are highly theoretical.

Chemistry and Physics

Applied Science and Technology Index. See entry under Engineering and Electronics.

Besancon, Robert M. *The Encyclopedia of Physics.* 3rd ed. New York: Van Nostrand Reinhold, 1985.

A one-volume encyclopedia with signed scholarly articles. Articles on major topics are less technical for general readers, while specific articles are more advanced.

Chemical Abstracts. Columbus, OH: American Chemical Society, 1907–. Weekly, with semiannual cumulations.

Provides access to the world's chemical and chemical engineering research literature. Besides a general subject index that uses a controlled vocabulary, it includes a chemical substance index, a formula index, an index of ring systems, a patent index, and an author index. All of these indexes provide access to the weekly abstracts, which are arranged by subject classifications. Available in electronic format, sometimes called *CAS* or *CA Search.*

CRC Handbook of Chemistry and Physics. Boca Raton: Chemical Rubber Co., 1913–. Annually.

A compilation of formulas, tables, and charts presenting data of use to chemists, researchers in the physical sciences, and mathematicians. Information is grouped in six broad categories with a subject index included at the end of the volume.

Information Sources in Physics. 3rd ed. London: Bowker-Saur, 1994.

A guide to the literature of the field, with evaluations and descriptions presented in narrative format.

Kirk-Othmer Encyclopedia of Chemical Technology. 4th ed. New York: Wiley,1991–.

A revision of the twenty-four-volume third edition, published in 1978. Consists of background articles on chemical technology and related issues, such as energy and toxicology. Approximately half of the articles discuss chemical substances and describe chemical properties and the manufacturing process; a separate index provides subject access to the entire set. *The Kirk-Othmer Concise Encyclopedia of Chemical Technology* (1985) is a one-volume digest based on the third edition. The complete set of the third edition and the fourth edition in progress are both available in electronic format.

Physics Abstracts. Surrey, England: Institution of Electrical Engineers, 1898–. Twice monthly, with cumulative subject and author indexes every six months. Available in electronic format as part of the INSPEC database.

Publishes abstracts for English-language journals, books, reports, dissertations, and conference proceedings on physics. Abstracts are grouped in ten major subject classifications with subdivisions. A detailed summary of the classification system as well as a subject index is given at the beginning of each issue. Each set of six months' cumulated index volumes contains the following indexes: subject, author, bibliography, conference, and corporate author.

Science: Chemistry. Internet. Available at http://yahoo/com/Science/Chemistry. Includes a solid list of Internet connections, including sites for chemical pictures, articles, the periodic table of elements, etc.

JOURNALS

American Chemical Society Journal. Washington, DC: American Chemical Society, 1879–. Biweekly.

Publishes research articles; brief articles discussing, correcting, or amending earlier research; and book reviews.

American Journal of Physics. New York: American Institute of Physics, 1933–. Monthly. Formerly *American Physics Teacher* (1933–1940).

Contains technical research and review articles on physical science, particularly the instructional and social aspects; short reports on new apparatus or new techniques; and book reviews.

Chemical Reviews. Washington, DC: American Chemical Society, 1924–. Bimonthly.

Reports research in chemistry and allied fields.

Physical Review. Lancaster, PA: American Physical Society, 1893–.

A vast publication, covering general physics, solid-state physics, nuclear physics, and particles and fields. *Physical Review Letters* covers current developments and is also available in electronic format from OCLC.

Classics

L'Année philologique; bibliographie critique et analytique de l'antiquité Greco-latine. Paris: Societé d'edition "Les Belles Lettres," 1924/26–. Annually.

The major index to classical research. Includes books and articles on all aspects of Greek and Latin culture, from archaeology to literature, and includes works in all languages.

Howatson, M. C. *The Oxford Companion to Classical Literature.* 2nd ed. New York: Oxford University Press, 1989.

A current and concise guide to classical literature, including some consideration of the social and philosophical context of the writers and works covered.

The Oxford Classical Dictionary. 2d ed. Oxford: Clarendon Press, 1970.

A useful guide to people, places, events, and topics in the classical world, and a handy resource for understanding classical references in Western art and literature as well as classical cultures.

Reid, Jane Davidson, *The Oxford Guide to Classical Mythology in the Arts, 1300–1990.* 2 vols. New York: Oxford University Press, 1993.

Traces the uses of classical imagery, mythology, and history in the arts: literature, graphic arts, theater, etc. A fascinating collection of references.

Thesaurus Linguae Graecae. CD-ROM. Irvine: University of California, Irvine, 1987.

A database of over 9,000 Greek texts from the eighth century BCE to 600 CE. Searchable by word or letter strings using the software provided. A valuable tool for scholars and historians in the field.

JOURNALS

American Journal of Philology. Baltimore, MD: Johns Hopkins, 1880–. Quarterly.

The oldest U.S. journal in the field, it publishes long, scholarly articles on classical languages, philology, history, and literature.

Bryn Mawr Classical Review. Bryn Mawr, PA: Bryn Mawr College, 1990–. Five times a year.

An electronic journal providing reviews of new publications in classics. Each issue contains fifteen to twenty lengthy review essays. To subscribe send an e-mail message to listserv@brynmawr.edu with the message: subscribe bmcr-1 [your name].

Classical Antiquity. Berkeley: University of California Press, 1982–. Quarterly.
This journal emphasizes literary studies and offers a half dozen lengthy, scholarly articles in each issue.

Journal of Hellenic Studies. London: Society for the Promotion of Hellenic Studies, 1880–. Annually.
An important journal containing long research articles, reviews, and brief notes.

Communications (Radio, Television, Speech, Journalism)

American Orators of the Twentieth Century: Critical Studies and Sources. New York: Greenwood, 1987.
A useful survey of important orators and their speeches, including bibliographic information. A companion set covers nineteenth-century orators.

Blum, Eleanor, and Frances Goins Wilhoit. *Mass Media Bibliography: An Annotated Guide to Books and Journals for Research and Reference*. 3rd ed. Urbana: University of Illinois, 1990.
Nearly 2,000 entries for works published between 1980 and 1987, with sections on broadcasting, print, film, advertising, and so on and with subject and author-title indexes.

The Broadcast Communications Dictionary. 3rd ed. New York: Greenwood, 1989.
Provides definitions relating specifically to broadcast communications.

Communications Abstracts. Beverly Hills: Sage, 1978–. Quarterly.
Abstracts articles from more than 150 journals as well as research reports and books in communication theory, mass communications, journalism, broadcasting, advertising, speech, and radio and television. Subject and author indexes appear in each issue and cumulate in each year's final issue.

Comserve. Internet. Available by subscription from comserve@vm.its.rpi.edu.
A collection of several electronic conferences and databases relating to various aspects of human communication. Includes a New Books hotline and discussion groups on semiotics, information technology, and other areas. Maintains an index to some communications journals.

DeVito, Joseph A. *The Communication Handbook: A Dictionary*. New York: Harper & Row, 1986.
Includes mostly brief definitions of over 2,000 terms in communications. About 100 topics are discussed in in-depth essays.

Index to Journals in Communication Studies. Falls Church, VA: Speech Communication Association, 1974–.
Covers key journals in speech and communications, giving complete tables of contents, a classified subject list, and alphabetical subject and author indexes. Often called *Matlon* after its first compiler. New editions come out every few years.

International Encyclopedia of Communications. 4 vols. Philadelphia: Annenberg School of Communications; New York: Oxford University Press, 1989.
Publishes signed articles covering communications. Articles range from historical treatment of communication techniques to the psychological, sociological, and anthropological treatments of communication processes. Most

articles are followed with a brief bibliography. The back of volume 4 contains a topical guide to the contents and an index.

Longman's Dictionary of Mass Media and Communication. Ed. Tracy Daniel Connors. New York: Longman, 1982.

Gives brief definitions of terms and acronyms used in broadcasting, advertising, journalism, marketing, publishing, and other communications-related fields.

Paneth, Donald. *The Encyclopedia of American Journalism.* New York: Facts on File, 1983.

Attempts to cover all aspects of American journalism: the gathering, evaluating, and dissemination of news and information, fact, and opinion. It looks at each form of journalism from print to electronic media and the history and technology of each form. Cross-references and bibliographies are included, as is a subject index at the back of the volume.

Speech Index. 4th ed. Metuchen, NJ: Scarecrow, 1966. With supplements.

Indexes speeches found in over 250 published collections and anthologies. A supplement published in 1982 covers works published between 1966 and 1980.

JOURNALS

Columbia Journalism Review. New York: Columbia University, 1962–. Bimonthly.

Publishes articles for lay readers and professionals analyzing issues in journalism. The Briefings section gives short reviews of symposia, books, and media productions. Book reviews are included.

Communications Quarterly. University Park, PA: Eastern Communication Association, 1953–. Quarterly. Continues *Today's Speech.*

Contains scholarly articles on all aspects of communication, including public speaking, nonverbal communication, and interpersonal communication, as well as lengthy book reviews.

Journal of Broadcasting and Electronic Media. Washington, DC: Broadcast Education Association, 1956–. Quarterly.

Publishes research articles on issues in broadcasting; some shorter research reports and industry commentary; and lengthy book reviews.

Journal of Communication. Philadelphia: Annenberg Press, 1951–. Quarterly.

Covers communication theory and practice. In addition to research articles, each issue focuses on a specific review topic, such as the international flow of information. The Intercom section provides professional news, book reviews, and commentary.

Journalism Quarterly (JQ). Columbia, SC: Association for Education in Journalism and Mass Communications, 1924–. Quarterly.

Presents scholarly articles reporting research in mass communications and journalism; brief research reports; book reviews; and annotated bibliographies of articles on mass communications.

Quarterly Journal of Speech. Annandale, VA: Speech Communication Association, 1915–. Quarterly.

A scholarly journal concentrating on speech research and education at the college or university level. Articles focus on historical, critical, empirical, and theoretical issues; a section of book reviews is included.

Computer Science and Mathematics

ACM Guide to Computing Literature. New York: Association for Computing Machinery, 1977–. Annually. Continues *Bibliography of Current Computing Literature.*

Contains seven sections: bibliographic listing, author index, key word index, category index, proper noun subject index, *Computing Reviews* (a reviewer index), and source index. Covers the literature of computer science, including papers from conferences and the major journals of computer science.

American Mathematical Society Gopher. Internet. Available at gopher.e-math. ams.com.

Maintained by a major scholarly society. Includes peer-reviewed research articles, preprints of forthcoming research, and multiple connections to other related Internet sites.

Companion Encyclopedia of the History and Philosophy of the Mathematical Sciences. 2 vols. London: Routledge, 1994.

A detailed examination of mathematics as a cultural phenomenon, giving lengthy articles followed by bibliographies.

Computer Abstracts. London: Technical Information Co., 1957–. Monthly, with annual author and subject indexes.

Abstracts of books, journal articles, proceedings, and government documents in classified arrangement with monthly author and patent indexes.

Computer Literature Index. Phoenix: Applied Computer Research, 1980–. Continues *Quarterly Bibliography of Computers and Data Processing* (1968–1979). Quarterly.

A comprehensive index to the professional literature, covering periodicals, books, conference proceedings, trade journals, and technical reports. Entries are arranged by subject classifications and cover computer hardware, software, and applications; brief abstracts are given for most entries.

Encyclopedia of Computer Science and Engineering. 3rd ed. New York: Van Nostrand Reinhold, 1993.

Contains signed articles on computer hardware and software, information systems management, theory and methodology of computing, and computer applications. Articles are arranged alphabetically, with a general classification system described in the front of the volume to guide reading on general subject areas; some articles have bibliographies. Appendixes provide helpful information in the form of acronym lists, lists of journals and of universities offering Ph.D. programs in computer science, and a glossary of major terms in five languages.

James, Robert C. *Mathematics Dictionary.* 5th ed. New York: Van Nostrand Reinhold, 1992.

Explains in fairly simple terms the meanings of mathematical words and phrases, often including figures and formulas.

Mathematical Reviews. Providence, RI: American Mathematical Society, 1940–. Monthly, with semiannual cumulation.

Contains comprehensive coverage of pure and applied mathematics literature. Abstracts are arranged according to a classification system with semiannual author and subject indexes. Another publication, *Current*

Mathematical Publications, covers newly published literature. Both are available in electronic format, under the name *MathSci.*

JOURNALS

ACM Communications. New York: Association for Computing Machinery, 1958–. Monthly.

Presents research and review articles on the design and applications of computers. Occasional issues focus on topics such as computer science education and professional news.

American Mathematical Monthly. Washington, DC: Mathematical Association of America, 1894–. Ten issues per year.

Publishes expository and review articles directed at a college-level mathematics education. Issues include book reviews and a section on "elementary and advanced problems."

American Mathematical Society Bulletin. Providence, RI: American Mathematical Society, 1894–. Quarterly.

Includes detailed articles on current issues of interest to mathematicians. This journal publishes practical and theoretical articles and covers all areas of mathematics.

Association for Computing Machinery Journal. New York: Association for Computing Machinery, 1954–. Quarterly.

Includes technical articles on programming languages, system analysis, computing theory, and artificial intelligence.

Byte: The Small Systems Journal. Peterborough, NH: McGraw-Hill, 1975–. Monthly.

Contains twelve to eighteen feature articles per issue as well as reviews of books, software, hardware, and computer languages. Selected programs, computer news, and an international calendar of events are presented.

Datamation. New York: Technical Publishing Co., 1957–. Twice monthly.

Contains news and review articles on developments in computer hardware and software along with descriptive reviews of hardware and software.

Criminal Justice. *See* Law and Criminal Justice.

Drama and Dance

Breed, Paul F., and Florence M. Sniderman, eds. *Dramatic Criticism Index.* Detroit: Gale, 1972.

A bibliography of books and articles on modern American and foreign playwrights. Citations are arranged alphabetically by playwright and by name of play; indexes of play titles and critics are included.

Carpenter, Charles. *Modern Drama Scholarship and Criticism, 1966–80: An International Bibliography.* Toronto: University of Toronto, 1986.

A classified, selective list of some 27,000 items of criticism on world playwrights since Ibsen. Includes alphabetical index of playwrights and of authors of criticism.

Cohen-Stratyner, Barbara Naomi. *Biographical Dictionary of Dance.* New York: Schirmer, 1982.

Covers prominent figures in dance in Europe and the Americas, including composers, impresarios, artists, choreographers, and dancers.

Ganzl, Kurt. *The Encyclopedia of the Musical Theatre*. 2 vols. New York: Schirmer, 1994.

An up-to-date survey of musical theater, giving detailed profiles and background.

International Dictionary of Ballet. 2 vols. Detroit: St. James Press, 1993.

Covers world ballet in 800 entries, with articles contributed by an international panel of dance authorities. Entries on individual dancers include teachers, roles danced, companies; other entries detail the history and interpretations of particular works.

McGraw-Hill Encyclopedia of World Drama. 2nd ed. 5 vols. New York: McGraw-Hill, 1984.

Provides articles on dramatists, directors, national, regional, and ethnic dramas, as well as on aspects of performance, such as makeup and costume. Articles on major dramatists give biographical and critical information, bibliographies, and plot summaries for the plays. Volume 5 includes a glossary with definitions of concepts and terms, a play title list giving authors' names, and an author/title/subject index.

The New York Times Theater Reviews. 10 vols. New York: New York Times, 1971–.

A chronological reproduction of theater reviews appearing in the *New York Times* from 1920 to 1970. Volumes 9 and 10 have indexes by title, by production company, and by personal name; volume 9 also has an appendix listing theater awards and prizes and summaries of productions and runs by season.

Simons, Linda Keir. *The Performing Arts: A Guide to the Reference Literature*. Englewood, CO: Libraries Unlimited, 1994.

A guide for researchers, covering resources of interest to theater and dance students, performers, and scholars.

The World Encyclopedia of Contemporary Theatre. 5 vols. London: Routledge, 1994.

A new, authoritative guide to the current world of theater, providing an international perspective.

JOURNALS

Dance Magazine. New York: Dance Magazine, 1926–. Monthly.

The longest continuously published dance publication in the country. Covers current dance in the United States, with attention paid to ballet, modern, and Broadway styles.

Drama: The Quarterly Theatre Review. London: British Theatre Association, 1919–. Quarterly.

Prints reviews of British drama, interviews with directors and actors, and book reviews.

The Drama Review (TDR). Cambridge, MA: MIT Press, 1955–. Continues the *Tulane Drama Review*. Quarterly.

Covers the international avant-garde in performance art and theater. Each issue contains six to ten articles focusing on a single topic, such as French theater. TDR also includes short descriptive reports on contemporary works, short plays, and book reviews and is well-illustrated with photos.

Theatre Journal (TJ). Washington, DC: University and College Theatre Association, 1949–. Quarterly. Continues *Educational Theatre Journal*.

Contains five or six scholarly articles per issue; theater review and book review sections; and a list of recent books, arranged by subject.

Theatre Research International. Oxford: Oxford University Press, 1958. Three issues per year. Continues *Theatre Research*.

Provides scholarly historical and critical articles on drama along with lengthy book reviews.

Earth Sciences.   *See* Environmental and Earth Sciences.

Economics.   *See* Business, Accounting, and Economics.

Education

Berry, Dorothea M. *A Bibliographic Guide to Educational Research*. 3rd ed. Metuchen, NJ: Scarecrow, 1990.

A guide to research sources in education. The book is an annotated bibliography arranged by type of information source, such as bibliographies, indexes, research studies, government documents, nonprint materials, and reference books. These categories are subdivided by area of education, such as special education, curriculum, international education, and educational technology. The final chapter focuses on guides to research. The guide also includes an author/editor index, a title index, and a subject index.

Buttlar, Lois. *Education: A Guide to Reference and Information Sources*. Englewood, CO: Libraries Unlimited, 1989.

Twenty chapters cover resources ranging from series to reference books to databases. Each chapter deals with a special area, such as special education, administration, or evaluation.

Digest of Education Statistics. Washington, DC: Department of Health and Human Services, 1975–. Annually.

Contains current education statistics, including numbers of schools and colleges, enrollments, and financial information. Another useful annual publication is called *The Condition of Education*.

Education Department Gopher. Internet. Available at gopher.ed.gov.

Education Department Home Page on the World Wide Web. Internet. Available at http://www.ed.gov.

The gopher site provides resources for educators and researchers, including statistics, research reports, links to other education sites on the Internet, and access to the AskEric service, through which requests for ERIC searches can be made and digests, publications, and lesson plans can be accessed. The department's Web site includes national education goals, the texts of legislation and speeches, and information for researchers and teachers about the department and its mission.

Education Index. New York: Wilson, 1929–. Ten times a year, with annual cumulations.

A subject and author index to English-language periodicals, monographs, and yearbooks in educational administration; teaching from preschool through adult; and curriculum and teaching methods in all subject fields. From 1961 to 1969, author indexing and book reviews were omitted; since 1969, book reviews have been included. Available in electronic format.

The Encyclopedia of Education. Ed. Lee C. Deighton. 10 vols. New York: Macmillan, 1971.

Contains 1,000 articles on educational history, philosophy, theory, and practice, concerned mainly with education in America. Entries are signed and have bibliographies. Volume 10 has a directory of contributors, a guide to articles (grouped by subject area and giving cross-references), and a subject index. Though dated, this set is still a valuable place to find overviews of issues and topics in American education.

ERIC (Educational Resources Information Center). *Current Index to Journals in Education (CIJE).* Phoenix: Oryx, 1969–. Monthly, with semiannual cumulations.

A subject index to almost 800 journals; access is through a controlled vocabulary, the Thesaurus of ERIC Descriptors. Each citation includes a list of assigned descriptors and an abstract. An author index and a journal contents index are also included. Available in electronic format.

ERIC (Educational Resources Information Center). *Resources in Education (RIE).* Phoenix: Oryx, 1969–. Monthly, with semiannual cumulations.

A companion to *CIJE, RIE* indexes educational research reports, books, government publications, conference papers, and unpublished manuscripts. Documents are available on microfiche or in hard copy through the ERIC Document Reproduction Service. An abstract is given for each document. In some electronic formats, *CIJE* and *RIE* can be searched as one file. Available in electronic format.

International Encyclopedia of Education: Research and Studies. 10 vols. Oxford: Pergamon, 1985. With supplements.

Substantial articles, signed and with bibliographies, cover all aspects of education, with an emphasis on scholarship and research. Covers educational systems throughout the world.

Shafritz, Jay M. *The Facts on File Dictionary of Education.* New York: Facts on File, 1988.

Gives definitions and explanations — some brief and others more interpretive — of terms, concepts, individuals, laws, organizations, and tests of interest to educators.

JOURNALS

American Educational Research Journal. Washington, DC: American Educational Research Association, 1964–. Quarterly.

Contains empirical research articles on issues in education.

American Journal of Education. Chicago: University of Chicago Press, 1893–. Quarterly. Continues *School Review* (1893–1979).

Presents research and review articles and book reviews. Some issues focus on a specific topic such as the development of literacy in American schools.

Harvard Educational Review. Cambridge, MA: Harvard University, 1931–. Quarterly. Continues *Harvard Teachers Record.*

Publishes scholarly articles reporting research and opinion on educational topics as well as both extended and brief book reviews. Special issues treat topics such as education and the threat of nuclear war.

Journal of Educational Psychology. Washington, DC: American Psychological Association, 1910–. Bimonthly.
  Presents original research on psychological aspects of learning.

Engineering and Electronics

Applied Science and Technology Index. New York: Wilson, 1958–. Continues *Industrial Arts Index.* Quarterly, with annual cumulations.
  Subject index to more than 300 English-language journals in engineering, earth sciences, food technology, textile production, energy, computer science, petroleum, metallurgy, physics, electronics, and other related fields. Book reviews are listed by author in a separate section. Available in electronic format.

Engineering Index. New York: Engineering Information, 1884–. Monthly, with annual cumulations.
  Provides abstracts for the world's literature in engineering sciences taken from journals, technical reports, books, and conference proceedings; the abstracts are arranged by subject with additional access through an author index and an author affiliation index. Available in electronic format under the name *COMPENDEX.*

Information Sources in Engineering. 2nd ed. London: Butterworths, 1985.
  Covers patents, standards, abstracts services and databases, and reference sources in fluid mechanics, stress analysis, automotive engineering, and electronics.

INSPEC. Piscataway, NJ: IEEE, 1969–. Monthly.
  An electronic file covering physics, engineering, information technology, and computer science. The full online file contains over 3 million bibliographic records with abstracts. A CD-ROM version covers publications from 1989 on.

The New IEEE Standard Dictionary of Electrical and Electronics Terms. 5th ed. New York: Institute of Electrical and Electronics Engineers, 1993.
  Each entry in this alphabetical list has a number that keys it to a source in the back of the book. There is also a separate list of abbreviations, symbols, code names, project names, and acronyms.

JOURNALS

Electronics Week. New York: McGraw-Hill, 1930–. Weekly. Continues *Electronics.*
  Contains articles on new developments in technology and news of the electronics industry; one section covers previews of new products.

IEEE Spectrum. New York: Institute of Electrical and Electronics Engineers, 1964–. Monthly.
  Prints technical articles on new technological developments and their applications; articles on systems and analyses of specific problems; and book reviews.

Mechanical Engineering. New York: American Society of Mechanical Engineers, 1906–. Monthly.

Reviews developments in mechanical engineering; contains sections on computer applications, information on new products, society news, and book reviews.

Environmental and Earth Sciences

Allanby, Michael. *Dictionary of the Environment.* 3rd ed. New York: New York University Press, 1989.

Covers over 6,000 words and phrases used in all sciences touching on the environment. Acronyms, abbreviations, and some personal names are included.

Beacham's Guide to Environmental Issues and Sources. 5 vols. Washington, DC: Beacham, 1993.

A large and current bibliography and guide to interdisciplinary aspects of environmental sciences.

Environment Abstracts. New York: Environment Information Center, 1971–. Monthly.

An abstracting and indexing service covering books, articles, films, television programs, government studies, and conference proceedings. Abstracts are arranged in broad categories, with author, subject, and industry indexes. *Environment Index* is a printed cumulated index to the series, with an annual overview of legislation on environmental issues. An electronic version of this series can be found in *Enviroline* or in *Enviro/Energyline Abstracts Plus.*

Environmental Protection Agency Gopher. Internet. Available at gopher.epa.gov.

Includes current press releases, information about grants and fellowships, EPA air information, and data from the Environmental Monitoring and Assessment Program.

Geological Society of America. *Bibliography and Index of Geology.* Alexandria, VA: American Geological Institute, 1933–. Monthly, with annual cumulations.

Indexes the world's literature (books, periodicals, reports, maps, and North American theses and dissertations) on geology. Each month the Field of Interest section gives bibliographic citations for all documents covered, grouping the citations by subject category and then by document type; each issue also contains subject and author indexes. In the annual cumulation, citations in the Fields of Interest section are in alphabetical order. Until 1969, did not cover North American Geology, which was separately indexed in the *Bibliography of North American Geology,* published by the U.S. Geological Survey. Available in electronic format under the name *GeoRef* or *Geological Reference File.*

The Information Please Environmental Almanac. Boston: Houghton Mifflin, 1991–. Annually.

A handy compilation including facts and statistics on the environmental state of the countries of the world.

Information Sources in the Earth Sciences. 2nd ed. London: Bowker-Saur, 1989.

Includes detailed bibliographic essays covering reference sources, textbooks, and special resources for the various subdisciplines of geology.

Meredeth, Robert W. *The Environmentalist's Bookshelf: A Guide to the Best Books.* Boston: Hall, 1993.

An annotated list of recommended titles, including a short list of the most influential books on the environment.

Pollution Abstracts. La Jolla, CA: 1970–. Bimonthly.

Covers international technical publications on the environment, including technical reports, books, journal articles, proceedings, and government publications. The subject areas covered include air and water pollution, solid wastes, noise, pesticides, and radiation. Available in electronic formats including *Pollution/Toxicology CD-ROM.*

Publications of the Geological Survey. Washington, DC: Government Printing Office, 1934–.

An index to the vast number of publications included in the work of the Geological Survey. Covers such series as the Bulletins, Open File Reports, Professional Papers, and Water Supply Papers. To some extent, these series are also covered in the Bibliography and Index of Geology and in the Monthly Catalog, both of which have electronic versions.

United States Geological Survey–HTTP Server–Home Page. Internet. Available at http://www.usgs.gov.

A visually interesting site, offering declassified intelligence service satellite photos, earthquake information, volcanic observations, news on relevant government policy and legislation, and a survey and guide to Geographic Information Systems (GIS).

World Resources: A Report by the World Resources Institute and the International Institute for Environment and Development. New York: Basic Books, 1986–. Annually.

A guide covering a wide range of environmental issues — such as land use, water resources, and population — with many comparative statistics and analyses.

JOURNALS

Earth Science Reviews. Amsterdam, 1966–. Quarterly.

Articles in English from many countries on current developments and research. Each issue contains two long articles with extensive bibliographies. An especially valuable news supplement to each issue, Atlas, lists the contents of selected other geological journals and contains eight to ten book reviews.

Ecology. Tempe, AZ: Ecological Society of America, 1920–. Bimonthly.

Concerned with the study of organisms in relation to the environment, this journal contains research articles (about twenty-five per issue), a notes and comments section, and lengthy book reviews. *Ecological Monographs* (same publisher) is a quarterly journal for longer articles (more than twenty pages).

Environment. Washington, DC: Helen Dwight Reid Educational Foundation and the Scientists' Institute for Public Information, 1958–. Ten issues per year.

Contains technical articles (about three per issue) on environmental problems and solutions as well as abstracts for these articles in the table of contents. Also included are short book reviews and an overview of current environmental topics.

Environmental Geology and Water Sciences. New York: Springer-Verlag, 1975–. Quarterly.

Prints international research articles on natural and human pollution in the geological environment; also includes environmental impact studies.

Journal of Geology. Chicago: University of Chicago Press, 1893–. Bimonthly.

Contains four to six research articles, with abstracts, on all aspects of theoretical and applied geology; a section titled Geological Notes; and book reviews of varying lengths. Occasional issues are devoted to particular subjects.

Film

Film Literature Index. Albany, NY: Film and Television Documentation Center, 1973–. Quarterly, with annual cumulations.

A subject and author index to the world's periodical literature on film covering more than 200 magazines and newspapers. Citations indicate whether the articles include screen credits, biographical information, interviews, or illustrations.

Fisher, Kim M. *On the Screen: A Film, Television, and Video Research Guide.* Littleton, CO: Libraries Unlimited, 1986.

Annotated coverage of over 600 English language reference sources, as well as directories of research centers, societies, archives, and organizations, listed geographically. With author, title, and subject indexes.

Halliwell, Leslie. *Halliwell's Film Guide 1994.* New York: HarperPerennial, 1994.

A quick way to locate information about all sorts of films — good, bad, and awful. Includes brief and opinionated synopses, release dates, and basic facts about production.

Katz, Ephraim. *The Film Encyclopedia.* 2nd ed. New York: HarperCollins, 1994.

A handy one-volume encyclopedia covering a wide range of film history in nearly 1,500 pages.

Main Page: The Internet Movie Database. Internet. Available at http://www. msstate.edu/Movies.

A Web site based in Wales but with mirror sites around the world. Offers ratings, reviews, top movie lists, and searches by title, actor, genre, country of origin, year of release, production company, and so on. Includes information on about 4,000 films.

New York Times Film Reviews. New York: Times Books, 1913–1968. Biennial supplements.

A collection of film reviews from the *New York Times* arranged chronologically and including films made since 1913. Entries are reproductions of the actual signed reviews and include the credits and photographs (if any accompanied the original review); indexes by title, personal name, and corporate name are included.

The Oxford Companion to Film. Ed. Liz-Anne Bawden. New York: Oxford University Press, 1976.

Publishes short unsigned articles on all aspects of cinema, including film production, actors, directors, and movies. Lists of films by specific actors or directors are not always comprehensive; cross-references to related articles are included.

JOURNALS

Film Comment. New York: Film Society of Lincoln Center, 1962–. Bimonthly.
Each issue has three or four extended articles and several brief articles on films, directors, and actors.

Film Quarterly. Berkeley: University of California Press, 1945–. Quarterly.
Contains articles for nonspecialists and specialists on film, film production, and specific movies; articles and interviews with directors and actors; book reviews and film reviews on foreign and domestic films, documentaries, and experimental films.

Sight and Sound: The International Film Quarterly. London: British Film Institute, 1932–. Quarterly.
Presents articles about film and film production worldwide with emphasis on Great Britain; has film and book reviews.

Geography

Dictionary of Human Geography. New York: Free Press, 1981.
Covers specialized terminology and concepts in about 500 entries, many followed by a bibliography of recommended sources.

Encyclopedic Dictionary of Physical Geography. Oxford: Blackwell, 1985.
Over 2,000 terms are defined here, some briefly and others in longer, signed articles. Covers terminology for topics such as biogeography, climatology, geomorphology, and hydrology.

Geographical Abstracts. Norwich: Elsevier/Geo Abstracts, 1972–. Bimonthly.
Called *Geo Abstracts* and published in several parts until 1989, it now appears in two parts: Human Geography and Physical Geography. Covers topics such as landforms, climatology, economic geography, and sedimentology in broad categories, with a regional index. Available in electronic format as *GEOBASE.*

A Geographical Bibliography for American Libraries. Washington, DC: Association of American Geographers, 1985.
An excellent bibliography of works, most published from 1970 to 1984, essential to the field. Each citation includes a brief critical annotation. For earlier publications, consult *A Geographical Bibliography for American College Libraries* (1970).

Hammond Atlas of the World. Maplewood, NJ: Hammond, 1994.
Includes sections on interpreting maps, global relationships, the physical world, maps of the world, and statistical tables. Also includes information on energy resources, global warming, living standards, and politics, as well as physical and political maps.

Modern Geography: An Encyclopedic Survey. New York: Garland, 1990.
Covers influential people, institutions, concepts, subfields, and the history of the discipline from 1890 to the present.

Xerox PARC Map Viewer. Internet. Available at http://pubweb.parc.xerox.com/map.

A geographic information system that allows users to view locations in the United States and the rest of the world. The system lets users zoom in for more detail, shows borders and rivers, and provides information from the U.S. Geographic Name Server (an online gazetteer) about specific locations.

JOURNALS

Association of American Geographers Annals. Washington, DC: Association of American Geographers, 1911–. Quarterly.
Publishes scholarly research reports in all aspects of geography; includes papers from the association's meetings, commentary, and book reviews.

Geographical Review. New York: American Geographical Society, 1916–. Quarterly.
Contains scholarly research and review articles, brief reports in Geographical Record, and book reviews.

Journal of Historical Geography. London: Academic Press, 1975–. Quarterly.
Prints research and review articles on historical geography and related subjects, such as agriculture, archaeology, and anthropology; includes an extensive book review section.

Geology.   *See* Environmental and Earth Sciences.

Government.   *See* Political Science and Government.

History

America: History and Life. Santa Barbara: ABC-Clio, 1955–.
A bibliography, with abstracts, of publications on Canada and the United States, covering history and culture and including articles, books, and dissertations. An important research tool for the historian, along with *Historical Abstracts,* below. Available in electronic format.

American Historical Association. *Guide to Historical Literature.* New York: Oxford University Press, 1995.
Assists in historical research for all areas of the world. Following a section on general works and references, the book is divided geographically and then chronologically. Within each section, sources are arranged by form: bibliographies, reference works, geographies, anthropological and demographic studies, histories, biographies, government publications, and periodicals. Evaluative annotations are particularly helpful.

Carruth, Gorton. *The Encyclopedia of World Facts and Dates.* New York: HarperCollins, 1993.
A guide to the chronology of world history. A companion volume, *The Encyclopedia of American Facts and Dates* (1993) covers the United States in more detail.

C.R.I.S.: The Combined Retrospective Index Set to Journals in History, 1838–1974. 11 vols. Washington, DC: Carrollton, 1977.

A comprehensive key word index for 243 periodicals covering all historical periods and geographic areas. The first nine volumes are subject indexes grouped geographically (with four volumes for world history and five for American history); volumes 10 and 11 are author indexes.

Dictionary of American History. Rev. ed. 8 vols. New York: Scribner's, 1976.

A collection of articles arranged alphabetically on all aspects of American history and life. Articles are signed and each has at least one bibliographical reference. For biographical information, consult *The Dictionary of American Biography.*

Encyclopedia of American Social History. 3 vols. New York: Scribner's, 1993.

A survey of social history, including coverage of labor movements, women and minorities, religion, family history, and migration. Includes long topical essays followed by bibliographies. There is an index to all three volumes.

Freidel, Frank, ed. *Harvard Guide to American History.* Rev. ed. Cambridge: Belknap–Harvard University Press, 1974.

Volume 1 contains background articles and bibliographies on research methods and materials, biographies, comprehensive and regional histories, and histories of special subjects, such as economics, immigration, and education. The bibliographies in volume 2 are arranged chronologically; volume 2 also contains a subject index and an index of names to both volumes.

Fritze, Ronald H. *Reference Sources in History: An Introductory Guide.* Santa Barbara, CA: ABC-Clio, 1990.

An introduction to reference works for all periods and regions, emphasizing English language materials on Western history, but including Asian, African, and Latin American history. Each entry has a lengthy annotation.

Grun, Bernard. *The Timetables of History: A Horizontal Linkage of People and Events.* 3rd ed. New York: Simon and Schuster, 1991.

A chronology listing developments in various areas — politics, the arts, science and technology, daily life, religion, and philosophy — in tables, year by year, allowing you to make connections between different disciplines. With a detailed index. For a specialized chronology, see James Trager's *Women's Chronology: A Year-by-Year Record from Prehistory to the Present* (1994).

Historical Abstracts. Santa Barbara: ABC-Clio, 1955–.

Covers modern world history, excluding the United States and Canada, from 1450 to the present. Books, articles, and dissertations are covered, with abstracts provided. Available in electronic format.

The Historical Text Archive. Internet. Available at http://www.msstate. edu/Archives/History/index.html.

A World Wide Web interface for the oldest FTP site for historical archives. Includes texts, programs, images, bibliographies, and guides. Emphasizes U.S. history but is increasing its coverage of Latin America and Asia.

The New Cambridge Modern History. Ed. G. R. Potter. 14 vols. Cambridge: Cambridge University Press, 1957.

The classic scholarly history of the Western world from the Renaissance through World War II. Each volume has its own subject index; volume 14 is a historical atlas. The *Cambridge Ancient History* and the *Cambridge Medieval History* cover prehistoric time through the fifteenth century. The same publisher has put out many multivolume sets, such as *The Cambridge History of Africa.*

JOURNALS

American Historical Review. Washington, DC: American Historical Association, 1895–. Five issues a year.
Contains four or five scholarly articles per issue as well as research notes, an extensive book review section subdivided by geographic region and period, and a section listing documents and bibliographies.

English Historical Review. Harlow, England: Longman, 1886–. Quarterly.
Publishes scholarly articles covering all fields of history; also includes research notes, book reviews, and an extensive section of short notices.

Journal of American History. Bloomington, IN: Organization of American Historians, 1914–. Quarterly. Continues *Mississippi Valley Historical Review.*
Prints research articles on American history; also extensive book reviews, a bibliography of articles and dissertations, and lists of bibliographies and archive acquisitions.

Journal of Modern History. Chicago: University of Chicago Press, 1929–. Quarterly.
Publishes research and review articles on modern European history since the Renaissance and lengthy book reviews. Special issues focus on topics such as political practice in the French Revolution.

Law and Criminal Justice

Black's Law Dictionary. 6th ed. St. Paul: West, 1990.
Standard law dictionary for ready reference.

Cohen, Morris L. *Legal Research in a Nutshell.* 5th ed. St. Paul: West, 1992.
Intended to provide students with a brief introduction to the main areas of legal literature. Appendixes list state research guides, loose-leaf services, official state reporters, and titles in the national reporter system.

Criminal Justice Abstracts. Hackensack, NJ: National Council on Crime and Delinquency, 1977–. Quarterly. Continues *Crime and Delinquency Literature* (1968–1976).
Contains in-depth abstracts of current books, journal articles, dissertations, and reports published worldwide. Many issues include a review or bibliographic essay on a current issue in criminal justice. This is a classified index with a separate subject index. Available in electronic format.

Encyclopedia of Crime: Criminal Justice, Criminology and Law Enforcement Dictionary. 6 vols. Willimette, IL: CrimeBooks, 1989.
The first four volumes of this set include unsigned articles covering aspects of crime and law enforcement internationally. Volume 5 is a dictionary, containing over 20,000 specialized terms. The final volume is an index of names and subjects.

Encyclopedia of Crime and Justice. 4 vols. Ed. Sanford H. Kadish. New York: Free Press, 1983.
Covers the nature and cause of criminal behavior, crime prevention, punishment and treatment of criminals, administration of criminal justice systems, law that defines criminal behavior, and the application of criminal law. Articles are signed, with bibliographies. Volume 4 contains an index.

Index to Legal Periodicals and Books. New York: Wilson, 1908–. Monthly, with annual cumulation.

Subject and author index to English-language periodical literature on legal topics. Includes a table of cases and a book review index. In 1994 began to cover books as well as articles. Available in electronic format.

Legaltrac. Menlo Park, CA: Information Access, 1980–. Monthly.
An electronic index to over 800 legal publications selected by an advisory committee of the American Association of Law Libraries. Also called *Legal Resources Index.*

Lexis. See entry for *Nexis/Lexis* under Indexes to the Popular Press.

The Oxford Handbook of Criminology. New York: Oxford University Press, 1994.
An up-to-date manual on topics, concepts, and basic facts in the field of criminology.

THOMAS: Legislative Information on the Internet. See entry under Political Science and Politics and Government.

JOURNALS

American Bar Association Journal. Chicago: American Bar Association, 1915–. Monthly.
This official journal of the membership of the American Bar Association contains articles of interest to legal practitioners and the public. Special columns include What's New, Supreme Court Report, and Computer Corner. Book reviews are included.

Crime and Delinquency. Beverly Hills: Sage, 1955–. Quarterly.
Publishes articles on all aspects of crime and the administration of justice.

Harvard Law Review. Cambridge, MA: Gannett House, 1887–. Eight issues per year.
Contains lengthy articles on all aspects of law.

Journal of Criminal Justice. Elmsford, NY: Pergamon, 1973–. Bimonthly.
Written for professionals and academics, this scholarly journal covers all aspects of the criminal justice system. A regular feature publishes short descriptive abstracts of recently published books.

Literature

Alex. Internet. Available at gopher.rsl.ox.ac.uk.
An index to full-text books available on the Internet. Though not complete and not devoted exclusively to literary texts, it can help you find electronic versions of literary works. It covers texts produced or loaded through Project Gutenburg, Wiretap, the On-Line Book Initiative, Eris, the English Server, and the Oxford Text Archive. Search options include browsing by author, title, date of original publication, and language.

American Literary Scholarship. Durham, NC: Duke University, 1963–. Annually.
An annual review of the year's scholarship in American literature. Chapters cover individual major authors, periods, and genres, discussing new research in essay format. This complements the *MLA International Bibliography* by providing an evaluative and comparative framework for criticism. For similar evaluative coverage of research in English, American, and Commonwealth literature, see *The Year's Work in English Studies* (1921–).

American Women Writers: A Critical Reference Guide from Colonial Times to the Present. Ed. Lina Mainiero. 4 vols. Volume 5 supplement issued in 1994. New York: Ungar, 1979–82.

Contains biographical data, critical assessments, and bibliographical lists for 1,000 women writers. Volume 4 contains an index to names and subjects. Volume 5 updates coverage in volumes 1 to 4 and adds new writers.

American Writers. 4 vols. New York: Scribner's, 1979–1982. With supplements.

Profiles prominent American writers in lengthy biographical sketches intended for a general audience. Includes bibliographies of works by and about the writers. Related series include *European Writers* (1983–) and *British Writers* (1979–).

Black American Writers: Bibliographical Essays. Ed. M. Thomas Inge, Maurice Duke, and Jackson R. Bryer. 2 vols. New York: St. Martin's, 1978.

A good preliminary source for the study of black writers, these volumes evaluate biographical and critical writings about selected black authors and offer suggestions for further study. Essays are organized by topic, such as slave narratives and the Harlem Renaissance, as well as by individual author.

The Bloomsbury Guide to Women's Literature. New York: Prentice-Hall, 1992.

A guide to women's literature of the world, including lengthy and detailed country surveys in the front section, then covering writers, works, and topics alphabetically.

Columbia Literary History of the United States. New York: Columbia University Press, 1987.

A successor to several editions of the *Literary History of the United States,* covering women's and minority literature in greater depth than earlier efforts. Lengthy chapters cover American literature thematically and chronologically.

The Concise Oxford Dictionary of Literary Terms. New York: Oxford University Press, 1990.

An excellent short guide to literary critical terms, including classic topics and trendy new developments. A handy place to define befuddling terms encountered in critical texts.

Contemporary Authors. Detroit: Gale, 1972–.

Records biographic information about living international authors writing in all subject areas. Each entry includes biographic information, a list of works published, and works in progress. Because entries are often updated and revised, check the most recent cumulative index to find complete listings. Other related series published by Gale include *Contemporary Literary Criticism* and *Dictionary of American Biography,* extensive collections of biographical and critical material. The indexes in all three sets include references to the other series.

Encyclopedia of World Literature in the Twentieth Century. 2nd ed. 5 vols. New York: Ungar, 1981–1985.

Contains short articles (one to two pages) on authors who have produced their major works in the twentieth century and on national literatures, genres, and movements. Articles on authors give brief biographical information, discuss and list their major works, and supply further references.

Harner, James L. *Literary Research Guide: A Guide to Reference Sources for the Study of Literatures in English and Related Topics.* New York: Modern Language Association, 1989.

An in-depth guide to literary research, listing reference tools and providing lengthy annotations. Includes core journals, library collections and catalogs, and databases. Though the focus is on English and American literature, there are also chapters on foreign language literature, comparative literature, and translation.

Hart, James D. *The Oxford Companion to American Literature.* 5th ed. New York: Oxford University Press, 1983.

A one-volume encyclopedia with brief articles on American authors, (including biographic information and bibliographies), literary works, and allusions as well as persons and events important in social and cultural history. Articles on individual literary works give summaries of the works and include verse form for poems. A chronological index lists a parallel chronology of American literary history and social history.

The MLA International Bibliography of Books and Articles on the Modern Languages and Literature. New York: Modern Language Association, 1921–. Annual.

A classified list of international periodical articles, *Festschriften*, books, and dissertations on modern languages, literature, and folklore. Citations are grouped by national literature and then chronologically. Available in electronic format.

New Cambridge Bibliography of English Literature. Ed. George Watson. 5 vols. Cambridge: Cambridge University Press, 1974.

A comprehensive bibliography of English literature from A.D. 600 through 1950. Arranged chronologically, each section lists general works and genre studies and then individual authors. For each author, bibliographies and information on special collections or location of manuscripts are given; collections are listed chronologically. Also included is a comprehensive international bibliography of criticism. Besides the index in each volume, volume 5 contains an index to the whole set. This bibliography is especially useful if your topic is highly specialized or if you are looking for older critical approaches. If you are looking for current criticism, see the *MLA International Bibliography.*

The Oxford Companion to English Literature. Ed. Margaret Drabble. 5th ed. Oxford: Clarendon, 1985.

A one-volume encyclopedia with brief articles on English authors (some American authors are included), literary works, literary societies, characters, and allusions. Facts about each author's life and a list of major works with dates are given. Oxford Companions have been published for many world literatures, including French, German, Canadian, Spanish, and Australian, as well as for theater, film, and children's literature.

JOURNALS

American Literature: A Journal of Literary History, Criticism, and Bibliography. Durham: Duke University Press, 1929–. Quarterly.

Publishes scholarly historical and critical articles on American authors; includes twenty to twenty-five lengthy book reviews per issue with an additional section (Brief Mention) of short book reviews. Each issue also contains a selected annotated bibliography on American literature.

ELH (English Literary History). Baltimore: Johns Hopkins University Press, 1931–. Quarterly.

Provides about ten lengthy critical articles on British literature in each issue.

Modern Fiction Studies. West Lafayette, IN: Purdue University, 1955–. Quarterly.
Publishes literary criticism and bibliographic articles on modern (post-1880) fiction together with lengthy book reviews; two issues each year focus on one writer or on a special topic, such as modern war fiction.

Modern Poetry Studies. Buffalo: Media Study/Buffalo, 1970–. Three issues per year.
Prints critical studies of modern poets and poetry as well as original poetry.

PMLA (Publication of the Modern Language Association). New York: Modern Language Association, 1884–. Six issues per year.
Contains scholarly articles on themes, critical approaches, and other aspects of modern languages and literature along with association news and commentary.

Mathematics.   *See* Computer Science and Mathematics.

Medicine and Nursing

Centers for Disease Control Gopher. Internet. Available at gopher.cdc.gov.
Full-text access to current issues of the *Morbidity and Mortality Weekly Report,* which contains national and international news and research reports on epidemiology and disease, very up-to-date advisories on medical precautions to take if traveling to different regions and countries, and information on AIDS, smoking, and women's health, among other medical topics.

Cumulative Index to Nursing and Allied Health Literature. Glendale, CA: Glendale Adventist Medical Center, 1977–. Continues *Cumulative Index to Nursing Literature* (1956–1976). Bimonthly, with annual cumulations.
Indexes approximately 300 English-language journals in nursing, health, and health care–related fields; pamphlets, audiovisual materials, and book reviews are included. A list of subject headings (organized in a hierarchical structure) is used to assign terms for a subject index. Available in electronic format, sometimes under the acronym *CINAHL.*

Encyclopedia and Dictionary of Medicine, Nursing, and Allied Health. 4th ed. Philadelphia: Saunders, 1987.
A concise handbook for practitioners, with an emphasis on patient care. Includes information on nursing diagnosis and conceptual models of nursing.

Harrison's Principles of Internal Medicine. Ed. Kurt J. Isselbacher et al. 13th ed. 2 vols. New York: McGraw-Hill, 1994.
This textbook on internal medicine is a major source of background information on health concerns. After an introductory section on clinical medicine, two volumes are divided into sections on disease: the clinical manifestations, biological aspects, biological and environmental causes, and organ systems. The section on each disorder includes a definition and background information, description of symptoms, complications, diagnosis and treatment, and additional references. An index at the end of each volume provides access by specific disease or disorder.

Haselbauer, Kathleen J. *A Research Guide to the Health Sciences: Medical, Nutritional, and Environmental.* New York: Greenwood, 1987.

Covers over 2,000 sources in clinical medicine, social aspects of medicine, and sources for medical specialties. Entries have lengthy annotations, and selections have been made with the novice researcher in mind.

Index Medicus. Bethesda: National Library of Medicine, 1960–. Monthly, with annual cumulations. Continues *Quarterly Cumulative Index Medicus* (1928–1959) and *Index Medicus* (1879–1927).

Indexes periodical literature in medicine worldwide; subject access is through headings assigned from *Medical Subject Headings (MeSH)*, which arranges terms from general concepts to specific terms. There is also an Author section (all authors are cross-referenced) and a Medical Reviews section. Available in electronic format under the name *MedLine.* At some libraries, Grateful Med, bibliographic software for downloading and managing references in *Medline,* is available. You can purchase Grateful Med software for your own IBM PC or Apple Macintosh for $29.95. To get details or to order, call the National Technical Information Service at (703) 487-4650.

National Institutes of Health Gopher. Internet. Available at gopher.nih.gov.

Offers information on grants and research opportunities, as well as health and clinical information and connections to AIDS resources, a cancer network, and molecular biology databases.

Stedman, Thomas Lathrop. *Stedman's Medical Dictionary.* 25th ed. Baltimore: Williams and Wilkins, 1990.

Includes brief definitions of terms in fields such as medicine, endocrinology, immunology, genetics, psychiatry, and molecular biology.

JOURNALS

American Journal of Human Genetics. Chicago: American Society for Human Genetics, 1949–. Bimonthly.

Publishes research and review articles on heredity and genetic applications in sociology, anthropology, and medicine; book reviews and society news.

American Journal of Nursing. New York: American Journal of Nursing, 1900–. Monthly.

Publishes articles reporting developments in techniques and treatment in clinical medicine as well as brief clinical news reports and professional news.

JAMA: Journal of the American Medical Association. Chicago: American Medical Association, 1848–. Weekly.

Contains brief reports on medical news; original research articles and case studies in clinical medicine and related areas; association news; and book reviews.

Journal of Nutrition. Rockville, MD: American Institute of Nutrition, 1928–. Monthly.

Contains scholarly articles reporting original research on the physiology of nutrition.

New England Journal of Medicine. Boston: Massachusetts Medical Society, 1812–. Weekly.

Prints articles reporting original research and case studies, editorials, commentary, correspondence and occasional book reviews.

Music

Baker, Theodore. *Baker's Biographical Dictionary of Musicians.* 7th ed. rev. by Nicolas Slonimsky. New York: Schirmer, 1984.
An excellent source for concise biographies of musicians, including some popular musicians; a good choice when the articles in *Grove* (see below) offer more than what is needed.

Duckles, Vincent. *Music Reference and Research Materials.* 4th rev. ed. New York: Schirmer, 1994.
An annotated guide to references for music and musicology divided by type of reference book, such as dictionaries, histories, bibliographies, and discographies. Indexes provide access by subject, title, and author/editor/reviewer.

The Music Index. Detroit: Information Coordinators, 1949–. Monthly, with annual cumulations.
An index by subject, author, and title or work to periodicals on music and dance. Book reviews are listed alphabetically by author; reviews of performers and music are listed under the performer's or composer's name, and record reviews are listed under Recordings. Available in electronic format.

The New Grove Dictionary of Music and Musicians. Ed. Stanley Sadie. 6th ed. 20 vols. London: Macmillan, 1980.
A scholarly encyclopedia on all aspects of music. Entries cover terminology, performers, theory, instruments, composers, history, music of all regions of the world, and folk music. Many articles include bibliographies and lists of works. A glossary of terms used in non-Western music is included in volume 20.

New Oxford History of Music. New York: Oxford University Press, 1986–.
A multivolume history covering music ancient to modern. Each volume is written by an expert on the period. New editions of the original ten volumes are appearing on an irregular basis.

JOURNALS

Acta Musicologica. Basel: International Musicological Society, 1928–. Two issues per year.
Publishes articles by international scholars on musicology.

American Musicological Society Journal. Philadelphia: American Musocological Society, 1948–. Three issues per year.
Prints scholarly articles on musicology; issues contain lengthy book reviews and lists of publications received.

Journal of Music Theory. New Haven: Yale School of Music, 1957–. Two issues per year.
Contains scholarly articles on music theory, lengthy book reviews, and bibliographies of books and articles on music theory.

Nursing.   *See* Medicine and Nursing.

Nutrition.   *See* Medicine and Nursing.

Philosophy and Religion

Adams, Charles J. *A Reader's Guide to the Great Religions.* 2nd ed. New York: Macmillan/Free Press, 1977.

Contains bibliographic essays describing resources for research on primitive religions; religions of the ancient world, Mexico, and China; Hinduism, Buddhism, Sikhism, Jainism; religions of Japan; early, classical, medieval, and modern Judaism; Christianity; and Islam. Author and subject indexes are given.

Alex. Internet. Available at gopher.rsl.ox.ac.uk.

An index to full-text books available on the Internet, including many religious texts such as versions of the Bible, the Koran, and the Book of Mormon. It covers texts produced or loaded through Project Gutenburg, Wiretap, the On-Line Initiative, Eris, the English Server, and the Oxford Text Archive. Search options include browsing by author, title, date of original publication, and language.

American Philosophical Association Gopher. Internet. Available at apa.oxy.edu.

American Philosophical Association Home Page. Internet. Available at http://www.oxy.edu/apa/apa.html.

Includes news relating to the association, information about grants, an international preprint exchange, software for philosophers, and e-mail directories.

Anchor Bible Dictionary. 6 vols. New York: Doubleday, 1992.

A monumental work, compiled by an international and ecumenical group of around 1,000 Bible scholars. Includes information on the history, figures, texts, and images in the Bible, and covers topics such as "abortion in antiquity," "feminist hermeneutics," and "computers and Biblical studies."

Brandon, S. G. F., ed. *A Dictionary of Comparative Religion.* New York: Scribner's, 1970.

Provides brief descriptive entries on all aspects of world religions, including deities, religious leaders, concepts, sects, geographic locations, rites, and rituals. Many articles have bibliographies.

DeGeorge, Richard T. *The Philosopher's Guide to Sources, Research Tools, Professional Life, and Related Fields.* Lawrence: Regents Press of Kansas, 1980.

An annotated guide to the literature of philosophy that includes a guide to research tools and a bibliography of sources on the history of philosophy and the various branches, schools, and national philosophies. The bibliography also includes a section on philosophical periodicals and professional issues, such as publishing, associations, and research centers. An index by author, title, and subject is provided.

Encyclopedia Judaica. 16 vols. New York: Macmillan, 1972.

Contains signed scholarly articles as well as brief descriptions of topics in all areas of Jewish history, religion, and culture; most articles have short bibliographies. Volume 1 indexes the entire set.

The Encyclopedia of Philosophy. Ed. Paul Edwards. 8 vols. New York: Macmillan, 1967.

Publishes scholarly articles on Eastern and Western philosophy and on philosophers, concepts, and theories from ancient to modern times; bibliographies are given at the end of each article. Volume 8 includes a subject index.

Encyclopedia of Religion. Ed. Mircea Eliade. 16 vols. New York: Macmillan, 1986.
Covers important ideas, beliefs, rituals, myths, symbols, and persons that
have played a role in religious history from paleolithic times to the present.
Articles are signed and include bibliographies. Volume 16 is an index.

Nelson's Complete Concordance to the Revised Standard Version Bible. Ed. John Elli-
son. 2nd ed. New York: Thomas Nelson, 1984.
Arranged alphabetically, this reference gives the context and location of
nearly every word in the RSV Bible. Nelson also publishes *Young's Analytical Concordance to the King James Version of the Bible* (rev. ed., 1982), which
gives the context, location, and Hebrew and Greek words from which the
English was translated. *Young's* contains a Universal Subject Guide to the
Bible.

The Philosopher's Index. Bowling Green: Philosophy Documentation Center,
1967–. Quarterly, with annual cumulations.
Indexes all English-language philosophy books and English, French, German, Spanish, and Italian philosophy journals as well as some journals in related fields. Abstracts are provided for many of the citations in the author
index. Also included are a subject index and a book review index. Available
in electronic format.

Religion Index One: Periodicals. Chicago: American Theological Association,
1977–. Continues *Index to Religious Periodical Literature* (1949–1976).
Indexes more than 300 journals in religion and theology. Abstracts are included for many of the citations in the author index. A subject index and
Scripture index are also provided. This index can be searched using the Religion Index database (1975–). Book reviews were included until 1985 and
are now indexed in a separate publication, *Index to Book Reviews in Religion.*
A companion of this set is *Religion Index Two: Multi-Author Work,* which indexes composite works by author and subject. Available online under *Religion Index* or *Religion Indexes.*

JOURNALS

Ethics: An International Journal of Social, Political, and Legal Philosophy. Chicago:
University of Chicago Press, 1890–. Quarterly.
Publishes scholarly articles on the social, ethical, and legal aspects of philosophy; book reviews and book notes; short discussions; survey articles; and
reviews.

Journal of Biblical Literature. Chico, CA: Society of Biblical Literature, 1882–.
Quarterly.
Contains scholarly papers on the Old and New Testaments, lengthy book
reviews, a section on essay collections, and a list of books received.

Journal of Philosophy. New York: Journal of Philosophy, 1904–. Monthly.
Presents scholarly papers in all areas of philosophy; some issues include papers from various symposia as well as comments and criticism.

Journal of Religion. Chicago: University of Chicago Press, 1882–. Quarterly.
Publishes critical, scholarly articles on theology and related religious studies, review articles, and book reviews.

Journal of Symbolic Logic. Providence: Association for Symbolic Logic, 1936–.
Quarterly.
Publishes technical articles on symbolic logic and related fields, such as
mathematics and philosophy; includes book reviews and association news.

Physical Education and Sports

Encyclopedia of Physical Education, Fitness and Sports. Ed. Thomas K. Cureton, Jr. 3 vols. Salt Lake City: Brighton, 1980.

Each volume covers one area of physical education in detail and has its own table of contents, index, and biographical directory. Volume 1 covers the philosophy and history of physical education and programs for schools, the armed forces, and the handicapped. Volume 2 has sections on training and conditioning, nutrition, and fitness for children and adults. Volume 3 contains articles on types of sports, dance, and related physical activities.

Physical Education Index. Cape Girardeau, MO: Ben Oak, 1978–. Quarterly.

Indexes English-language periodicals covering physical education, physical therapy, health, dance, recreation, sports, and sports medicine. Entries include research reports, legislation, biographies, and reports from associations; a book review listing is given.

Sport Bibliography/Bibliographie du Sport. Ottawa: Sport Information Resource Center, 1983–1987.

Covers journal literature, conference papers, books, theses, and dissertations on various sports as well as physiology, exercise, biomechanics, coaching, and counseling. Updated by *Sport Bibliography Update* (annual). Available electronically as *Sport Discus,* updated semiannually.

JOURNALS

American Journal of Sports Medicine. Baltimore: American Orthopaedic Society for Sports Medicine, 1972–. Bimonthly.

Publishes review and research articles on the medical aspects of sports and sports injuries, society news, book reviews, and an annual bibliography on sports medicine.

Journal of Physical Education, Recreation, and Dance. Reston, VA: American Alliance for Health, Physical Education, Recreation, and Dance, 1896–. Monthly except July.

Contains brief news and research reports, review articles on issues and techniques in sports and physical education, and book reviews. Issues occasionally focus on one topic, such as gymnastics.

The Physical Educator. Indianapolis: Phi Epsilon Kappa Fraternity, 1940–. Quarterly.

Publishes articles on the history, theory, and philosophy of sports and physical education. Each issue focuses on one of four themes: special populations, program development, foundations, or human performance.

Research Quarterly for Exercise and Sport. Reston, VA: American Alliance for Health, Physical Education, Recreation, and Dance, 1930–. Quarterly.

Presents lengthy, scholarly articles reporting the results of empirical research and short articles reporting research in progress.

Physics. *See* Chemistry and Physics.

Political Science and Government

ABC Pol Sci: Advance Bibliography of Contents, Political Science and Government. Santa Barbara: ABC-Clio, 1969–. Bimonthly.

A subject index and an author index provide access to the tables of contents of more than 300 U.S. and international journals in political science and related subjects, such as area studies and sociology. Available in electronic format.

Blackwell Encyclopedia of Political Thought. Oxford: Blackwell, 1987.
Covers theory, doctrines, and ideologies in historical and contemporary contexts. Emphasizes Western politics but includes selected concepts from Islamic, Hindu, and Chinese cultures. Articles are substantial and signed and include bibliographies. A related title is *The Blackwell Encyclopedia of Political Institutions* (1987).

Congressional Quarterly's Guide to the Presidency. Washington, DC: Congressional Quarterly, 1989.
A massive collection of information on the presidency as an institution. Historical, cultural, procedural, and political aspects are considered. Similar works include *Congressional Quarterly's Guide to the U.S. Supreme Court* (1989), *Congressional Quarterly's Guide to Congress* (1991), and *Congressional Quarterly's Guide to U.S. Elections* (1985).

Holler, Frederick L. *Information Sources of Political Sciences*. 4th ed. Santa Barbara: ABC-Clio, 1986.
A detailed, annotated guide to research resources. Holler begins with a general section on political science research and then discusses specific tools classified as general reference sources, social sciences, American government and politics, international relations, political theory, and public administration. It contains indexes by subject, author, title, comparative and area studies, and typology.

International Political Science Abstracts. Oxford: Blackwell, 1955–. Quarterly.
Prepared by the International Political Science Association and designed to cover the international literature of political science. Abstracts in English or French are arranged in broad categories, with subject and author indexes.

Kalvelage, Carl, Albert P. Melone, and Morley Segal. *Bridges to Knowledge in Political Science: A Handbook for Research*. Pacific Palisades, CA: Palisades, 1984.
A practical guide for students of political science organized around the process of writing a term paper. It includes annotated bibliography of political science reference materials.

Political Handbook of the World. New York: Published for the Council on Foreign Relations by Harper & Row, 1927–. Annually.
A country-by-country survey of political structures and situations, including charts of government organization, historical background, and political parties; and analysis of contemporary issues.

Politics in America. Washington, DC: Congressional Quarterly, 1981–. Biennially.
Includes profiles of members of Congress, with analysis of their interests, leanings, and effectiveness. Lists of their voting records and committee memberships are also included. Arranged geographically, with profiles of states and districts provided.

Public Affairs Information Service Bulletin. See entry under Social Sciences.

Thomas: Legislative Information on the Internet. Internet. Available at http://thomas.loc.gov.

A database of congressional information offering full texts of legislation searchable by key word or bill number. The text of the *Congressional Record* is searchable by keyword. Coverage starts with the 103rd Congress.

United States Political Science Documents. Pittsburgh: University of Pittsburgh, 1975–. Annual.

Published by the University of Pittsburgh's University Center for International Studies in conjunction with the American Political Science Association. Indexes more than 120 American journals in the political, social, and policy sciences. Each year's volume is published in two parts. Part 1 contains five indexes: author/contributor, subject, geographic area, proper name, and journal. Part 2 has 100- to 200-word abstracts for each citation. Available online.

U.S. Government Manual. See entry under Government Documents.

JOURNALS

American Journal of Political Science. Austin: University of Texas Press, 1957–. Quarterly.

Published for the Midwest Political Science Association. Articles are concerned mainly with American politics, but some deal with international affairs.

American Political Science Review. Washington, DC: American Political Science Association, 1906–. Quarterly.

Presents scholarly papers on American government, political science, and related fields, such as area studies, law, and economics. It also contains extensive book reviews and review essays grouped by subject.

Congressional Quarterly Weekly Report. Washington, DC: Congressional Quarterly, 1956–. Weekly.

Not a research journal but a weekly update on happenings in Congress. An excellent place to find out about new developments, the progress of legislation, or news on a particular member of Congress. Includes its own detailed index.

Foreign Affairs. New York: Council on Foreign Relations, 1922–. Five issues per year.

Publishes articles expressing opinions and discussing issues in international relations, occasionally written by national and international political leaders. Includes brief book reviews and bibliographies of relevant government documents and other related publications.

Journal of Politics. Gainesville, FL: Southern Political Science Association, 1939–. Quarterly.

Publishes scholarly articles on political science, research notes, book reviews (including review essays), and association news.

Psychology

American Psychological Association Gopher. Internet. Available at gopher.apa.org.

American Psychological Association Home Page. Internet. Available at http://www.apa.org.

Includes information for students, announcements of research opportunities and grants, conference information, and connections to related Internet sites.

Diagnostic and Statistical Manual of Mental Disorders: DSM-IV. 4th ed. Washington, DC: American Psychiatric Association, 1994.
A glossary and classification system for mental disorders, including diagnostic criteria and descriptions. Includes a glossary and list of changes from the third edition. An essential tool for professionals and an authoritative guide to mental disorders.

Encyclopedia of Psychology. 2nd ed. Ed. Raymond J. Corsini. 4 vols. New York: Wiley, 1994.
Includes signed background articles on all aspects of psychology and biographical articles on important psychologists. Some articles have bibliographies, and all references mentioned in the articles are listed in complete form in a single bibliography in volume 4. Volume 4 also includes a name index (persons and titles) and a subject index.

Mental Measurements Yearbook. Highland Park, NJ: Mental Measurements Yearbook, 1941–.
A listing of tests available, giving descriptions, availability, reviews, and research on the construction and use of tests. Indexes cover test titles, publications, and test classification. Available in electronic format.

Psychological Abstracts. Arlington, VA: American Psychological Association, 1927–. Monthly, with semiannual cumulations.
A bibliography with abstracts of the world's literature in psychology and related fields. Entries include journal articles, books, technical reports, and dissertations. Abstracts are grouped in sixteen subject classifications with more specific access through subject and author indexes. Available in electronic format under the name *PsycInfo* or *PsycLit.*

Reed, Jeffrey G., and Pam M. Baxter. *Library Use: A Handbook for Psychology.* Washington, DC: American Psychological Association, 1992.
A guide to library research in psychology. It begins with topic selection and works through the research process for writing a paper. Detailed instructions for using sources such as *Psychological Abstracts* and citation indexes are provided.

JOURNALS

American Psychologist. Washington, DC: American Psychological Association, 1946–. Monthly.
Issues contain review articles and articles reporting empirical research, a section titled Psychology in the Public Forum, association news, and a commentary section.

Journal of Counseling Psychology. Washington, DC: American Psychological Association, 1954–. Quarterly.
Publishes research articles on counseling arranged by subject: counseling process and outcomes, counseling assessment, career development, group intervention, special populations and setting, professional issues and training, and research methodology. There are also brief research reports and a comments section.

Journal of Personality and Social Psychology. Washington, DC: American Psychological Association, 1965–. Monthly.

Publishes scholarly articles covering empirical and theoretical studies grouped in three sections: attitudes and social cognition, interpersonal relations and group processes, and personality processes and individual differences.

Psychological Bulletin. Washington, DC: American Psychological Association, 1904–. Bimonthly.

Presents review articles evaluating and synthesizing research and methodological studies in psychology as well as articles on quantitative methods in psychology.

Religion.   *See* Philosophy and Religion.

Space Science.   *See* Astronomy and Space Science.

Sociology

Bart, Pauline, and Linda Frankl. *The Student Sociologist's Handbook.* 4th ed. New York: Random House, 1986.

Covers writing papers in the field, research materials, journals, government data sources, and use of computers in sociological research, with over 500 resources and journals discussed.

Book Review Index to Social Science Periodicals. See entry under Social Sciences.

Boudon, Raymond. *A Critical Dictionary of Sociology.* Chicago: University of Chicago, 1989.

An abridged translation of the *Dictionnaire critique de la sociologie,* first published in France in 1982. Provides long articles on theory and concepts, such as beliefs, ideologies, and social control.

C.R.I.S.: The Combined Retrospective Index Set to Journals in Sociology, 1895–1974. 6 vols. Washington, DC: Carrollton, 1978.

A comprehensive index to journals in sociology and related fields, such as anthropology, covering the literature since 1895. Articles are arranged in the first five volumes by subject key word within eighty-six subject categories. Volume 6 is an author index.

Encyclopedia of Social Work. 18th ed. 2 vols. Silver Spring, MD: National Association of Social Workers, 1987.

Contains 225 articles on interdisciplinary topics such as adolescent pregnancy, homelessness, homosexuality, immigrants, and workfare — each a lengthy, signed article with a bibliography. Emphasizes social work practice and professional issues.

Encyclopedia of Sociology. 4 vols. New York: Macmillan, 1992.

A current and scholarly exploration of the theories, issues, and terms used in the field. Articles are substantial and include bibliographies.

Sociological Abstracts. San Diego: Sociological Abstracts, 1952–. Five issues per year.

A bibliography with abstracts of the periodicals in sociology and related fields, such as education and anthropology. The abstracts are grouped in thirteen subject classifications. Available online, sometimes under the name *SocioFile*.

JOURNALS

American Journal of Sociology. Chicago: University of Chicago Press, 1895–. Bimonthly.
   Publishes articles reporting empirical and theoretical research in sociology and related fields, such as social psychology. It also includes research notes, review essays, discussion, and lengthy book reviews.

American Sociological Review. Washington, DC: American Sociological Association, 1936–. Bimonthly.
   Contains scholarly papers on research and theoretical methodological developments in sociology. Research notes, comments, and articles on professional issues are included.

Sociology and Social Research: An International Journal. Los Angeles: University of Southern California, 1916–. Quarterly.
   Presents research and review articles on sociology and related fields, such as urban sociology, sociology of education, and family studies; also contains book reviews.

Sports.   *See* Physical Education and Sports.

Women's Studies

Carter, Sarah. *Women's Studies: A Guide to Information Sources.* Jefferson, NC: McFarland, 1990.
   A sourcebook including over 1,000 annotated listings of reference works and other resources on women such as African-American women, law and politics, and spirituality.

Feminist Activist Resources on the Net. Internet. Available at http://www.igc. apc.org/women/feminist.html.
   A well-organized guide to resources, including Internet sites relating to women's studies, people, government agencies, and libraries. Includes news and documents of interest to feminists.

Humm, Maggie. *The Dictionary of Feminist Theory.* Columbus: Ohio State University Press, 1990.
   Gives brief but pithy discussions of terms relating to feminism. Includes a useful bibliography.

Searing, Susan. *Introduction to Library Research in Women's Studies.* Boulder, CO: Westview, 1985.
   A discussion of search strategies, library use, and reference tools specific to the field, including databases, special collections, and microfilm sources. Contains a list of review essays in the journal *Signs* (see entry for *Signs*, next page).

Stineman, Esther. *Women's Studies: A Recommended Core Bibliography.* Littleton, CO: Libraries Unlimited, 1979.
   A reader's guide to materials, giving lists of recommended books under a variety of topics and including useful annotations. Supplemented by

Catherine Loeb's *Women's Studies: A Recommended Core Bibliography, 1980–1985* (1987).

Women Studies Abstracts. Rush, NY: Rush Publishing, 1972–. Quarterly.
Covers scholarly work in women's studies from an interdisciplinary perspective, offering lengthy abstracts of most of the works listed. An alphabetical index covers the entire year.

Women's Studies Encyclopedia. New York: Greenwood, 1989–1990.
A three-volume collection of essays on various aspects of women's studies. Volume 1 deals with science and the social sciences, covering medical, economic, legal, political, and behavioral research. Volume 2 covers women in the arts — both as artists and as represented in the arts. Volume 3 covers history, philosophy, and religion.

Women's Studies Index. Boston: Hall, 1991–. Annually.
A selective author and subject index to articles in about seventy-eight scholarly and popular periodicals.

JOURNALS

Frontiers. Albuquerque, NM: University of New Mexico, 1975–.
An interdisciplinary journal of women's studies, often publishing theme issues in which a common topic is approached through the lenses of different disciplines. Includes literary writing as well as research articles.

Journal of Women's History. Bloomington, IN: Indiana University, 1989. Three times a year.
A scholarly journal focusing on history and historiography, with a global scope and interdisciplinary perspective. Includes book reviews and annotations of new publications.

NWSA Journal. Norwood, NJ: Ablex, 1988–. Quarterly.
Published under the auspices of the National Women's Studies Association, this journal includes scholarship as well as articles on learning and teaching. Includes announcements, calls for papers, reviews, and reports on research in progress.

Signs: A Journal of Women in Culture and Society. Chicago: University of Chicago, 1975–. Quarterly.
A leading journal in the field, founded by Catherine Stimpson. Long, scholarly articles from all disciplines are published, along with useful review essays, book reviews, and announcements.

Using Footnotes
or Endnotes
to Document Your Paper

The system of using notes at the bottom of each page or at the end of the paper (called footnotes, endnotes, or notes) is often called the Chicago style. Though this system of citation has been replaced in many periodicals by the author-date system, many writers and publishers in the humanities, especially in history and the fine arts, prefer to use Chicago style.

Despite the fact that this system uses numbers to refer to the sources, it differs from the citation-sequence system. The citation-sequence system (see Chapter 12) requires a list of references that are assigned numbers (the list is organized according to order of reference in the text of the paper). A number is repeated as many times as the source is used. In the note system, a note is used each time a source is referred to; accordingly, though numbers are not repeated, a source is repeated as many times as it is used. The notes themselves usually serve as the list of references or bibliography. The following explanation of the Chicago style is based on the *Chicago Manual of Style* (14th ed., 1993).

In-text Citations

Refer to the source of your information by placing a number in the text either half a space above the line or in parentheses on the line. Put the number outside all marks of punctuation except the dash. Try to place numbers at the end of a sentence or at a break in structure or meaning. Here are some examples:

    The Indian Vedas[1] are a collection of theories about the
    origins of the cosmos and mankind.

    (The Babylonians also taught Sumerian in their
    schools.)[2]

```
Hinduism combines religion, cultural tradition, and so-
cial structure³--it is a complex philosophy.
```

The corresponding note is placed either at the bottom of the page on which the number appears or in a list at the end of the paper or book. A bibliography is often supplied in addition to the notes, but if full citation is given in the notes, a bibliography is not necessary. Occasionally a bibliography is added to give additional related sources not specifically cited.

Notes

Spacing of notes varies greatly from one book or journal to another. For a student paper, the best format is to indent the first line of each note three or five spaces. Single-space within each note if it is at the bottom of the page; double-space between notes placed at the end of the paper. Number footnotes consecutively throughout the paper. If you place your notes at the end of your paper, begin them on a separate page following the body of the paper with the heading Notes or Endnotes. The first reference to a source should give the complete citation, even though the author or title is given in the text. For subsequent references, give the last name of the author, followed by a page number.

```
        1. Elsie B. Washington, Uncivil War (Chicago: The
Noble Press, 1996), 15.
        2. Washington, 17.
```

If the note refers to the same source as the immediately preceding note, some writers use the abbreviation Ibid., for *ibidem,* meaning "in the same place."

```
        3. Kenneth Clark, Feminine Beauty (New York: Rizzoli
International Publications, 1980), 65.
        4. Ibid., 42.
```

If the whole citation, including the page number, is the same as the preceding reference, you can use just the abbreviation.

```
        5. Ibid.
```

More and more writers and journals are dropping the use of all Latin abbreviations in footnotes and endnotes. The abbreviations Loc. cit. and Op. cit. are no longer recommended by the *Chicago Manual of Style,* and Ibid. is only reluctantly included as an option.

Repeat the title as well as the author's name when you have cited more than one title by the same author. When you repeat a source with a long title — either a book or an article — use a shortened title consisting of key words from the title (do not change word order).

FULL TITLE

The American Writer and the European Tradition

SHORT TITLE

American Writer

Here are some commonly used footnote or endnote forms.

BOOK WITH ONE AUTHOR

6. Clarence Page, Showing My Color: Impolite Essays on Race and Identity (New York: HarperCollins, 1996), 47.

BOOK WITH TWO AUTHORS

7. Michael L. Conniff and Thomas J. Davis, Africans in the Americas: A History of the Black Diaspora (New York: St. Martin's Press, 1994), 31-35.

BOOK WITH MORE THAN THREE AUTHORS

8. Jiu-Hwa L. Upshur et al., World History, vol. 2 (St. Paul: West, 1991), 381.

BOOK WITH ANONYMOUS AUTHOR

9. Wild Animals of North America (Washington, D.C.: National Geographic Society, 1960), 21.

Begin the reference with the title of the book or article. Do not use Anonymous or Anon.

EDITOR OR TRANSLATOR

10. Jacob Simon, ed. Handel: A Celebration of His Life and Times (London: National Portrait Gallery, 1985), 32.

11. Rachel Adler, "A Question of Boundaries," in Tikkun: An Anthology, ed. Michael Lerner (Oakland: Tikkun Books, 1992), 465-71.

12. Gustave Flaubert, Madame Bovary, trans. Paul De Man (New York: W. W. Norton, 1965), 121.

JOURNAL ARTICLE

13. Colin A. Palmer, "From Africa to the Americas: Ethnicity in the Early Black Communities of the Americas," Journal of World History 6 (Fall 1995): 224.

The volume number precedes the date; only the page or pages of the portion cited in the text are provided. Inclusive page numbers for the entire article would be provided in a bibliography.

MAGAZINE ARTICLE

14. John Horgan, "Plotting the Next Move," Scientific American, May 1996, 16.

In a note for a magazine article, only the specific page cited is given; in a bibliography, the inclusive pages of the article are given.

BOOK REVIEW IN A NEWSPAPER

15. William W. Warner, "The Call of the Running Tide," review of Looking for a Ship, by John McPhee, Washington Post, 9 Sept. 1990, Book World section, 1.

The word *section* is spelled out when it is not followed by a number or letter; the abbreviation *p.* or *pp.* is not necessary.

GOVERNMENT PUBLICATION

16. Senate Select Committee to Study Governmental Operations with Respect to Intelligence Activities, Alleged Assassination Plots Involving Foreign Leaders, 94th Cong., 1st sess., 1975, S. Rept. 94-465, 22.

ENCYCLOPEDIA

17. Encyclopaedia Britannica, 15th ed., s.v. "English horn."

The abbreviation *s.v.* stands for *sub verbo*, meaning "under the word." Topics are organized alphabetically in the reference work, so no other information is needed.

BOOK WITHOUT PUBLICATION INFORMATION

If the publisher or place is not given, use the abbreviation *n.p.* for each. If no date is given use *n.d.*

18. Clark Wissler, Indians of the United States (New York: n.p., 1940), 42.

MATERIAL FROM AN INFORMATION SERVICE

Include standard publication information, followed by any other information, such as file numbers, that would help others access the source.

19. Leslie R. Brody et al., "Gender Differences in Anger and Fear as a Function of Situational Context," Sex Roles: A Journal of Research (New York: Plenum Publishing, January 1995), 32, Dialog, ERIC, Ed 504407.

ONLINE DATABASE

Include the description *database online* in brackets after the title of the source and conclude with the electronic address or other information to help others access the source.

20. Gus Chavez, "Economic Boycott Begins," in Immigrant Rights in California [database online] (Los Angeles: University of California, 1994- [cited 7 December 1994]), available from gopher://latino.sscnet.ucla/edu/00/Researcher/Social%20Sciences.

ELECTRONIC JOURNAL OR BULLETIN BOARD

Include the description *electronic journal* or *electronic bulletin board* in brackets after the title of the source and conclude with the address and, if applicable, the type of network.

21. Bruce R. O'Brien, review of Land, Law, and Lordship in Anglo-Norman England, by John Hudson, in Bryn Mawr Medieval Review [electronic journal] (Oxford: Clarendon Press, 1994-[cited 14 November 1995]), file no. 95.3.4; available from listserv@cc.brynmawr.edu;INTERNET.

COMPUTER PROGRAM OR SOFTWARE

22. Lotus 1-2-3 Rel. 4. Lotus Development Corporation, Cambridge, Mass.

"Rel. 4" indicates that this is the fourth release.

Bibliography

A bibliography is sometimes used with notes, especially if it contains works of general interest on the subject in addition to the works cited in the notes. In a bibliography the works are listed alphabetically by the last names of the authors. The punctuation is also different, as the following examples show.

Notes

   1. Patricia J. Williams, <u>The Rooster's Egg: On the Persistence of Prejudice</u> (Cambridge, Mass.: Harvard University Press, 1995), 68.

   2. David Scott, "A Note on the Demand of Criticism," <u>Public Culture</u> 8 (Fall 1995): 43.

Bibliography

Scott, David. "A Note on the Demand of Criticism." <u>Public Culture</u> 8 (Fall 1995): 41-50.

Williams, Patricia J. <u>The Rooster's Egg: On the Persistence of Prejudice.</u> Cambridge, Mass.: Harvard University Press, 1995.

A P P E N D I X 3

Style Manuals
and Handbooks
in Various Disciplines

One of the four documentation styles explained in this book and illustrated in Chapters 10, 11, 12, and in Appendix 2 can be used in most of the papers written by college students. The style manuals and handbooks listed in this appendix are useful especially for those wishing to publish in a specific discipline. They contain detailed information about bibliographic format and about such matters as punctuating and spelling scientific terminology. Some of them contain suggestions on the process of research and writing in particular subject areas.

Agronomy
American Society of Agronomy. *Publication Handbook and Style Manual.* Madison, WI: American Society of Agronomy, 1988.

Art
Barnet, Sylvan. *A Short Guide to Writing About Art.* 4th ed. Glenview: Harper-Collins, 1993.

Biochemistry
The Practical Handbook of Biochemistry and Molecular Biology. Ed. Gerald D. Fasman. Boca Raton: CRC Press, 1989. Series of multivolume handbooks in four areas.

Biology
CBE Style Manual Committee. *Scientific Style and Format: The CBE Manual for Authors, Editors, and Publishers.* 6th ed. Chicago: Council of Biology Editors, 1994.
McMillan, Victoria E. *Writing Papers in the Biological Sciences.* 2nd ed. Boston: Bedford, 1997.

Business. See also Economics.

Smith, Charles B. *A Guide to Business Research: Developing, Conducting, and Writing Research Projects.* Chicago: Nelson-Hall, 1991.

Chemistry

Dodd, Janet S. *The American Chemical Society Style Guide.* Washington, DC: American Chemical Society, 1986.

Earth Science, Geology

Bates, Robert. *Writing in Earth Science.* Alexandria: American Geological Institute, 1988.

Economics. See also Business.

Officer, Lawrence H., Daniel H. Sachs, and Judith A. Saks. *So You Have to Write an Economics Term Paper.* East Lansing: Michigan State University Press, 1985.

Engineering

Michaelson, Herbert B. *How to Write and Publish Engineering Papers and Reports.* 3rd ed. Phoenix: Oryx Press, 1990.

Film

Corrigan, Timothy J. *A Short Guide to Writing About Film.* 2nd ed. Glenview: HarperCollins, 1994.

Geography

Lounsbury, John F., and L. Lloyd Haring. *Introduction to Scientific Geographic Research.* 3rd ed. Dubuque: William C. Brown, 1992.

History

McCoy, Florence N. *Researching and Writing in History: A Practical Handbook for Students.* Berkeley: University of California Press, 1974.

Marius, Richard, Marcia Stubbs, and Sylvan Barnet. *A Short Guide to Writing About History.* 2nd ed. Glenview: HarperCollins, 1995.

Rampolla, Mary Lynn. *A Pocket Guide to Writing in History.* Boston: Bedford, 1995.

University of Chicago Press. *The Chicago Manual of Style.* 14th ed. Chicago: University of Chicago Press, 1993.

Law

The Columbia Law Review, et al. *A Uniform System of Citation.* 16th ed. Cambridge, Mass.: Harvard Law Review Association, 1996.

Linguistics

Linguistic Society of America. "LSA Style Sheet." *LSA Bulletin.* December 1995. Annually.

Literature

Gibaldi, Joseph. *MLA Handbook for Writers of Research Papers.* 4th ed. New York: Modern Language Association, 1995.

Mathematics

American Mathematical Society. *The AMS Author Handbook: General Instructions for Preparing Manuscripts.* Providence, RI: American Mathematical Society, 1994.

Swanson, Ellen. *Mathematics into Type.* Providence, RI: American Mathematical Society, 1987.

Medicine

Huth, Edward J. *How to Write and Publish Papers in the Medical Sciences.* Baltimore: Williams & Wilkins, 1990.

Iverson, Cheryl, et al., *American Medical Association Manual of Style.* 8th ed. Baltimore: Williams and Wilkins, 1989.

Modern Languages.   See Literature.

Music

Helm, Ernest Eugene, and Albert T. Luper. *Words and Music: Form and Procedure in Theses, Dissertations, Research Papers, Book Reports, Programs, and Theses in Composition.* Valley Forge: European American Music, 1982.

Holoman, D. Kern, ed. *Writing about Music: A Style from the Editors of* 19th Century Music. Berkeley: U of California P, 1988.

Physics

American Institute of Physics. *Style Manual: Instructions to Authors and Volume Editors for the Preparation of AIP Book Manuscripts.* 5th ed. AIP Press, 1995.

Political Science

American Political Science Association. *Style Manual for Political Science.* Rev. ed. Washington, DC: American Political Science Association, 1993.

Goehlert, Robert U. *Political Science Research Guide.* Monticello, IL: Vance Bibliographies, 1982.

Stoffle, Carla J., Simon Karter, and Samuel Pernacciaro. *Materials and Methods for Political Science Research.* New York: Neal-Schuman, 1979.

Psychology

American Psychological Association. *Publication Manual of the American Psychological Association.* 4th ed. Washington, DC: American Psychological Association, 1994.

Religion

Sayre, John L. *A Manual of Forms for Research Papers and D. Min. [Doctor of Ministry] Field Project Reports.* 5th ed. Enid, OK: Seminary Press, 1991.

Science — General

American National Standard for the Preparation of Scientific Papers for Written or Oral Presentation. New York: American National Standards Institute, 1979.

Day, Robert A. *How to Write and Publish a Scientific Paper*. 4th ed. Phoenix: Oryx Press, 1994.

Social Work

National Association of Social Workers. *Writing for NASW*. 2nd ed. Silver Spring, MD: NASW, 1994.

Sociology

Cuba, Lee J. *A Short Guide to Writing About the Social Sciences*. 2nd ed. Glenview: HarperCollins, 1993.

Gruber, James, and Judith Pryor. *Materials and Methods for Sociology Research*. New York: Neal-Schuman, 1980.

Sociology Writing Group. *A Guide to Writing Sociology Papers*. 3rd ed. New York: St. Martin's, 1993.

Acknowledgments (continued from p. vi)

Choice, from M. Silverman's review of *A Software Law Primer* by Frederic William Neitzke. Copyright © 1985 by the American Library Association. Reprinted with permission from *CHOICE,* a publication of the American Library Association.

Congressional Information Service Annual, from *Abstracts of Congressional Publications,* January–December 1988. Copyright © 1989 by the Congressional Information Service. Reprinted with permission of Congressional Information Service (Bethesda, MD). All rights reserved.

Consumer Reports, from "Soaping Up." Copyright © 1990 by Consumers Union of United States, Inc., Yonkers, NY 10703-1057. Excerpted with permission from *Consumer Reports,* October 1990.

Encyclopedia Americana, last paragraph and bibliography from the "Pirandello" entry. From the *Encyclopedia Americana,* © Grolier, Inc. Reprinted with permission.

Encyclopedia of Associations, "Native American Rights Fund (NARF)" entry. From *Encyclopedia of Associations,* 28th edition. Copyright © 1993, Gale Research, Inc. Reproduced by permission. All rights reserved.

Essay and General Literature Index, from "Atwood, Margaret" entry. *Essay and General Literature Index,* 1985 to 1989. Copyright © 1985, 1986, 1987, 1988, and 1989 by The H. W. Wilson Company. Material reproduced with permission of the publisher.

Ann Gibson, "Universality and Difference in Women's Abstract Painting: Krasner, Ryan, Sekula, Piper, and Streat." From *The Yale Journal of Criticism,* vol. 8, no. 1. Copyright © 1995. Reprinted by permission of the Johns Hopkins University Press.

Humanities Index, "Yeats, W. B." entry. From *Humanities Index,* September 1995. Copyright © 1995 by The H. W. Wilson Company. Material reproduced with permission of the publisher.

Bill Katz and Berry G. Richards, *The Nation* and *National Review* entries. From *Magazines for Libraries,* 8th edition. Copyright © William A. Katz. Reprinted with permission.

Library of Congress Subject Headings, "Solar heat" and "Solar heating" entries. From *Library of Congress Subject Headings,* 18th edition, vol. IV. Copyright © 1995, Library of Congress. Reprinted with permission.

The Literary Essays of Thomas Merton, edited by Brother Patrick Hart, from copyright page. Copyright © 1981 by the Trustees of the Merton Legacy Trust and Our Lady of Gethsemani Monastery. Reprinted with permission of New Directions Publishing Corp.

MLA International Bibliography, from Subject Index, and *MLA International Bibliography Classified Listings,* from Author Index. Copyright © 1993. Reprinted with permission of the Modern Language Association of America.

Ogden Nash, "Song of the Open Road." From *Verses from 1929 On* by Ogden Nash. Copyright © 1932 by Ogden Nash. First appeared in *The New Yorker.* Reprinted with permission of Little, Brown, and Company.

The New Encyclopedia Britannica, from the *Propaedia, Macropaedia, Micropaedia,* and *Index.* From *Encyclopaedia Britannica,* 15th edition. Copyright © 1994 by Encyclopaedia Britannica, Inc. Reprinted with permission from *Encyclopaedia Britannica.*

Elizabeth A. Nist, from "Tattle's Well's Faire: English Women Authors of the Sixteenth Century" by Elizabeth A. Nist, in *College English* 46.7 (November 1984). Reprinted with permission of the National Council of Teachers of English.

The Oxford English Dictionary, definition of "educate," prepared by J. A. Simpson and E. S. C. Weiner. From *The Oxford English Dictionary,* 2nd edition. Copyright © 1989 by Oxford University Press. Reprinted with permission of Oxford University Press.

PsycLIT abstract printout from the PsycINFO Database. Citation reprinted with permission of the American Psychological Association, publisher of *Psychological Abstracts* and the PsycLIT Database, all rights reserved.

Readers' Guide to Periodical Literature, "Skin" and "Bishop, Elizabeth" entries. *Readers' Guide to Periodical Literature,* 1989. Copyright © 1994 by The H. W. Wilson Company. Material reproduced with permission of the publisher.

Carl Sagan, from *The Dragons of Eden: Speculations on the Evolution of Human Intelligence.* Copyright © 1977 Carl Sagan. All rights reserved. Reprinted with permission of the author.

Social Sciences Citation Index, from the Citation Index, Source Index, Permuterm Subject Index, and Corporate Index, 1994. Copyright © 1995 Institute for Scientific Information, Inc., 3501 Market Street, Philadelphia, PA 19104. (215) 386-0100. ISSN: 0091-3707. Reprinted with permission.

"Techniques of Gestalt Therapy" from *The Encyclopedia of Psychology,* 2nd edition. Copyright © 1994 John Wiley & Sons, Inc. Reprinted with permission.

Ulrich's International Periodicals Directory, entry for "Psychological Bulletin." From the *Ulrich's International Periodicals Directory^{TM},* 33rd edition (1994–1995). Copyright © 1994–1996, Reed Elsevier Inc. All rights reserved. Reprinted with permission of R. R. Bowker, a Reed Reference Publishing Company, a Division of Reed Elsevier Inc.

Sidney van den Bergh and James E. Hesser, "How the Milky Way Formed." From *Scientific American,* January 1993. Copyright © 1993 by Scientific American, Inc. All rights reserved. Reprinted with permission.

Gore Vidal, from *Writers at Work,* George Plimpton, editor. New York: Penguin, 1981. Reprinted with permission.

Subject Guide to Books In Print, entry for "Martin Luther King." From the *Subject Guide to Books in Print^{TM},* 1994–1995, vol. 2. Copyright © 1994–1996, Reed Elsevier Inc. All rights reserved. Reprinted with permission of R. R. Bowker, a Reed Reference Publishing Company, a Division of Reed Elsevier Inc.

Walford's Guide to Reference Material, Social and Historical Sciences, Philosophy and Religion entry, edited by Alan Day and Joan M. Harvey. From *Walford's Guide to Reference Material,* 6th edition, vol. 2, 1994, published by Library Association Publishing. Reprinted with permission.

Index

Directory to Documentation Models

AUTHOR-PAGE STYLE (MLA)